GRISHA

The Story of Cellist Gregor Piatigorsky

by
M. Bartley

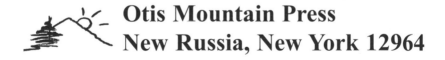

**Otis Mountain Press
New Russia, New York 12964**

**2008
FOURTH EDITION**

GRISHA

Copyright® 2004 by Margaret Bartley

Photographs courtesy of the Piatigorsky family
and the author's collection.

Cover Photo: Gregor Piatigorsky taken about 1914
while a student at the Moscow Conservatory.

Back Cover: Gregor Piatigorsky taken in
Elizabethtown, New York by Carl Huttig

Publisher's Cataloging-in-Publication

Bartley, M.
    Grisha : the dramatic story of cellist Gregor
Piatigorsky / by M. Bartley. -- 2nd ed.
    p. cm.
    Includes bibliographical references.

    LCCN 2004095992
    ISBN 0-9760023-0-2
    ISBN 0-9760023-0-2 51995
    ISBN 978-0-9760023-0-7

    1. Piatigorsky, Gregor, 1903-1976.
    2. Violoncellists
    Biography.   I. Title.

ML418.P63B37 2004   787.4'092
                      QBI04-800055

Gregor Piatigorsky

CONTENTS

This book is dedicated to Jacqueline Piatigorsky, without whose help it could never have been written.

AUTHOR'S NOTE

GRISHA was written as the result of a gift I received from Joram Piatigorsky. In July 1999, he visited his old home in New Russia, New York, and gave me copies of his parents autobiographies. Inspired by what I read, I dug deeper into the history of Gregor Piatigorsky and eventually wrote "Sanctuary Among the Birches", which was published by Adirondack Life magazine in June 2001. However, I felt a magazine article couldn't do justice to Piatigorsky's incredible and fascinating life.

"My father was always on the run," Jephta Piatigorsky Drachman told me when I interviewed her. *"First he ran from the pogroms in Russia, then the Bolshevik Revolution and finally the Nazis. He didn't stop running until he came here."*

With her support, and help from her mother, Mrs. Jacqueline Piatigorsky, I decided to bring Gregor Piatigorsky's story to life. I have chosen to present the biography as a dramatic narrative, telling it from Gregor's point of view and reconstructing it as accurately as possible. I am indebted to his family, friends, colleagues and students for sharing their memories of this remarkable man.

Margaret Bartley

FOREWORD

The story of Gregor Piatigorsky's life was one of adventure, struggle, success and love. He was a man with a heart too big to fill, a mind that was both penetrating and wide open, a talent rich in its agility and expressiveness, and a sense of humor as warming as his enormous smile.

Piatigorsky's life was dedicated to finding what was beautiful. He found beauty everywhere-in nature, in art, in people, in life itself, and of course in music.

Gregor Piatigorsky's cello was his lifelong companion and "weapon" as he referred to it. He admired it, loved it, was in awe of it, fought with it, and shared it with people in every corner of the world. He brought the cello to places that had never seen one. He taught and inspired dozens of fine cellists to become artists. They learned about music from the inside, not merely about technique. They also learned the important values of honesty and quality.

Piatigorsky told stories, not only with words, but he spoke through music, and he always spoke from the heart. Piatigorsky gave to the world of music the cello as a solo instrument and, along with it, a voice of warmth, imagination and infinite humanity.

Jephta Piatigorsky Drachman

In his autobiography, The First Man, Albert Camus writes of the eerie feelings aroused as he contemplated the foreign world of his late father's life. Reading Margaret Bartley's book based on my father's life brings forth those same emotions.

Margaret has done a wonderful job of researching my father's life, from the frightening hardships of the Russian pogroms, his escape from the Bolshevik Revolution and the insanity of Hitler and World War II. She tells of his struggles as a talented young cellist and his success as a great artist. She captures my father's remarkable life in extraordinary times, his vulnerabilities and his strength as a survivor.

When I was a boy, I heard my father's own account of these events, and I can state with first-hand knowledge that she has recreated the highlights of his life in her own words with feeling and sensitivity. I can hear my father's voice and see my father gesticulating as she recounts his adventures. This book has its own music. I regret that my father is not alive to read it himself, but I'm certain that he would approve.

Joram Piatigorsky

PREFACE

I have not made a contract with nature,
That there will be a tomorrow,
Or that there will be sunshine or rain.
These things are gifts,
Treasures, bestowed upon us,
And for that,
There is no end to the gratitude I feel.
Gregor Piatigorsky
1903-1976

Polish-Russian Border
1921

They crouched in the shadow of the chicken house, barely visible to each other in the darkness. Gregor's legs ached and he shifted, letting one knee drop to the ground. Cold wetness seeped through his pants, but he didn't dare move. Beside him, he felt rather than saw Mischa stretch. His friend's joints popped. In front of him, Madame sniffled. Her arm bumped him as she wiped her nose.

"Shhhh," Sergei hissed.

God help us, Gregor thought. If she starts crying we're doomed. He squeezed his eyes shut and tried to concentrate on something else. Should he find a better fingering for the Tchaikovsky? What could he do about the chipped peg, the one that slipped every time he held more than four beats on the C string?

Someone coughed. The chickens on the other side of the flimsy stockade wall squawked. Gregor sank lower, dropping his head and rounding his shoulders, no longer caring about the mud. If he were caught, the Commissar would order him shot, dirty clothes and all.

The cello felt snug against his shoulder, but Gregor ran his hand over the canvas case anyway. Would they confiscate it? Would they give it to another artist or would he still be carrying it when they shot him? The bullets would go through his body and shatter the instrument. The thought made him wince. Better that he give it away before he was shot.

Behind him, he heard the sucking of boots in mud. Someone moved beside him and he held his breath.

"Give me your money."

Gregor recognized Ivan's voice, a trace of German in the man's otherwise flawless Russian.

"All of it. Give me your rubles and kopeks." The man squatted with his back against the chicken house wall. "You cannot use rubles in Poland."

The quartet had met Ivan that afternoon in the livestock barn. The four of them had just completed an underappreciated performance of pieces from *Carmen* for the Comrade farmers. As they packed their instruments, Ivan approached them.

"You want to go west?" His tone was casual. "I can guide you. One hundred rubles each."

Six hours later, their money in Ivan's pocket and their luggage abandoned, they were at this man's mercy.

"How much more must we pay?" Sergei said.

"How much do you have?" Ivan chewed on a sliver of wood while they dug through their pockets,

"Not much." Gregor handed over two rubles he had hidden in the side of his sock.

"You will need more."

Mischa produced a few coins and managed to drop one in the mud.

"This is all?" Ivan spat splinters at their feet.

"We gave you everything." Mischa said, apologetic. "Please, you must take us across."

"Your party papers, ration cards and military identification." Ivan seemed to lose interest in the coins.

"Why?" Gregor shoved his hand deep in his pocket, keeping a firm grip on the bundle of papers that meant life or death.

"No papers can cross." The man's accent grew thicker. "Give them to me!"

"Grisha," Mischa said as he handed the man his identity card. "Give him your papers."

Still, Gregor hesitated. Without his passport and ration card, he had no protection. If he were caught and executed, his body wouldn't be identified. Mama and Papa would never know what had become of him.

"I don't have my papers," Sergei said. "I left them in my luggage at the dormitory."

"Here's mine," said Madame. She was short and blonde, a soprano who always cried for more than her ration of food. She pressed her papers into Ivan's hand. "Grisha, please. You won't need them in Poland. None of us can go unless you give him your papers."

Gregor sighed then handed over his documents. Now he felt naked, exposed. He wanted a cigarette, but lighting one would have been suicide.

"Leave all your possessions," the smuggler said. "Carry nothing. Tonight you must move quickly."

"I won't go without my cello." Gregor tightened his grip on the strap.

"My violin is small," Mischa pleaded. "I can carry it."

"Be ready to throw them away. This is not an easy journey." Ivan stood. "No more talking."

Gregor lifted the instrument onto his shoulder and fell in line behind Mischa. If he had to run, he didn't want the cello banging the back of his legs.

They moved in single file across a freshly plowed field. Wet soil clung to Gregor's boots making them heavy. It had to be past midnight. The thin crescent of a waning moon, soft and fuzzy through the ground fog, gave off just enough light for him to see figures moving ahead. Without warning, Mischa stopped and Gregor ran into him.

"Watch it, you dumb ox," Mischa said.

"Get down," Ivan whispered. "Stay low."

Gregor dropped to the ground, his hands and knees sinking into the soft earth. The smell of manure reached his nose, but he didn't care. He would have wallowed in manure if it would get him to Poland. His feet grew numb and he shifted, trying to keep his cello off the ground. He waited. His breath was too loud. He pressed his hand over his nose. Why didn't they move? He closed his eyes and tried to swallow, but his tongue, dry as paper, stuck to the roof of his mouth. Something tickled his nose and he felt the urge to sneeze.

"Shhhh. Shhhh, my little Grisha." Mama's lips pressed close to his ear. *"God will protect us if you are still."* Memory of her warning sent a shiver through his body. Cold sweat dampened his shirt.

Here's the river." The smuggler's voice was barely audible. "The bridge is on the right. Stay together when you reach it."

"Do the guards have guns?" Madame's voice quivered.

"*Ja* and they shoot people. If you try to swim, the water will slow you. The soldiers have more time to kill you."

Gregor heard Mischa move forward and he followed. Underbrush narrowed the path and branches scraped the side of his cello. He slid the instrument off his shoulder, lifted it overhead then turned sideways. It was awkward, but moving was easier.

Ivan stopped and again they waited. Gregor's arms ached and he rested the cello on his head. Sweat trickled down his cheek. His chest felt tight, like someone was choking him. The craving for a cigarette became unbearable.

"Go," the smuggler whispered. "Run. Now!"

For the third time in his life, Gregor ran.

PART I

Chapter One

By the Authority of Nicholas II, Tsar of Russia, Sovereign of the Caucasus. To all subjects between the Baltic, the Bosporus, the Caspian and the Black Sea and all others who live in and under his domain. To tolerate no anarchy, civil disobedience, unrest or destruction of property. Except against those who do not acknowledge the dominion of God and his son, Jesus Christ our Holy Savior. All loyal Christians will be protected against seizure, confiscation or injury by any Infidel, Socialist, Anarchist or Jew.
A.B. Neigart, Governor: City of Ekaterinoslav

Ekaterinoslav, Russia
October 1909

"No school today," said Papa from the doorway of the back room, his face unshaven. "Stay inside. Do you understand? No one leaves the house."

"Is it a holiday?" Gregor said as he slid out of the bed he shared with Leo, and stood shivering in his nightshirt. Without another word Papa disappeared down the hall toward the kitchen.

"No, stupid." Leo pushed back the covers and tossed his nightshirt under the bed. "It's pogroms. My teacher told us. The Black Hundreds are coming."

"What's a pogrom?" Gregor pulled on his uniform. Even with no school, he didn't know what else to wear on a Tuesday. "Are they really black?"

"They're Cossacks. They catch children who can't run fast, like you." Leo poked Gregor's shoulder.

"Why?"

"Because they're hungry."

Gregor sat on the floor lacing his shoes and tried to imagine such a thing. If Cossacks were hungry they should go home to supper.

"Don't let anyone in." Papa's voice carried down the hall. "Keep it locked." Gregor heard the door slam shut. He peeked from his room in time to see Nadja slide the bolt in place. Mama hugged his big sister's shoulder and stroked her hair. "Don't cry," Mama said. "Papa knows what to do."

Nadja pressed her face into Mama's chest and Gregor heard her sobbing. He would have gone to comfort his sister, but Leo grabbed his arm and dragged him back into the room. "Come on," Leo whispered. "Let's see what they look like."

"But Papa said stay inside."

"We'll only go to the gate." Without waiting, Leo swung open the window and scrambled over the ledge. Gregor had to follow.

Leo lied. He didn't stop at the gate. Instead, he pushed it open and hurried past the alley that led to Pradid's carpentry shop. Then he ran to the end of Philosofskaya Street and up the gently sloping hill to the wide-open grassy spot where all the children played. Now it was empty.

Gregor looked over his shoulder only once to see if Mama was watching, but the shutters on the house were fastened. Nothing moved.

Along the path, Leo picked up two stones. Bouncing them in his hand, he tested their weight then handed one to Gregor and made a sharp downward motion. "This is your weapon. Hit them hard."

Gregor squeezed his fingers around the rock and made the same striking motion. "I can do it," he said. "I'll smash their heads."

They pushed through the tall grass and ran until they reached a place where they could see everything below. The city of Ekaterinoslav stretched toward the river, strangely quiet in the early morning light. No smoke rose from the tall stacks of the Belgian Ironworks. The cluster of wooden cottages, including their own home, sat like an afterthought at the end of the street.

Beyond, the grassy steppe stretched as far they could see, all the way to the Dnieper River. Barges piled high with coal and iron ore snaked toward the quay. The log-filled barges should have been moving, but they weren't. In the distance, almost to the opposite shore and lost in the early morning haze, a huge coal ship sat heavily at anchor.

Ahead of them, at the end of the path, Gregor saw Papa standing alone, a solitary figure against the big open sky. Papa looked very small.

"Grisha, get down." Leo tugged at Gregor's sleeve. Papa must have heard them. Before Gregor could move, Papa turned and looked right at him. Sweat dampened the back of Gregor's neck despite the cool October breeze. He froze.

Leo pulled him to the ground. "Did he see you?"

"I–I think so."

"Stupid." Leo stretched up and peered over the tall grass. "I'll see—." He gasped, his mouth dropping open, a sob escaping his lips. From across the steppe a cry pierced the air as if ripped from a dozen throats.

"What is it?" Gregor felt his heart jump.

Before Leo could reply, Papa cried, "Run Grisha!"

Gregor stood and stared across the waving heads of pale yellow grass. In the distance dark figures on horseback moved against a bright autumn sky. Gregor squeezed the stone in a tight fist and raised his arm.

"Run!" Leo cried. "They'll eat you." Then he was gone.

Gregor turned and ran. Moving as fast as he could, he pushed aside tall grass, willing himself back toward the cluster of cottages at the foot of the hill. But the grass was high and his shoes, Leo's old shoes, were too big for his six-year-old feet.

"Faster!" Leo's voice grew faint as he disappeared down the path.

Gregor felt the Cossack's hot breath on his neck. They had guns and knives. Leo had told him so. And they ate children. The stone could not protect him.

Weeds pulled at his feet and tangled around his shoes. He pitched forward, the stone flying from his hand. The ground came up hard like a fist, slamming into his chest, knocking breath from his lungs. Bright flashes of light danced before his eyes. He couldn't move, couldn't breathe. He waited for the knife, helpless as a stunned chicken.

Footsteps. Heavy breathing.

Pulling his knees to his chest, Gregor curled his arms over his face. Big hands grabbed him, circling his waist, lifting him from the ground. As his captor ran, Gregor hung face down, the ground bouncing beneath him. He wanted to throw up.

"Let me go." He kicked, and his heels found a soft target. There was no reply, only panting as he was carried down the hill. Then they were through the front door and the hands released him. He fell to the floor and lay there, unable to move, staring at Papa's black shoes.

"Nadja—come—here," Papa gasped. "Help your grandfather into the cellar. Leo, get your instrument."

From a crumpled heap on the floor, Gregor watched his brother push back the carpet and lift the trap door. When Leo's head disappeared below the floorboards, Papa handed down his viola and Leo's violin.

"They're coming." cried Nadja as she ran from the bedroom waving her arms. "They're going to kill us."

Old Pradid limped behind her, imploring in his ancient voice. "Quiet child. The Cossacks will hear you." But Nadja wouldn't be quiet.

"They'll kill us," she sobbed.

"Shut your mouth." Gregor had never heard Mama speak like that before. "Get down the ladder. Hurry."

Gregor hated the cellar. It was damp and smelled of mold and thick with cobwebs. If he went down there, he would be trapped, unable to run. Instead, he rolled to his knees and headed for the back door, toward light and freedom. He made it only as far as the kitchen table before Papa's big hands scooped him up and passed him through the hole in the floor. Into the darkness he went, kicking and clawing at the hands that grabbed him.

"No, no—."

Mama's fingers squeezed his mouth shut and passed him deeper into the void. The last bit of light disappeared as Papa came down the ladder, pulled the trapdoor shut, then used a string hanging through a nail hole to pull the rug back in place.

The air felt thick and Gregor had trouble breathing. Distant voices screamed and cursed. Sounds grew closer. Heavy footsteps pounded the floor above his head. Bits of dust drifted onto his face and stung his eyes. He felt a sneeze move up his nose, but fought it off.

"Where are they?" The guttural words made him shiver. The question was followed by the sound of breaking glass. Mama flinched.

"Not a god damn Jew left in here." The voice had a Cossack accent. "Damn *Zhyds*. Nothing but vermin." Something heavy hit the floor, then a chorus of laughter.

Silence. Gregor became aware of rough hardness pressing against his cheek. Leo's shoulder pushed him into the damp stone wall. For sure he felt spiders crawling down his neck. "Get off me—." He tried to shove Leo away, but Mama's hand covered his mouth.

"Shhhh. Shhhh, my little Grisha." Her lips pressed close to his ear. "God will protect us if you are still."

How long? Hours? It seemed like eternity. Gregor's stomach told him breakfast had passed, maybe even lunch. Above them the house grew still. He fell asleep against Mama's arm. When she moved, he opened his eyes. Leo sniffled and Nadja whimpered. Gregor needed to use the toilet.

Papa moved. Slowly he pushed open the trapdoor and Gregor watched him lift his head above the level of the floor.

"I'll see if it's safe." Papa climbed the ladder then closed the door behind him. Darkness again. They waited. Papa's slow footsteps crunched overhead. More silence. At last the trapdoor opened and Gregor saw Papa silhouetted by bright sunlight.

"Don't rush." Papa's voice was too loud for the tiny cellar. "One at a time."

As light illuminated the hiding place, Gregor saw everyone clearly. Nadja's wide, unblinking eyes reminded him of a cat. In the corner, Pradid rocked back and forth, eyes closed, his wrinkled lips moving silently in prayer.

Gregor couldn't bear the cramped space a moment longer. Uncurling numb legs, he followed Leo up the ladder into the kitchen. The acrid smell of smoke hit his nose first, followed by the odor of urine. Someone had used the kitchen table for a toilet. Broken glassware crunched under Papa's shoes. Mama's china cabinet lay face down. The parlor window had a gaping hole. The front door hung askew on a single hinge. Only the piano was undamaged.

Gregor and Leo followed Papa into the front yard, down the path, past broken crockery and a shattered chair. Papa pushed open the gate to Philosofskaya Street then stopped. "Stay back." His voice was hard and he stretched his hand out. "Back inside, both of you."

They both disobeyed. Gregor peeked around Papa's long legs and saw Aunt Rosie lying in the middle of the street, strangely still, reminding him of a doll thrown to the ground, her hair fan-like around her head. She watched the sky, her eyes unblinking. Gregor's gaze moved from her face to her shoulders, then down her torso. His fingers gripped Papa's leg, but he couldn't take his eyes off Aunt Rosie.

Her blue dress was pushed above her waist, her white legs bare, like newly risen bread dough. One of her shoes was missing. From the slit in her belly a lumpy purple snake slithered into the dust. Beside her, face down in the dirt, lay her brother Samuel. Two lines of red flowed from their bodies, merging into a single stream. Gregor reached down and touched the red. It felt warm and sticky, like new jam.

"No!" Papa yanked him back. "Don't touch it."

Mama's hand went to her mouth, stifling a sob. "Not Rosie," she cried.

Papa turned and pushed them all back up the path and inside the house. Then he pulled the broken door shut. "Quiet now." He wrapped his arms around Mama. "You'll frighten the children."

But Mama would not be quiet. She pressed her face into Papa's chest. "Why did they do this?" Her voice was muffled. "Why did God let this happen?"

Gregor didn't know why God had let such terrible things happen. Didn't the Cossacks do it? If it was God's fault, then they could never escape. God knew everything, even their hiding place.

Clinging to Papa's leg, he squeezed his eyes shut and pushed his face into the itchy wool of his long pants.

"Nadja," Papa said. "Take your brothers back to the kitchen yard." Gregor felt Papa's leg move and his arms were pried lose. "I'll take care of Rosie and Samuel."

"Don't leave." Gregor tried to follow Papa out the shattered doorway. "Papa don't go—."

Papa knelt before him. Gregor had never seen his father's face so dark. "They've had their fill of killing. They won't come back."

"I don't want to be like Aunt Rosie." Gregor kept his voice low so Mama couldn't hear him. "I don't want to be..." He couldn't say the word.

"It won't happen again." Papa squeezed Gregor's hand. "Rosie had a baby. She couldn't run fast enough."

Gregor felt Nadja pull his hand free. Her fingers were like ice "Let's go to the back yard," she said. Her voice trembled. "We can sit under the grape arbor. It will smell better there."

* * *

"Even the Torah scrolls are gone." Papa's voice penetrated Gregor's sleep and he rolled over then rubbed his eyes.

"Ruined, all of them. They set the marketplace on fire and the bakery. How can they hate a bakery?"

Wide-awake, Gregor propped his head on his hand and listened.

"The cemetery stones are broken." There was a moment of silence followed by the clinking of the glasses and the hiss of the samovar.

"Do they think they can hurt the dead?" Pradid's voice was soft. Gregor heard the familiar sound of the old man sucking his pipe.

"They threw an ox cart wheel through the synagogue window." Papa's voice grew louder. "Only those who painted a cross on their door escaped." The anger in Papa's voice made Gregor's stomach tighten.

"We're being punished for our Jewishness," Mama said, then sniffled. Gregor imagined her sitting at the kitchen table, hands over her face, holding back tears.

Throwing off the blanket, he tiptoed across the cold floor to the bedroom door. At the end of the hall he saw Papa's shadow moving back and forth.

"They hung a man from the big tree near Putkin's butcher shop. Soaked his clothes in oil and set him on fire." There was a moment of silence. "I couldn't recognize his face but I think it was Shem Rabinowitz."

"The teacher at the Yeshiva?" Pradid's voice quivered.

"Don't let the children hear," Mama whispered. Gregor heard a chair scrape the floor. He ran back to the bed, pulling the covers over his head.

"They'll know soon enough." Even under the blankets he could still hear Papa. "You can't protect children from the truth."

The truth? Gregor slid closer to Leo, reached out and touched his brother's shoulder. "Leo, wake up."

No response.

He pushed harder. "Leo, I'm afraid."

Leo's only reply was a grunt and a sharp kick to the shins.

Gregor pulled back and pressed his hands to his eyes, but he still saw a man on fire, a rope around his neck, skin peeling from a blackened face. What did it feel like to die that way? How bad did it hurt? Next time they would catch him. He couldn't run fast enough. He might not make it to the cellar. He would be the one they burned alive.

* * *

The next morning Papa and Pradid slashed the lapels of their coats. Papa put his razor and soap away. Gregor watched as dark stubble took over his father's face. It made him look angry.

Mama covered all the mirrors with cloth. Crying and wiping tears, she helped Rabbi Levinsky's wife bake bread. Then she and Nadja cleaned the house, scrubbing every floor with hot soapy water. The whole family sat Shiva for Rosie and Samuel, but few people came. Every Jewish family in the city was in mourning.

Night after night, while Leo slept, Gregor lay awake listening for the sound of approaching soldiers, imagining the feel of fire on his skin, planning his escape. No matter what Papa said, Gregor knew in his heart they would come back. This time the Cossacks would find him, and Mama, and Nadja, and Leo and Pradid.

For weeks the schools remained closed. Most of Papa's music students, especially the Christian ones, stopped coming to the house for lessons.

Gregor and Leo stayed outside during the day, hiding in the tall grass on top of the hill that overlooked the city and the Dnieper River. From there they watched the horizon, waiting with rocks and sticks in hand, ready to sound the warning if the Cossacks returned. But the wide, wind-blown steppe remained empty.

Chapter Two

February 1910

"Grisha." Gregor felt a hand shaking him and opened one eye. In the darkness of early morning he saw Mama standing over him. The soft glow of the oil lamp lit her face, making the shadows under her eyes even darker. She set the lamp on the bedside table and reached across the bed. "Leo, get up. Today is school."

Gregor gathered his clothes and headed for the warm kitchen. Papa stood in front of the big tile stove adding a shovel full of coal to the embers. Still, the air was chilly and Mama pulled her shawl tight around her shoulders. While Gregor dressed, he watched her put a pot of kasha on the iron cookstove. The air was thick with silence. Papa sat at the head of the table, cleared his throat then waited. Nadja tiptoed down the hall in bare feet and slid into her place at the table.

"Today is an important day." Papa folded then unfolded his big hands, finally placing them flat on the table. "Our school has reopened and there is a new primary teacher. Mr. Schelmosk comes to us from Moscow." He pointed at Gregor. "I expect you to be his best pupil."

Gregor looked at Mama. Her mouth smiled, but her eyes didn't. "He will do the best he can." She reached out and ran her hand over his hair then straightened his jacket collar. "Won't you Grisha?"

"I will." Gregor gave her his best smile. "But Leo and Nadja have to be the best too."

Papa reached for his glass of tea and Mama filled it to the brim. "The other teachers are nothing important." He added a heaping spoon of sugar and stirred. "None of the other teachers have been farther than Kiev." He paused as Mama scooped hot cereal into smaller bowls. "A new teacher from Moscow, now that's someone important. One day the name Piatigorsky will mean something."

* * *

"I have a special surprise for you," Papa announced on a mild March afternoon. The leftover lumps of snow, now dirty and brown, melted in the bright winter sun and left muddy trickles across the packed earth. Together, Gregor and Papa walked toward the center of the city, past the cottages and factory houses on Philosofskaya Street, then alongside the lumberyard near the railway station where stacks of new white boards were piled as high as a house. After crossing the narrow stone bridge that marked the edge of the business district, they reached Empress Catherine Boulevard, the main thoroughfare through the heart of the city.

"Today you will see and hear something completely new," Papa said. They joined the crowds strolling past fancy stores where windows filled with expensive goods from faraway places beckoned buyers.

"Is it the circus?" Gregor felt his heart race. "I love the circus."

"You've never been to the circus, so how can you say that?"

"If you did take me to the circus, I know I would love it."

A streetcar rattled by, its metal wheels making *clickety-clack* on the steel rails embedded in the cobblestones.

"Can we ride the streetcar?" Riding a streetcar looked like fun.

"Our feet belong to us," Papa said. "And they are free. Why should we waste precious kopeks on the streetcar? That would only make us fat and lazy, like so many in this city."

They passed the Empress Catherine Royal Museum with its white marble columns, then walked through the public gardens where a fountain, made of three green fish, spouted water in the air. Gregor decided he would try to perfect spouting water like that when he got home.

When they reached the far side of the park, Papa stopped before a large two-story building. In front of the doorway a group of well-dressed people formed a line. Gregor sounded out the word Concert Hall above the arched doorway.

"The Imperial Orchestra has come to our city," Papa said as they joined the queue. "Never before have you heard such beautiful music."

"Is it circus music?" Gregor stood close to Papa as they inched their way toward the ticket counter.

"No." Papa shook his head. "This is what people in Moscow listen to every day. Today you will hear Brahms and Mozart. It's the best music in the world and well worth the price."

The man with the tickets was as round and doughy as a matzo ball. Gregor tried to imagine him floating in a bowl of soup, bobbing up and down like a dumpling. The thought made him giggle until the ticket man glared at him.

"One ruble for you," the ticket man said. "And fifty kopeks for the boy."

"My son is not yet seven." Papa pulled money from his pocket and handed the man three coins. "A child's ticket is only twenty-five kopeks."

"That boy is almost as tall as I am." The man kept a tight grip on the pasteboard squares. "He's nine at least, probably ten."

"I'm almost seven," Gregor said, before Papa could protest. "Leo's ten, but I'm taller."

"Taught the boy to lie, I see," said the man.

Papa leaned forward. "My son does not lie." His words were soft but chilling. "And he never will." He snatched the tickets from the man's hand and they entered the hall. As they moved through the big double doors Gregor turned and looked back.

The ticket man scowled. "Cheap *Zhyd*," he said to the next couple in line.

"Ignore him." Papa moved forward into the lobby and didn't look back. "We won't let him spoil the performance for us."

They took seats in the second tier, above the patrons dressed in furs and fancy hats. Before them the stage stretched wide in both directions. A huge piano, much larger than the one at home, filled the far end of the stage.

"Papa?" Gregor tugged at his father's sleeve. "Can I play the piano? A big one like that?"

"No. Piano is a woman's instrument."

"But I like piano music."

"Shhhh."

Though it was still light outside, the concert hall was gloomy. A skinny boy dressed in all black entered from the left carrying a long taper. One by one he lit the lamps ringing the front of the stage.

"Can I be a lamp boy?"

"Lamp boy?" Papa frowned. "Today you will hear the finest musicians in the world. Someday it will be you on stage performing, not lighting lamps."

Gregor slumped in his seat. Lighting all those lamps looked like fun. Leo played violin and Papa made him practice for hours while Gregor played soccer in the street with other children.

There was motion to the left of the stage and the orchestra walked in. They were mostly men, dressed in black suits, carrying instruments of all sizes. Even the pianist was a man. The only woman, a beautiful dark-haired girl, sat at the harp. A tall man with a short, trimmed beard came last. In his arms he held the biggest violin Gregor had ever seen. It was so large that when the man sat he propped the instrument between his knees.

"Why is his violin so big?"

"It's not a violin, it's a cello. That is Maestro Kubatzky, the best cellist in all Russia."

"Can I play the cello?"

"It's a very difficult instrument, the violin is much easier. Besides, there are few positions in an orchestra for cello."

"But Leo plays violin. I want something different."

"Shhhh. Listen to the oboe. The orchestra will tune to his A."

The musicians rearranged chairs and music stands then settled themselves into places facing the center of the stage. The man with the oboe held a note and everyone in the orchestra played the same note. It sounded so awful that Gregor put his fingers in his ears. "It's terrible."

Papa grabbed Gregor's hands and pulled them down. "This is not the music we came to hear. You've heard me tune my viola before."

"It didn't sound like that."

"There are at least sixty musicians in the orchestra. Of course it sounds different."

Gregor looked around at the rest of the audience who were chatting and ignoring the musicians on stage. After a few more minutes of squawks and squeals, Papa put his finger to his lips.

"Shhhh," he said. "Here comes the conductor."

A white-haired man in a long old-fashioned frock coat walked slowly to the front of the stage. The musicians grew still. The conductor bowed to the audience then turned and raised his baton for silence. The chattering from the audience subsided. When all was finally quiet, the conductor raised his arms. With his downward stroke, an enormous sound swept across the hall.

Gregor closed his eyes as the music washed over him. High notes and low, melodies he knew and rhythms he had never heard. It was part of a great sea, an ocean of sound. The rest of the audience, the orchestra, the lamp boy, even Papa were gone. He was alone. He floated on the music rising and falling with each swell. In the midst of that ocean, a single note broke through all others and he was lifted, as if by a hand high above the water.

He opened his eyes and saw the cellist. The man seemed alone, the only performer on stage. The music was no longer the ocean but the voice of a bird flying far above all others. Gregor wanted to be that bird, soaring far above the steppe, his house, his school and Ekaterinoslav.

"I don't want to be the lamp boy anymore," he announced on the walk home. "I want to play the cello."

* * *

The smell inside Pradid's shop was like perfume, and cedar wood smelled best. Gregor liked to pick up splinters from the dusty floor and hold them to his nose, inhaling the sweet aroma. The carpenter's shop had squatted forever, long and low beside their house. Gregor was sure that it was in this very shop that Pradid had been born, already old and wrinkled, even as a baby.

"Pradid, I want you to build me a cello," he said. "It must be this big." He stretched his arms up over his head. "And this wide."

Pradid looked up from the chair he was repairing. "Perhaps you should build it yourself."

"Yes," Gregor said, excited at the idea of making such a thing of beauty. "I want to make it from cedarwood. And I'll take it to school."

"In the back." Pradid pointed to the rear door. "Find something in the scrap pile. I'll cut it if it's too big."

Gregor dug through the discards of lumber, saving several pieces, throwing others aside. A wide panel from a door would do for the body of the instrument, while a long thin splinter from a broken curtain rod made a perfect bow. "Listen to me play," he said as he perched on the crooked stool in the front of the shop. With the wide plank between his knees, he drew the curtain rod across it. There was a scratching sound as the two pieces of wood met, but in his head he heard the cello sing. It was glorious.

"Mama," Gregor cried as he ran across the yard. "Listen to me—." He stopped short at the kitchen door.

"I will not go begging at his doorstep again," Papa said, his voice loud, his arms waving in the air.

"But you have so few pupils." Mama tried to grab his hand. "My father can't feed us all. He has only his carpentry shop and no one to help."

"What would you have me do?"

"Ask your father for help. Surely he will not turn you away this time, not with a baby coming soon." Mama's hand went to her swollen belly. "How will we feed another child?"

"My father understands nothing but his own stubborn pride."

"And what of your pride?" Mama sank into the chair at the end of the table. "Christian parents don't want a Jewish music teacher. They are afraid of us." She pressed her hands to her face. "They won't send their children near our home and you are no longer welcome in theirs."

"Music is music. Why should they care what my name is? It's all stupidity."

"Perhaps so, but we can't change how they feel. What about Leo and Grisha? Do you want them to work in the iron foundry like other boys, while you . . . you..."

"While I what?" Papa leaned forward over the table.

"While you . . . While you try to win a position in the orchestra."

"I will become first viola." His tone was low, but the words sent a shiver through Gregor. "And my sons will attend the music academy. It's necessary if they're ever going to gain admission to the conservatory." The flat of his hand hit the kitchen table. "I will have them baptized Christian if that's what it takes."

"But surely you will be discovered."

"Not if you keep quiet and don't shout it all over the marketplace."

"You can't—." Mama stopped, her hand flying to her mouth as her eyes met Gregor's. "Oh Grisha," she cried as she hurried from the table and pushed him back into the yard. "Go find Leo. Tell him I need more coal for the stove."

"But Mama—." He hated it when they quarreled. "I want to show you—."

"Not now Grisha. Go, do as I say."

Turning away from the house, he let his new cello drag in the dirt. He didn't know where Leo had gone and he didn't know where to find him. Instead, he made his way back to Pradid's shop and sank onto the stool beside the door. Behind him the tap, tap, tap of the hammer sounded like the ticking of a clock. Closing his eyes, he laid the bow on imaginary strings and began to play. As the sound of music grew inside his head, it almost drowned out the angry voices still drifting from the open kitchen window.

* * *

"Nadja?" Mama spooned hot kasha into the breakfast bowls. "Is the iron hot?"

Nadja pushed back from the table, wrapped the hem of her apron around the wooden handle of the flat iron and tested it with spit. The hot metal sizzled. "It's ready."

"Grisha, Leo." Mama motioned to them with the wooden serving spoon. "Find your good white shirt and black pants."

Gregor rubbed his hands across his sleepy eyes and propped his chin on his palm. Nadja had woken him while it was still dark. "Why?" he said then yawned, forgetting to cover his mouth. "It's still night time."

"No." Mama took her chair at the women's end of the table beside Nadja, tucked baby Alex in the crook of her elbow and let him take her breast. "Papa has business in the city. You and Leo will go with him." With one hand she scraped the last of the porridge into her own bowl. "And bring me your shoes. They need shining."

In their back room, Gregor pulled his good clothes down from the hook on the wall then looked under the chair for his shoes. "What's Papa's business?" He lowered his voice so it wouldn't carry down the hall. "Do you think he'll make us visit the Queen of Spades?"

"I hope not." Leo dropped to his belly, reached under the bed and pulled out two pairs of dusty shoes. "Better not let Papa hear you call grandmother that name."

"He hates her too." Gregor grabbed socks from the basket at the foot of the bed. "I know he does. He never likes to go to her spooky house."

"It's not spooky." Leo tossed Gregor the worn shoes. "It's just her bones rattling when she walks."

"She even creaks when she sits." Gregor headed toward the kitchen."And she has ugly teeth." He made a face baring his teeth. "Why can't we wear boots today?"

"Papa wears shoes when he goes to the city." Leo pushed past him and made it to the kitchen first. "Only ignorant *mujiks* wear boots."

"I'm not an ignorant *mujik*," Gregor said then stopped. Papa stood in the doorway.

"What is all this noise?" Papa's voice filled the room. Leo cringed as he slid onto the bench at the far side of the table. With head down, he stirred his cereal as if it were the most important thing in the world.

"Papa?" Gregor said, as he sat beside his brother. "Leo says only ignorant *mujiks* wear boots instead of shoes."

"In the city that is true." Papa took his chair at the end of the table."Give your clothes to Nadja. Today you must look presentable."

"Why?" Gregor handed Nadja his pants and shirt.

"We have business to attend to. Men's business, and you must look your best."

"What's men's business?" Gregor dug his spoon into the kasha. It had grown cold and stiff so it was hard to stir. Papa didn't answer. Gregor looked up, aware that the room was too quiet. The sound of spoons scraping bowls and rapid chewing took the place of answers. Men's business was something no one wanted to talk about.

* * *

A crowd of beggars squatted on the steps of Cathedral of the Holy Assumption, each one vying for attention.

"Have mercy," a man with one eye pleaded as he stretched out a dirty hand. "Have mercy on a poor, blind soldier."

Gregor pulled back, expecting Papa to shove the grimy hand away. Instead, he watched Papa reach into his pocket, extract a kopek and drop it onto the man's outstretched palm.

"God bless you," the man said, as he tried to pat Leo's head. "And God bless your boys. May Jesus be merciful and never send them to war."

Papa's gift sent a signal to the other beggars. A crowd moved forward, the strong and young elbowing the older and weaker ones aside. Papa grabbed Gregor and Leo's hands and hurried them toward the entranceway.

"Have mercy," cried a frail voice. Gregor looked down and saw a woman sitting on the muddy ground, rooted as if she were a shrub. "Have mercy on a crippled mother." She pressed a scrawny, rag-wrapped infant to her chest. Leo averted his eyes and screwed up his face as if smelling something bad.

Papa gave nothing to the woman or any of the other beggars. Instead, he yanked on the handle of the big wooden door. "Come quickly." As he pulled open the door, he removed his hat. "Take off your caps," he instructed.

How strange, Gregor thought as he stuffed his wool cap in his coat pocket. At the synagogue everyone wore a hat, but here in the cathedral hats came off.

Inside the dark, cavernous room statues stared down from niches in the wall. For a moment Gregor pulled back. The eyes were everywhere, following him as he tried to slip behind Leo. Papa placed the flat of his hand on Gregor's back and pushed him forward. "Come," he whispered. "Don't be afraid."

The great room with a domed ceiling seemed to press down on the old people who stood and bowed and muttered unintelligible words. Some knelt on the stone floor. Gregor wanted to kneel too, just to escape those eyes. Smoke rose from clusters of candles, making the air seem close and thick. Papa moved forward past a *babushka*, clutching a golden cross to her forehead, then her lips and finally her chest. She dropped to her knees, bowing again until her face touched the floor.

"I want to go home," Gregor whispered. "I don't want to be here."

"Shhhh." Papa's fingers dug into Gregor's arm and hurried him forward.

"Stop crying," Leo whispered. "We have to do this."

"Do what?"

"Do as Papa says."

"But I don't..." Gregor protested, but too late. Before them stood a decorated screen, behind it, shuffling and chanting, people on the move. A great bearded man in a long cloak stepped from behind the screen and stood like a mountain before them. Papa bowed his head and Leo did the same. Gregor looked up at the tall man, made even higher by the funny black hat perched on his head.

"Holy Father," Papa said, while his head was still lowered. "These are my sons."

The man leaned forward and Gregor wanted to run. He turned, but found himself staring at the buttons on Papa's black vest.

"Are they ready?" Holy Father said. "Do they understand?"

Gregor felt Papa's hands on his shoulders. "They understand."

Gregor knew better than to argue with that tone.

They followed Holy Father around the screen and up two steps to a platform ringed with burning candles. White wax dripped and formed small hard puddles on the stone floor. As Papa and Holy Father spoke in hushed tones, Gregor stared down. The tip of Holy Father's shoes peeked from under his robe. They looked lumpy and worn, like he had pebbles in them instead of toes. Hanging straight from his big belly, a silver chain nearly touched the ground. It swung back and forth as the man moved, making a tinkling sound.

Leo shuffled his feet and scratched at his collar. Gregor saw Papa's fingers dig into his brother's shoulder until he grew still. From behind, Gregor heard the swishing of rough cloth and turned to see a boy, not much older than Leo, step onto the platform. He also wore a long black robe with a cross around his neck. In his hands he carried a large silver bowl half filled with water. Gregor smiled at the boy, but the newcomer kept his eyes down.

Holy Father began speaking in words that made no sense to Gregor. As the voice droned on Gregor's attention wandered to the painting of a mother and baby high up on the wall. Holy Father must like mothers and babies. Maybe he didn't know there was a hungry baby outside the cathedral door. Maybe Holy Father would give the mother some kopeks so she could buy milk for her baby.

"Leonid Piatigorsky," Holy Father said. Leo stepped forward, his back stiff, his shoulders hunched up around his ears. More strange words which to Gregor sounded backward and inside out. The boy with the bowl moved closer. Nothing much happened except that Holy Father dipped his hand in the bowl and touched Leo's head. Then he handed him a silver cross on a chain. Maybe this wasn't so bad.

It was Gregor's turn. He stepped forward and the ritual was repeated. The drops of water on his forehead were cold and he felt some of them run down his nose, but it seemed impolite to wipe them off with his sleeve. Holy Father handed him a cross. It was pretty but a girlish sort of thing. Maybe he would give it to Nadja.

Papa bowed again to Holy Father then reached into his pocket and offered money, but Holy Father turned away as if the coins were somehow dirty. Instead, he motioned to the boy who put his bowl down and retrieved a wooden plate from a small table. Papa placed ten rubles on it. Then he reached down and took Gregor's and Leo's hands. Again Papa bowed as Holy Father stepped from the platform and disappeared around the screen. Leo bowed too and this time Gregor joined them. When Holy Father was gone they followed the boy back into the great sanctuary.

Papa's grip tightened on Gregor's fingers as they hurried past the kneeling *babushkas*. The air still smelled sickly sweet and Gregor saw an older boy, also dressed in black, swinging a silver basket on a chain. Smoke billowed out around him and seemed to catch on the hem of his long gown, a trail of white following him as he walked between the kneelers.

Then suddenly they were outside and the bright sunlight almost blinded Gregor. He tried to shield his eyes, but Papa's grip tightened as he pulled them past the beggars. He didn't let go of their hands until they were well beyond the cathedral and into the park.

"Give me your cross," Papa demanded, when they stopped beside the fountain.

Gregor held open his hand. In the sunlight the cross and chain shone like a jewel. "Can I give it to Nadja? It's pretty. I know she'll like it."

"No," Papa said, as he took both crosses and slid them into his pocket. "If anyone asks you, tell them your cross is in a safe place at home. Do you understand?"

"Yes, Papa," Leo said.

"But don't tell your grandparents," Papa added.

"Why?" said Gregor. The bright sunlight made his head hurt and the bubbling fountain reminded him he needed to urinate.

"Because." Papa's said, his voice low. "They would not understand."

Chapter Three

April 17, 1910

"Do, re, mi, fa, sol, la, ti. Wake up."

Gregor felt the cold morning air on his bare legs as the blanket was pulled away. Through sleepy eyes, he looked up and saw Papa standing over him.

"What did I just sing?" Papa said.

"C major," Gregor mumbled as he rubbed his eyes.

"How many notes?"

"Seven." He pulled his knees to his chest and tried to grab the blankets, but Papa yanked them to the foot of the bed.

"That's right and today you are seven. It's your birthday."

Gregor sat up in bed, now wide-awake. "Can I go to the circus?"

"Not the circus. Come. Hurry. There's something waiting here for you."

Gregor followed Papa to the parlor door where Mama, Leo and Nadja were waiting in their night clothes. The somber look on Nadja's face was unusual.

"Go on," Mama said.

Gregor started into the room then stopped, his mouth dropping open. Leaning against the piano bench was a cello just his size. He stared at it, unable to move.

"It's yours," Nadja said. "Try it."

He looked up at Papa. "Can I touch it?"

"Of course. It belongs to you."

Gregor approached the cello and stood before it, studying it. His eyes followed the curves of the instrument, from the scroll at its head to the wide belly. Hesitating, he reached out and ran his hand down the strings. With even the lightest touch they hummed beneath his fingers. "It's beautiful," was all he could say.

"I will teach you to play," Papa announced. "Sit. Hold it between your knees."

Gregor wrapped his arms around the polished wood, hugging it to his chest. With his knees spread wide, he looked up at the scroll of wood. It looked like the uncurled head of a new fern. He loved this cello more than anything else in the world.

"Papa?" Nadja asked. "Can you play the cello?"

"Violins? Violas? Cellos?" Papa handed Gregor the bow. "They're all one big family."

But Papa was wrong. His skill as a violist did not work with the cello. Under his instruction, Gregor produced only offensive squeaks and scratches. After several attempts Papa gave up. Gregor began cello lessons with Mr. Gubarioff once a week after school.

His new teacher was short, only slightly taller than Gregor. His triple chin and loose jowls provided a perfect resting-place for the neck of his instrument. With his belly protruding between his knees, Mr. Gubarioff's cello seemed to stand by itself.

"You see," said the teacher. "You must do it this way. Hold your hand up high and let the bow flow over the body of the instrument."

Gregor stretched his left arm near his head and pressed his fingers as hard as he could against the strings. It felt awkward, not the way he was used to practicing at home. Still, he wanted to please Mr. Gubarioff and make Papa proud, so he did exactly as the teacher instructed.

At home that night he took the pillow from his bed and placed it on his stomach, recreating his teacher's enormous size. The cello sat out so far he had to stretch his arms to lay the bow on the strings.

"What is this?" Papa peered into the tiny parlor and pointed at the pillow.

"I'm playing the way my teacher does." Gregor puffed up his cheeks to make his face fat.

"What has this man taught you?"

"He taught me to play the C note. He said I should play like this." Gregor stuck his elbows out and leaned over the cello.

"That is absurd," Papa cried. "The man is an idiot." Lessons with Mr. Gubarioff ended.

Gregor's next instructor was a visiting cellist from the Kiev Orchestra, a young man named Kilkulkin. He had once studied with Professor Julius Klengel in Leipzig and Papa was in awe of him. After much pleading on Papa's part, the man agreed to hear Gregor play. As he fidgeted in the straight-backed chair, a knock on the front door announced the teacher's arrival. Gregor felt his stomach tighten.

"Where is the boy?" the man asked, ignoring the usual courtesies.

"Here." Papa led the teacher into the parlor. The man's face was thin and he wore a sour expression.

"Can you play "Marzuka" by Popper?"

"I . . . I think so."

"Of course he can," Papa said.

Gregor laid the bow on the strings and tried to remember the opening phrase. For a moment his mind went blank.

"Grisha?"

At the sound of Papa's voice, he played the melody he had practiced all week. His fingers slid to fourth position, but his stretch was short. Did the teacher notice? Did Papa? When he finished, he looked up at Papa's somber face. Was it good enough?

The teacher looked bored as he shifted his weight from one foot to the other, all the while cleaning his fingernails with a toothpick. Papa and Gregor waited. The man finally tapped his clean fingers on the table. "Listen carefully," he said, turning to Papa. "I strongly advise you to choose some other profession for your son, one that better suits him. He has no talent for the cello."

With that edict, music lessons ended. Gregor, not wanting to see the disappointment in Papa's face, returned to the streets and his playmates. For weeks he played soccer every afternoon. Papa hardly spoke to him. The cello stood alone in the corner of the parlor, untouched.

But after supper Gregor couldn't help glancing at the instrument, which remained in the corner, patiently waiting for him. When he walked past it on his way to bed, he reached out and let his fingers slide over the strings.

"What bothers you?" Papa asked.

"I miss it," Gregor said, as he stood next to the instrument. "I keep hearing music in my head."

Papa sighed and folded his newspaper. "Then play it. Fate does not ask for advice. The instrument is calling you."

The next morning Gregor rose before dawn. After rekindling the fire in the stove, he warmed his fingers under his armpits. Not wanting to wake the others, he devised a way to practice without sound. With his left hand on the fingerboard, he moved his bow through the air just above the strings. In his head he heard every note.

In the evening, cello music filled the house. After school, Gregor hurried home, ready to practice. At night the instrument was his constant companion. He carried it around the house and it rested beside him at the dinner table. While he slept, the instrument stayed in the corner next to his bed, close enough for him to reach out and touch it.

Papa found a new cello teacher, Mr. Maltova, a man with a beautiful instrument. He had once played in the Odessa Theater orchestra. Mama said his entire family had been killed when the Cossacks set fire to the city and that was why he had moved to Ekaterinoslav. Gregor thought he had a sad face. No matter how well his students played, the man never smiled.

"Papa," Gregor said one evening. "My cello is ugly. It's the color of mud." He laid the offending instrument on the kitchen table. "Can I have a new cello, a big one like my teacher plays? His is all red and gold and the wood is so smooth it feels like silk."

"Yours is a sturdy instrument," Papa said, scowling. "And not easily damaged." He handed the cello back to Gregor. "When you play well enough to win a scholarship to the music academy, you'll have earned yourself a new instrument."

* * *

Outside the parlor window the rain tapered off, but the drip, drip, drip of water running off the roof kept time with Leo's foot. Gregor leaned close, trying to see the bottom line of the score. The oil lamp flickered and the notes seemed to jump on the page. Leo's foot grew louder as he played the fugue, his bow flying across the violin's strings. Gregor tried to keep up, his arm moving faster, *accelerando.*

Leo lowered his bow. "Grisha," he said. "Tempo, tempo."

Gregor pressed the bow against the strings, his eyes following the rapid succession of sixteenth notes. He had to catch up.

"Grisha!" Leo rapped the end of his bow on Gregor's hand. "Stop playing."

Gregor lifted the bow and looked up. "What's wrong?"

"You're playing too fast. You're two bars ahead of me."

"I am?" Gregor looked at the sheet of music propped up on the end table, held in place by volume two of Slatesky's History of the World.

"Follow my tempo." Leo tapped his foot in four-four time. "Like this."

Gregor nodded then turned his eyes toward the kitchen. Everything was quiet, a momentary lull in the argument that had come through the wooden door. Playing loud and fast was the only thing that could drown out the sound of angry voices.

"Why are you doing this?" It was Mama's voice. "Would you leave us to starve?"

Gregor cringed and closed his eyes. He wished he could close his ears as well.

"I'm doing this for you and for the children," Papa said. "It's the only way I'll ever have a chance at a position in a real orchestra." His voice grew louder. "I won't spend the rest of my life playing dance tunes at bar mitzvahs and weddings."

"You can find more students. Surely there must be more parents in the city who will pay you to teach their children."

"They are all idiots with wooden heads and no ears. Can I teach donkeys to play?"

"But you can't leave. What will you tell your father? He's offered you a job in his bookstore."

"I'm not a clerk and I am not a rabbi. I am a musician."

"There are other jobs. We need the money."

"I will not work in your father's carpentry shop. Look at what the saws and hammers have done to his hands. My career would be ruined."

"What about the children?" Mama's voice rose and Gregor recognized the familiar quiver that preceded a crying spell. "If you go to St. Petersburg we'll starve. Your music can't feed us."

"I'll sell the piano. I already have a buyer in mind. Kushkin offered me enough money to last you through the winter."

"You would sell my mother's piano to a Christian?"

"What does it matter? Christian rubles will fill our belly as well as Jewish ones."

"Does your father know what you've done?"

"I care nothing for what he thinks."

"He doesn't know, does he?"

"Know what? Do you think I should tell him about the baptism? How else can I keep my sons alive or get them into the conservatory school? What else would you have me do?"

Gregor heard Papa's shoes pace the kitchen floor.

"We'll starve." Mama sobbed. "We can't live on piano money unless we eat only borscht and kasha until spring."

"Enough." There was a crash and Gregor flinched at the sound of Papa's hand hitting the table. Whenever they fought he wanted to jump in between them, push them apart, yell at them and make them stop.

Looking for help, he turned to Leo, but his older brother stared at the floor in silence. Leo, always the stupid coward, never said or did anything.

Gregor dropped his bow and started for the kitchen, but his brother grabbed his arm, digging his fingers into flesh. "No!" Leo pushed him back into the chair. "Leave them be."

"I hate it," he cried, pulling his arm free. "Make them stop."

"Leo? Grisha?" The door swung open and Papa stood there, his face dark. "Let me hear you play."

They quickly put bows to strings and started a Bach prelude. The door closed and music filled the parlor. Above the sound of Leo's violin, Gregor could still hear Mama's voice.

"And what if the director of the academy finds out? Your lies cannot protect them."

"I told them they had to be careful," Papa said, his voice dropping so Gregor could barely hear him. "To drink nothing in the morning. If they don't visit the lavatory, and if they remember to wear their crosses, no one will know they're Jews."

Chapter Four

Rain streaked the windows of the music academy practice room, making it nearly dark at four in the afternoon. Gregor buttoned his coat, shifted the strap of the cello case over his shoulder and headed for the door.

"Wait for me," Vasi called.

Gregor turned and saw the younger boy packing his new violin in a shiny leather case. The cost of that violin alone would feed his family for a year.

"My grandmother came to visit for Easter." Vasi sat on the floor and pulled on his tall India rubber boots. "She's making kielbasa and latkes tonight. Come home and have supper with me and I'll show you my new music."

Vasi's supper sounded delicious and Gregor felt his stomach growl at the mere mention of latkes. "I can't," he said, as he headed for the door. "I have to visit my grandfather. Mama wants me to work in his book store."

"Work? Why do your parents make you work?"

"I don't have to work for long, just until Papa comes home. He's studying viola at the conservatory in St. Petersburg. He'll be the best violist in all Russia." Gregor slid a hand into his coat pocket and felt the hard lump of bread he had saved from lunch. He didn't want to show such a poor supper to Vasi. "When he comes home we'll eat cutlets and latkes every night."

"If there are any latkes left." Vasi buttoned his coat. "I'll bring you some tomorrow, but don't tell Leo."

"I won't." If Vasi brought latkes tomorrow, he would share them with Leo anyway.

He walked down Empress Catherine Boulevard toward the center of the city. Carriages and the occasional motorcar passed by, the lights on the cars illuminating the twilight, creating halos in the cold drizzle. The great white marble of the royal museum looked dull in the rain. Gregor didn't mind the long walk. It gave him time to think about what he would say.

"I want you to talk to Grandfather Piatigorsky," Mama had told him at breakfast. "Tell him we have no money and little Alex is hungry." As she spoke she wrapped a potato roll and hardboiled egg for his lunch. "Look sad. Perhaps he will have pity on you. Ask him to let you sweep out his bookstore."

"Why can't Leo do it? He's older."

"Leo is helping Pradid in the carpentry shop and Nadja's doing laundry for the butcher's wife. Besides, Grandfather Piatigorsky likes you best." She put her arm around him and gave him a hug. "It won't be for long. Papa will be home soon, I just know he will."

He remembered her words and his pace slowed. Streetcars rattled by full of dry passengers and he wished he was one of them, but Papa's words popped into his head. *Our feet belong to us and they are free.*

It was a long way to Grandfather's shop. The cello grew heavy and his shoulder ached. When he reached the great stone synagogue, he sank onto the front steps. Ladders leaned against the side of the building and he smelled new paint. The building looked so shiny and clean, it was hard to believe it had ever been burned.

He reached in his pocket for the bread and picked the lint off before gnawing at it. His stomach grumbled, but finally grew quiet with the offering.

When he felt dampness seeping through the seat of his pants, he got up and started for the footbridge that spanned the narrow tributary which dumped storm water and sewage into the Great Dnieper River. On the far side was the Jewish business district, old and squeezed together in a small space. He paused at the railing to stare down at the rushing water, muddy and high. On impulse, he picked up a few dead leaves from the curb. One by one he dropped them into the foamy water and watched them disappear. Against the torrent, they didn't stand a chance.

On the other side of the bridge were big houses where rich people lived. Two blocks down the narrow alley, past the kosher butcher, he came to Grandfather's shop. Above the door hung an old-fashioned sign that read: *BOOKS: New and Used.* It was the same store Papa had once worked in and Grandfather Piatigorsky before that, when he was a boy. Papa hated the place and Gregor knew why. It smelled awful, like dirty leather shoes and mouldy cellar dust. A bell rang as he opened the door.

"I know why you're here." Grandfather peered over the top of his narrow glasses. Only his stern square face showed above the stacks of holy books. "Why doesn't your father send money?"

"He has no money. He has to pay Professor Auer for lessons." Gregor tried to sound convincing. "Papa will be a great musician when he comes home. Someday he'll play for the Tsar and the Tsarina."

"Not likely," Grandfather said. "I see he's already filled your head with the same useless garbage." He waved a stubby finger at Gregor's cello. "Give up that thing. Prepare yourself for Yeshiva and study the Talmud. Promise me that and I'll help your mother. There's plenty of work to do here in my shop."

"But I'm the best cellist at school." Gregor stretched up on his tiptoes and tried to see over the wall of books. "And Papa is the best violist in Ekaterinoslav."

"And the poorest one, no doubt." Grandfather moved from behind the stack of books to the counter and ran his hand over worn wood, pushing aside imaginary dust. "What about your mother's father? Have you gone begging at his door?"

"Pradid is a carpenter. Papa said I should not risk my fingers sawing wood."

"I offered your father work here in my shop if he would give up his fiddle." The old man's mouth turned down in an ugly scowl. Leaning over the counter, he tapped his hand on a thick copy of <u>Commentary on the Prophets</u>.

"Your father imagines himself too good for honest labor." Grandfather moved from behind the counter and shook his finger in Gregor's face. "I predicted this would happen." His voice rose and he sounded so much like Papa that Gregor wanted to run from the wretched shop. Instead, he stood frozen.

"Tell your mother I won't give her a single kopek." Grandfather's wrinkled lips trembled. He turned and hunched over a pile of books, opening them, running his hand lovingly over the pages. "You're a big boy," he said. "You look like you eat well enough." He closed one book and opened another. "What kind of fool wastes his time on music?"

Gregor had no answer. As quietly as possible he tiptoed out the front door. He walked back across the dark city, the cello case scraping the ground when his arm grew too tired to hold it up. He stopped more often, resting the instrument on the top of his shoe so it wouldn't get wet.

In his mind he saw Mama's worried face. Did he dare tell her the truth? No. She would tell him it didn't matter and they would get by somehow, if God willed it.

"Grandfather wasn't there," Gregor said as he slipped out of his coat. "His shop was locked." Sinking onto the chair, he folded his arms on the kitchen table and dropped his head. For the first time in weeks he was too tired to practice. What did it matter? With no money, he and Leo would have to quit school and find jobs.

"The other children already ate," Mama said. She ran her hand over his damp hair then set a bowl in front of him. "It's borscht, as good as yesterday's. But look, today we have bread, only one day old. Nadja got it from the butcher's wife. Dip it in your soup and it will soften."

Gregor lifted his head and ate. The borscht was thin, but he didn't care. Neither did his belly. Tomorrow he would have to find work. If he didn't there might not be any more supper.

* * *

Gregor picked up his cello and headed for the door of the Yellow Café. "Sorry," Mr. Shimolsky called after him. "But I have an accordion player. Why don't you go into the city and play in front of the cathedral? People there are more charitable."

Back on the street, Gregor jammed his hands in his coat pockets, massaging his fingers to keep them warm. The smell of fresh bread drifted from a bakery window, making his empty stomach growl.

Pulling the strap of the cello case over his shoulder, he headed toward the center of the city. Maybe the cathedral was the place to play, along with all the other beggars. As he passed the butcher shop, he turned away from the sight of chickens and salted herring hanging in the window. Why did the sight and smell of food assault him at every turn?

As he crossed the butcher's alley, he saw a young man in a fashionable suit dash across the street, a violin case tucked under his arm. A musician? He ran after the man but wasn't fast enough. The man disappeared through a windowless door in a narrow brick building. Before Gregor could knock, the door swung open, almost hitting him in the face. A tall gray-haired man emerged carrying a violin case.

Gregor grabbed the man's sleeve. "Please, sir. What is this place?"

The man frowned as he pulled his arm away. "What do you want?"

"Are you a musician? Is this a music hall?"

"It's the hiring hall. There's an agent inside looking for musicians." The man glanced over his shoulder. "Unfortunately the idiot doesn't recognize talent and the pay is an insult."

"Can I try? I'm a cellist."

The man raised an eyebrow in disbelief. "Why not? You're probably just the kind of musician he's looking for, someone young and cheap."

Gregor hesitated, sweating despite the cold air. This might be his only chance at a job, but did he dare try? Running his fingers through his hair, he wished he had let Mama trim it the night before. Taking a deep breath, he opened the door.

Inside the dimly lit hall, he joined a line of people waiting to audition. One man with a missing leg balanced himself on a crutch while holding an accordion over his shoulder. Another white-haired man looked to be a hundred years old. He held a silver flute to his wrinkled lips and played the same merry little tune over and over again. There were no chairs, so people leaned against the walls.

Now he was glad he hadn't eaten. Papa always said a full belly before a performance was a bad thing. Still, he felt nauseous. What chance did he have here among all these grown-ups? What if he failed? Would they laugh at him?

"Stop!" cried a loud voice. "No. No. I don't need a flute player. Not even a dancing flute player."

Gregor peered around the corner into the next room and saw a stout man sitting at a table next to a sorry looking piano. The man didn't look happy.

"Next." The man motioned to a hunchback violin player. "Come here. I don't have all day. Let me hear something."

"Hey, kid." Someone grabbed his collar and yanked him back in line. "Wait your turn like the rest of us."

"Why don't you go home?" said a hawk nosed woman carrying a mandolin. "Your mother is calling you." She threw her head back and cackled. Others joined and their teasing brought heat to Gregor's face.

"Stop it," he cried "I'm the best cellist in the music academy."

"Oh, he's all high and mighty," said a young man with a trumpet. His thin moustache looked liked it was painted on his upper lip. Bowing to Gregor in mocking reverence, he stepped aside. "Let the maestro pass."

Their laughter continued and all Gregor could do was turn his back, face the wall and put his fingers in his ears. By the time he reached the front of the line his hands had grown cold. Ignoring their taunts, he tucked his fingers under his armpits, trying to restore some feeling. Now he wished he had never come. This was a stupid idea. Most of the applicants had been dismissed. Only a pretty young lady that played piano left smiling, a slip of paper in her hand.

"Next," called the contractor. Gregor moved forward into the audition room. The man didn't look up from his ledger. As he stood waiting, Gregor wished he had used the latrine, but it was too late. He slid the canvas cover off his instrument, extended the cello's endpin and tightened the bow. He was ready.

The man looked up. "What do you want?"

"A job." Gregor tried to keep his voice steady.

"You're a kid. How old are you? Ten? Eleven?"

"Almost eleven." What did adding two more years matter?

"And your parents allow you to work?"

"They sent me here."

"Have you played before? Performed anywhere?"

"At home, trios with my father and brother." Gregor took a deep breath, stood tall and gave the man his best smile. "I'm a student at the music academy. I've studied cello for five years," he said, adding three more years to his resume. "I am the best cellist in my class."

"I don't need string trios. Do you know dance music? Gypsy tunes?"

"Papa taught me some. He's studying violin in St. Petersburg. When he comes home, he'll play for the Tsar."

"I don't need that kind of musician." The man stood and pointed to the chair. "Have a seat. Let me hear you play something snappy."

The chair felt warm from the contractor's ample buttocks. Closing his eyes, Gregor took a deep breath and ignored the knot in his stomach. With the bow gently on the strings, he slid his hand up the neck of the instrument until it felt at home on the fingerboard. Then he imagined the sound of Leo's violin and Papa counting out time.

The first piece was a gypsy tune called "Marussja." Gregor hummed the violin part as he played, keeping time with his toe. It was the harder of the two pieces, especially without Leo's help. Then he moved into a variation of "Dark Eyes." One he had worked out himself.

"Why don't you use sheet music?" the man asked when he finished playing.

"It's all in my head." Gregor smiled again. Please give me the job, he thought.

"There's an opening at the North Star Klub, but the owner wants gypsy dance music."

"I can do it. I'd like the job very much."

"What will your parents say?"

"They'll be happy I have a job."

"Can you start tomorrow?"

"Yes. Yes." Now he couldn't hide his excitement.

"Good." The man extended his hand and Gregor stared at it, unsure of what to do. Then standing, he reached out and shook the man's hand like Papa did when he made a deal.

"Thank you, sir."

"Here's the address. Report to the North Star Klub at eight. What's your name?"

"Gregor Piatigorsky."

He watched the man write *GREGOR PIATIGORSKY* in the ledger with the word *CELLIST* next to it. "The pay is one ruble a night. Tell Gelko I sent you."

* * *

Each evening, after a hurried supper of borscht and bread, he walked into the city, past the synagogue and across the rickety footbridge that spanned the tributary to the Dnieper. He didn't tell Mama where he worked. She would never have let him walk that far after dark. Instead, he told her he was entertaining the customers at Mr. Shimolsky's Yellow Café.

The North Star Klub was located in a rundown log building near a shallow creek that ran brown with foul-smelling sewage. The owner was a Pole named Gelko who brought girls from Warsaw to work in his Klub.

Vera was the prettiest. Her long golden hair tumbled around her shoulders and she spoke Russian with an accent that rolled off her bright red lips like music. Gregor loved to listen to her speak and she smiled more than the other girls. While he played, the girls danced and sometimes tried to sing, but most of them weren't very good.

"Why does she pretend to play?" he asked Gelko one night as Vera caressed her mandolin, swaying her hips as she glided across the raised platform in front of the customers. "I could tune it, make it sound pretty for her."

"Don't bother," Gelko said, adding a little water to a bottle of vodka and pouring the mixture into a glass. "It is just for decoration. You make the music. The customers don't care about her playing any more than they care about what they drink."

Gregor realized Gelko was right. The customers, they were always men, didn't seem to mind the girl's lack of talent. No matter how bad the performance, the men cheered and rolled coins onto the stage.

Dancing was hard work. Late in the evening, Vera would discard her red gown and perform in her shift. She was the most popular dancer and Gregor knew why. When business was slow she would sit beside him. As she ran her fingers through her hair, he inhaled her perfume. It reminded him of the wild roses growing along the Dnieper, the ones that bloomed in the spring after a hard rain. Never before had he smelled anyone as good as Vera.

When customers filled the dark room, Vera would walk from table to table, bending low, talking to the men. Then she stepped up on the stage and it was time for him to play. By the sound of their applause, the customers seemed to like his music. But when a customer asked for a private dance, Vera would leave, often for hours. Another of the girls would dance, but the applause was never as loud.

"Why do they make you leave?" he asked Vera one night as she sat beside him, cooling herself with a peacock fan.

"I dance for them in the back room. Some customers like it when I perform for them in private."

"But who plays music for you?"

"Gelko gave me an Edison phonograph. It's from America and plays any tune you want." She lifted her golden curls and fanned the back of her neck. "Everyone in America has one."

"Really?" Gregor didn't quite believe her. "Can I see it?"

"Gelko doesn't want you back there. He told me so."

"Why?"

"He said it would be bad for business."

"Why would hearing your phonograph be bad for business?"

"Never mind. You're too young to understand." As she fanned, waves of warm perfume drifted over him. He saw the beads of sweat shining like jewels along her brow. "It's pouring outside," she said, shaking her head. The golden curls bounced on her bare shoulders. "Why don't you come home with me tonight? You can ride in my carriage so you won't get wet."

"Can I bring my cello?"

"Of course." She laughed with a voice as sweet as her perfume. "You can play a special little tune for me."

"Mama won't know where I am."

"She'll be glad you aren't walking home in the rain."

The carriage ride was short since Vera lived only a few blocks from the North Star. The driver let them off in front of a two-story house with green shutters. Vera's room was located in the rear courtyard. Gregor followed her down the narrow alley, hunching against the rain, trying to protect his instrument. At the end they reached the iron gate, which protected her private entrance.

Once inside, he leaned his cello in the corner then stared in awe at her room. It was mostly filled with an enormous bed covered in a rich red brocade counterpane. When she lit the oil lamp, the room was bathed in a warm pink light. Sitting in the middle of the bed was a terrier doll with one black eye and one white one. It looked so much like a real dog that Gregor reached out and touched it.

"He's my special pet," Vera said. Her laugh sounded like music. "He keeps me company when I have to sleep alone."

Gregor pulled his hand back suddenly, feeling self-conscious but not sure why. Instead, he jammed his fists in his pockets and shifted from one foot to the other. Now he wished he hadn't come. Mama might be angry if she knew he was here.

Vera moved closer. She reached out and touched his hair. "My, my. Your hair is all wet from the rain." She gently twisted a lock around her finger and again he inhaled her perfume. Her chest rose and fell before his eyes. He decided to look at her face instead.

"Grisha?" she said, her voice almost a whisper. "Do you like girls?"

"Yes. I have—have a sister."

"How old are you?" She leaned closer and he felt the heat from her body rising onto his face. "Tell me the truth."

"You won't tell Mr. Gelko?"

"Of course not. It will be our little secret."

"I'll be nine in two weeks."

Her hand stopped moving, her fingertips still on his cheek. Then the expression on her face softened. She closed her eyes and exhaled slowly. "You are a big little boy, aren't you?"

"I'm taller than my brother. He's twelve."

Her fingers slid down his cheek, pausing beside his lips. He didn't dare move.

"I had a boy once." Her voice was barely audible. She looked away, but her fingers remained on his cheek. "I was only fourteen, but the priests took him from me. He would be nine now."

"Does he visit you?" Gregor asked, hoping the sad look in her eyes would go away.

"No." There was a long uncomfortable silence, then she shook her curls and seemed to compose herself. "Would you like some cocoa?" she said.

He didn't care for chocolate, but didn't want to be rude. "I would like some very much."

"Take off your jacket and hang it by the stove."

He obeyed, but there was only one chair in the room and he felt awkward taking it. Instead, he hung his jacket on the back of the chair and remained standing. Someone had obviously been here earlier and had started a coal fire in the iron stove. The room was already quite warm.

Vera handed him the cup of warm chocolate then poured one for herself. "Come sit." She patted the edge of the bed. "I'm going to change out of these silly clothes." As she stepped behind a folding screen, he carefully lowered himself onto the big soft bed.

"How did you get to be such a fine musician at your age?" Her voice floated over the screen.

"Papa is a great musician—." Gregor paused as he pushed the toes of his boots against the carpet to keep from sliding off the bed. "He's in St. Petersburg studying viola with Professor Auer. The professor is the greatest musician in the world. He played for the Tsar and Tsarina's wedding."

"So you come by your talent naturally." Vera stepped from behind the screen. The cup of chocolate stopped halfway to Gregor's lips. Vera wore a thin, white gown that didn't look like it would keep her warm. He swallowed hard.

"I would like to play for the Tsar. That's why my father sent me to the music school."

"I'm sure someday you'll be a great cellist and all the kings of the world will applaud." She sat beside him on the bed. "It's late and the rain is worse." She reached back and pulled down the counterpane. "Stay here with me tonight. When my driver comes back in the morning, I'll have him take you home."

"But Mama won't know where I am," he said. "She'll be worried."

"You'll be safe here with me. Take off your boots and pants. Tomorrow morning I'll press them and send you home clean."

The bed did seem inviting and the warm chocolate made him want to do nothing more than sleep. He did as Vera told him, hanging his pants on the chair and setting his boots before the stove. Now the air in the room felt chilly and his long shirt left his legs uncovered.

He crawled under the blankets, hugging the edge of the bed. His body sank into the thick feather mattress, as soft as a cloud. On the other side of the bed Vera blew out the lamp and climbed in beside him. He felt her move under the blanket as her hand reached out to touch his neck. A shiver ran down his spine.

"Good night my big little boy," she whispered.

"Good night," he mumbled, his face pressed into the sweet smelling pillow. The last thing he remembered was the soft touch of her fingers stroking his hair.

* * *

"Grisha!" Mama cried as she pulled him into the kitchen. "Where have you been?"

Gregor saw dark circles under her eyes and knew she had been crying. "I'm sorry. I..."

Her fingers dug into his upper arm. "I sent Leo to the Yellow Café looking for you. The owner doesn't even know your name."

"I was . . . I was at the . . ." He couldn't think up a good lie.

"I haven't slept all night." She alternately shook then hugged him, running her hand over his hair. "What is that smell?" Her eyes grew wide as a look of horror filled her face.

"It was raining last night and . . . and Vera took me to her room. I rode in her carriage so my cello wouldn't get wet."

"Vera? Who is Vera?"

He looked past Mama and saw Leo's laughing face peeking through the crack of the kitchen door. "Vera is... she ironed my clothes and let me use hair tonic. She told me it was all right. I'm sorry." He dropped his head and stared down at the tips of his boots. "She has a boy too. He's nine, but not as tall as me."

Mama released his arm and ran her fingers through his oiled hair. Her calloused hand didn't feel like Vera's soft one. "Where have you been working? Certainly not at the Yellow Café."

He pushed his hand into his pocket and pulled out three rubles, his pay for the past three nights. "The café only pays fifty kopeks a night so I got a job at the North Star Klub. Mr. Gelko pays me more."

"A *bardak*?" Mama cried, her hands flying into the air. "My son works in a brothel?"

"Brothel? The girls dance and I play gypsy music for them, that's all. Vera's the best."

"I want you out of those clothes," she said, pulling him toward the basin. "And I want that awful smell washed from your hair."

"But I have to go back tonight. You need the money."

"Money? What will people think of us?" As she spoke, she rubbed a wet dishtowel over his head. "Would you want your sister working there?"

Nadja work at the Klub? The thought had never occurred to him. Some of the girls probably were Nadja's age. "Mama, I don't think Nadja would like it there. It's . . . It's . . ."

"What would Papa say?" She let go of his arm and collapsed into a chair. "How have we come to this?" she sobbed, holding her head in her hands. "Your father gives all our money to Professor Auer while we starve."

Tears filled his eyes. He couldn't bear to see her this way. "Please, Mama." He pulled a chair beside her and patted her thin arm. "It's a good job. They pay me well and Mr. Gelko likes my music."

"Grisha, Grisha." Her head fell on her arms. "What am I going to do?"

In the end she couldn't argue with the money. Gregor returned to the North Star Klub, but something had changed. He still sat in the chair to the left of the platform, his cello between his knees. He played the same tunes he always played. Why did he feel different? Why did it feel wrong now?

When the new girl, the one from St. Petersburg that looked a little bit like Nadja, danced across the stage, he turned his head. Nadja never wore paint on her face like this girl. And Nadja would never sit on a soldier's lap and wiggle.

When customers called Vera to dance, a knot formed in his chest and he felt sick to his stomach. The very sight of the drunken men beckoning her made his fists tighten. Ashamed, he turned away so his eyes would not meet hers.

Night after night he worked, but he grew to hate the Klub. He also dreaded the long walk from school, across the footbridge, into the city. As the winter darkness fell, he hurried past the warehouses along the riverbank, the ghostly stacks of logs and lumber looming high above him. Under the railway bridge tramps huddled around fires warming themselves. Sometimes they shouted at him to join them in their drunkenness.

During the day it was hard to stay awake at school. When his head drifted toward the desk, the sting of the teacher's switch brought him back to attention. During lunchtime the other boys played games, but now they seemed childish.

"Grisha," Josef called. "Come play soccer."

"I can't," he answered from the edge of the field. "I'm too tired. I had to work last night."

"Only poor boys have to work," Josef shouted then laughed as he ran toward the rest of the boys, the soccer ball under his arm.

Even Vera treated him like a child, but he felt old. He tried not to watch her and turned his chair so she didn't dance directly in front of him. But it felt no better. If it weren't for Mama's sigh of relief when he handed her his wages, he would have quit.

It was Sunday night when a thick man with a beer-stained jacket staggered into the club. He ordered drink after drink, grabbing at Vera as she served him. When it was her turn to dance, the man climbed onto the stage and slid his ham-like arm around her narrow waist.

"Dance for me," he demanded as he stuffed coins down the front of her shift. "Just me." He tried to kiss her neck.

Gregor's bow stopped in mid-air. He watched the swine run his hands over her hips and up her inner thigh. At that moment he felt something break inside. "Stop it!" he screamed, dropping the cello and lunging from the corner. With the bow clenched in his fist, he swung at the man. "Take your hands off her! Leave her alone."

"*Chyort Pobery?*" the man swore. "Is this a kindergarten or a whorehouse?"

"Grisha." Vera turned from her customer. "Go back to your chair." Her voice was hard.

Gelko slid from behind the bar and Gregor felt cold fingers grab his collar, yanking him down from the stage. "I knew this wouldn't work," the man said, as he shook him like a puppy. "You're bad for business."

"Let go of me!" Gregor's arms flailed as he tried to push the man away.

"You're fired!" Gelko reached into his pocket and threw two coins on the floor. "Take your pay and go home."

For a moment Gregor stood there, stunned, shaken. Why didn't Vera help him?

"Do you hear me?" Gelko bellowed. "Get out of here."

Stumbling backward, Gregor dropped to his knees and ran his hands along the floor searching for the money. Customers laughed. One man stretched out a leg and kicked the coin beneath a table.

On hands and knees, Gregor crawled across the sticky beer-splattered floor, ducked under the table and retrieved the precious ruble. When he emerged, two men threw kopeks at him.

"Here's a tip," yelled a soldier. "Let's see how many you can catch."

The sound of their catcalls stopped him. He rose, facing his tormentors, anger welling up inside. No longer could he stand to see their snarling faces and smell their foul breath.

"You're all dirty, drunken pigs," he screamed. Helpless, he felt hot tears run down his cheek. "I hate you. I hope you all die!"

Vera stepped from the platform, picked up the cello and handed it to him. "Go home to your mother," she said softly. "Don't come back here anymore."

Chapter Five

Gregor missed Papa. He even missed his anger. Without Papa's outbursts and occasional smile, Gregor didn't know when he was right or wrong. Days were long and nights too short. With Papa gone only two things mattered, food and music.

Unlike Leo, who hurried through his music, Gregor never thought of practicing as a chore. Sometimes he woke before the rest of the family. On those mornings he tiptoed through the chilly kitchen to the parlor. The stove was cold. Coal was too precious, Mama said, to waste on nighttime heat. Wrapping his blanket around his shoulders, he sat in the straight-backed practice chair, the cello between his knees. Holding his cold fingers to his lips, he exhaled slowly, warming them with his breath the way Mama had done when he was little. Then he slid his palms up the strings, warming them as well.

With his bow in the air above the belly of the instrument, he closed his eyes and heard music. Humming softly as he played, his bow arm moved in the air above the strings, his mind hearing every note. Early morning music was never the silly dance tunes he had played at the North Star Klub. It was real music, Bach and Beethoven, Brahms and Vivaldi.

It was summer when Grandfather Piatigorsky died. Papa came home from St. Petersburg without a ruble in his pocket. But Mama seemed happy and Gregor felt like a great weight had been lifted off of him. Everything would be better now that Papa was home, even if he did yell and pound the floor with his big feet when he was angry. For the first time in months Gregor slept without nightmares.

"I care nothing for my mother's wishes." Papa's voice carried down the hall, penetrating Gregor's sleep. He rolled onto his back and threw his arm over his eyes. "Half is mine," Papa said. "The magistrate made it so."

"But what of Julia?" Mama said. "Your sister expects you to work all day in the shop and still give her half the money?"

Gregor opened his eyes, yawned and looked at the window. Was it morning already? Breakfast time? No. The narrow slice of night sky visible from his bed was still inky black. Leo snored beside him, oblivious of the angry voices coming from the kitchen.

Gregor rolled to his side and covered his ears but could still hear them arguing, though not so loud.

"I'll find a buyer," Papa said. "Then we'll leave this wretched place."

"I can't leave Pradid. He is so old and he has no one. What if he becomes ill?"

"You have brothers.It's their duty to care for their father."

Leave? Gregor sat up, suddenly wide-awake. Was Papa going to leave them again? What if this time he took Mama? What would he do? He and Leo could never work hard enough or earn enough money. *No, Papa.*

Gregor slid out of bed and tiptoed to the door. From the hallway there was silence, then footsteps and hushed voices moving toward him.

"But we have no papers to travel." Mama's voice quivered. "The soldiers will stop us as soon as we cross the river."

"I've already arranged it." Papa always had a ready answer. "I have connections. My friend put in the fix. For a price he can obtain papers for all of us."

"But what about a job? Jews are not allowed to work in Moscow."

"I'm sure I can win a seat in one of the state orchestras." Papa made no attempt to lower his voice. "A big city is the only place I can hope to succeed."

Their bedroom door closed and the voices faded. For a moment Gregor stood with his forehead pressed against the wall. They were all going to go. Where and when, he didn't care. Just as long as Papa didn't leave again. He shivered, though the room wasn't cold. In darkness, he felt his way along the wall then crawled back in bed. When he pulled the covers to his chin, Leo rolled over and mumbled. "Don't want to—Stop!"

Stop what, Gregor wondered. Had Leo heard them arguing? Was Leo afraid too? He pushed his brother's arm, hoping he would wake up so they could talk. But Leo rolled away, let out a sigh and began snoring again. Gregor sank back and stared into the darkness. No more school, no more friends to play soccer with, no more Pradid. This house, the only place he had ever lived, the only bed he had ever slept in, was too still. He squeezed his eyes shut, but sleep wouldn't come.

*   *   *

The bookstore was sold and Papa gave half the money to Aunt Julia. A month later she, her husband and their three children left for America. Uncle Leonid tried to convince Papa to come with them. In America the leaves of the trees were made of money and all one had to do was reach up and pick it.

Everyone becomes rich in America, some doing it in just days with no hard work at all.

"Papa," Gregor pleaded as they finished supper. "Can we go to America too? Everyone in America has an Edison phonograph."

"And no one there speaks Russian." Papa pulled out his pipe.

"But what about Aunt Julia?" Leo said. "How can she live in America? She doesn't speak American."

"In America everyone speaks English." Papa tapped tobacco into the bowl and lit it. A cloud of bitter smoke billowed toward the rafters. "Just you wait. She and Uncle Leonid will be home before the year has passed and all her money will be gone." He rose and walked to the back window that looked onto the kitchen yard. "Besides, there is no work there for musicians. All they care for is cinema and jazz."

"What is jazz?" Gregor joined him at the window, holding his arm the same way Papa did, pretending he too had a pipe. The very word jazz sounded foreign and exciting.

"I heard jazz in St. Petersburg. Terrible stuff. Professor Auer calls it jungle music."

"What does jungle music sound like? Gregor imagined monkeys with trumpets and orangutans playing bass."

"It's noise and banging, not music at all." Papa scowled. "No real artist would play it." He puffed on his pipe and the cloud of smoke circled his head. "Ekaterinoslav is too small," he said. "I've decided we're moving to Moscow."

"Moscow?" Gregor said. "Do people in Moscow speak Russian?"

"Of course," Papa said. "The people there are just like us, only they live in grand houses and go to the opera or theater every night."

"Then it's better than America."

Nadja frowned. "But I like it here." She picked up the dinner plates. "I don't want to leave."

"Why?" Gregor followed her into the kitchen. "It will be wonderful, everything new."

"I don't care." She handed Mama the dirty dishes. "I don't want to go."

"We'll do what Papa wants," Mama said.

"He doesn't know anything," Nadja said. She poured hot water in the dishpan too fast and it spilled on the floor. "I don't—."

"Papa knows what is right." Mama cut her off. "I don't want any more of your crying."

* * *

Everything was sold. Day after day people arrived at the front door, negotiating with Papa over how much they were willing to pay for a table or a chair. When the beds were sold, Gregor and Leo made a pallet on the kitchen floor near the stove. The house grew empty and their voices echoed off the bare walls. Gregor slept with his cello by his side, worried that someone might want to buy it too. By month's end most of the furniture was gone.

"I have contracted for a concert tour," Papa announced. It was suppertime and they sat on plank benches around the rickety table that once belonged in the kitchen yard, the one Mama and Nadja used for laundry. The big kitchen table had long since been sold to the butcher and the chairs went to the Rabbi's wife.

Mama looked up, a startled expression on her face. "A concert tour? How can that be?"

"Grisha and Leo will go with me to Kharkov. I know a man there who has arranged for two performances. Then we'll play in Penza and maybe Tula on our way to Moscow. By the time we arrive the Piatigorsky name will be well known."

"Will we play in a concert hall?" Leo said. "In front of a great audience? Will there be a conductor and orchestra?"

"Of course," Papa said as he stroked his thick black mustache. "And glowing newspaper reviews which I will add to our portfolio."

"What will we play?" Gregor said, his mind already racing through the repertoire. "I want to play the Bach piece I just learned." Turning to Leo, he punched his brother in the shoulder. "It will be grand. We can play Haydn, the Gypsy Trio."

"You don't even know the Gypsy Trio."

"I'll learn it. You can teach me. Mama, you and Nadja sit in the front where you can see us."

"Mama, Nadja and Alex will stay here with Pradid," Papa said. "When we get to Moscow, I'll send tickets."

Mama looked at Papa, then down at her hands. "How long before we can come?" she said.

"The Kharkov performance is in ten days. We should be in Penza two days after that and Moscow by the first of the month."

"But I want Mama to hear me play," Gregor said.

"It is best this way." Mama reached out and ran her hand over his hair. "You can tell me all about it when we come to Moscow. It won't be long."

"Nadja," Papa said. "Make sure your brother's clothes are clean and shoes polished before we leave."

Gregor looked across the table and his eyes met Nadja's. Her lips turned down and her eyes stayed focused on her plate.

"Yes, Papa." Nadja looked so sad that Gregor wanted to reach out and give her a hug.

The day before they were to leave, Mama and Nadja filled a basket with food and packed three suitcases with clean clothes. Papa added a few books, which made the bags very heavy. Mama sniffled and wiped away tears, all the while hugging Gregor and Leo every chance she could. Nadja sulked and after supper Leo escaped to his friend Ivan's house.

On the last night in the only home he had ever known, Gregor heard muffled sobs coming from Nadja's room. He knew she didn't want to leave her girl friends, but he also knew she would miss Peter, the butcher's son. Opening the door, he tiptoed in and sat on the floor beside her mattress.

"Go away," Nadja said. Her voice was muffled as she pressed her face into the pillow.

"It won't be so bad," Gregor rubbed her shoulder. "You'll make new friends in Moscow. We all will."

Nadja turned her head and he saw red-rimmed eyes. Tears streaked her swollen face and it hurt his heart to see her so sad.

"Papa doesn't understand." She sniffled and rubbed the back of her hand across her damp face. "I'll never see any of my friends. Not Elana, or Katerina." She hiccuped. "And I'll never see Peter again." A moan escaped her lips and she dropped back onto the pillow, her shoulders heaving.

Gregor leaned over and tried to hug her. "There are other boys in Moscow," he said. "You'll meet someone wonderful there. All the boys will like you. They'll want to take you dancing."

This was the wrong thing to say.

"I don't want to find anyone else," she wailed. "Go away and leave me alone."

Feeling like a fool, he retreated and shut the door. Mama stood at the end of the hall, a pile of winter coats on her arms. "There's nothing anyone can do for her." She handed him the clothes. "Nadja doesn't know it, but she'll make new friends in Moscow."

Gregor saw the shadows under Mama's eyes and little lines at the corners of her mouth he hadn't noticed before.

"It's always easier for children," she said, as her rough hand touched his cheek. "You're the one that has to be strong for all of us."

On the morning of the departure Pradid brought his wagon to the front door to carry their luggage to the rail station. Gregor was amazed at how old Pradid looked, as if he had shrunken to the height of a child. His steps were hesitant and he held Mama's hand as he walked with her to the street.

Gregor and Leo rode in the back, their legs dangling off the tailgate. Nadja, jammed between the suitcases in the wagon bed, held Alex on her lap while the adults rode in the front. The May sun, already hot, made Gregor sweat inside his black jacket. The wagon wheels kicked up clouds of dust as they started down Philosofskaya Street. They rolled past the crooked wooden fences that marked the dusty yards of their neighbors' homes. Gregor looked down the narrow path that led to Pradid's carpentry shop and felt an awkward cramp in his chest. He rubbed it with his fist but it wouldn't go away.

The street sloped toward the factory workers' houses, squat structures built close with no yards. When they passed the industrial school, the wagon turned onto the cobblestones of Empress Catherine Boulevard where the Jewish shopkeepers were just opening for business. It was Friday and because they would close their shutters early for *Shabbat*, customers were already lining up at the bakery. The smell of fresh baked *Challah* drifted all the way to the street. When the wagon reached the entrance to Potemkin Park, Gregor looked for the spouting fish. But the fountain was not flowing and the bronze fish looked parched in the bright sun.

The railway station, a huge brick building topped with towers on either end overlooked the river near the center of the city. Green spires pointed skyward and a flag fluttered in the ever-present wind. Parallel tracks stretched right and left along the backside of the building, while the main entrance faced Potemkin Park. Inside the high vaulted room, crowds of people sat and stood clustered around piles of luggage. Papa went to purchase tickets while the rest of them encamped by the tall windows.

"Mama, can we go to the park?" Leo asked as he peered out the window.

"No!" Mama's voice was sharp. "Sit right here." She handed two-year-old Alex to Nadja. "No one leaves this spot."

Nadja sank down on the bench as Alex squirmed on her lap, her face long and sad. Gregor sat beside her, his back against his suitcase, his cello case between his knees. Leo walked in circles. As they waited, Mama and Pradid stood to one side, speaking softly, their heads close together so Gregor couldn't hear their words.

This should be a happy time, he thought as he watched travelers coming and going, but he didn't feel happy. From the bench he could see the whole length of the great station. Above him the domed ceiling was covered in yellow tiles and ornate lamps as big as wagon wheels hung from black chains. He saw a policeman who, despite the early summer heat, wore a long gray coat with official markings on collar and cuffs. The man moved from person to person, demanding permits and documents, his right hand resting on a thick black stick stuck in his belt. Men and women rummaged through pocketbooks and bags, producing the papers necessary to satisfy him.

From the far side of the station Gregor saw Papa moving through the crowd, tickets in hand. Before he could make it to the place where they sat, the policeman stepped in his path. The din of voices made it impossible for Gregor to hear what was said, but the expression on Papa's face and his waving hands meant there was trouble.

"Look," he whispered to Nadja. "What's the policeman doing with Papa?"

"Policemen do whatever they want." Nadja stood Alex on the floor, but kept a tight grip on the back of his shirt so he wouldn't run off.

Gregor watched, pressing his knuckles to his chin. The policeman was big, a head taller than Papa, but not as muscular. As the discussion grew more animated, the policeman whose back was all Gregor could see, pulled the stick from his belt. Gregor had seen this happen before. Turkish peddlers, Armenian water carriers, even beggars in Potemkin Park, they were easy targets for the police. The beatings he had seen on his way to school were not unique. No one, not even grownups, dared interfere. Papa's voice rose and Gregor cringed.

"My papers are in order," Papa said, his voice loud as he waved the documents in his hand. "Right here, it says I have permission to travel to Moscow."

Gregor couldn't hear the policeman's reply but saw Papa's face grow red. "I'm going to help him," he said to Nadja as he rose and placed his cello on the bench.

"No." Nadja grabbed his arm and in doing so released Alex. The child immediately toddled off toward the middle of the station. Gregor ran after his brother, scooped him up and returned to the bench. Suddenly aware of the commotion, Mama turned from Pradid, her face pale and tear-stained.

"Pavel, what is it?" she cried as she hurried toward him. The policeman seemed to lose interest when Papa reached into his pocket and handed him something.

"Idiot," Papa sputtered as he joined them, his face still crimson. "Thieving Cossack dog."

"Shhhh, Pavel. You mustn't speak like that." Mama grabbed his arm, but he shook it off.

"What was it?" Gregor asked and he joined them, tugging at Papa's coat. "What did the policeman want?"

"What they all want. Money," Papa said. "Swine. My papers are good. Why should I pay him to make them so?"

"Pavel." Mama pulled at his sleeve. "You can't put yourself at risk arguing with him."

"I paid the bastard." Papa retrieved his suitcase and viola. "And I won't pay him again."

The sound of an engine whistle pierced the air and a clot of people formed near the door. Like a beast with one mind, they surged onto the rail platform. Papa pushed his way to the front of the crowd, while Leo and Gregor struggled to keep up.

"All with tickets get on," sang out the conductor. Gregor climbed the steps, holding his cello in front of him, trying to protect it with his arms. On the platform he turned and saw Mama and Nadja waving. He wanted to wave back, but the crowd pushed him forward.

"Make way, make way," cried the conductor. "More coming on." Before he could even acknowledge Mama, Gregor was pushed into the car. Inside, he and Leo wrestled their luggage onto overhead shelves then found places to sit on the fourth-class benches. Gregor peered out the window as the train pulled away from the station, leaving behind Mama, Pradid, Nadja, Alex, their old wooden house at the edge of the city, the wide grass covered steppes and everything he had ever known.

As the engine picked up speed the big train snorted and shook like a living beast. Inside the passengers were rocked side to side as they struggled to remain seated. When the engine surged forward Gregor grabbed the back of a bench and let his body sway with the motion. It was almost fun, but it made his stomach queasy. Papa pulled out a deck of cards and moved to the end of the car where he and a wizened little man with a scraggly beard played "Nines" and "Roll-Over" using the bench between them as a table. Kopeks and a few rubles changed hands.

With noses pressed against the window, Gregor and Leo watched the countryside slip by. For hours the wide-open steppes stretched unbroken to the horizon. Tall grass rippled in the wind and only the occasional hovel or *mujik* leading a horse broke the monotony. Much more interesting were the towns where Gregor and Leo counted things: cathedrals, electric street lamps and even the occasional automobile. The railway car was crowded and the benches were hard, especially for sleeping. But Mama had packed them salted fish and bread and cabbage rolls. For Gregor, every meal felt like a holiday and there were no dishes to wash.

The second day, they pulled into Kharkov. Passengers struggled into early morning wakefulness and several banged on the car doors trying to get the conductor's attention. Vendors on the rail platform hawked meat pies and fresh bread, but passengers couldn't reach them since most of the windows were nailed shut.

"No one leaves this car," announced the conductor when he pushed the door open. Behind him stood a policeman, his hat pushed back on his head. The conductor stepped aside and the uniformed man moved down the center aisle.

"Documents and papers. No one enters Kharkov District without proper identification." He paused at each bench. Gregor watched Papa pull out his wallet.

"Remember what I told you," Papa said, his voice low. "You know what to say."

Gregor's hand went to his throat and he felt the chain that held the little cross. He hated the feel of the thing against his skin, but Papa made him wear it. If you are asked, tell them you are Christian and show them your cross, Papa had said, but only if you're asked.

The policeman worked his way through the car, examining documents, his stick gripped in his right hand, occasionally poking a passenger in the chest. He was young, too thin, with the first wispy hairs of a moustache shading his upper lip. In a barking voice, he tried to make up for his lack of stature.

"Where are you going?" he demanded when he reached Papa.

"We are musicians," Papa said as he stood to face the man. "My sons and I have a contract to perform in Kharkov."

Gregor watched Papa hand over his documents, then saw him rub his moustache, the way he always did when things were not going well. Leo pulled back, his eyes fixed down on his shoes. Gregor looked down too. Maybe being meek was the best way to behave. As he sat, he felt daggers in his gut. His mouth went dry. What if the man didn't believe Papa? He imagined the feel of the stick hitting him, or worse yet, hitting Papa.

"Pee—ti—gors—ky?" The officer mispronounced the name. "You don't look like musicians. You look like *Zhyd*. The city of Kharkov is closed to *Zhyds*."

"We're Christians." Papa motioned Leo to stand, then pushed him forward. "You see, my sons wear the sign of Jesus Christ." Papa pulled open Leo's shirt exposing the cross.

"Any *Zhyd* can buy a cross." The young policeman said as he frowned.

"But no *Zhyd* would wear one," Papa said. The response seemed to satisfy the policeman and he moved on. Papa sank onto the bench and Gregor slid close beside him, not caring how hot it was. He didn't dare speak but stared at his folded hands, slick with sweat. What if the policeman noticed? He spread his hand flat on his knees and closed his eyes. Aunt Rosie, wide eyes, dress pushed up over her belly, a purple snake lying in the dust.

He held his breath. Behind him, the policeman continued his interrogation. Then the car door clanged shut and Papa exhaled.

"Papa? Will he come back and—."

The conductor opening the door at the front of the car interrupted him. "We stop for ten minutes in Temel," he said, loud enough for all to hear. "Four more hours until we reach Kharkov."

* * *

"I expected a concert hall," Papa said as he pointed to the gazebo that stood in the park across the street from the Kharkov Cathedral. "Not a bandstand in a hay field."

"This is a summer concert series," replied Mr. Rybin, who despite the heat was dressed in a formal gray coat and high-collared shirt. His face was already red and Gregor saw lines of sweat running down his cheek. "It's not as if your sons can command a large audience, at least not enough to fill the concert hall. Besides, an Italian opera company has it reserved for the remainder of the week."

He pulled a rolled up sheet of paper from his coat pocket. "See, I have posted these notices throughout the city."

Papa held out the concert announcement and eyed it. "World famous child prodigies direct from Vienna and Rome? Hear them play Bach and Haydn?" He lowered the poster. "My sons have never been to Vienna or Rome."

"No one but us needs to know that. I prefer to give the public more for their money."

"What's this?" Papa pointed to the fancy script at the bottom. "Study with Shulinov and Sokonitz and your child will become a brilliant musician."

"The music school teachers asked me to give them some exposure."

"For a price no doubt." Papa rolled up the poster then handed it back. "Child prodigies can't be expected to perform in a hay field."

"I'll see that the grass around the stage is cut."

"What about a piano?"

"I'll arrange for a spinet to be in place by tomorrow night."

"It will sound terrible."

"The public won't notice."

"I was promised payment of forty rubles?"

"Maybe. Your fee is fifty percent of the ticket sales after expenses."

"I expect a full accounting."

"Of course." The man smiled and reached to shake Papa's hand. Gregor watched as his father hesitated. Leo looked away and wrinkled his nose as if he smelled something bad. Finally Papa extended his hand and the deal was made.

Rehearsals began after lunch. Since the piano was not in place, they followed Mr. Rybin to the Christian grammar school. After much waiting and confusion a young lady named Anika arrived. She was slim and pretty, her dress bright yellow and her hair dark red. Papa seemed less anxious after she settled herself at the piano. He didn't even say good-bye when Mr. Rybin left.

"I'm accustomed to playing for singers," Anika said as she ran her fingers over the keys. "We have a great many opera companies performing here. I even helped Chaliapin rehearse when his own pianist was indisposed." Her face glowed as she spoke. "He is very tall and so handsome."

Papa frowned. "Have you ever played Haydn's Gypsy Trio?"

Her smile disappeared. "I don't think so. Do you have a score?"

Papa took a deep breath and ran his hand over his face. "Haydn. Tell me you know something by Haydn."

"Of course I know Haydn." She sounded indignant. "But I am accustomed to getting the material at least one month in advance."

"Not possible." Papa handed her the score for the Gypsy Trio. "We'll start with this piece. Come boys, let's begin."

The audience for the evening performance was sparse, the Italian Opera attracting most of the prosperous citizenry. Those who came to hear the unknown trio were young, elderly, or families with small children. The price of admission, fifty kopeks for adults and children free, meant that little ones outnumbered their parents. Those who couldn't or wouldn't buy a ticket simply sat in the long grass beyond the fence and listened for free.

From the edge of the stage, Gregor looked out on the scattered islands of people, many with supper baskets and blankets spread on the newly cut lawn. He scanned the crowd wishing, as if by some miracle, he would see Mama and Nadja. They could have taken a later train and been here by now. But they weren't. Glancing at the cloudless sky, he prayed it would rain and cool the dry summer air. Inside his black wool jacket, his shirt was already glued to his back. At the rear of the bandstand, Papa paced while the perspiring Mr. Rybin tried to keep up with him.

"The piano needs tuning," Papa said. "How can my sons perform with an instrument like that?" He pointed to the portable keyboard that produced such a weak sound under Anika's fingers that it was inaudible a short distance from the stage.

"She'll just have to play louder, as will your sons," Mr. Rybin said.

"You go first," Gregor whispered. He and Leo stood in the shade at the edge of the stage. He watched his brother tighten his bow then tuck the violin under his chin. "Then you'll be done first."

"Just remember to follow my lead in the second part of the Haydn." Leo drew his bow over the strings, checking the sound of each note. "If you go too fast we'll be two bars apart by the end."

"The tempo feels slow to me." Gregor pointed to the second page. Leo had spread the sheets of music across the low railing. "Right here where it goes——."

"That's the way Papa wants it," Leo said. "Remember, play as loud as you can, not as fast as you can."

"I don't like playing outdoors." Gregor smacked at a fly that landed on his neck. "The sun is in my eyes."

"You can turn your music stand toward me," Leo said. "But not too much."

"I wish Mama and Nadja were here." Gregor rested his elbows on the rail and cupped his chin in his hands.

"Unpack your cello." Leo motioned to the canvas case. "Tune to my A."

As Gregor set up his instrument he glanced at Papa, who was still arguing with the promoter.

"How many tickets have you sold?" he heard Papa say. "You promised a full accounting."

"So far, sixty-three. My assistant is still at the gate and will collect from the late arrivals."

"That's not even sixteen rubles for us. You promised me at least twenty."

"Don't forget we have to deduct expenses, the pianist and the grass cutting fee."

"This is not acceptable." Papa's voice rose. Leo looked down at the music, turning the pages of the Haydn score as if nothing else mattered in the world.

"If your sons perform well tonight word of their success will spread. It will be easier to sell more tickets tomorrow night."

"Will we be successful?" Gregor whispered, wondering what would happen if they weren't.

"I know I will," Leo said. "Just do what Papa says." He gathered up the music as Mr. Rybin climbed the back steps and strode across the stage. The promoter raised his arms and waved at the crowd. From where Gregor stood he saw dark circles of sweat on the man's suit coat. The chattering audience grew still.

"Welcome, citizens of Kharkov. You are honored today to hear music never performed before in this city. I have arranged an experience for you, a musical delight. I present to you the renowned Piatigorsky brothers direct from the capitals of Europe. Leonid Piatigorsky is only eleven years old but already he is an extraordinary violinist and has studied with the greatest teachers in Germany and France. Along with a piece by Schubert, he will perform two works by Bach, music rarely heard outside of Germany."

The introduction was such a series of wonderful lies that Gregor wished he were in the audience.

"What pieces?" he whispered to Leo. "I thought you were playing Bach preludes."

"I am," Leo said, his voice low.

"The two brothers will also play the beautiful "Gypsy Trio" by Haydn." Mr. Rybin made a flourish with his hand and paused as if to let the audience absorb his words. "Finally, you will be privileged to hear three pieces presented by young Gregor Piatigorsky, an exceptional cellist who began studying this rarest of instruments at the tender age of five. Now nine years old, he is as accomplished as any adult. Today he will play a piece by Tchaikovsky followed by the music of Saint-Saens and Davidoff. Miss Anika Mostokov will join them on the piano."

There was a polite scatter of applause.

"Why did he say I was nine?" Gregor asked, tugging at Papa's sleeve. "I turned ten already and Leo's twelve."

"Quiet," Papa muttered then motioned Leo forward. "You're first."

Leo stepped to the front of the stage, tucked the violin under his chin and waited. Gregor watched Papa motion to Anika, but she was too busy smoothing her skirt over her knees to notice his signal.

"Now!" Papa hissed and Anika looked up. Realizing her mistake, she started with the opening chord but didn't hold it long enough. Leo hesitated and the whole piece started to fall apart. He hurried to catch up, missing a note and sliding into another. Papa covered his face with his hands and Gregor sank against the back wall. Somehow Leo and Anika managed to reconnect and the piece stumbled to its conclusion.

Poor Leo, thought Gregor. He was a good musician, but the audience wouldn't understand it wasn't his fault.

The applause was tepid. The second piece by Bach went better. Anika seemed more comfortable with the simple rhythm, but the violin was almost drowned out by her chords. They finished together and Leo took a stiff bow. The audience clearly liked the second offering over the first and their applause was more spirited.

"The trio." Papa motioned Gregor forward, then picked up the straight-backed chair and moved it into position, placing the music stand in the middle. Gregor sat and adjusted the end-pin since the chair was too low. Papa waved to Anika. This time she played an A on his cue and Gregor tuned his instrument.

Across the park the sun glinted off the white stucco wall of the cathedral. Gregor squinted, turning a bit to the right to lessen the glare. Still, the notes danced before his eyes. When he rubbed his hand across his face, Papa cleared his throat. It was time to play.

Anika began with the theme, faster than he was used to. Nadja was a much better accompanist, Gregor thought, wishing she were here. On the third line he and Leo entered at the right moment and from that point the sound of the violin and cello overpowered the piano. During a two bar rest, he glanced up and saw a few people had moved closer to the stage.

During the second variation the tempo slowed and Leo came in a bit late. Gregor adjusted his pace so they remained together, but he knew that if they had been at home Papa would have made them start over again. Still, they managed the ending, a rondo in Hungarian style and were at least together on the last note.

Lowering his bow, Gregor looked left to where Papa stood in the shadows. He stroked his moustache, a dark frown on his face. Finally, he nodded and Gregor knew the performance, if not great, was at least acceptable.

The audience applauded with more enthusiasm than they had for Leo's solo. Gregor stood and they bowed together, just the way Papa had taught them. *This is not China*, Papa once said when Gregor had bowed too low at a school recital. *You don't have to kowtow. You're an artist, not a slave.*

When the applause subsided, Leo walked to the edge of the stage and stepped behind the narrow wooden partition that constituted the only area out of sight of the audience. Gregor glanced at Papa then at the audience. More people were repositioning themselves closer to the stage.

"Go on," Papa whispered as he removed the music stand. Mr. Rybin waited until Papa was again out of sight before approaching the edge of the stage. From behind, Gregor noticed the man's starched paper collar had come unbuttoned from his shirt and was close to falling off.

"Now you will hear three wonderful pieces, the first by our very own Peter Ilych Tchaikovsky, then the always popular *Swan* and finally, *At the Fountain,* composed by master cellist Davidoff." Rybin bowed again as he backed off the stage, the wings of his collar flapping.

Gregor sat alone before the hushed audience. Playing solo was harder than playing with Leo. He ran his tongue over his dry lips, tried to swallow and wished for water. Turning his chair a fraction to the right, he managed to lessen the glare of the bright sunlight.

Anika began, but her introduction to the Tchaikovsky variations was too soft and too slow. Papa's threats during rehearsal seemed to have no effect on her playing. There wasn't time left for nervousness. Starting fast, Gregor immediately felt more comfortable as he worked his way through the opening. Anika did her best to pound out the accompaniment. *Louder, not faster,* he remembered Leo's words. It felt like he and Anika were competing for volume. The excitement increased in the final variation and miraculously he and Anika ended together, neither one dominating the other.

The applause was louder and more sustained than it had been for Leo. Gregor kept his eyes down, remembering Papa's admonition not to make visual contact with the audience until the program was finished. The second piece was "The Swan" by Saint-Saens, a softer piece, and this time it felt as if the piano would overpower him. Still the audience seemed to like it and the applause was respectable.

Finally, Davidoff's *At the Fountain.* He knew the piece by heart and liked it. It sounded difficult but was really easier than the slower pieces. And it was short, only three minutes. No time for the audience to get bored.

Before he knew it, he was done. The applause was loud and when he stood so did quite a few people in the audience. Several children ran forward to the stage and one little girl placed a handful of wildflowers at his feet. He took a stiff little bow, exactly as he had been taught and found himself looking down at the little clutch of purple and white blossoms. The girl, about seven, smiled up at him and clapped her hands, pure excitement glowing on her face. Without thinking, he stooped, took the flowers and bowed again, this time to her.

"You should never kneel before the public," Papa said. They stood together behind the bandstand waiting for Mr. Rybin to count out the receipts. The man's sweat-stained paper collar now hung loose at his neck, threatening to take leave of his shirt altogether. The assistant, a young man with a wispy goatee, pulled coins and bills from his coat and pants pockets and lay them on the table.

"I know I sold more. Yes, here is another ruble and forty kopeks," said the nervous young man.

"How could you have forty kopeks?" Mr. Rybin held four coins in his palm. "The price of admission is fifty kopeks?"

"Some one must have cheated me."

"Never mind forty kopeks," Papa said. "How many rubles did you collect?"

"I have a total of . . . of . . ." Mr. Rybin's hand slid into his coat pocket. "Here. Thirty-nine rubles, forty kopeks, minus the costs, which came to twelve rubles eighty."

"Twelve rubles! What cost twelve rubles?"

"Five for the pianist, three to rent the piano, two for use of the bandstand, which included cutting the grass, and two rubles eighty for the tickets and posters."

"That leaves us less than fifteen rubles."

"Thirteen rubles, thirty kopeks to be exact," Mr. Rybin said as he handed Papa half of the proceeds. "I get the same as you for all my efforts."

"There had better be more customers tomorrow night," Papa snapped as he pocketed the money. "Come, boys. We'll have very little to eat until we get to Moscow."

Chapter Six

Moscow was a dark and dirty place, unlike the open steppe and great windy sky of the Ukraine. Even in summer, when the sun shone until midnight, the light in Moscow was gray. Waiting for them in the late twilight at the railway station was a skinny man wearing a round city hat. He spoke funny sounding Russian so fast, Gregor could hardly understand him. Papa said he was a friend from St. Petersburg, a man with important connections.

"I have just the place for a big family like yours," the man said. "A real bargain."

With the remainder of the inheritance money Papa bought the old two-story building on Ogorodnya Street. The place was made of thick logs, unpainted and black with soot from years of breathing dirty Moscow air. It contained six apartments, five of which were already occupied. A solid stockade fence surrounded the front courtyard and the only entrance was through the rusty iron gate.

A week later, Mama, Nadja and Alex arrived. Just in time, Gregor thought. He and Leo had grown tired of eating bread and cabbage soup in the dusty kitchen while Papa went out at night with his friends from St. Petersburg. Mama and Nadja quickly made things right and soon the apartment was cleaned and smelled of kasha and fried fish.

Every two weeks Papa collected the rents, but the tenants often paid late or not at all. When the money wasn't there, Papa cursed and stomped his feet loud enough so the downstairs tenants could hear him.

The space beyond their courtyard and across the alley was filled with unpainted wooden shacks occupied by people much worse off. Ragged men with dented samovars strapped to their backs peddled cups of tea. Exotic Chinese women with black eyes and smoky skin sold magic herbs and potions to Muscovites too poor to hire a doctor. The smell of foreign food wafted up from open windows, mixing with factory fumes and the odor of sewage from ancient latrines. Tartars, who lived in log hovels along the smelly canal, sold home brewed *samogon* but never drank it. Allah would not allow such a transgression.

The Gypsies had secret ways of making quick money and for a ruble would tell you how. On the next block a Polish tailor lent money to anyone willing to pay a fee. If a borrower could not pay, his son or daughter would work off the debt in the tailor's shop. The *Kalmucks* did no work at all but sent their women and children into the streets to beg and collect empty bottles to sell back to the brewery.

But there were too many vodka and samogon shacks and the ground around them was littered with broken glass. The Tartar children threw shards of glass at one another when they had no new targets. A few streets away, filling an entire block, stood the chocolate factory. Day and night steam belched from the black smokestack bathing the entire neighborhood in a sickly odor that clung to clothes and skin.

When payday came, wives and mothers stood in the doorways waiting for sons and husbands to come home from the factory, hoping to extract enough money from the men's pockets to feed their children. The men, intent on reaching the vodka shacks, beat their wives as they tried to hold onto their rubles.

On each block some adults and most of the children formed gangs and fought with one another over vodka, cigarettes, cards and whores. When there was nothing left, they fought over race, religion and even recipes for cooking cabbage. The children did little damage beyond bloody noses, but when the grown-ups fought, people sometimes died.

"Stay clear of the troublemakers," Mama warned.

"Stand your ground," Papa said. "Don't let anyone get in your way."

The one group everyone hated was the police. They came to the vodka shacks and loudly demanded free drinks, threatening anyone who got in their way. The proprietors always paid.

From the lower apartments Gregor fell asleep to the sound of coughing, crying and cursing. Late into the night husbands and wives fighting kept Gregor awake.

"Worthless whore," a drunken husband bellowed. "This meat isn't fit for a dog." His complaints were usually followed by the sound of a woman's scream.

"Cossacks," Mama muttered. "Stay away from them."

"Why are they so angry?" Gregor asked.

"Living here too long makes them so," she said as she handed him a stack of dinner plates.

"Will we become like them if we stay?"

Mama turned away and placed the bowl of beets and onions on the table. But she didn't answer his question.

Papa auditioned for the Bolshoi Orchestra and was rejected. "Idiots," he bellowed when he stormed through the front door. "The director is a fool and the first viola has never studied outside Moscow."

Mama's red hands twisted the dishtowel into a knot. "What will we do? Grisha needs new boots. He can't audition for the conservatory in rags."

"I'll fix his shoes with glue," Papa said. "You can cut his hair. Nadja, press Grisha's pants and jacket." Papa had already forgotten his own failure. "Tomorrow it is your turn to audition. I know you'll succeed. By the New Year you will be performing for the Tsar."

"Are you scared?" Leo said that night as they undressed for bed in the narrow room at the end of the hall.

"I'm scared." Gregor climbed onto the cold mattress. He pulled the heavy blanket to his chin and shivered. "I had a bad dream last night. The conductor hit me on the head with his baton."

"That can't happen. It's not allowed."

"How do you know?"

"Papa would have said."

"I hope it's like the auditions back home."

"Don't take all the covers." Leo yanked the blankets to his side of the bed. "What if they don't accept you? What will you do?"

"I don't know. What do you think Papa will say?"

"He'll yell," Leo said, his voice muffled. "And he'll stomp his foot a lot and call them all idiots."

"I don't want to disappoint him."

"But if you fail we can all go home." Leo rolled over and propped himself up on his elbow. "I hate it here."

"You do?" Gregor pushed Leo's shoulder. "Why?"

"I miss my friends. It's boring. There's no one to play soccer with. Nadja hates it too."

For a long time Gregor lay in the dark, staring at the ceiling, unable to sleep. If he won the scholarship, he would work hard and become the best cellist in the conservatory. Papa would forget his disappointment and be proud. But Leo, Nadja and maybe even Mama would be miserable.

If he failed at the conservatory, Papa would be angry and Mama would be disappointed, but maybe secretly she would be happy. If he failed, then they could all go home. Leo would have his friends and Nadja would laugh again. No matter what he did, someone would be miserable. Rolling over, he buried his face in his pillow. At that moment he wished he had never laid eyes on a cello.

* * *

The Moscow Conservatory was a huge three-story faded yellow building that covered several city blocks. Classes were divided into vocal and instrumental, with the string classes located in the west wing. The air inside the practice rooms was clammy and smelled of mildew after a hard rain.

The gloomy hallway leading to the large concert hall was crowded with parents and children, all hoping to capture one of the few scholarships available for the poor. Papa said the children of wealthy Muscovites could attend no matter how badly they played, just so long as their parents paid the tuition.

Inside the hall, straight-backed chairs had been set in clusters at the corners of the room. Cellos and violas auditioned on the stage, while basses and violins auditioned near the back wall. Cacophony filled the hall and spilled out into the entryway.

The director of cellos sat in the corner barking orders while two older students, dressed in stiff uniforms, stood by looking bored. He allowed no more than a minute of playing, two minutes if the performance was exceptionally good. Almost as quickly as they arrived, most of the applicants were dismissed.

"Next," called the director who sat at a small table, his back to the parents. The line inched forward. Papa ran his fingers over his mustache and Gregor mimicked the same action on his own lip. Parents didn't speak to one another and children eyed each other with curiosity or suspicion.

"Next." The word hung heavy and Gregor felt a chill. It was his turn. Papa had to stand aside with the rest of the anxious parents while he took the chair and faced the judges.

"Play the third Duport etude," the director said.

Gregor wished he could turn and look at Papa, but he didn't dare. Instead, he closed his eyes and ignored the sick knot in his stomach. With his left hand, he felt the strings as he held the bow above the cello's body, imagining the correct sound. His hand trembled a little and he willed it to stillness. Touching the bow to the strings, he ran through the technical drill with ease. So far so good.

He looked at the director who sat with his chin propped on his stubby fingers. The man seemed to be asleep.

"Do you know the Dvorak?" the man asked without opening his eyes.

"Concerto for Cello. First movement?"

"Let me hear it."

Relieved he hadn't asked for something new, Gregor laid his bow on the strings and started playing pianissimo. Surprise them, Papa always said. Start soft then build, draw in your audience. Now Gregor poured every bit of energy he had into the music. He felt the notes flow from one bar to the next.

"Stop." The director's voice startled him just as he was building to the crescendo. "That's enough!"

Gregor looked to Papa, hoping for reassurance. Instead of smiling, Papa dropped his head and covered his face with his hands. Failure?

The director rose and walked to the corner where he whispered something to the two older students. They shook their heads. The director walked past Papa and stopped in front of the waiting parents.

"The scholarship position for cello is filled," he said. "The rest of you can go home."

A cry of protest rose from the waiting parents, but the director turned his back on them. "Your son is accepted," he said to Papa. "Classes begin on Monday."

Papa straightened up and pounded Gregor's shoulder. With his back turned to the other grumbling parents, he announced in a loud voice. "My son will be first cello before the year is finished. Then he will play for the Tsar."

In his wildest dreams, Gregor had never believed he would be chosen. Was he really good enough for the Moscow Conservatory? Good enough to play first cello? What if he disappointed Papa? What if he failed?

For the next two nights he tossed and turned, unable to sleep. Fear of the unknown hung over him like a dark cloud. Because of him the whole family was stuck in Moscow. Now Nadja and Leo would hate him.

Walking from Ogorodnya Street to the conservatory took Gregor an hour. He didn't mind it in good weather, especially when he joined other boys along the way. At first he hung back, avoiding the questions and stares of the older students, but in time he found a place among them.

Most of the students had never traveled farther than the Moscow River or Sokolniki Park. Gregor found a ready audience when he told fantastic stories of the bandits who lived on the open steppes and wild boat rides down the Dnieper River. His imagination ran wild, but most of the younger boys believed him.

Mathematics and geography classes were boring, but music theory was fun and chamber music was best. There were competitions between the viola, violin and cello students, but they always joined forces on the soccer field to beat out the brass and woodwind players.

The morning walk to school was usually uneventful, since the Tartar children were still asleep and the vodka shacks closed. The walk home was different. He had to endure verbal harassment from the Tartar boys who loitered near the bridge. They approached him on the pretense of selling their homemade cigarettes or picking his pockets, but he had no money.

Sometimes they followed him, yelling *"Boom, boom, boom"* as they pointed to his cello, making obscene gestures with sticks they found along the path. Still, the Tartars didn't frighten him. They were short and their funny way of speaking reminded Gregor of small yapping dogs.

Only in the courtyard, when he passed the drunken Cossack's son, Dimitri, did he raise his guard. The stocky dark-haired youth, dressed in a telegraph office uniform, stood in the courtyard every afternoon smoking a stubby cigarette.

"Hey, music boy," he called as Gregor climbed the stairs to his apartment. "Why don't you play something for me on that big fiddle of yours."

Gregor paused and slid the cello from his shoulder and leaned it against the door. Perhaps talking about music with Dimitri was the safest way to deal with him. "What kind of music do you like?"

"Whatever kind would get that pretty sister of yours to lift her skirts." He thrust out his hips and made a crude gesture with his hand. "Tell her I have plenty of money."

Gregor froze. For a moment he could not reply. In Dimitri's face he saw the same vulgar eyes and vile smirk he had seen on the faces of men at the North Star Klub.

"Shut your dirty mouth!"

"Make me."

Dimitri outweighed him, but wasn't much taller. Jaw hard and fists clenched, Gregor flew down the stairs intent on smashing the Cossack's face.

"Hey, music boy." Dimitri pointed to his own big square chin. "Want to try?"

"I'll kill you." Gregor swung, but his adversary jumped away. "*Zhyd* boy with the big fiddle." Dimitri laughed again.

"Dimitri, you lazy son of a whore," a slurred voice called from the lower apartment. "Where's that bucket of coal I sent you for?" The apartment door opened and Dimitri slipped inside, grinning as he made good his escape.

Gregor stood alone in the courtyard, shaking with rage. His breath came in short sobs as tears welled up. Humiliated, he swung at the door but missed and his fist hit the frame. Pain shot through his hand and up his arm. From the other side of the door he heard laughter.

With breath coming in ragged gasps, he grabbed his instrument and ran up the stairs. I'll kill him, so help me I'll kill him, the voice in his head screamed. When he reached the third floor landing, he sagged against the doorframe, his torn knuckles pressed to his lips. He didn't dare tell anyone, not Mama, not Nadja and most of all, not Papa.

Chapter Seven

Moscow, Russia
June 1914

"Come here, boys," Papa called from the dining room. "I have great plans for the summer."

Gregor dropped his schoolbooks on a chair then propped his cello in the corner.

"Are we going home?" Leo asked. "Back to Ekaterinoslav? Are we all going? Will we see Pradid?"

"Forget that place." Papa sat at the dining room table with a large sheet of paper spread in front of him. "There's no future for us there. Grisha, look at this."

Leo slid into the chair and propped his elbows on the table as Gregor peered over Papa's shoulder. In large ornamental print the poster announced: HISTORIC SUMMER OPERA EVENT!! SENSATIONAL PRODUCTION OF "EUGENE ONEGIN!!" Musicians wanted for three-month tour.

"A friend of mine recommended us to Mr. Susow," Papa said. "He's the manager of the Summer Opera Company. I met him today and we are hired for the entire tour." He pushed back his chair and stood erect as if he were facing a live audience.

"May I introduce myself? I am Pavel Piatigorsky, first viola." Pointing to Leo, he said. "This is my eldest son, a fine violinist." He placed his big hand in the middle of Gregor's back. "And my son Gregor. He is the best cellist in the Moscow Conservatory." Papa took a stiff bow to the imaginary crowd.

"Bravo! Bravo!" Gregor cried, clapping as he jumped up and down. "Where will we perform? Can all of us go? Even Mama and Nadja and Alex? She can accompany us on the piano." He looked to Leo who hadn't said a word. "It's going to be wonderful. I can't wait to tell my friends at school." His questions came tumbling out. "Will we be paid real money? Can I get a new bow and a new black jacket? It's going to be such fun!"

Before Papa could reply, Gregor ran to the kitchen. "Mama, did you hear? We're going on tour."

* * *

"I wish you could come, too," Gregor told Nadja, as they waited on the crowded platform beneath the sign that marked Track Three. "You're a wonderful pianist."

"I wish I could." Nadja shifted Alex from her right hip to her left. "If Mama wasn't sick every morning, I know Papa would let me go." The three-year-old squirmed and she sat him on Gregor's suitcase. "It will be awful here with all of you gone."

"You must make some new friends." He knelt next to Alex and tickled his brother's bare feet. Alex giggled and tried to pull Gregor's hair. "You should find someone who loves music as much as you do."

A smile lit up Nadja's face and she knelt beside him. "Don't tell Papa," she whispered. "But I know someone who likes my music. He heard me playing."

"Really?" Gregor felt relieved. It was good to see her happy. "Who?"

"The boy downstairs." She kept her voice low. "He walked with me to the market last week."

"Not Dimitri."

"Shhhh," she said and he saw pink come to her cheeks. "He's very nice."

"No. He's a . . . a . . . ." He wanted to say *Grubnii Durok,* but Mama did not approve of such language.

"Keep your voice down." Nadja stepped away from him and said loudly. "I know you're going to have great fun. You must promise to write and tell us everything. And don't forget to have your photograph taken so we don't forget what you look like."

Gregor glanced at Papa then back at his sister. How stupid could she be? "Dimitri is not—"

"Promise me you'll write every week," she interrupted.

"I will." Gregor sighed. She was hopeless. "I'll write, but you must write and tell me everything."

"How can I? There is no place to send you a letter." She moved toward Leo, who ignored her. "Good-bye, Leo. I'll miss you too." She gave Leo a hug, but he stiffened and tried to pull away.

"Nadja," Gregor said, hopping up to sit on the edge of a wooden baggage cart. "I'll buy picture postcards and send them so you can see all the cities we visit."

"That would be fun," she said. "I've never gotten a postcard before."

Gregor heard the train whistle in the distance. He looked toward the end of the platform where his parents stood. Papa had his arms around Mama's shoulders, but she was too busy crying and rubbing her eyes to actually speak. At her feet, Alex clung to her leg and joined in the chorus of sobs. Leo retreated and with his back to both parents, seemed to wish he belonged to some other family.

"Train for Samara, train for Samara," cried the railway officer as the engine steamed into the station. "Get on now or be left behind."

"Everything will be wonderful, you'll see," Papa said. He kissed the top of Mama's head, patted her shoulder then picked up his viola case. "We'll return with our pockets full of rubles and our careers assured."

Nadja hugged Gregor, then kissed his cheek. He wanted to say something, anything to change her mind about the filthy pig Dimitri, but all that came out was, "Be careful."

They boarded the train and Gregor scrambled over empty seats then pulled open the window. As the train moved, he waved to the figures on the platform. He kept on waving until the track curved and the platform slipped out of sight. From somewhere below his throat, he felt a sudden pressure, as if his body had grown too heavy. He glanced at Leo who rubbed at his eyes.

"Did you get cinders in your face?" Gregor felt his own eyes fill with tears.

"Yes," Leo said, sniffling. "Must have."

As the train picked up speed Gregor spread his feet wide and held onto the back of the seat. The car shook and rolled, first left then right. "But the wind is blowing the other direction." He looked at the clouds of black smoke billowing past the window. "And I didn't feel any cinders."

The opera company filled the entire third-class railcar right behind the engine. Mr. Susow assigned Papa, Leo and Gregor to a compartment that slept four. Their roommate was a rotund woman who sang soprano in the chorus. She smelled like ripe cheese.

While Papa retrieved their suitcases from the aisle, Gregor tried to squeeze past their traveling companion. The compartment was so narrow that her hips filled the entire space between the two lower seats. When she sat, she spread out filling an area meant for two.

"And keep your belongings off the floor," she snapped. "Or I'll step on them."

"Stop," Papa cried, as he opened the door, suitcases tucked under both arms. "There are three of us. You can't take up all this space."

"They don't count," she said, waving a meaty finger. "They're just children."

"Boys, wait in the corridor," Papa said, as he dropped the luggage and held open the door. Gregor and Leo slipped under his outstretched arm.

"She is really, really big, like an ox," Gregor whispered to Leo who leaned against the sooty window.

"She smells bad too," Leo puckered up his nose. "Like she took a bath in honey and garlic."

Through the closed door Gregor heard Papa's voice, at first low then louder. "I will not tolerate your taking all the space. I am first viola and my son Leo is concertmaster. Grisha is first cello. You are only a member of the chorus. You will have to leave."

"I don't care who you are," the shrill voice replied. "I will not vacate. The three of you can sleep in the freight car for all I care."

"I'll complain to Mr. Susow," Papa said. "He wouldn't tolerate this injustice."

"Go ahead, Mr. Important. I was here first."

The door flew open and Papa stomped out. "Don't move," he said and headed to the next car.

Gregor looked at Leo's glum face. "Do you think he'll find us a new compartment?"

"I doubt it. I heard the conductor say every seat is filled." Leo backed away from the compartment door as if he were afraid the cheese lady might come charging out. "What if she's sitting on your cello?"

Gregor gently turned the door latch. Opening it just a crack, he peeked inside. The woman's back was to him, her red streaked hair falling lose as she removed her hat. Then her coat and her skirt came off, followed by her blouse and shoes. His mouth fell open as he saw mounds of starchy white flesh rising above her shift. Her flabby upper arms reminded him of churned butter.

She turned away from the window and lifted her shift, revealing her bare backside. Gregor couldn't hide the giggle that burst forth from his lips, but the rattle of the train saved him from discovery. Her great huge thighs reminded him of Pradid's white mare. Finally, she pulled a greasy pink robe from her suitcase and slipped it over her head. Once she was fully covered, she dropped onto the seat and opened a lunch basket. On top of the lid she set out cheese, apples and a big loaf of bread.

"She's eating," Gregor whispered after he shut the door. "Do you think she'll share?"

"Of course not." Leo sank to the floor and pulled his knees to his chest. "That's why she's as fat as a cow."

"This is an outrage!" Papa's voice came from the end of the car. A moment later he charged down the aisle, waving his hands at Mr. Susow.

"There's nothing I can do," said the manager. Gregor knew the situation was hopeless.

For the next two days the three of them tried to stay out of the woman's way by visiting with the other musicians. Gregor and Leo played cards to pass the time, but at night they had nowhere to sleep but in the compartment. The heat from the woman's enormous body and the odor of her greasy cheese made the air in the cramped car reek. Gregor fell asleep on the top bunk, his nose pressed into the rolled-up jacket he used for a pillow.

On the evening of the third day the train pulled into the Samara railway station, an elegant stone building with great tall windows that let in the bright noonday sun. Without a single tree nearby for shade, the heat inside the station was oppressive. Still, it was good to be off the train and not dodging hot cinders in order to get fresh air. The members of the opera stepped off the railcar, laughing and shouting at one another like children set free from school. Their luggage remained behind in the car, which the engineer detached from the rest of the train. The railcar became their hotel.

Mr. Susow announced they would walk into the city and carry their own instruments since no wagons were available. Gregor was happy to stretch his legs, but their roommate, who had nothing but her own weight to carry, muttered and complained the entire way.

"Come on," Leo cried. "Let's race to the end of the station."

"Wait," Gregor called as he struggled with his cello. "It's not fair. Your violin is small."

"Ha, ha," Leo yelled over his shoulder. He ran the length of the platform, stopping only when Gregor had no chance of winning.

"Look… we are… famous," Gregor said, when he caught up to Leo. As he leaned against a baggage truck he pointed at a poster glued over remnants of earlier announcements.

HISTORIC EVENT! ORCHESTRA AND CHORUS! FAMOUS STARS!

"If we were famous," Leo said. "We'd be riding in a carriage and eating cake for supper."

The Samara Opera House was an old wooden structure near the open-air market. Paint peeled from its massive black doors and the heat of the late morning sun made Gregor's head hurt. They waited outside, sweating, while Mr. Susow went searching for the hall manager. A Tartar boy, about Gregor's age, approached them from the market, a tray of fruit balanced on his head.

"You buy? Good to eat." He dropped to one knee, brought the tray down and balanced the offering on his thigh. "Only five kopeks."

"Can we, Papa?" Gregor's stomach growled at the sight of purple grapes.

"After rehearsal," Papa said. "If you play well."

Gregor shrugged and the boy returned the tray to his head and moved down the line of musicians. "You buy? Good to eat," he chanted, his tone unchanged by rejection.

The admission price to the opera was only one ruble. On the day prior to the performance the line at the ticket window stretched around the block. The promised orchestra, which Susow advertised as having one hundred musicians, was a lie. In reality there were only seventeen. The conductor doubled as the only French horn player, which left him unable to speak or use his hands as he stood at the podium.

The concert manager, Mr. Susow, also sang tenor opposite the girl who had been hired to play the part of Tatiana, a virgin maiden who is seduced by the hero. The young lady had neglected to inform Susow of her advanced state of pregnancy, which was now apparent for all to see.

"Virgin maiden?" the manager complained loudly to anyone willing to listen. "What if she gives birth during the performance?" He declared she would be replaced as soon as possible, but the schedule of performances allowed no time for auditions.

Inside the great dark hall the air was musty but cool. With his jacket off and his shirtsleeves rolled up, Gregor found himself facing four stands, each holding music for a different instrument. At times he played the cello parts, then filled in for the missing clarinet, oboe and trumpet. Changing from bass clef to treble then back again was confusing. With faint light coming in the high windows, he had trouble even reading the notes.

They had only one afternoon to rehearse and the orchestra sounded awful. The chorus was even worse. It was dark by the time they finished. Gregor was exhausted and Leo's feet dragged as they headed back to the railcar. Outside the hall, the market was deserted and the fruit boy nowhere in sight. For supper Papa bought cabbage rolls from a vendor at the railway station. They sat outside the station on a baggage cart, hoping to catch the wisp of a night breeze.

"Don't leave the station," Papa said after supper. "I have important business to attend."

"What business?" Gregor hopped off the baggage cart. "Can we come too?"

"Men's business." Papa ran a comb through his black curly hair then buttoned the collar of his shirt. "I expect you to be here when I return." Papa waved to Mr. Susow as the manager exited the railcar. Gregor climbed back on the cart and pushed Leo's feet out of the way.

"Did you see how many people bought tickets?" Leo said. He stretched out on his back and made a pillow with his folded jacket "We'll make a lot of money tomorrow."

Gregor dangled his legs over the edge and watched a skinny cat stalking a cricket. The hissing gas lamps gave the station a yellow glow and the lined-up carts cast huge shadows. "I don't think we sounded very good today. I can hardly see the notes."

"It doesn't matter." Leo yawned. "The audience won't care. All they want to see are the singers, not us."

"Maybe I should practice some more," Gregor said. "If I memorize the cello and viola parts, all I have to do is read for the trumpet and oboe." He dropped off the cart and headed for the dark railcar. "Come on, practice with me."

"No, I'm tired," Leo said. He rolled onto his side, his face away from the lamp and made a pillow with his hands. "I'm sick of this tour anyway. I wish we'd never come."

"Papa said it will be better when we get to Saratov." Gregor climbed into the empty railcar. "And he says Astrakhan is even better. By then we'll sound wonderful."

"Hmmppph," Leo grunted. "You are a fool. You believe everybody and everything."

"You believe Papa." Gregor said. "Don't you?"

Leo didn't answer and Gregor didn't ask again.

The next afternoon Gregor sat near the front of the small orchestra, surrounded by a wall of music stands. Papa and Leo were on his right, the string bass player on his left, a vodka bottle protruding from the man's coat pocket. The conductor stepped onto the platform and bobbed his head, marking the tempo with his French horn.

When the house lights dimmed they played the overture and the laughing, chattering audience grew still. Determined to make up for their lack of numbers, the orchestra played with as much volume as possible. But the poor acoustics and bad timing became apparent as the opera progressed. The two trumpets entered a bar too late then stopped altogether. Leo's violin trill could barely be heard and the crowd grew restless. The chorus persevered as the rumble of hisses and boos grew louder. Gregor glanced at the double bass player beside him. When he wasn't playing either the second cello or bass part, the man turned his back to the audience, pulled his vodka bottle from his pocket and took a long swallow.

When Mr. Susow sang the aria to Olga, the pregnant actress feigned indifference. Suddenly, Susow's voice cracked and there was silence. The conductor lowered his French horn and stared at Susow, who broke into a fit of coughing. In desperation the conductor pointed at the bass player. "Sing!" he hissed.

The man lowered his vodka bottle and stepped forward, his instrument in his left hand. "Olga, good-bye forever," he sang, his voice gurgling as he swayed right then left, as if he were on the deck of a rolling ship. Finally, unable to retain his balance, he pitched forward, crashing down on top of his instrument.

The audience went wild. "We want our money back," someone cried. Several patrons ran toward the stage, shaking their fists in the air. Gregor pushed his chair back as a man in a dirty army uniform crawled onto the stage. Before he knew what to do next there was a wild scramble as everyone around him, musicians and singers alike, raced for the back door. Music stands and chairs toppled.

"Get out!" Papa cried.

Gregor tried to run but the endpin of his cello snagged the leg of a chair. Lifting it into his arms like a baby, he dodged those around him until he made it to the street, the audience in pursuit.

Leo was faster, his violin easier to carry than the cello. But Papa's long legs outraced everyone. They reached the railway car, breathless, sweating, hearts pounding. Safely locked inside, Gregor and Leo crouched on the floor. Mr. Susow, the singing manager, was nowhere in sight.

"Do you— think— they killed him?" Leo asked, gasping for air.

"I didn't see him." Gregor scrambled into the smelly compartment.

"We can't let anyone in." Leo's hands shook as he slid the door latch shut. Not that it would do much good. A few well-placed kicks and the door would be splinters.

"I think they want their money back," Gregor said. He pushed his cello on the upper bunk then sank to the floor below the window. Outside, he heard people yelling, as they pounded on the sides of the train. From his hiding place Gregor heard Papa's voice, "Get the locks and barricades. Keep them out," followed by the sound of the railcar door slamming shut.

They waited side by side in silence, listening to the noise on the other side of the wall. A bead of sweat trickled down Gregor's neck. He saw a fly land on Leo's forehead and for a moment considered swatting it, but didn't. Finally the angry voices began to wane.

"Here's Mr. Susow." Papa's voice echoed down the corridor.

Gregor lifted his head and peered out the dirty window. He saw the manager limping toward the railcar, his clothes disheveled, blood running from his nose, his left eye swollen shut.

"Open up!" the man cried. The door was unlocked and he scrambled on board.

"Come on," Leo said. "Let's go out there." He unlatched the door to their compartment and they crawled out, standing when they were past the windows.

"Under duress," Mr. Susow said as he wiped sweat and blood from his face with a white handkerchief. "I have returned the night's receipts to the theater owner. That should satisfy the audience."

"What about our money?" Papa demanded. "You promised we would be paid tonight."

"We must improve our performance." Susow paused to accept the vodka bottle from the drummer. He tilted his head back, took a long swallow, then wiped his mouth with his sleeve. "Or none of you will receive a single kopek."

Back in their smelly compartment, Gregor tried to sleep on the hard upper bunk while the cheese lady snored below them. She had waddled back to the railcar long after the altercation, her satchel stuffed with food. Papa spent the night playing cards with the drummer, refusing to enter the compartment.

Sometime after midnight the railcar was reconnected to a southbound train and they began their journey. Gregor felt the car lurch forward and almost rolled off his bunk. The rocking motion made the lady snore louder. He slept the remainder of the night with fingers pressed in his ears.

The three scheduled performances of Eugene Onegin in the next town turned out to be only two. The audience was more tolerant, or perhaps more drunk and they didn't seem to notice the production's flaws.

Mr. Susow gave each member of the opera company three rubles. When the train left for the next destination, the Volga River resort towns of Astrakhan, one third of the performers, including their fat roommate, were not on board.

Two days later, what was left of the opera company arrived at the rail station and unloaded their belongings onto the platform. Susow left to arrange for their next performance and never returned. Gradually, orchestra members and singers drifted away, some intent on buying return tickets to Moscow while others looked for more lucrative work. Gregor, Leo and Papa sat alone on the rail station bench.

"I'm sure Mr. Susow will return," Papa said. "He's an honorable man and I signed a contract." He pulled the official looking paper from his pocket. "We'll wait a little longer."

"What if he doesn't come back?" Gregor asked.

Papa ran his hand over his black moustache and appeared deep in thought. "Then we'll make this our vacation." He rose and retrieved his suitcase. "This is a famous resort town known for its sunny weather and healthful climate."

Chapter Eight

The cheapest room Papa could find was a tiny shack behind the pastry vendor's stall, near the riverside amusement park. For one ruble a night Leo and Gregor shared a narrow bed while Papa slept on the lumpy couch. In the morning they ate overripe melons, grapes and day-old bread the fruit peddler sold them for twenty kopeks.

On the first day of their vacation they explored the entire amusement park. Gypsies told fortunes as they tried to entice customers into their colorful tents. A man with an accordion had two little monkeys perched on his shoulders. Gregor knelt in front of the monkeys, coaxing them to take a peanut from his hand. One creature scurried forward, did a backward flip, then reached out and snatched the peanut. Gregor would have stayed there all day playing with the monkeys, but the man with the accordion wanted money for the animal tricks. Papa said they couldn't afford it.

In the center of the amusement park stood an ornate full-size calliope. A woman in a long red dress with black hair flowing down her back sat at the keyboard. But the sound coming from the instrument was shrill and out of tune. Papa said it wasn't music at all, though Gregor thought it sounded like fun.

In the evening Papa met a man who took them to a low dark building with a wide hole in the dirt floor. Around the hole squatted men who shouted and called each other names. Some wore the baggy trousers of Tartars, but others looked like ordinary Russians. One dandy wore a fine black suit but swore like a policeman. A swarthy looking Turk entered the pit then waved toward two men who joined him, each carrying a wooden cage.

"Are the men going to fight?" Leo asked, his eyes wide. "I want the tall one to win."

"Not the men," Papa said as he bounced several coins in his hand. "Roosters. This is a cockfight."

It made no sense to Gregor. "How will they know which rooster wins?"

"Which ever bird is still alive is the victor."

"One of the birds has to die?"

Gregor stared at the animals as their keepers extracted them from the cages. The birds looked tough and all had long sharp spurs on their heels. One rooster wore a black ribbon around its neck, the other a red one.the circle of men began yelling as the Turk began collecting bets.

"Two rubles on Red," Papa said and handed the man his coins. "If Red wins," he explained. "I'll make back at least ten." He clapped as the birds flapped their way into the circle. Gregor and Leo did the same.

The fight was fast and furious. Feathers flew as the animals attacked. Specks of blood spotted the hard packed dirt. Black was the tougher. Even when Red went down, Black kept attacking, pecking at his foe's eyes and neck. Gregor turned away, his supper souring in his belly. "Get up, you stupid bird." But his cries did no good and the rubles were gone.

"It was worth it," Papa said, his face glowing as they left the cockfight arena. "So what if Red did lose. We'll come back tomorrow and I'll bet on Black. This is a marvelous vacation."

* * *

"Come on," Gregor called to Leo. It was the afternoon of their third day and the sun was unbearably hot. "Let's swim." At the river's edge Gregor stripped to his shorts and threw himself into the murky water. With his pants legs rolled up to his knees, Papa waded in, but Leo removed only his shoes and socks, content to get just his feet wet.

On the horizon huge steamers moved slowly upstream, barges piled high with coal and lumber snaked by. Smaller sailboats turned to catch the wind. The moving air felt delicious on Gregor's wet skin as he lay on the beach under the shade of the railroad trestle. Leo sat beside him while Papa wandered off in search of something to drink.

"I love it here." Gregor rolled over and stared up at the ribbed pattern of light and dark the bridge made above him. "This is the best vacation I've ever had."

"This is the only vacation you've ever had." Leo brushed sand off his pants and pushed down the cuffs.

"What do you want to be when you're old, as old as Papa?" Gregor said.

"I don't know." Leo poked at a beetle with the grass straw, flipping it over then waiting for it to right itself. "I never think about it."

"Don't you ever wonder?"

"I don't like to think about it. Papa will tell us what we must do."

Gregor rolled onto his side and propped his chin on his hand. "I want to be the best cellist in all Russia. No. I want to be the best cellist in the whole world."

"That's not possible."

"Why not?"

"Because to be the best you have to be rich. You have to go to the finest schools and have the best instrument, one specially made for you by a master, not that old thing you play on."

"How do you know?"

"I heard Papa say. He told Mama the reason he was never chosen for the Imperial orchestra was because he wasn't well connected and because..." His voice trailed off as he picked up a shard of a broken vodka bottle and threw it into the water.

"Because what?"

"Because the Tsar doesn't want too many Jews in his orchestra." Leo pushed the sand with his toes, making a little mound ahead of his feet. "Besides, Papa said you have to know someone who can fix things for you."

"Fix what things?"

"The fix. It means you have to have connections in all the right places and you have to pay money to someone to fix things, to get you the best job. That's why Papa came home from St. Petersburg. He had no money for the fix."

"I could earn enough money, save it and pay for things so I wouldn't need the fix."

"You could never earn that much money, not in a thousand years."

Behind them, Gregor heard footsteps and sat up. From the bushes near the bridge trestle a man in a ragged coat stumbled forward. Without even glancing at them, he staggered to the river's edge, dropped to his knees and urinated.

"Come on," Leo said, getting to his feet. "Let's find Papa."

For supper Papa bought two terra cotta bottles of fresh milk and pastries filled with ground meat. The three of them sat on the stone wall circling a fountain in the center of the marketplace eating their supper and watching the crowds ebb and flow around the vendors' stalls. Beautiful ladies and chubby *Babushkas* with grandchildren in tow strolled along the boardwalk. Gregor spotted pious-looking rabbis and Turks, exotic in their colorful head wrappings. Everywhere he saw people buying and selling things, haggling over the prices as the peddlers called out their wares.

"You see that man," Papa said, as he pointed to a tall fellow in a smartly cut suit and bowler hat. "He's a lawyer, you can tell by his clothes. And that man over there, he's a doctor. Only doctors wear glasses like that."

"How do you know?" Leo asked.

"I saw men dressed like that in St. Petersburg."

"What about that lady in the green dress?" Leo pointed to the young woman at the bookseller's booth.

"Hmmm," Papa said, as he ran his fingers through his hair. "I will attempt to find out." He rose from the wall and made his way through the crowd to the bookseller's stall. Gregor watched as Papa picked up a book and appeared to examine it. Then he moved closer to the woman and a moment later they were talking. Gregor got a better look at the woman as she turned and gazed up at Papa, her pretty face breaking into a smile at something he said. Her smile seemed too friendly, like the one Vera used when she danced for men at the North Star Klub. He glanced at Leo, but his brother slouched, chin on his fist, kicking his heels against the wall.

"Come on," Gregor said, as he dropped off the wall. "Let's find out who she is."

"Why?" Leo picked up a grasshopper that climbed up the wall and flicked it into the street. "I don't want to look at some old books."

"I do." Gregor grabbed Leo's elbow and pulled him through the crowd. "Papa, we're tired," he announced when he reached the stall. "Can we go home now?"

Papa's face darkened and for a moment Gregor thought he might start yelling, but just as quickly he recovered his composure and smiled. "These are my sons, Grisha and Leo. They are both fine musicians."

"How nice to meet you." The young lady said and smiled, her very white teeth showing behind her pink lips.. "Your father's been telling me all about your travels."

"We won't be in Astrakhan very long," Gregor said. "Papa told Mama we'd be home before school begins."

The smile faded from the young lady's face as she looked at Papa. Gregor saw Papa's face turn dark red. Wordlessly, he picked up a book titled <u>History of China and Nippon.</u>

"I'm sure your mother will be happy when you all arrive home safely," she said in a chilly tone, then walked away.

* * *

"Papa?" Gregor kept his voice low. Papa didn't reply. Gregor rolled to the edge of the narrow bed and sat up. Though it was late, it was still too warm in the tiny room. He and Leo slept back to back on top of the blankets. "Papa, I wish Mama and Nadja were here. They'd love the sun. It's prettier than Moscow." There was no answer from across the room.

Gregor stood and tiptoed to the couch. The weak light of the oil lamp illuminated one end of the sofa where Papa lay, a book on his chest, his big hands covering his face.

"Papa?"

"Go to sleep," he growled. Gregor crept back to bed, but the itchy wool of the blanket stuck to his sweaty skin. In the darkness the close, damp air was suffocating.

"Papa?" Gregor said. No answer. He didn't try again.

The next morning after breakfast Papa rented a rowboat for three rubles. Gregor sat in the bow as lookout, while Leo took the stern. Though the air was warm, the wind off the water felt wonderful and clean. Leo trailed his fingers in the water as they moved downstream, while Gregor lay forward watching the waves come up and slap the hull.

The river, actually a tributary to the Volga, flowed just below the city of Astrakhan where the two bodies of water met before entering the Black Sea. Papa had Gregor and Leo take turns naming all the countries that bordered Russia. Near the shoreline, but still separated from the mainland by a narrow channel, they came upon a deserted island, overgrown with tall grass, marsh flowers and scraggly shade trees. Papa declared that they had reached their destination. Perspiring from rowing, he decided they should all take a swim. This time no clothes were necessary. With the boat pulled up on the muddy bank, Papa and Gregor stripped and jumped in.

"Leo, don't be an old lady," Gregor called out as he splashed his brother. But Leo remained seated on the stern of the beached boat.

"I don't want to get in," he said. "It's all dirty and slimy."

"It's good for you," Papa said. "This place is the Garden of Eden." But Leo was not convinced.

When their skin turned soft and wrinkled, Gregor and Papa stretched out in the grass, letting the sun dry their bodies. Leo chose a shady spot under a willow tree for a nap, but Papa couldn't lie still for long.

"Come, Grisha," he whispered. "Let's explore the rest of Eden."

They donned their pants and shirts to save their skin from the insects, which were the principal inhabitants of Eden, but remained shoeless as they pushed their way through the thick underbrush.

"I shall name this island Africa," Papa said. "This is surely as wild a jungle as there ever was on that dark continent."

Gregor felt something cold on his foot and looked down to see a shiny green snake slither through the grass. Fascinated, he knelt and searched for more exotic creatures. Between the blades of grass, he saw a wriggling nest of baby snakes, each no bigger than a worm. When he moved their cover of grass aside, they scattered in all directions. What wondrous creatures, he thought. There was nothing like them in dusty Ekaterinoslav and certainly not in the stony streets of Moscow.

He stood and a rotten odor tickled his nostrils. A short distance away stretched a pool of bubbly yellow liquid. "Ughhhh." He held his nose. "Papa, something smells dead."

"I've read that in Africa such pools are medicinal and used for curing various ills." Papa stepped forward and put his bare foot in the yellow slime. "This could be such a place."

Tentatively Gregor followed him into the pool, still holding his nose. The soft warm muck oozed up between his toes. Bubbles of yellow liquid tickled his ankles and he wondered if there were tiny fish nibbling at his skin.

"Ahhhhh." Papa sighed as he closed his eyes and moved deeper into the spa. "I can feel the healing power flowing through my body."

Gregor closed his eyes and tried to imagine swimming in the surrounding slime. It was not a pleasant thought. While Papa meditated in the midst of the pool, Gregor backed out and tried to wipe off the yellow residue by rubbing his feet in the grass. Instead, the substance dried like glue and made his toes stick together.

"I will register this find with the local authorities," Papa announced. "Perhaps this elixir can be bottled and sold to the public. A vendor's stall at the marketplace would be perfect. We could make a great deal of money and return home rich."

*   *   *

Papa stared at the coins in his hand. "Twenty-eight rubles are all we have left."

"What are we going to do?" Gregor rinsed melon juice off his hands in the bubbling water of the public fountain near their room where they sat eating breakfast. After only four days of vacation, none of them were smiling.

"I'm tired of this place," Leo said. "Can we go home?"

"We don't have enough money to get home." Papa slid the coins back into his pocket.

Gregor looked at his father's melancholy face and didn't know what to say. Since yesterday's disaster at the city office, Papa had hardly spoken.

"Who are you?" the clerk had asked when Papa presented him with a milk bottle filled with yellow slime. "And what is that stench?"

"This is an elixir that promotes good health and can cure all manner of illness." Papa pulled the cardboard lid from the bottle. "I want to register my find with the proper authorities, then I'll arrange to have this potion bottled and sold all over the world."

The clerk picked up the bottle and peered inside, wrinkling his nose. "Looks like sewage from the distillery to me. Where did you get it? Down by the river?"

"I will not disclose my source."

"Get that stuff out of here," the man said. "Take yourself and those thieving rascals with you."

"You can't treat us like common criminals." Papa's fist hit the counter and the milk jar bounced.

"I know your type, down here for the summer to pick the crowds clean. Get out of here before I call the police."

They left the office in a hurry. At the entrance to an alley, Papa took one final look at his elixir then threw the bottle to the ground where it shattered splattering yellow slime on the stucco wall.

"It's not your fault, Papa," Gregor said again as he flicked melon seeds off the stone wall. "If this was Africa, that pool would have been a healing spa."

"A sewage pond," Papa muttered, shaking his head. "What kind of people spoil a beautiful island with sewage?"

"I'm glad I didn't go in it." Leo tried to tie his frayed shoelace. "I told you that river was disgusting."

"Enough of your complaining." Papa stood and began pacing. "What to do? What to do?" He ran his fingers through his hair. "We are doomed."

"Maybe I can find work," Gregor offered. "How much do we need?"

Papa stopped and again pulled the coins from his pocket. "A ticket to Moscow costs twelve rubles. We have enough for two tickets, but not three."

"You're not going to leave me behind?" Leo cried.

"You two wait here," Papa said. "I'll look for work. All we need is eleven more rubles for a third ticket and a little extra for food."

Gregor watched him head toward the amusement park. "I don't think he'll find work here."

"But he promised Mama we would bring home lots of money," Leo said.

"I know, but Papa's not good at making money. Mama knows that."

They sat on the fountain wall for a long time, Leo kicking the stones with his heels while Gregor tried to come up with a plan. Around them produce shanties and pastry salesmen opened their stalls. Chickens roamed the alley between the booths, pecking at piles of garbage. Leo flicked melon seeds toward them and the birds eagerly gobbled them up.

"Maybe I can find a job in a dance hall," Gregor finally said.

"Do you think you can earn enough to get us home?" Leo sounded doubtful.

"If no one will pay for music, we can work in the amusement park." The idea of working with animals made Gregor feel better. "I'd like a job with the snake man. Did you see the way it wrapped around his arm? It looks like fun."

"Papa won't let you work with snakes," Leo said. "He'd say it's undignified."

"Papa thinks most work is undignified." Gregor dropped from the wall. "I have an idea. Let's stand on the corner by the accordion player."

"What will we do?" Leo said.

"We can play. I'll leave my cello case open. Maybe people will like our music and give us money."

"I'll play "The Bumble Bee", Leo said as he broke into a run.

"Wait for me," Gregor cried, but Leo had a head start and beat him to the door.

They set up their instruments along the main thoroughfare, between the dart throwers' booth and the accordion player. The accordionist had already drawn a crowd but not because of his music. Gregor noticed the ancient instrument leaked and the low C sounded only intermittently. It was the small dog that walked upright on its hind legs that drew people in.

"Hey," the man cried when Leo opened his violin case. "This is my corner. These are my customers." He shook his fist and the dog ran toward Leo, snapping at his ankle.

"Come on," Gregor said and they quickly moved to the other side of the dart throwers. The accordionist seemed satisfied.

Leo started with a minuet and the fast tempo caused people strolling by to pause. Gregor added a pizzicato beat then repeated the melody. It was hard to play standing up even with the endpin all the way out. A lady with two small children stopped in front of them. Leo increased the tempo. Gregor laughed at the toddlers who jumped up and down. When the mother threw five kopeks in the violin case, Leo took a bow.

A young couple joined the group and a few more tourists paused. More coins dropped into the case and Gregor tried counting them from where he stood. Ten, maybe twelve kopeks and they had only been playing a few minutes. At this rate they would all be home soon.

"Grisha? Leo? Where are you?" Gregor heard Papa's voice calling from behind the crowd.

Leo ended the piece with a flourish and they both bowed. A few more coins fell from people's hands.

As the audience melted away, Gregor looked up and saw Papa's angry scowl.

"Did I raise my sons to be beggars?" He grabbed Leo's violin case and dumped the money on the ground. "What else will you do to embarrass me?"

"But Papa." Gregor scrambled after the kopeks. "We can make enough this way to go home. All of us."

"That money is filth." He grabbed Gregor's arm. "Come with me. I found real work, a respectable job, one that will not bring you shame."

"For all of us?" Leo asked.

"No." Papa headed toward the shack. "Just Grisha. The amusement park orchestra lost its cellist. The pay is two rubles a day if he fills in."

"What will you do while I work?" Gregor felt his heart race at the thought of a real orchestra job.

"Leo and I will go home." Papa pulled two suitcases from under the bed.

"I'm staying here—alone?" Gregor felt like he had been hit in the belly. "Can't you stay until I earn enough money?"

Papa threw the suitcases on the bed then held out his open hand. "This is all we have. It will take twenty-four rubles for two tickets home. We'll spend three more on food." He handed Gregor one ruble, twenty kopeks.

"How will I live?" Gregor clutched the coins.

"I told the conductor you must be paid each day. The fruit vendor has agreed to let you keep this room for fifty kopeks a night. If you spend no more than that on food each day you'll have a ruble left. In two weeks' time you'll have fourteen rubles. Then you can buy a ticket home."

"You can do it," Leo said. "You'll have a marvelous time. Tell us all about it when you get home."

Gregor looked first at Leo's smiling face then at Papa's serious one. Papa looked away. "Grisha, if we stay here with you none of us will get home."

Gregor steeled himself. "I can do it." He wanted to sound confident but felt his voice quiver. "If I don't eat much I can come home sooner."

"That's my boy." Papa squeezed his shoulder.

Leo jammed his clothes in the suitcase then pulled his violin from under the bed. Gregor watched, helpless to stop them.

"Come," Papa said, his voice too cheerful. "Bring your instrument so the conductor can hear you play. I told him you were the best cellist in the Moscow Conservatory. You'll be a great addition to his orchestra."

Gregor hugged his cello and followed Leo into the alley. Papa locked the shanty door. "I told the conductor you were thirteen," he said, as he handed Gregor the key. "I didn't think he would hire you if he knew you were eleven."

The amusement park pavilion was empty at nine in the morning. Sun streamed in through the high painted glass windows, creating colored patterns on the walls. It was a pretty place with colored streamers hanging from the ceiling and pictures of great steamboats, merry-go-round and people dancing were painted across the walls.

"This is my son," Papa said, as he pushed Gregor forward. "I know he will prove satisfactory."

The conductor's black eyes peered over round glasses. His sharp nose and tiny mouth reminded Gregor of a crow. "Can you play Grieg?" he said. "How about Mozart or Brahms?"

"He can play all of those," Papa said. "But remember, he must be paid every evening, otherwise he will not return to work the next day."

"I'll pay what I promised." The man shook Papa's hand. "Won't you be here to collect it?"

"Leo and I have musical engagements in Moscow," Papa dropped his voice, but not so low that Gregor couldn't hear him. "We cannot disappoint our benefactors. In two weeks my son can leave for Moscow. He is the best cellist in the conservatory and his teacher insists he return for the new term."

"All right, let me hear him play "The Swan" by Saint-Saens." The conductor waved to an empty chair.

Gregor sat, adjusted the endpin and glanced at the music. It was a popular piece, one he had played many times, but he took his time tightening the bow and tuning the cello. Anything to keep Papa from leaving.

"My son is an excellent musician," Papa said. "He will not disappoint you." Then he patted Gregor's shoulder. "Leo and I must leave now. We have to make the next train."

Gregor sat motionless, staring at their backs as they disappeared out the door. Before it swung shut he saw Leo turn and wave. He waved back, then they were gone. The room began to spin. If he had tried to stand, he would have fallen. *Please Papa, please don't leave me,* he begged, but no words escaped his lips.

"All right, young man," the conductor said. "Let me hear you play."

He fought back tears, unwilling to let the man see him cry like a child. The music was slow and sad. When he pressed his knees hard against the body of the instrument, it felt like the strings were crying with him. He rested his cheek against the fingerboard. The cello was all he could hold onto.

* * *

"Your shoes must be polished for tonight's performance," the conductor told Gregor when the rehearsal ended. "Also, wear a clean shirt and dark socks."

"Yes sir," Gregor replied. "But I don't have shoe polish or a clean shirt."

"Temkin." The conductor pointed at the young man who played first violin. "See what you can do for him."

The violinist looked annoyed. "Just use grease on a rag," he whispered. "It will shine your shoes. Mix it with lamp soot if you want to really please the old bastard."

"What about my shirt? I only have one other and it's no cleaner than this."

"Just wash the collar and the front part where it shows." Temkin tucked his violin in a case lined with blue velvet. "And take a damp cloth to your jacket. Even if you put the shirt on wet, it will dry as you wear it."

"Thank you," Gregor said, grateful for the advice. "Nadja takes care of my clothes at home. She's my sister."

"She's not here with you?"

"No, she's in Moscow with Mama."

"You're all alone?" Temkin's eyebrows shot up and for the first time he looked interested.

"Yes. I have to earn enough money to buy my ticket home."

"Do you have money now?"

"Only one ruble."

"Let me see it."

Gregor pulled the coin from his pocket. "I pay fifty kopeks for my room and save the rest for food."

"Would you like to drink *samogon* after the concert?"

"*Samogon*? I've never had *samogon*."

"You haven't?" Temkin said, smiling a broad toothy grin. "You'll love it."

"When will the concert be over?"

"Not until late, but you can sleep in tomorrow morning. Rehearsal isn't until noon." Temkin pulled a flat metal box from his pocket, lit a stubby cigarette and blew a long plume of smoke into the air. "This Armenian I know lives behind the concert hall. He sells *samogon* very cheap. It tastes like shit, but after a couple of drinks you won't care if it tastes like a morning whore."

At eleven they stopped playing and the electric lights in the hall went dim.

"Hurry up," Temkin said as his closed his violin case. "Or the Armenian will lock his doors." The alley behind the pavilion was so dark Gregor could hardly see where he was walking, his only guide, the sound of Temkin's feet crunching on the gravel. "Wait for me," he called out, scared he would get lost in the maze of shacks, stalls and piles of rubbish. There was a scurrying in front of him and his foot came down on something soft. "Agghhh?" he cried and fell back against a brick wall as high-pitched squeals rose from the dark.

"Just rats," Temkin said and laughed. "They won't bite if you don't mess with them."

They turned a corner and Gregor saw a small lantern hanging crooked on a wall, its timid glow barely penetrating the darkness. Temkin stopped in front of a low door. "Give me your ruble," he said, holding out his hand.

"But I need it to pay for my lodging," Gregor said. "Here, I have twenty kopeks." He held out the small coins that Papa had left him.

"Holding out on me?" Temkin grabbed the money. "This will get us started." He pushed open the door and Gregor followed him inside the squat building.

An oil lamp burned on the wall, casting a yellow light over the room. Clusters of chairs and small tables lined the walls where half a dozen men sat. The hum of conversation stopped for a moment as the patrons eyed them.

"Hey, Temkin, I see you found a baby?" A man cried and the hum of conversation resumed.

"This is my new patron," Temkin said slapping Gregor on the back. "He's taking care of me tonight."

A swarthy looking man wearing a dirty fez rose from the back table. "You want *samogon*? I got special drink. Very strong." He spoke in a hoarse voice as he poked Gregor's chest with a stubby finger. "Make you a man." He dropped his hands to his crotch and gestured with two fingers. "Make you a man!" he repeated then laughed, the black stubs of his teeth showing.

"Here's twenty kopeks to get us started." Temkin handed the man Gregor's coins.

What would Papa think of him now, Gregor wondered as the Armenian handed him a small glass filled with clear liquid. If he was old enough to work and live alone then he was old enough to drink *samogon*. The smoke and the heat of the room made him thirsty. He grinned and held his glass up the way he had seen Papa do it. "*Za vashe zdorovye*," he said, tipped the glass and swallowed.

* * *

The headache felt like a nail driven into his skull. Even before he opened his eyes, he covered his face with his hands and tried to block the light. It did no good. Sunlight lapped like flames inside his eyelids. In his dreams little Tartar boys chased him, hitting him on the head with a long pole that sprouted broken pieces of glass.

He groaned as he rolled off the bed onto the floor, landing on his belly. Pressing one hand against his temple, he grabbed the edge of the bed and pushed himself to his knees. Holding his head still in his hands, he dug his elbows into the mattress and finally made it to his feet. When he stood, a wave of nausea rose from his gut. It was all he could do to stagger to the washbowl, pour a dipper full of water from the bucket and splash his face. Only then did he open one eye and stare at the bleary image in the cracked mirror.

"I will never drink *samogon* again," he said to the pathetic boy in the glass. "I swear it."

There was no money left in his pocket for food, but it was just as well. If anything had hit his stomach it would have come right back up.

With the cello strap over one shoulder, he managed the walk to the concert hall, but his legs felt like they were weighed down with stones. He had no idea if it was early or late. The cool dark room was deserted except for the bass player who stood alone at the back of the stage, tuning his instrument.

"Hey, you're not looking so good," the man said. "Are you sick?"

"I am." Gregor sank into his chair. "I drank *samogon* last night."

"You're too young to be drinking that rot." The man plucked the strings of his big bass fiddle, turning the pegs just a hair. "Where are your parents?"

"In Moscow."

"That's very far away." He pulled a folding knife from his pocket and trimmed the broken bow hairs. "What kind of father leaves his kid all alone in a place like this?" he muttered, shaking his head. "Swine."

Gregor started to open his mouth, ready to defend Papa, but a pulse of pain made him squeeze his eyes shut. What would Papa say if he were here? He would be angry. *Stupid! Idiot*! he would shout. *Why are you wasting money on samogon*? But Papa being angry was better than Papa being gone.

Gregor slumped in his seat and held his throbbing head in his hands. Other musicians drifted in and he tried to practice, but it was impossible with pain stabbing like a spike through the middle of his skull. The sound of their voices and the dissonance of their instruments only added to his suffering.

"Piatigorsky?"

Gregor looked up. The conductor and a heavyset man in a wrinkled jacket, carrying a cello, approached from the far end of the stage.

"Boy? It looks like you're out of work," the conductor said. "Our cellist has returned."

"But you told my father I could have this job."

"That's because our regular cellist was in Kiev." He pointed to the man who stood beside him. "But fortunately his sick father did not die. Let him have his chair back and give him the music."

"Please," Gregor begged. "I need the job or I'll never be able to get home."

The cellist moved forward and glared at him. "You'd better run home to your mother," he said. "Move it."

Gregor slid from the chair and the man settled his ample form on the seat then balanced his cello against a barrel sized chest. "Let a real musician show you how it's done."

"But you promised." Gregor tugged at the conductor's sleeve. "You gave your word. My father will be very angry."

The man's face softened ever so slightly. "I do need someone to play second violin."

"But I don't play violin."

"They're not that different." The conductor walked to a cabinet and returned with a scarred instrument. "Here, give it a try."

Gregor took the tiny violin in one hand and the cello in the other. As he dropped into the last chair of the violin section, he kept his cello close enough to touch.

When Temkin showed up for rehearsal, he laughed at the sight of his new partner. "Want to go out again tonight and celebrate your promotion?" A sadistic grin lit up his face.

"Leave me alone." Gregor pulled his chair away from his tormentor. But he needed money, so he tried his best to keep up with the rest of the violins during rehearsal. Every note he played sounded awful and the high pitch so close to his ear made his head hurt.

Rehearsal ended in midafternoon. Gregor stumbled back to the shack and slept until his headache subsided. The grumbling of his empty stomach woke him but he had no money for food. Sitting on the edge of the bed, he propped the musical score on the rickety chair and tried to practice the violin. The fingering was similar to the cello, but the angles were all wrong. He hated the ugly little instrument. On particularly difficult passages, when the notes ran together in a black smear of ink, he dropped the instrument between his knees and played it like a miniature cello. Immediately he felt more in control and could make his way through the piece with a reasonable sound, even adding vibrato. If he could just hold on for two weeks, he would have enough money to go home.

At sundown he headed back to the concert hall, pausing on his way at the fruit vendor's stall.

"Ahhhh," the mistress of the booth said. "I see you have changed instruments."

"I was promoted to second violin," he said, as he eyed the thick bunches of purple grapes and golden yellow melons.

"Have you eaten supper yet?"

"I have no money, not until I finish work tonight."

"Here, these grapes are a little wrinkled." She handed him a bunch from the back of the booth. "And this melon has a soft spot. Go ahead. I would just have to throw them away."

"Thank you," Gregor said and took his dinner to the fountain. Where were Papa and Leo now? Had they made it home yet? This job could have been Leo's. Then he could be the one riding the train with Papa.

Around him were few people, the afternoon crowd of mothers and children having thinned out. Soon the evening throngs would come to the amusement park. These were the young dandies and the pretty girls dressed in their best clothes. How he envied them, so rich and full of self-confidence. They seemed to have not a care in the world.

He washed his hands in the fountain then ran his wet fingers through his hair. It was time to perform. No matter what instrument he played, he must do his very best. Papa always expected that much of him.

* * *

"Look," cried someone in the first row of the audience. "Look at the boy with the violin."

Gregor heard them but didn't dare take his eyes off the score. This was the difficult passage of "La Boheme", the place where he dropped the violin between his knees. Applause broke out from somewhere in the audience and he heard shouts of Bravo! Bravo! Glancing at the conductor, Gregor saw deep furrows forming over the man's eyes.

When he returned the violin to its proper place under his chin, the applause died down. During a brief interlude, he glanced at Temkin. The violinist rolled his eyes, shook his head and mouthed the word *no*. But when he looked back at the score he saw the same crescendo passage repeated.

Again he dropped the violin between his knees and played. Once more the audience broke into applause. They like it, he thought. Isn't that what's important? Please the audience and you're a success, Papa always said.

He ended the piece with a flourish and the applause grew louder. They loved him. He felt it. When he rose and started to take a bow, he felt a heavy hand pressing down on his shoulder.

"Sit down, you idiot," Temkin said.

His knees folded under him and he sank back into the chair. "But the audience liked it."

"Shut up. You've caused me enough trouble."

At the conclusion of the performance and after only one encore, though the audience wanted more, the conductor stared down at him. "You made a circus of my concert," he shouted, pointing an accusing finger at Gregor. "And Temkin, you let him get away with it. I should fire you both."

"I didn't know he was going to do that!" Temkin threw up his hands. "I told him to play the right way, but he ignored me."

The conductor grabbed the violin from Gregor's hands. "You're fired. Get off my stage."

"But you owe me two rubles. I played the entire concert."

"I owe you nothing." The conductor's face turned red as he motioned to the door. "Get out before I throw you out."

Chapter Nine

In the center of the amusement park a clock chimed, missed a beat then chimed again as Gregor made his way through the crowd of late night revelers. He let his suitcase hang from his right hand, its weight balanced by the cello on his left shoulder.

His landlord, the pastry vendor, had been waiting for him outside the shack with an open hand. "Twenty five kopeks if you want to spend the night."

"But I didn't get paid." Gregor tried to smile. "Please let me stay. I'll pay you tomorrow. I promise."

"No." The pastry vendor shook his head. "I've got a magician and his assistant who want this room." He had kicked Gregor's suitcase into the alley, then pulled the door shut and locked it. "You'll have to find some place else to stay."

Defeated, Gregor headed back through the amusement park, passing the now silent calliope. He followed the dusty path between the dart throwers' booth and the empty circus ring. The last food vendors were locking their stalls as stray cats picked over piles of rubbish that lined the spaces between the booths. Exhaustion crept up on him and his legs ached. He leaned his cello against the wall of the shuttered café. A sign above the Café Chantant advertised tea and cakes, served between noon and dusk. Rickety chairs sat around little tables on a cobbled courtyard.

Sinking into a chair, Gregor folded his arms on the table and rested his head. He was too old to cry, but with his head on his arms, he felt the tears come. Why did Leo always have it easier? He was older. He should have stayed. They could have found work.

He would send a postal card home and tell Papa he had lost the job. Mama would make Papa come back. So what if Papa got angry. Angry was better than alone.

The cool midnight breeze blew over him and he wished for a blanket. The amusement park, with no one to share it with, was no fun. Eyes closed, he tried to dream. He was home in the kitchen, with Mama cooking, Nadja at the piano playing "Blue Danube", Papa smoking his pipe, reading the newspaper out loud. *"Come listen boys,"* he said. *"The Tsarina's birthday will be celebrated with a huge parade. Festivals and parties all over the city. There will be a great demand for music. This is our big chance."*

"Hey, kid." Someone shook Gregor's shoulder. "Are they open yet?"

Gregor lifted his head. "What? I don't know . . ." The nearly full moon illuminated a group of well-dressed older boys.

"This must be the place." Their leader, a tall boy in a bowler hat poked Gregor's shoulder. "Isn't it?"

"What place?" Gregor rubbed his eyes.

"The dance hall? The strip club. A fellow told us if we came to the Café Chantant at midnight we'd see naked girls."

"Naked girls?" Gregor looked around wondering how he missed such a thing. "No, I haven't seen any naked girls."

"Come on," another boy said. "The kid doesn't know a thing. Follow me. I bet it's down this alley."

The boys moved past him. Gregor grabbed his belongings and followed.

Behind the Café stood a low building with no name. The leader of the boys knocked three times then twice more. The door finally opened.

"You're early," said a bent gray-haired man, as he held out his hand. "The show doesn't start for almost an hour, but there's plenty to drink in the back room. One ruble." He collected money from each boy, but when it was Gregor's turn to pay he pushed his cello forward.

"I'm here to audition for the orchestra," he said.

"Orchestra? Ha. That's a joke." Still, the old man waved him inside. "Boris is up front, scar on his cheek. Tell him I could use some help. The last guy we had on cello couldn't keep his mind or his hands off his crotch."

Gregor moved around tightly packed tables that filled the sour smelling room. Near the low stage two men shared a vodka bottle. Taking a deep breath of stale air, he pushed the cello in front of him. "Excuse me, I'm here to audition for—." He hesitated. "For the position of musical accompanist."

The vodka bottle stopped midway between the two men. "You ever play for naked women?" asked a man with a long white scar that ran diagonally across his left cheek.

"I was accompanist at the North Star Klub in Ekaterinoslav."

"Then you know what to do. Start fast then slow down. These girls work to the tempo of the music. After they're down to their underclothes, take it even slower and make it last."

"I can do that," Gregor said.

"It's like sex," Boris said. "The customers don't want it to end too soon."

"He doesn't look like he's ever had sex," said his partner, a thick muscular man with no neck. "How old are you?"

"Fourteen."

"Don't lie to me," Boris said.

The knot in Gregor's stomach tightened. "I'm almost fourteen."

"You see," he said as he slid the bottle to his partner. "I can always spot a liar. Some girls tell me they're sixteen, but I know they're lying."

"I'm also an excellent musician."

"That hardly matters. Do you like naked girls?"

"I... uhhh." He chewed his lower lip. "I do, yes."

"I think the only tit he's ever seen was his mother's." Boris laughed. "What do you think, Ivan? Is he going to love working here?"

"He may love it too much if he's not careful." Ivan poured himself another drink.

Boris rose and pointed to a cluster of chairs below the lip of the stage. "Take that seat by the piano. I want you to play something fast then something slow." He waved to the old man who had let them in. "Get over here and show him the music." Then Boris pounded his fist on the edge of the stage. "Natasha," he called. "Get out here. Now."

A muffled voice came from behind the curtain.

"No. You can leave your clothes on for this fellow," Boris said. "Let me see if you can keep up with his tempo."

It was the North Star Klub all over again. Gregor sat between the bass player and the piano. The old man who had guarded the front door, dropped beside him on the bench, a cigarette dangling from his lips. With tobacco-stained fingers, he flipped through a dog-eared book of music.

"We start with this one," he said, talking around his cigarette. "Follow my lead and come in here." Gregor moved closer so he could see the music. It was a dance tune by Jean La Pierre, one he had never heard of before. He studied the score, straining to see it in the low light. It didn't look too difficult. After a heavy piano opening there were two repeats of the melody, but "4X" had been penciled above it, followed by a short cadenza.

"I'll open with the fanfare." The pianist jabbed his finger at the tops line. "Then you come in here. Repeat until I tell you to move on to this part." He pointed to the next page. "Here." He slid the music to the edge of the piano rail. "You keep your eyes on the score. I'll keep my eye on the girls."

Gregor positioned himself forward on the wooden chair. One leg was slightly shorter than the others, so the chair wobbled. He braced his toes against the floor as he ran his bow over the strings. "I'm ready."

The pianist began with a rumbling chord then the bass player matched him with a low C. On stage the curtain parted and Natasha glided out, a red silk gown low on her shoulders, black hair tumbling to the top of her breasts. Gregor watched fascinated as she moved, more snake-like than human. A long slit up the center of her gown exposed thigh-high black lace stockings as she pivoted on red high-heeled shoes. With a flick of her wrist, she pulled open one side of the long gown, revealing a momentary flash of red corset and white flesh. Gregor held his breath.

"Stop! stop!" Boris cried. "What is wrong with you?" He pointed at Gregor."Why didn't you play?"

The pianist halted mid phrase then spit on the floor. "Damn it. You have to keep your eyes on the music, not on her puss and tits."

Gregor felt his face grow hot and was grateful the cello hid his embarrassment.

"You'll get used to it," the bass player said. "After a while you won't care if the Tsarina herself undressed and offered to take care of you." He laughed and slapped his thigh.

Gregor locked his eyes on the music book, positioning himself to play. "I'm ready," he said, hoping the men couldn't see his face. They played and this time he didn't let his eyes wander.

After rehearsing only two pieces Boris called a halt. "The customers are here. Time to start the show." The thick-necked bouncer opened the door to the back room and several dozen men rushed into the hall, pushing and shoving as they tried to get seats close to the stage.

Tolerating only a minute of shouting and raucousness, Boris crossed the stage and stood before them. "Tonight we have something special for you. Our dancers have come to Astrakhan direct from Paris, France. The best looking tarts in all of Europe, young, beautiful and fresh." He made a smacking sound with his lips. "If you want them to stay, you must show your appreciation."

There was a loud chorus of cheers and someone yelled, "Get down. We want to see some ass, not your ugly face."

Boris didn't seem offended. Instead, he pulled back the heavy curtain then disappeared into the wings. The pianist began a trill in the lowest octave then pounded out the fanfare. Gregor's eyes moved briefly to the stage as Natasha emerged in a swirl of red. This time he dragged his attention back to the music, keeping time with his toe and entering when he was supposed to. The tune was repetitious and only the tempo changed, growing slower with each refrain.

They repeated the same eight bars for the fifth time, before Gregor glanced up. Natasha's gown was gone and she stood at the center of the stage, her black-sheathed legs spread wide as if she were ready to ride a horse. With her hands pushed up under her breasts, she thrust her hips back and forth. The crowd took up a chant. Huh, huh, huh, that kept cadence with her moves. Several men in the audience showered her with coins.

As she moved, she loosened button after button on her red corset. Gregor sucked in his breath and held it. He had never seen anything like this before, not even at the North Star Klub. It never occurred to him that women wore such things beneath their dresses and shifts. Surely Nadja didn't. Imagining such a thing made him feel dirty, but he only took his eyes off Natasha for a moment.

When the last corset button was undone, Natasha rolled her shoulders and the garment fell to the floor, leaving her great round breasts exposed. Below the corset she wore a red garter belt that held up her stockings. A black triangle between her legs was the only dark spot on her body. The audience cheered as she thrust her chest forward and shook her breasts. A soldier lunged from his seat, crawled onto the stage, both hands outstretched. Ivan was faster. With one hand the big man grabbed the offender's collar and pulled him off the stage.

"Hey, kid!" The pianist startled Gregor. "Back to work"

Gregor glanced at the music then looked up in time to see Natasha drop to her knees, as she continued to thrust her hips forward. For a moment he was mesmerized by the rhythm of her body. It was too hot in the room.

"Back to work," cried a loud voice. Gregor's chair was yanked hard to the left. Startled, he almost fell, but caught himself as he stared up at Boris.

"Tits and ass are too much of a distraction for a kid your age." The boss scowled and his black eyes shot daggers at Gregor. "I want your back to the stage."

"Yes, sir," Gregor mumbled.

As the evening grew late, the pianist sometimes nodded off at his keyboard, falling forward until his gray head hit the front of the upright piano. When it happened, Gregor or the bass player reached out with a bow tip and prodded the old man awake. At two in the morning the dance hall finally closed. Gregor was yawning and the doorkeeper-pianist looked more stooped than he had at midnight. Most of the customers staggered away when Boris announced it was closing time. The bass player packed up his instrument and headed for the kitchen while the bouncer picked up the last unconscious customer from the floor.

"Out you go." He dumped the drunk into the alley.

"You did a good job." Boris beckoned Gregor to his stage-side table. Before him he had stacks of coins and a few pieces of paper currency. "At least you did fine once you kept your eyes on your music instead of the girls. Here are two rubles." He dropped the coins into Gregor's palm. "You want to work again tomorrow night?"

"Yes, please." Gregor covered a yawn with the back of his hand. "But I have no place to sleep."

"Ask Natasha if she's got a cot. She and the girls have a cottage near the park gate." He laughed and Gregor thought he sounded evil. "For a few kopeks you can probably sleep with her. For half a man she should charge half price."

* * *

The buzzing of flies above Gregor's head woke him. With eyes still closed, he listened to the sound of birds clawing and pecking on the tile roof over head. Comfortable on the porch behind Natasha's cottage, he heard the tiny creatures chatter as they fluttered from the porch roof to the branches of a scraggly willow tree.

From his narrow cot, Gregor marveled at how quickly things had changed. Rolling over, he opened his eyes. Above him on rope strung between the rafters, the girls had hung their laundry. Green silk panties, a red and a black corset, white garters and tiny lace items. He let his imagination run wild and felt suddenly too warm. At the end of the clothesline a half dozen black stockings danced in the warm summer breeze.

The girls slept until noon, but Gregor couldn't stay in bed that long. First he washed at the water trough in the alley behind the cottage. Then he headed to the market in search of food. With two rubles in his pocket he felt as rich as a king.

He spent thirty kopeks on salami, bread and another fifteen on cheese and a melon. Enough food to last him a week. With his pockets and arms filled with groceries, he headed back to the cottage, nibbling at a piece of bread as he dodged mud puddles and stray dogs. The summer sun warmed his back and he thought about swimming.

"What do you have there?" The voice came from the cottage doorway. He recognized the barefoot dancing girl. She looked about Nadja's age but with long black hair and slanted gypsy eyes that made her seem older.

"I bought this at the market." He unloaded the food onto his cot.

"It looks delicious," she said, eyeing the salami. "Can I have some?"

"Of course. I have plenty."

He sat on the sagging wooden step and the girl joined him. Instead of the skimpy costume she had worn the night before, she was now dressed in a long black skirt and loose fitting red blouse trimmed in white lace. She was still barefoot, but he noticed that around her wrists and ankles were bands of tiny silver bells. They tinkled when she moved.

"What's your name?"

"Gregor Piatigorsky." He tore off a chunk of bread. "But my friends call me Grisha. I live in Moscow."

"I'm Irina." She spoke Russian with a slight accent that made her seem exotic. From the pleats of her skirt she produced a dainty cotton handkerchief and a folding knife. With deft fingers she peeled the cucumber then handed him a thin juicy slice. "I'm nearly sixteen, but don't tell Boris." She put her finger to her lips. "I'm from Kiev."

"We went through Kiev when I toured with the opera company," he mumbled, his mouth full of food. "It's a very big city."

"I wish I could go home," said Irina. She sighed. "I miss Mama and all my friends."

"Why don't you?"

"Boris lied to Mama. He told her I needed real dance experience before I could audition for the Bolshoi Ballet."

"You're a ballerina?"

"I took dance lessons at Madame Alexandra's studio for three years."

"I don't think Boris likes ballet," Gregor handed her the salami.

"I hate dancing for him," she said. Her voice sounded sad. "And I hate having to take off my clothes in front of those drunks." She sliced the salami into big circles then cut the cheese in wedges and handed him pieces of each. "The men don't really care what kind of dancing we do." She dropped her voice and motioned over her shoulder. "Natasha's so old and fat she waddles like a pig when she crosses the stage."

"How old is she?" Gregor asked.

"Nearly twenty-five and she's already had two babies. Did you see those lines on her belly?"

"Boris doesn't want us to watch the dancing," Gregor said, avoiding her eyes. "He says it's a distraction."

"You didn't see me dance?"

"I . . . I . . ." He felt his face grow hot. "You . . . uhhh. You dance very well."

Irina set the cucumber and salami on the porch then stood. "If you keep beat like this," she clapped her hands in two-four time. "I'll dance for you."

"Are you going to take your clothes off?"

"Of course not. I'll dance the ballet, just like Madame Alexandra taught me."

She stood in the middle of the backyard on the hard packed earth. A few scraggly weeds poked their heads through the dust, but mostly they were already brown. She stood tall, with her arms at her side, her right foot turned out. Then she closed her eyes and tilted her chin up high. Gracefully, she raised her arms and rose onto her toes. As she pirouetted, the tiny bells on her ankles tinkled.

Gregor kept time with his hands, but his eyes were transfixed on her figure as she danced around the yard, gliding, turning, then spinning on her toes. In his head he heard music, soft strings as she dropped low, her black skirt swirling around her legs. When she rose and spun on her right toe, he realized his hands were fingering the C major scale as he silently accompanied her.

"Bravo! Bravo!" he shouted when she finished and curtseyed. "You are a wonderful dancer."

"But I'll never get a chance to dance the ballet," she said with a sigh then sank onto the step beside him.

"Why don't you buy a ticket and go to Moscow. I'm sure you can audition for the Bolshoi."

"I have no money. Boris sends all my pay to my mother, but only after he takes out for food and the rent."

"I think you should dance the ballet for Boris," Gregor said, his mind already racing with ideas. "Once he sees how good you are, he'll understand you're really a ballerina. Let me choose a piece of music for you. We can practice until it's perfect, then show him."

"Oh, that would be wonderful." Irina clapped her hands. "I know exactly what I'll wear. I have a ballet dress I brought from Kiev. My mother made it for me when I performed the *Nutcracker*. Can you play something from that?"

"That would take a whole orchestra, but I know other pieces."

Irina returned to the step and finished cutting the remainder of the cucumber. He watched her hands move with the control of an orchestra conductor. The blade of the knife gleamed, razor sharp as the cucumber slices piled up on the handkerchief. Finally, she sliced the melon down the middle and handed him half.

"You are a nice boy," she said, cocking her head to one side as she studied him. "How old are you?"

"I'm—I'm almost twelve."

"That's good." She wiped the knife blade clean on the hem of her skirt.

"Why's that good?" He licked melon juice from his fingers.

"I don't like old men." She cut her half of the melon into cubes, speared one with the point of her knife and offered it to him. "Natasha does and so does Sophia, but I don't."

"Why don't you like old men?"

"They're all so hairy and some of them don't smell very good." She slid across the step, settling closer to him.

Gregor ate the melon cube but hardly tasted it. Then he looked down at his sticky hands. He felt awkward, as if his hands were suddenly too large and he needed a place to hide them. Irina inched closer and smoothed her skirt. The side of her bare calf touched his leg. If he pulled away she might take offense. But he didn't want to pull away.

"Grisha?" She had long dark lashes that looked very nice, he thought, especially the way they lay against her tawny skin. "Do you like me?" Her voice was soft.

His eyes dropped to her knees then moved up the fold of her lap and across the soft curve of her breasts. "Yes, I mean, of course . . ." He had difficulty getting the words out. "I like you very much."

"You may kiss me." She closed her eyes. "But only on the cheek."

Kiss her? More than anything else in the world he wanted to kiss her, touch her, put his sticky hands on her breasts.

Terrified that she might change her mind, he placed his palms on his knees and gripped hard. With his hands safely anchored, he leaned left, closed his eyes and pressed his lips against her cheek. Her skin was soft and cool and she smelled good.

"There." She pulled away. "That's enough, you can kiss me again tomorrow. But just you remember, I am no whore."

"No." Gregor exhaled. "Of course not. I would never think that."

"Good. Because a lot of men think that if a girl takes her clothes off to dance she must be dishonorable or a whore."

"I think you are very honorable."

"I'm glad." She stood and brushed breadcrumbs off her skirt. "Now get your cello. I want to hear you play."

He spent the next three mornings working on the new dance while Irina slept. "Souvenir de Spa" by Drdla was the ideal piece, with lots of movement and rhythm, and the ending would be perfect for ballet. Barefoot, he tried different moves, matching them to the melody that played inside his head. The pieces meter and tempo were just right. With each change in phrasing, he hummed out loud and danced. He worked in the alley behind the cottage, fearful that someone would ridicule his big feet and clumsy dancing.

At night he played the same repetitive dance tunes while the girls took off their clothes. When Irina came on stage, he made sure his chair was turned away and kept his eyes glued on the score, though he knew it by heart. The thought of seeing her dance naked made him queasy.

Still, when the piece ended and the men in the audience cheered, he couldn't help glancing up. Irina stood proudly with her head tilted back, her dark hair half covering her face. It fanned out over one bare breast as her hands slid down her thighs.

The sight of her body sent a wave of weakness through him. His bow hand trembled. Her eyes caught his and he held his breath. Could she see him? Could she see his face? He raised his bow in salute. A tiny smile played across her lips, a smile just for him. Then with a toss of her head, she disappeared behind the drapes.

Gregor squeezed his eyes shut, but she was still there. The curve of her back and the roundness of her breasts were burned into his brain. So was her smile.

"I think Irina likes your looks." The bass player rolled a cigarette during intermission. "She's a firm one, for sure."

Gregor looked at the man's shaggy beard and the yellow, tobacco-stained fingers that held the cigarette to his thin lips. The very idea of him thinking about Irina, of wanting to touch her, made him angry.

"She's no whore." Gregor turned the pages of the score, a little too hard. The music book fell off the piano rail and slid across the floor.

"Not a whore?" The man laughed as he blew smoke into the air. "They're all whores, every last one of them. Even your precious Irina."

"She is not."

"Leave him alone," the pianist said as he retrieved the music from the floor. "He's in love. Let him enjoy it while it lasts. Soon he won't care anymore than you or I do."

* * *

"I have the dance all worked out," Gregor said on Friday night as he and the girls walked back to the cottage after closing time. Natasha led the way with a lantern, while he and Irina followed. Boris had ordered Sophia to stay behind and she didn't look happy but dared not complain. Around them the vendors booths were shuttered and the only activity was the sound of rats scurrying inside the garbage barrels. A dog barked, which set up a howling response from several other beasts.

"The dance? You mean my ballet?" She kept her voice low.

"If you meet me by noon we can come back here and practice on stage." Gregor shifted his cello to his shoulder so it wouldn't bang against his leg. Natasha's lantern light bobbed ahead of them, but the path was dark and it was impossible to see. The clock in the center of the amusement park chimed two. Then Natasha's light disappeared leaving them in total blackness.

"I can't see." Gregor held back. If he tripped his cello could be broken.

"I know the way." Irina touched his arm then took his hand. "I've gone this way before."Her grip was strong and reassuring. Trusting her, he squeezed her hand as she led him through the darkness.

* * *

The dry heat vanished when they entered the side door of Café Chantant at noon the next day. Inside the low building it was dark and cool, almost as good as a dip in the Volga. Without the tobacco smoke, Gregor noticed the sour stench of *bragha* and vodka that soaked the wooden floor. "Change your clothes," he said. "I'll get my cello ready." He slid a chair to the corner of the stage.

"I'm scared," Irina said, her fingers toying with the handle of a straw bag. She glanced around the empty room, as if she had never performed there before. "What if Boris doesn't like ballet?"

"Don't worry," Gregor said as he leaned his cello in the corner then sat and pulled off his boots and socks. "He knows you're a good dancer and the men love you. That's what makes Boris happy."

As he tuned his instrument, Irina pushed the drapes aside and disappeared into the dressing room. He tightened the bow then laid it across the strings, a little too loose. He tightened the bow one more turn then ran quickly through the C and G major scales. Above the table where Boris and Ivan always sat were two high windows. They allowed enough illumination to see the stage, but not his music. It didn't matter. He could play it from memory. He wanted it to be perfect for Irina and he wanted to see her dance.

"Are you ready?" she called, her voice muffled by the drapes.

"I'm ready," he said. He positioned the cello between his knees and held the bow ready. There was a long pause. Nothing happened. Silence.

With a flourish, the drapes were thrown back. She was an angel, moving like air, hardly touching the floor. With bare arms and a tight fitting costume, she spun across the stage. No longer barefoot, she wore white ballet slippers with ribbons laced up around her calves.

"You are beautiful, wonderful," he said.

"*Merci.*" She affected a French accent, spun on her toes, then dropped into a low curtsy.

"I'll play four measures." He tightened the C peg. The dry heat made the wood shrink and all the pegs were slipping. "You start on the fifth measure."

The sound of the cello drifted across the empty room, much louder than it did when the place was filled with noisy, drunken customers. After a few bars he stopped and laid his cello on the chair. Side by side, they stood facing the empty hall.

"Start like this." He stood erect and stretched out his arms. Irina's eyes followed his every movement. Sometimes she laughed, her eyes sparkling with excitement, and she applauded each time he completed a pirouette. Then she duplicated his steps. Compared to him, she was a butterfly and he was an elephant.

They worked together all afternoon, he demonstrating the steps then playing the accompaniment, she taking them from idea to heavenly art. It grew warm and his shirt stuck to his chest. He slipped out of his jacket and rolled up his trousers to his knees.

"You're a wonderful artist." She danced beside him, touching his arm with one finger as she pirouetted around him.

"And you are a true ballerina." Gregor wished he could kiss her again. Instead, he replayed the passages while she added flourishes and touches he would never have dreamed of. His music and her motion became like one. By the time the daylight faded and the room grew dark, they were exhausted and hungry.

"Do you think I'm ready?" Irina wiped perspiration from her face and neck with a white handkerchief. "Will the audience like me?"

"They'll love you." Gregor packed up his cello. "Once Boris sees how talented you are, he might pay you more money. We should post signs telling people to come."

"I wish my mother were here," Irina said and knelt to remove her toe shoes.

"My mother too and my sister."

"You have a sister?" She paused and looked up at him. "Is she a dancer?"

"No, but she plays the piano. "Blue Danube" is her favorite."

"She's lucky. She doesn't have to take her clothes off to be a pianist."

"My father would never allow it." No sooner had he spoken than he wished he could take his words back.

"I wish I didn't have a father." Irina looked down at the floor and Gregor saw her shoulders sag. "If he were dead, I wouldn't be working here."

Gregor watched her in silence as she walked off the stage, her shoulders sagging.

* * *

Just before opening time, Gregor approached Boris's table. "Excuse me."

Boris ignored him as he poured another glass of vodka. Only after he downed it in one swallow did he acknowledge Gregor. "Don't tell me you want more money?" He winked at Ivan and Gregor saw the scar on his cheek move up toward the corner of his eye.

"No, sir. I have an idea."

The refilled vodka glass stopped halfway to the man's lips. "So what is it?"

"I've been working with Irina for the past several days and—."

"Aren't you a little young for that?" Boris laughed as he set the glass down on the table with a thud. "You like her?"

Gregor flushed with embarrassment. "Sir," he said, trying to keep his voice polite. "I've choreographed a new dance for her. She's very good. Someday she'll perform with the Bolshoi."

"Perform under the Bolshoi is more like it," Boris said.

"Will you let her dance tonight? It will be the greatest performance ever seen in this hall."

"Very well." Boris dismissed him with a wave. "Maybe the crowd will buy more beer."

"You'll love it," Gregor said. "I promise."

As the crowd of young and old men filled the hall, Gregor and Irina stood in the wings. She had laced her toe shoes with pink silk ribbons. Her arms were bare and she had darkened her eyelids with charcoal. The red she had used on her lips stood in bold contrast to her dusky skin. She had swept her hair up, but a few stray curls had escaped. Gregor knew she was nervous. Time after time she rose on her toes then dropped back. Perspiration made her skin shine.

Natasha and the other dancers waited nearby dressed in the flimsy undergarments they shed during the dance. "How are you going to get out of that outfit?" Natasha said as she fingered the stiff lace on Irina's costume. "It will take forever. These men are not patient."

"I'm dancing the ballet." Her tone was haughty. "Tonight my clothes stay on."

"This is all your fault." Natasha pointed a long red fingernail at him. "She's no ballet dancer."

"She's a fine ballerina. You're just jealous."

"You're an idiot and she's a fool. Boris will throw you both out."

At that moment the pianist began his overture. Gregor turned his back on Natasha and gave Irina his best smile. Then he walked on stage, took his seat, inhaled deeply, lay his bow on the strings and waited. Beneath his jacket he felt a tickle of sweat roll down his spine.

"We want the girls," a customer cried. "Bring us the dancers!"

The pianist finished with a loud, rumbling chord. The audience waited. Gregor took one more deep breath and began. As the notes filled the hall, Irina floated out from behind the curtain, moving like a butterfly, her feet barely touching the wooden floor. She was perfect. His music and her dancing created the greatest performance of their lives.

For the next few minutes he was aware only of Irina and the music flowing from his instrument. She glided, turned and spun on her toes. As quickly as it had begun, the dance was over. Irina made a final turn, pivoting with her arms thrown back, her chin held high. Then, like an elegant bird, she dropped low into a curtsy. For the first time Gregor took his eyes off her and glanced at the audience. At that moment something sailed past his head. Then a second object and a third landed on stage. The audience, hissing and booing, began to pelt them with stale bread.

"What do you think this is?" someone cried. "The Imperial Ballet?"

"Natasha, Natasha," they chanted. "Bring us Natasha."

Irina looked up at the crowd, her eyes growing wide. She jumped back as another small loaf rolled across the stage and landed at her feet. Natasha and the other dancers emerged from behind the curtain, strutting and thrusting their hips at the audience. The jeers changed to cries of "*Hurrah*" as the dancers opened their gowns, exposing their breasts. Natasha had been right.

Irina turned and ran from the stage, tears streaming down her face. Gregor stood, his cello and bow in hand, facing the crowd. He wanted to scream, throw things, kill them all. An empty bottle bounced across the stage, hitting his leg. There was nothing he could do. Booing changed to laughter. He laid the cello and bow on the floor, turned and walked off the stage. Outside the stage door he ran into Ivan who spread his arms, blocking the way.

"What are you trying to do?"

"Get out of my way." Gregor tried to push past him.

"You have a job to do." The man grabbed the back of his collar and dragged him toward the stage door. "Get down there with the other musicians and play for the girls. No man comes here to see the ballet."

"No."

"Then tell it to the boss." Ivan pushed him toward the dressing room.

The tiny dressing space had a doorway so low Gregor ducked his head. Even as he turned the knob he heard Boris screaming.

"Who do you think you are? This is a man's club. My customers want tits and bare ass, not the Bolshoi."

In the dim light of a single oil lamp Gregor saw Irina crumpled in the corner of a threadbare couch. Her face was red and tears had left dark streaks of charcoal makeup beneath her eyes. Towering over her, Boris looked like a bear ready to attack.

"I'm a ballerina," she sobbed. "I hate taking my clothes off for those pigs."

"I paid your mother good money for your ass." Boris shook a fist in her face. "I have a contract with your name on it. If you don't dance, I'll have you thrown in jail for theft."

"You can't make her." Gregor grabbed Boris's elbow. "You don't own her."

Boris shook him off. "I own her for the next eight months."

"I won't play for you anymore," he screamed. He saw Irina's dark eyes pleading for help.

"You can go to hell," Boris said, grabbed Gregor's shoulders and shoved him backward. "Get out of my club."

"I want my pay." Gregor tried to look past Boris, but the man's bulk blocked him. "I won't leave without it."

Boris reached into his pocket and threw a handful of coins at Gregor. The money bounced off his chest and rolled across the floor. "Now get out or I'll have Ivan throw you out."

"Irina." The door slammed in his face. There was no sound from the other side. "Let her go," he cried as he pounded the wood with a clenched fist.

"Hey, kid." Ivan's rough grip seized Gregor's collar and dragged him behind the curtain. "Here's your fiddle. Now get going while you can still walk."

"I need my money."

"I'll get it." Ivan went back to retrieve the coins.

If the musty stage curtains could have supported him, he would have collapsed into it. Instead, he sank to the floor and tried to catch his breath.

"Look, kid, you don't belong here." Ivan handed him the coins. "Go home."

"But Boris said he owned Irina. He can't do that."

"Her father's a Cossack and sold her. Boris can do whatever he likes with her now."

"I won't let him."

"You'll only get her in more trouble if you stay. By tomorrow it will be over if you're gone."

"But it was my idea for her to dance."

"Then it was a bad idea. Don't make it worse."

Chapter Ten

"Third class fare to Moscow?" the ticket agent behind the barred window said in a bored voice. "Twelve rubles."

"I only have nine." Gregor held the coins in his open palm.

"Nine rubles will take you to Samara."

"But I have to go to Moscow. My parents live in Ogorodnya."

"Then tell them to send you more money."

Gregor looked at the coins then pushed them across the counter. "I'll buy a ticket to Samara."

The agent scooped up the money but held onto the ticket. "There is also a two rubles charge for that big fiddle."

"No." Gregor hugged the instrument at his side. "I'll carry it myself."

"It will take up an extra seat."

"I'll sit on the floor."

"Let him on the train," a deep voice said. Gregor turned and saw a black-robed priest standing behind him. "I need a ticket for the ten o'clock train to St. Petersburg." The priest sounded irritated. "I can't be late."

The agent shrugged, stamped the word Samara on a pasteboard square and shoved it through the window.

"Thank you, sir." Gregor pocketed the ticket.

"Where are your parents?" the priest said. "Or are you running away from home?"

"No, sir." He picked up his cello and slipped the strap over his shoulder. "I'm going home."

The station was filled with vacationers, merchants and soldiers. Suitcases and trunks filled every available cart and wagon. Gregor headed to the far end of the platform and sat on a low brick wall. How far from home was Samara? Could he walk the rest of the way? Would he get lost? Would he have enough to eat? All that remained in his pocket were twenty-five kopeks.

When the smoke-belching engine pulled into the station, Gregor joined the crush of people pushing their way onto the train. There was no place safe to store the cello, and sitting in the narrow third class seat with it on his lap was impossible. Instead, he found room at the rear of the car near the toilet stall. It smelled bad, but he propped his instrument in the corner and sat on the floor with his back against the wall.

The train rattled and shook, waking sleeping babies who cried until someone pushed a thumb or a tit in their mouths. When he grew sleepy, Gregor curled up against the wall and used his suitcase for a pillow. He dreamed Irina was there beside him, laughing, the bells on her ankles jingling when she turned to touch his cheek. She had escaped, followed him and now they would go home to Moscow together. At the Bolshoi she would audition and win the lead in *Swan Lake*. Papa and Mama would watch from the balcony as he played and Irina danced. The audience would throw flowers on the stage in appreciation.

Gregor woke when someone kicked his foot on their way to the toilet. As he struggled to sit up, he was kicked again. Though he had tried to stay out of the way, he lost count of how many times this happened, especially after it grew dark.

The train's speed increased on the down slopes, creating a vibration that inched him forward until his head bumped the toilet stall wall. On the inclines, the engine labored, causing smoke to pour in the open windows. Everyone coughed or sneezed, and the ladies covered their faces with scarves.

"Hey, kid. Where's your ticket?"

Someone shoved his foot and Gregor looked up at the uniformed man. Scrambling to his feet, he pulled the pasteboard square from his pocket. "How far is it to Samara?" he asked, as he handed over the ticket.

"Two days but we stop overnight in Saratov." The conductor slid the ticket into the leather waist pouch.

"How much farther from there to Moscow?"

"By rail? Another day and a half, maybe two."

"How long if I walk?"

"Walk to Moscow?" The man frowned as he rubbed his bushy moustache.

"I didn't have enough money for the whole way."

The officer shook his head. "It might take ten days to walk that far."

"How will I know which way to go?"

"Follow this track west after you get to Pensk. Stay on the left track and it will take you straight to Moscow."

"Thank you, sir." Gregor slid down the wall and sat cross-legged on the floor. Two weeks? With no money he'd starve before he made it home.

"What kind of parents let their child travel alone?" the conductor muttered.

The train pulled into Samara at dawn. Sleepy passengers and grumpy children struggled to gather their belongings.

"This is your stop," the conductor said. Gregor shifted his cello sideways so a woman with a balky child could squeeze past him. "When you get off go straight across the station to the other side and follow the track toward the cathedral." The man paused to help a woman pull her bag from the shelf above her seat. "Near the clock tower, look for an old man selling meat pies," he continued. "Tell him Ilya sent you. He'll sell you a meat pie cheap."

"Thank you," Gregor said, hoping the pies would be very cheap.

The station was huge, filled with milling crowds, all on the move. Where was the pie man? He crossed the great room with a high vaulted ceiling and red tile floor, looking right then left. Around him crowded sausage vendors, tea sellers and gypsy girls peddling flowers, but no pie man.

In the center of the station stood a huge ornate clock atop a tall iron column. As he stared up, it sounded the hour with seven deep chords. What a wonderful music. When the last note faded away, Gregor dropped his eyes and saw an old man dressed in farm clothes, a tray of small pastries hanging around his neck.

"Meat pies," the man cried. "Sausage, fish and lamb."

"Do you know the train conductor?" Gregor asked as he slid his cello off his shoulder, balancing it on the toe of his boot. "His name is Ilya. He told me to find you."

The old man's face lit up. "He's my son."

"I didn't know."

"I sell more pies when customers have pity on a poor old man."

"I can't afford to pay much."

"For you a special price. Would you like lamb, beef or fish? Beef is the best, only fifteen kopeks. The rest are ten."

Gregor pulled his meager supply of coins from his pocket. "I'll take two fish pies."

"How far are you going?" The old man wrapped the pastries in a sheet of newspaper.

"To Moscow. My family lives there."

"But you missed the train to Moscow. It left less than an hour ago."

"I have no money for the train." He took the rolled up newspaper. "I'll walk to Moscow. How far is it?"

"Too far to walk." The old man took him by the arm and led him to a large doorway. "Listen to me. You see this place?" He pointed to the huge rail yard filled with cars and engines. "This is where the freight trains are loaded and unloaded. Walk along this track toward the cathedral domes. When you get beyond the fence, look for a boxcar with an open door, but don't board until dark."

"Do all these trains go to Moscow?" Gregor said, feeling hopeful.

"All the ones on this track do, but they run only at night." As he spoke he wrapped another meat pie in a piece of newspaper then stuffed it in Gregor's pocket. "You must get off in the morning. That's when the freight handlers do their work. If police don't catch you, you'll be home in a week."

* * *

The railway bed rose above the floodplain of the Volga, more a dike than a highway. Between the tracks and the water ran a narrow ribbon of scrub grass, stunted willow trees and the debris of a continent washed up by floodwaters.

Gregor moved along the shoreline, shifting the cello strap from his left shoulder to his right. It was easier walking at the water's edge than through the tall grass. Before him stretched his shadow, tall and intimidating. Tall was good. If he were as tall as his shadow, people would fear him and he would be safe, especially at night. But while the sun shone the world wasn't such a frightening place.

Grasshoppers jumped from thin blade to thin blade ahead of him. A crow perched in the willow tree cawed, watching him with a beady eye. In the distance, where the blue gray of the Volga met the horizon, a steamer left a trail of white against the summer sky.

Gregor's shoes squished in the mud and he looked down at the tiny worms slithering into the slime. Kneeling, he tried to dig one out with his finger but the wriggling creature burrowed deeper. As he stood and wiped his hands on his pants, he saw something floating at the water's edge. It was big, like a giant fish, maybe even a whale. He'd never seen a whale, but Papa said it was the largest of the fish, though not really a fish at all. The thing floated a few yards from the shoreline. He watched it rise and fall, the smooth surface wet and shiny. But this whale had arms and legs, and he knew it was a man.

A hand rose from the water and for a moment the fingers stretched toward him, but he saw no face. He sucked in a breath. The man beckoned him, reaching out for help. He hesitated then laid his cello at the edge of the grass beyond the reach of the waves. The water wasn't deep, no higher than his thighs. Maybe the man was unconscious, too weak to save himself.

Gregor reached out and grabbed the extended hand. His fingers sank into flesh. It felt soft, like uncooked eggs. He let go and the hand sank back into the water, but still beckoned him from beneath. Grabbing the sleeve of the man's jacket, he pulled him toward the shore. It was easy and the waves helped. For a moment it seemed the man moved, as if he recognized Gregor's efforts.

The body dragged in the shallow water settling on the muddy shore. The man was probably dead and there was no helping him now. Still, he rolled the man onto his back, just in case he started to breathe. Cracked purple lips curled back from blackened teeth. The eyes had already become a meal for fish. In the corpse's frozen expression, Gregor saw the look of the men who slept in gutters, empty vodka bottles by their sides. And he remembered Aunt Rosie, how she too had stared at the sky like this man with no eyes.

He wanted Papa, needed him, wished he were here. But Papa was in Moscow, a million versts away.

His knees wobbled as he backed out of the water and sank to the ground. With eyes squeezed shut, he let his head drop between his knees. If he had eaten that day, he would have thrown up. What was it like to drown, to struggle for air and suck in only water? What did it feel like to cry for help and have no one hear? What did it feel like to die? To be dead and have fish nibble your eyes?

When he raised his head, he looked past the body. From the corner of his eye he saw the arms and legs rise then fall with each wave. Before him the Volga sparkled in the sunlight. It was a beautiful river.

* * *

Smoke spiraling up at the water's edge was a warning. Gregor thought about climbing the bank to avoid whoever was camped along the shore. But the smell of fried fish made his stomach protest. He moved closer, stopping at a safe distance. Near the campfire tipped a two-wheeled cart hung with shiny pots and pans. The squatting man in a threadbare dress coat and wide brimmed hat looked like a typical orthodox tin peddler.

"How far to the rail yards?" Gregor asked.

The man didn't look up from his task. "Ten versts to the Simblok yards." He poked at the headless fish in his skillet. "Do you have money for the fare?"

Gregor held out his empty hands. "I have no money."

Still, the man didn't glance his way. "Then I guess I can't interest you in a nice new pot for your mother."

"My mother lives in Moscow. She has all the pots and pans she needs." He pressed his hand to his empty belly, trying to hide the growling. The peddler noticed anyway.

"If you've got a mother in Moscow, then I'm the son of the Pope in Rome."

"My mother does live in Moscow and my father too." He slid the cello case off his shoulder and balanced it on the tip of his shoe. "My father's a musician. He plays for all the important people in Moscow."

"Of course he does." The man flipped the crisp fish onto a wooden plate. He looked up. "That's why his son is wandering half starved along the Volga."

"It's not Papa's fault." Gregor felt heat come to his face. "The orchestra conductor promised to pay me wages, but he lied."

"Don't get angry at me because your father's a bastard." The peddler motioned him closer. "Better a bastard for a father than none at all."

"Papa's not like that."

"Never mind. If you've got something worth trading, I'll share my supper."
He peeled the blackened fish skin back with a fork and lifted a strip of white
meat. "But I can't give it away for free."

Gregor reached into the pocket of his cello case where he kept small things.

"Don't offer me that big fiddle." The man licked his fingers. "I've got
enough to carry."

"I have a comb and a bar of soap." Gregor peeled the paper from the soft
cake and held it out.

"Don't want your comb." The man picked up the smaller of the two fish by
the tail and handed it to Gregor. "I'll take the soap."

They sat on the sand in silence, chewing, picking bones, flicking slivers of
cartilage toward the water. A gull swooped down and salvaged the bones then
flew off to alert others.

"You're an orphan." The peddler picked at the fish carcass.

The question caught Gregor off guard. He sucked in a breath and a sliver of
bone stuck in his throat. "No—." He tried to answer, but coughed so hard the
peddler pounded him on the back. "I'm no orphan," he managed to gasp when
he could speak again.

"Might as well be." The man flung the fishtail toward a flock of squawking
birds. "I was alone at your age. My father died." For a moment he paused. "It
was a good thing. The bastard beat my mother until she couldn't take it any
more." He shrugged and wiped his fingers on his sleeve. "She gave up and died
first. It was easier that way."

"Papa wouldn't do that."

"Then why did you run away?"

"I didn't run away. Papa and Leo had to go home. There wasn't enough
money for all of us to ride the train."

"What kind of man abandons his own son?" The peddler rose and carried the
frying pan to the river where he washed it then dried it on his coattails. "A bastard
like that doesn't deserve a son."

"Papa isn't . . ." Gregor paused trying to think of the right words. "Papa isn't
very good with money."

"You don't need to stick up for him." He hung the pan with others on the
side of his cart. "My advice is, forget your father. Forget your whole family. You
need to look after yourself." He poked Gregor's suitcase with the toe of his shoe.
"What else have you got that's worth trading?"

* * *

The sun was red and low in the sky over Moscow as he walked the last few
blocks from the rail station to Ogorodnya Propst. It had been twelve days since

he left Astrakhan, only twelve, but it seemed like months. All that time he had dreamed of home, imagined sitting at the kitchen table eating Mama's borscht, sleeping in his own bed with Leo snoring beside him. Only a few more steps and he would be there. His legs ached and the sole of his left shoe was loose. With each step it scraped against the cobblestones, a stupid sound that would have embarrassed him had he not been so tired.

As he passed the chocolate factory, he detected the sweet odor of candy and for the first time it didn't sicken him. The Tartar children approached him near the iron gate, peddling their wares.

"Buy, buy. Only one kopek." A small boy pushed a dirty hand toward him, offering a loosely rolled cigarette. Another boy shoved the first aside and stuck out a fist full of sticky candy. "Buy from me."

"I have nothing." Gregor held out his empty hands.

The boys lost interest and turned away, heading for a Troika that approached from a side street. Like two yapping dogs, they ran directly in front of the horses so the driver had to stop. "Buy, buy from me. Only one kopek," they cried in unison.

The sound of their chant followed Gregor as he lifted the latch. Inside the yard he hesitated, looking up at the open parlor window. The sound of a violin drifted out over the street. He recognized Leo's vibrato.

Mama! Papa! He wanted to yell, but his mouth was parched and he hadn't the strength to be heard. He felt like crying and laughing and shouting all at the same time. Instead, he ran up the stairs, the sole of his shoe slapping time on each step, the cello banging the back of his legs. When he reached the landing, he stopped, trying to catch his breath. Tears welled up in his eyes, but he brushed them aside and pushed open the door.

The first thing he felt was the cool darkness of the apartment on his sweaty face. Mama stood at the dining room table, a wooden bread bowl in her hands.

"I'm… home," he said, still panting.

"Grisha!" Mama dropped the bowl and it bounced across the floor. A moment later he was wrapped in her arms, smothered by her breasts as she covered him with kisses. "Grisha. You're alive."

"I'm all right, Mama," he said, his voice muffled "I wanted to come home." He inhaled the aroma of onions and potatoes from her clothing and his stomach rumbled.

"I've been so afraid." She continued to kiss the top of his head. "Where have you been? Why didn't you write?"

Before he could answer someone pounded his shoulder. He pulled back enough to see Papa's smiling face. "You see," Papa said. "I told you he would come to no harm. And he made it home in time for school."

"Grisha, you're home?" Now it was Leo. He playfully punched Gregor's arm. "Mama thought you were dead, maybe eaten by wolves or stolen by gypsies."

"Leo, hush now," Mama said. "Go downstairs and find Nadja. Tell her Grisha has come home."

Gregor was escorted into the kitchen, but Mama's arm never left his shoulder. "Let me look at you." She studied him, holding him at arm's length. "You're filthy. Your hair is so long it's in your eyes." Her rough fingers pushed the locks from his face.

"I walked from Samara, except sometimes I rode a train. But only at night so the police wouldn't find me."

"Where's your suitcase and jacket?" Papa stood in the kitchen doorway looking down at Gregor's feet. "And what happened to your shoes?"

"It was a long walk and I ran out of money. I traded my suitcase and jacket to a peddler."

"I hope he paid well. That jacket cost ten rubles."

"He didn't give me money, only food."

"Never mind the jacket. We'll buy him a new one for school." Mama pressed her palms against his cheeks. "You must be starving,"

"Can I have goulash?" He felt his stomach growl with anticipation. "I haven't eaten since yesterday."

"You can have anything you want." Mama hugged him again.

"Grisha, my God!" Nadja's voice preceded her. Again he was enveloped, this time in Nadja's arms. She smelled of laundry soap and hot water. While she kissed him on his cheeks then on his forehead, she pulled him into the parlor where the afternoon light made everything rosy. "You look like you've been rolling in dirt."

"I rode in a freight car. One of them was filled with cows."

"Oh, Grisha." She hugged him again. "I thought we'd never see you." He wrapped his arms around her, returning her hug. Over her shoulder he saw another figure in the doorway. For a moment he froze as he and Dimitri locked eyes. He pulled away from Nadja, but she must have seen his face.

"It's all right, Grisha," She glanced over her shoulder. "Dimitri, I'll be down in a few minutes to finish your mother's laundry."

The boy's eyes didn't leave Gregor's face. "My mother wants the laundry done by tonight," he said. "She'll pay you extra if it's done sooner."

"Get out—." Gregor started toward him but Nadja squeezed his cheeks with her damp fingers. "Grisha, take those filthy clothes off and let me wash them."

She was protecting that disgusting pig. Was she mad? Gregor tried to pull free but too late. A grin of victory crossed Dimitri's face, then he turned and was gone.

Chapter Eleven

September 1914

"The Russian Army is now fighting Germany to protect our Serbian brothers." The teacher's voice was slow, as if each word weighed heavy on his tongue. "With God on our side, we shall prevail."

There was silence in the room, but a dozen eyes moved back and forth, everyone's face full of questions. Gregor raised his hand and the teacher looked at him over round glasses. But instead of the customary nod, which gave a student permission to stand and speak, the man turned away and stared out the window at the street below. "Your lesson for tomorrow is to transpose the etude from C major to G, then rewrite it in D."

That was it. There was no more talk of war, or of killing, or why the Germans were suddenly the enemy. Music, only music, it was all the teacher ever talked about. Gregor wondered if the man knew anything else. He imagined him living alone in a house surrounded by instruments, reading only musical scores, singing to himself.

"What do you think?" Gregor joined the crowd of boys surging downstairs toward the dining hall.

"I'd like to go to war." Sasha said, pushing past one of the younger students. "But my mother won't let me. She says I'd get shot like a stupid *Kulak*."

"My brother's going," Vladim said. "He told us last night, right there at the supper table. My father can't stop him."

"How old do you have to be to join the army?" Gregor pulled open the door to the long room filled with narrow tables. "Maybe they need musicians to keep the soldiers entertained?"

"Forget about music, I want to shoot a gun." Sasha took a seat at the end of the table and the rest joined him, shoving their way along the bench. "Besides, all the army wants are brass and drummers. You can't march with a cello."

"Do you think the Tsar will give your brother a gun?" Gregor slid his composition book under the bench then reached into his pocket for lunch money. All he found was a ten-kopek coin.

"A rifle for sure and maybe a pistol." Sasha made his hand a gun and pointed it at Gregor's head. "Bang, bang. Just like that. You're dead. He'll kill a dozen Germans."

"Not with those glasses." Vladim laughed and made circles around his eyes with his fingers. "Come on, Grisha, let's get sausage rolls. Only five kopeks. Smells good."

Gregor bounced the ten-kopek coin in his hand. If he spent it on lunch, even a bowl of cabbage soup, he wouldn't have enough for the streetcar home. "No, I'm not hungry."

"Is that all the money you've got?" Sasha elbowed him in the ribs.

"It's for the streetcar."

"Tell your father you need more."

"He doesn't like to hand out money." Gregor pocketed the coin.

Tonight Papa wanted him home before dark. He and Leo would have to stand by his side as he went door to door collecting the rents from the other tenants. Gregor despised rent day. Women wailing, men cursing, Dimitri's mother spitting on them and calling them dirty *Zhyds*.

"Are you poor?" Vladim dumped a handful of kopeks and rubles on the table.

"No," Gregor said too quickly. "My father owns a big apartment building with hundreds of tenants. And he's a famous violist."

"I've never heard of him." Sasha unbuttoned his jacket collar, which left a red mark on his thick neck. "Sounds like you're a peasant."

Gregor wanted to protest, but Vladim laughed. "I think it would be fun to be poor. No rules to follow, no one to tell you that your clothes aren't clean. You wouldn't even have to smell nice."

Sasha punched Vladim's shoulder, nearly knocking him off the bench. "*Vladnik*, you smell like a rose."

"Come on, Grisha." Vladim headed toward the kitchen. "Let's eat. Forget about going home tonight. You can stay in my room. We'll read Vivaldi, the solo parts only."

Gregor pulled the ten-kopek coin from his pocket, smelled the heavy aroma of sausage and felt his stomach grumble. "All right," he said and followed his friend. "I'll tell Papa we had rehearsal for the Saint Nicholas Festival. He'll understand."

* * *

January 1915

On the first morning after Saint Nicholas Day, Gregor lay in bed wide-awake. Skiing, sledding, even playing soccer in the snow, which should he do first? As the gray early morning light filtered through the frosty window, he exhaled slowly, watching his breath cloud above the rim of the blankets. Beside him Leo snored, occasionally sputtering and mumbling in his sleep. Reaching under the blankets, Gregor poked his brother's shoulder. Leo didn't move.

"Wake up." He pushed back the blankets and rolled off the bed. Breathing a circle of warmth on the frosty windowpane, he rubbed a spot clean with his sleeve. "Look, Leo, it snowed last night and it's still coming down." Below him the backyard and latrines lay clean and white.

Leo groaned. Only his dark head was visible, peeking from beneath the blankets.

"Come on, get out of bed." Gregor pounded his brother's back. "It's still snowing. No school for a week."

"Let me sleep."

"Not today." Gregor yanked the blankets back, uncovering Leo who curled into a ball, his hands over his eyes.

"When did you get home?" Leo mumbled through his hands.

"Last night." Gregor bounced on the foot of the bed. "Late. We had a farewell party for Vladim."

"I'm cold." Leo reached for the blankets, but Gregor pulled them away.

"I walked home. The streetcars weren't running." He wound the blanket into a ball and threw it at Leo's head. "Let's eat breakfast then wax our skis. The snow will be perfect in Sokolniki Park."

Leo untangled the blanket and disappeared beneath it. "Leave me alone." His voice was muffled.

Gregor abandoned his assault and pulled a clean pair of socks from the corner basket. "If you don't get up I'll ask Nadja to ski with me. She can use your boots."

Leo's head popped up, his dark hair sticking like broom grass from behind his ears. "Nadja can't go." He threw the blankets off and swung his bare legs over the bed. "Leave her alone."

"Yes she can." Gregor stepped into his thick wool pants. "I'll be ready before you will."

Leo didn't take the challenge. Instead, he sat on the bed, hugging his arms to his chest, his skinny legs dangling below his nightshirt. "Grisha, you can't ask Nadja."

"Why not?" He slipped on his sweater then started for the door.

"Grisha, wait." Leo tried to push the door shut, but wasn't fast enough. Gregor ducked beneath the outstretched arm and headed toward the kitchen.

Before he made it to the end of the hall, Leo grabbed Gregor's shoulder and yanked him back. It was gloomy in the hall, but there was enough light to see Leo's pale face.

"Nadja's not here," Leo whispered.

"Let go." Gregor pulled free. "I'm going to wake her up."

"You can't—I mean." Leo's voice quivered the way it did when he was upset. "You can't ask her, not now."

"Why not? She loves to ski."

"Shhhh." Leo put his finger to his lips. "Keep your voice down."

Footsteps sounded from the kitchen and they both looked up. Papa stood in his nightshirt, his unshaven face gray, like he'd taken ill.

"Grisha." Papa paused and ran his hand over his eyes. "Grisha, you haven't been here. You're the only one who doesn't know."

"Know what?"

"Nadja is married." Papa sounded weary. "Love is as sacred as life."

"What? That's absurd. She just-."

"She can and she is." Papa cut him off. "Some children grow up and fly away like birds. Nadja has only moved downstairs with Dimitri now. We'll all be here when her child is born."

The air had been sucked out of his body. His knees weakened and he reached for the wall. "No! You can't make her do this."

"Keep your tongue in your head."

"It's not a few steps— downstairs." He could barely get the words out. "It's— it's a cesspool."

"You will not argue." Papa moved into the hall, close, and Gregor saw beads of sweat dotting his forehead. A trickle ran down into the stubble on his cheek.

Taking a deep breath, he tried to control his anger. "Papa. Nadja is only sixteen. She doesn't know Dimitri. You don't know him. He's a filthy pig."

"She knows him well enough to be mother of his child." Papa's nostrils flared.

"Dimitri will beat her." The words spilled out. "Just like his drunken father beats his lazy mother. They're Cossacks. They won't protect her."

"She is married." Papa's voice shook. "No daughter of mine will be called a whore."

"Is that all you care about?" Gregor felt pain between his eyes. "What people will think of you?"

From across the room he became aware of Mama. "Stop it, both of you. I can't bear it."

They ignored her.

"You can't make Nadja do this. She'll hate you forever." He sucked in a deep breath. "And so will I."

"You ungrateful, worthless boy," Papa screamed. His hand flew back and the blow landed so hard it knocked Gregor sideways, slamming his shoulder into the wall. Legs buckling, he slid down the wall to the floor. The room swaying around him. For a moment there was silence, as if everyone in the room had turned to stone.

"Don't hit him." Mama screamed. She grabbed Papa's arm. He shoved her back and she fell against the kitchen table.

Alex came running from the bedroom, his nightshirt so big it tangled around his legs. "Mama, Mama," he cried, then tripped, fell and lay on the floor, his piercing wail unanswered.

"Grisha will obey me." Papa threw his hands in the air. "Or he will leave this house."

From the floor Gregor stared up, tears of rage blurring his vision. "You are a monster." It hurt to speak. He tasted blood and spit a mouthful of red on the floor. "I hate you. I will always hate you. I am no longer your son."

"She—is Dimitri's wife." Papa punctuated each word with his finger. "It is finished."

Gregor rolled to his knees, reached for the wall and pulled himself up. His eyes met Leo's.

"Please, Grisha, don't do this," Leo pleaded.

Leo, always the coward. Turning, Gregor raised a fist and shook it in the monster's face. "I swear, if you make her do this, you will never see me again."

There it was, an ultimatum he could not take back. Pushing past Leo, he yanked his coat from the hook by the door.

"Grisha," Mama cried. "You can't leave."

He turned and his eyes met hers. Tears streamed down her face and for a moment he was struck by how old she had grown. "Mama, Nadja is your own flesh and blood."

"You don't understand." She reached out to take his hand but he pulled away. "You're still a child," she said. "You must obey Papa. He knows what's best for Nadja."

"I am not a child." He wanted to shake her, make her understand, make her love Nadja the way a mother should. But already Mama was pulling away.

"Pavel," she said. "Talk to him, make him understand."

"I will not live here if you let this happen," Gregor said. "And I will never come back."

"Grisha," Mama said. "Don't say that."

Gregor looked once more at Papa. His father's black eyes met his, then turned away. With arms crossed, Papa stared out the window, looking down to the street. Mama hesitated, then moved to Papa's side and plucked at his sleeve. "Pavel, you can't mean this."

Papa didn't move. He stood with shoulders hunched, his back stiff.

"You will never see me again." Without waiting for a reply, he grabbed his cello from the corner and left, slamming the door behind him.

If he had met Dimitri at the bottom of the stairs, he would have killed him with his bare hands. Or died trying. He stopped in front of the hated door, ready to kick it in. Nadja was somewhere on the other side. With a clenched fist he pounded the door. "Nadja, Nadja," he called. No response. He pounded again, then kicked the door until his foot ached. Nothing.

Backing away, he wiped his damp face with his sleeve. New snow blanketed the empty courtyard, crunching cold and dry underfoot. Everything was quiet. No smoke rose from the chimney pipe that protruded out the log wall. Dimitri had taken her away.

In the street he turned and looked up at the windows of the apartment. Surely Mama would come. She would call to him and beg him to come back inside. She would make Papa understand. He moved outside the gate to get a better view of the upper window, searching for her familiar face at the curtains. The windows remained dark behind the veil of icicles that hung from the roof. Why? Nothing made sense. He despised them all.

The air didn't feel cold as he paced back and forth, moving from one end of the fence to the other. The heat of anger kept him warm. Papa was not his father. He was a monster. What made him so full of hate, so uncaring? How could he give his daughter to Dimitri? And Nadja, where was she? Was she already in that hell? Why didn't she run away? Why had she let that pig touch her? The thought of them together, of Dimitri kissing her, touching her, undressing her, made him nauseous.

He slung the cello strap over his shoulder. Surely Mama was watching. Now she would have to call him back. Crossing the street, he paused with his back to the building. He waited. No one called from the window, no familiar voice beckoned him to return.

Standing against the wall of the neighboring vodka shack, he felt icy wind cut through his coat. His feet felt numb and he pounded one foot, then the other on the snow, stamping out anger, trying to restore feeling in his toes.

Papa. He hated him, always hated him, ever since he had left them and gone to St. Petersburg. He was no different than Boris or Gelko. No better than drunken Cossacks who sell their daughters into slavery.

He could never go back, never apologize. It was over. He wiped his runny nose on his sleeve then spit a clot of blood, bright red onto the snow. Without another look at the windows, he walked away.

Fresh snow, deeper than his boots, slid up his pants legs, melted and soaked his socks. Faster, faster, he began to walk, without purpose, toward nothing, going nowhere. Over the footbridge that spanned the frozen canal, past unpainted houses trimmed in sparkling icicles, beyond the chocolate factory, running, then walking, then running again until the frigid air burned his lungs and he couldn't draw another breath. The street was unfamiliar, the houses low and dirty. A skinny dog barked at him from behind a fence.

The cello grew heavy, like an anchor pulling him down. He was lost. He turned left into a narrow street. A shuttered shop and stable stood next to a frozen ditch. His legs felt like stones. Sinking to his knees, he covered his face with his bare hands. With his breath he tried to warm them the way Mama did when she would hold his frozen fingers to her lips. But even his breath was cold. Beside him the hard stone horse trough made a windbreak from swirling snow.

Never again would he play the piano with Nadja, or ski in Sokolniki Forest with Leo. Gone were nights drinking hot tea from the samovar, or warming his feet by the kitchen stove. Tears welled up, but he didn't have the strength to weep. His lip felt fat, his tongue swollen. The salty taste of blood turned sour in his mouth.

Slumping against the trough, he pulled his knees to his chest, hugging his arms around them. Snow settled on his head and melted. Icy water ran down his neck. He didn't care. Beside him lay his cello wrapped in the canvas cover Mama had made. Gradually, it too disappeared beneath a blanket of white. What did it matter? Music was pointless. Life meant nothing.

Troikas and sleigh wagons rumbled by at the far end of the alley, their metal runners muffled by the packed snow, but he was alone in the alley. He didn't know where he was, nor did he care. Anger settled like stones in his belly, the weight pinning him to the ground. With hands over his face, he slumped to one side, resting his head on the cello. If God were merciful, if there was a God, he would let him die right here. All he had to do was wait.

Ekaterinoslav with Dnieper River in background

Ekaterinoslav Synagogue

Ekaterinoslav: Jewish shopping district with music store on left

Piatigorsky family about 1912
(Standing L to R) Uncle Leo and Aunt Julia Agronoff, Maria and Pavel
Piatigorsky. (Seated) Grandmother and Grandfather Piatigorsky, Gregor, Nadja,
Alex, Leonid Piatigorsky. Others: children of Leo and Julia

Pavel and Maria Piatigorsky

Moscow Conservatory

PART II

Chapter Twelve

"God in heaven, the kid's frozen stiff. You'd better run for the doctor. Shutkin, can we use your place?"

Voices pricked at the edge of Gregor's consciousness but seemed a long way off.

"Of course. Let me pick him up."

"No. He's too big and you're too old. Take his fiddle. I'll carry him."

Mercifully, the sounds faded into darkness. Then suddenly he was lifted, bounced and turned on his back. Searing heat hit his face. He tried to open his eyes, but everything blurred. Faces, arms and hands. All indistinguishable. Motion, drunken and violent.

"Quick... blankets... a pillow."

He was dropped on a hard surface, wooden and unforgiving. Something soft was slid beneath his head. Nothing else. Darkness.

A thousand shards of broken glass rained down on him. From below, he was lying on knife blades. "Stop!" He thrashed, rolling left then right, desperate to escape. "Please. Make it stop." He wanted to cry, but crying hurt too much.

Above him a wrinkled, bearded face appeared. "Shhhh, my boy. I'm Shutkin. My friend Ivan found you asleep on the street. You were covered with snow." The man's gnarled hand touched Gregor's head and gently stroked his hair. Gregor flinched, but the old man's touch didn't hurt.

"The doctor came last night," Shutkin said. "He bandaged your hands and feet. Your hands were the worst." The wrinkled face smiled again. "You'll heal but the pain is only beginning. That's what happens when a body melts."

"It hurts— I hurt—." Even speaking caused invisible knives to cut into his flesh. "Please— help me. I can't bear it."

The old face vanished, returning a moment later with a glass. "Drink this. It will ease your pain." He slid his arm under Gregor's neck and lifted his head high enough to place the glass at his lips. "At least for me it always does."

What he swallowed felt like fire. Raw vodka burned his tongue and scorched his throat, but it was nothing compared to the pain in his hands. "I am sorry you must lie on my table, but I have no bed." Shutkin dragged a chair over and sat beside the table. He spoke as if nothing were seriously wrong. "You see, I sleep on that couch. But you are such a tall fellow you would never fit. In any case, I'm too old to climb up there and take your place. It is certainly no worse than a *doss* house and maybe better than factory lodging."

Gregor couldn't reply. Even the tiny movements it took to speak were excruciating.

"You see," Shutkin reached across Gregor's chest and pulled the curtains shut. "I display my best items here on this table. When people walk by, they might be tempted to spend a ruble or kopek in my shop."

Gregor turned his eyes but not his head. All he saw was dusty fabric bunched up against the window. "I don't think the sight of you lying here will invite any buyers." Shutkin chuckled. "Not unless they are in need of a badly used boy."

The old man disappeared. Gregor closed his eyes and counted each breath. In. Out. In. Out. Breathing out hurt more than breathing in. He continued until he reached one hundred. Then he did it again. In the midst of the third set Shutkin reappeared with a steaming bowl.

"Try this. It will warm your belly." He spooned salty soup into Gregor's mouth. At least swallowing didn't hurt. Instead of counting breaths, he counted spoonfuls of soup. Anything to keep from crying. When the soup was gone, Shutkin heated bricks, wrapped them in rags and tucked them along the edge of the table. At first the heat felt like flames licking at his arms and legs. Gregor clenched his teeth and returned to counting, this time imagining he was conducting, 4/4 then 3/4 time. It was better than counting to one hundred.

The man shuffled out of sight. From somewhere in the room Gregor heard the ticking of a clock. He counted the beats, 3/4 time. One hundred measures, then two hundred. He lay very still, breathing as slowly as possible, motionless, not moving so much as a muscle or a hair. If he kept counting and breathing, the pain subsided, just a little. Very slowly, without turning his head, he let his eyes roam the room.

It was a strange and interesting place. Above him was a low ceiling made of logs, with flaking plaster between the beams. Tools and gardening implements hung from hooks on the wall and piles of books filled narrow shelves at the far end. There was even a violin hanging from the ceiling.

He turned his head a fraction and saw a row of dusty glassware and ancient dishes crowding the top of a bookcase. Everything looked old and unused. At the edge of his vision sat a faded brocade sofa and at the far end of the room a fire in an old stove. He couldn't actually see the fire, only the bits of light dancing on the walls.

"Where am I?" He managed to speak without breathing too deeply. "What is this place?"

Shutkin reappeared. "This is my store. I sell some of everything, but mostly I sell nothing."

"You have no customers?"

"I think people do not like my wares." He lit a long-stemmed pipe and Gregor saw the plume of smoke rise in the air. It smelled acrid, like burning hair.

"How do you live?"

"As you see, I don't live very well."

"I'm sorry— to take— your table." The words seemed to stick to his tongue. The warmth of the vodka and the soup were taking effect. As the old man spoke, Gregor felt his eyelids grow heavy.

"It has been a long time since I used my table to serve company," he said. "I'm glad it suits you." Gregor remembered no more. In sleep he was home again.

He faced them from the kitchen doorway. On his right Nadja stood, her belly swollen, a bruise darkening the side of her face. She stretched out her hand to him, her eyes pleading, then turned away and buried her face in Mama's shoulder.

"Grisha." The voice cut into him and he cringed. Papa loomed over him, tall and dark. Gregor crouched, making himself small.

"Please, Papa," he wanted to cry but his voice failed him. Papa's open hand landed hard against his cheek. Tears blurred his vision, but he wiped them away. "I hate you. I am not your son."

He stood. In the distance he saw Dimitri behind Papa. The Cossack moved in a pus-colored cloud, laughing his wild-animal laugh. Helpless, Gregor watched him drag Nadja toward the stairs. The sound of her cries cut his heart. He stood before the door, bloodying his fists, trying to break it down. "Papa, help me. Don't let him take her."

Papa turned his back and walked away.

* * *

"The young fellow will thaw out in no time. *Da?*"

"He's already more supple," Shutkin said. "Less likely to break."

Gregor opened one eye then the other. Everything around him was blurred, out of focus. Gradually, he made out someone tall standing over him. It was a man rolling a cigarette.

"I'd better get back to the factory before my boss throws me into the street and I end up like our young friend here."

"Who are you?" Gregor said. His tongue and lips felt thick. Shifting a fraction to the right, he relieved the pressure of the hard wood on his hip and shoulder. For the first time it didn't hurt to move.

"I see you're now awake. Good." The tall man lit his cigarette then spit on the floor. "Shutkin, your tobacco tastes like dried cow dung." The man tipped his hat and disappeared.

"That is my friend Ivan," Shutkin said. "He thinks you're an army deserter. Are you?"

"I'm not old enough to be a soldier."

"I didn't think so, but there are many young men who don't want to fight the Germans."

Gregor tried to lift his head, but pain gripped his chest like a giant claw. He collapsed back onto the table. "Where's my cello?" he asked when the pain subsided. "Is it here? Did someone take it?"

"You mean that big fiddle?" Shutkin disappeared and Gregor heard the old man's feet scuffing across the floor. "Here it is." He raised the instrument close so Gregor could see it. "It was very wet, so I took the cover off and stood it near the hearth to dry."

Gregor cringed. The fingerboard would probably warp and if it got too hot, the body would crack. "Is it damaged?" he said as he tried to sit up.

"There now, don't try to move." Shutkin put a firm hand on Gregor's shoulder and pulled the blanket up over him. "Don't worry. I asked my friend who plays violin how to dry your big fiddle. It will need tuning but it's no worse for the experience."

"Thank you." Gregor closed his eyes and sank back onto the table.

"It's a serious musician who cares more for his instrument than for himself."

"I study at the Imperial Conservatory. Someday I'll be the best cellist in Moscow and play for the Tsar and Tsarina."

"How old are you?"

"I'll be thirteen in April."

"You are as tall as a grown man." Shutkin shuffled to the hearth and returned with a glass of tea.

"I have my student identity card." Gregor tried to move, but his arm felt like wood. "My papers are in my coat pocket. The director makes us carry them if the police stop us."

"As well they might when they see a boy your size." Shutkin again slipped his arm under Gregor's head and tried to lift him. "Drink, but first you must sit up."

Gregor struggled to move to a sitting position at the edge of table. At first the room tilted right then left like a rocking boat. Shutkin kept a firm grip on his shoulder until he opened his eyes. "I'm stiff. I can't move."

"You've been lying on that hard table for three days." Shutkin placed the tea glass in Gregor's bandaged hands. "See if you can hold this."

By pressing on the sides of the glass with his palms, he managed to raise the glass to his lips. It was hot, sweet and strong. The liquid slid into his empty stomach and he realized he was hungry.

"I can hear your belly complaining." Shutkin opened a cupboard and returned with a half loaf of black bread, dusty with flour. "Here, eat this. You're a growing boy."

"Is this all you have?" Gregor tried to carefully set the glass on the table, but managed to spill some of it on the blanket. "I can't take food from you."

"My old body needs very little." Shutkin eased himself onto the sofa then patted the space beside him. "Come down off your hard perch and sit with me."

Gregor stretched down with one leg and tested his weight, but a jolt of pain shot up his foot. Keeping his weight balanced on his heels, he staggered the few steps to the sofa and collapsed next to the old man.

"You are doing very well for a boy just back from the dead." Shutkin broke off a small chunk of bread for himself then handed the rest to Gregor. "You see. There's enough for both of us."

It was awkward eating with bandaged hands. His fingers felt like boiled sausages and he couldn't bend them. Still the bread calmed the devils in his stomach. He gnawed at the tough crust and when he was finished his belly felt better.

"Are you ready to go home now?" Shutkin brushed the crumbs from his lap. A skinny cat crept from beneath the sofa and licked them up.

"I can't go home." Gregor sank back into the lumpy sofa and let his head drop onto the brocade.

"Why is that?"

"It is impossible. Papa—, I mean, my father told me I could never come home again."

"Those are very strong words."

"He cares only about himself."

"And who do you care about?"

"I tried—." His voice faltered and he felt tears welling up. Throwing his arm over his face to hide his shame, he swallowed hard. "I care about my sister Nadja, and my mother, even my brother Leo. But there is nothing I can do for any of them."

"You are only a boy. It's not your job to take care of them."

"I had to. Papa went to St. Petersburg, so I worked." He hesitated and pulled his knees up on the sofa, wishing he could be small. "Something always went wrong and I got fired."

"It's a boy's place to make mistakes." Shutkin puffed on his pipe, sending the bitter odor of bad tobacco into the air. "That is how a boy must learn."

"I can't make anymore mistakes. Every time I try to do something, I only make it worse." Memories of past disasters flooded back. "I couldn't help Vera, or Mama, or Nadja. When Papa came home I thought everything would get better, but it only got worse."

"You're a stubborn boy." Shutkin sucked in loudly and coughed. "Don't be angry with your father. I think he is hurt too. It's a hard thing for a man to lose a son."

"It doesn't matter. I'm no longer his son."

"For now," Shutkin said softly. "Maybe, just for now."

"Can I stay here with you?" Gregor looked at the wrinkled old man. The thought of going back out in the cold was more than he could bear. "I have no place else to go."

"Of course. You're not ready to go home yet."

"Thank you. I'll work hard. I'll get a job and pay for whatever I eat."

"No, no." Shutkin pushed himself slowly up from the sofa. "You must go back to your studies and play your instrument. But first let me look at your hands. A musician's hands are his most valuable tools."

He stood in front of Gregor and leaned forward like a tree ready to topple in the wind. Slowly the old man unwrapped the bandages. As the cloth strips came off, the air touched Gregor's raw skin. It felt like fire. With eyes squeezed shut, he took deep ragged breaths, again counting, until both hands were free of the cloth.

"It seems you are not ready to return to the conservatory." Shutkin made a clucking sound with his tongue that reminded Gregor of Mama. Reluctantly, he opened his eyes. The pair of hands before him were not his own. From the last knuckle to the fingertips the skin was as white as tallow wax. Each finger was so swollen, he was sure the skin would burst.

"You are damaged. If your fingers don't heal they may turn black and fall off."

"No," Gregor cried as he stared at the strange objects attached to his arms. "Please. If I can't play my cello I'll die."

"We may be able to save them. I will try goose grease." Shutkin hobbled to a lopsided wooden cabinet and returned with a small pot. "I'll rub this on your hands. I think if we do it several times a day until your fingers turn pink, your hands might be saved. But I must warn you, it will be most painful."

"Do it," Gregor said without hesitation, stretching out his hands.

Shutkin scooped the grease onto his palms then gently massaged the right hand. The first few strokes were so excruciating, Gregor thought he would faint. Each stroke was like having needles driven into his swollen flesh. He bit his lip to keep from crying as he squeezed his eyes shut. Looking at the bloated flesh was more than he could bear.

Again Shutkin spoke and his voice became a welcome distraction. "A boy like you could be my great-grandson. If my son had lived he might have had a son who in turn might have had a son. A boy such as you could be sitting with me right now."

He paused, as he switched to the left hand. "It's been a long time since I had company so I am not used to talking. The young have no patience for an old man and the middle-aged prefer to hear themselves speak. The old people don't hear very well and besides, they only talk about their ailments."

"How old are you?" Gregor asked.

"Not old enough to think of death. We all know that we will die, but not when we will die. It's a trick of nature that makes us feel immortal." He smiled. "I couldn't watch my own birth, but I hope to witness my own death. It should be most interesting."

Seven days passed before Gregor could sit on the sofa and hold his cello. The familiar weight between his knees felt comfortable and reassuring. His bandaged hands were still too swollen to hold the bow or press the strings. But he closed his eyes and with an empty bow hand moving through the air, imagined all the parts of Tchaikovsky's *Swan Lake*, or at least the ones he remembered.

Twice a day Shutkin removed the bandages and massaged Gregor's stiff fingers, and each day the pain became slightly more bearable. By the end of the week the swelling started to subside, but the skin along the edges of his fingers cracked, oozing a clear sticky substance that dried as hard as glue. Shutkin made soup of warm salt water and butter. Every night before going to sleep Gregor soaked his swollen hands in the slimy concoction.

By the second week, he could bend his fingers well enough to hold the bow in a fist. But he still couldn't put pressure on the fingerboard. His hands, callused by years of playing, were now as tender as baby skin. The slightest pressure on the strings caused excruciating pain. Yet, even without the use of his left hand, he was able to draw the bow across the strings.

For hours he practiced with a limited repertoire of sounds. But as he played he also forgot the pain. Only the emptiness in his heart did not fade.

"Soon I'll look for work," he said. "I'll get a job and give you all the money I earn."

Shutkin shook his head. "You must study and practice. You shouldn't think of being a burden or earning money." The old man shuffled to the closet and returned with a folded piece of paper. "For you. The director at the Conservatory gave it to me when I went to explain your absence."

"You went there?" A knot of dread gripped Gregor's stomach. "Why?"

Shutkin shrugged and turned toward the boiling pot of *kasha* simmering on the stove.

Gregor unfolded the paper. It was Leo's handwriting.

Grisha, we heard you were well and have a new place to live. Papa told the conservatory that you are working for a shopkeeper. He can't find work, so we're going home to Ekaterinoslav. Please come visit us. Mama sends her love and I miss you. Also, I took your skis. Leo.

He read it three times before folding it in half then folding it again. "How did he know I was here?"

"I sent word to your parents," Shutkin said. "I didn't want them to worry."

"No!" His voice sounded too loud but he couldn't help it. "You had no right to do that."

Shutkin poured water into the dented samovar. "You are safe here and you know where your family is. But they didn't know what has become of you."

Shutkin had betrayed him. "I won't go home," he shouted. "Not now. Not ever."

"Maybe not now." A smile creased Shutkin's wrinkled face. "By spring your hands will be healed. Then you must go back to the conservatory. I spoke to the director. There is a new cello teacher, Professor Von Glehn. If you prove yourself, the director said you could be promoted to the master class by autumn."

* * *

Among the cluttered belongings of Shutkin's store Gregor felt secure. As his hands healed, the blisters of black flesh split and peeled like a snake losing its skin. Emerging from the old, his new fingertips were red and tender. Every day he soaked them in warm salt water, drying the blisters until calluses began to form.

Without printed music still he practiced, improvising his own cadenzas to music he knew by heart. When spring began to melt the snow, the new term began at the conservatory. On the day before Gregor's first class, Shutkin declared it was time for a real haircut.

"Tomorrow my young friend returns to the music conservatory," he told the barber. "He will need to make a good impression on his new teacher if he hopes to advance."

"Better his teacher than the army recruiter." The barber snipped too close to the ear and Gregor flinched, but the barber didn't seem to notice or care. "All I hear is that the war goes badly, all defeats and no victories."

"Wars always go badly." Shutkin tapped a bit of tobacco into the bowl of his pipe. "Even when our leaders claim victory. I have seen my share of those victories."

Gregor listened to the two old men talk of battles and generals, hardships and the stupidity of men with too much power. Why do countries go to war? What was the point?

Through the window of the barbershop Gregor saw ragged men in torn uniforms hobble by on crutches. In the alley broken men huddled around trash fires to stay warm. The military bands that once played patriotic music for new recruits as they marched to the railway station were gone now. Instead, conscription squads prowled the streets looking for deserters or anyone healthy enough to hold a gun. Still, to Gregor the war seemed far away, and the German Kaiser as distant as the moon.

On his first day at the conservatory, Gregor faced his new teachers. All morning he sat in academic classes where he was taught basic Russian grammar, mathematics and world history. But as a music student no one expected him to do well. He rarely did his homework and his grades were poor.

In mathematics class he sat on a wooden bench between an opera student old enough to sport a mustache, and a boy violinist who couldn't write his own name. All three of them failed their examinations. No one cared.

Finally, after lunch came music. "Forget all your bad habits," said the cello teacher, a thin man with a tired voice. "Everything you have been taught, all that you have known previous to this day, must be put aside. From this day on you are all beginners. None of you will be accepted into Professor Von Glehn's master class until you improve your basic fingering and bowing technique."

"Piatigorsky." The teacher looked over his little glasses. "You're next. Keep the bow arm high."

In the straight-backed chair Gregor sat stiff, his bow in the proper position, his fingers pressing the strings. He looked at the teacher's dull face then glanced at his classmates. Most of them were new. In his absence all his friends had been promoted to the next level.

Laying his bow on the strings, he played the practice etude by Duport as if he were sawing wood. It sounded awful. Surely the teacher would chastise him for such a terrible performance and demand better.

"That's enough," the teacher said, dismissing him with a wave of his hand. "Next, you there, what's your name?"

"Alexanderov," replied the boy whose hunched shoulders made him look like an old man.

"Let me hear you play."

Each boy took a turn, some were awful, others mediocre, a few showed marginal promise. Then the teacher presented a history of the cello and the appropriate fingering technique. Gregor thought the man sounded bored with his own lecture. Finally, the students were sent to the practice rooms.

"Grisha," Alexanderov said as the group moved down the hall. "You were here last fall. I remember you from mathematics class."

"I had to drop out," Gregor said. He turned away so his embarrassment wouldn't show.

"Why?"

He hesitated. Should he explain his sorry life to this hunched boy? "I joined the circus," he said. "We traveled to Paris and I met the King of France." He felt the lie grow. "I even played at the royal court. I ate stuffed goose and turtledove soup. Our bread was pure white and covered with red currant jelly. All the ladies wanted me to stay, but the King said I had to return to my studies."

Alexanderov's face twisted in disbelief. "You did not."

"I did." His story seemed to take wings and fly. "I even spoke in French. *Parlez-vous français*? And I taught the princess how to dance."

"I thought you could play a lot better." A frown crossed Alexanderov's little puckered face.

"I'm an excellent cellist," Gregor said. "I don't belong in this class. I'm not a beginner." Backing into the practice room, he slammed the door. He hated Alexanderov.

For a long time he sat on the practice chair, staring out the window. But he didn't play. The high collar on his wool uniform irritated his neck and he scratched at it. Still, he didn't raise the bow. He felt strange, as if he were someone else, separated from his own body, no longer attached to the earth.

He looked down at his hands. The fingers had healed and there was no longer any sign of frostbite. But why had he performed so badly for the teacher? The man was not unkind, yet he didn't seem to care whether his students failed or succeeded. How could he make the man care?

Gregor sighed and laid his bow on the strings. What did it matter? Ignoring the etude he had been assigned, he played everything he loved. The music swept him away. He was no longer at war with Papa, sleeping on a table in a junk shop, missing Mama. In music he escaped. The cello was home.

At night, back in the shop, Shutkin was his audience. Gregor tried new pieces and replayed old ones.

"You are very talented," Shutkin said as he lowered himself onto the sofa. "Your teacher must be happy to have you in his class."

"My teacher hates music. He should be selling shoes or driving a troika."

"How do you know this?"

Gregor lowered his bow then placed it near the bridge and pressed hard, dragging it across all four stings. "You hear that? I play out of tune and he says nothing. I slow the tempo and he yawns."

"You should play for him well. Let him hear your beautiful Bach."

"I will not waste Bach on his stupid ears."

Every afternoon, when it was time to perform for the teacher, he played the same Duport etude in the same wooden fashion, sawing away at the strings like a beginner. He let the bow bump and thump the edge of the instrument. The teacher said nothing, only nodded then pointed to the next student.

One week then two went by. Nothing changed. The teacher stopped calling on him and Gregor sat idle, watching the other students play. His resentment grew. Why didn't the man demand he play something else? Why didn't he stomp his feet and wave his hands the way Papa did? Why didn't he care?

"On Friday we will have our first recital in the small concert hall," the teacher announced. "Make certain your shoes are polished, your clothes pressed and your hair combed. This is your chance to show the other conservatory students what you've learned."

When class ended, Gregor approached the teacher. "Sir, will I be allowed to perform on Friday with the others?"

"You want to play the cello?" The man's bushy eyebrows shot up. "If I allow you to play, you will have to perform first. I save the best students for last."

"Yes, sir."

"Very well." The teacher shook his head. "I hope you find something else to play. We are tired of hearing your etude."

"Yes, sir."

On Friday morning they all marched into the concert hall, bowed to the audience and took seats in two parallel rows.

"The students from the string instrument section will now perform from their repertoire," the teacher told the audience of first-year opera, brass and woodwind students. He turned and motioned to the front of the row. "Gregor Piatigorsky."

Gregor rose and took a seat on the wooden chair at center stage. The familiar sick knot of fear rose in his belly as he looked out at the crowd of bored faces. He had sat through many such tedious recitals for oboe and clarinet.

Surprise your audience. Papa's words filled his head. Today there would be no Duport etude. Closing his eyes, he lifted his bow and let go with a tune he had once played in the cinema, "Souvenir de Spa." It was a showy piece, the kind audiences loved.

As he played with the normal tempo, he noticed the mood of the audience change. From the crowd he heard tapping feet and clapping hands. He repeated the piece, increasing the tempo until the entire audience was completely engaged. The sound pulsated around him and he couldn't stop. The music and his own heartbeat had become one.

A firm hand shaking his shoulder finally startled him and he looked up to see the stunned face of his teacher. *You see*, he thought. *This is what I am. This is what I can do.*

"Enough! Off the stage."

When the recital concluded, the teacher peered down at him over his tiny glasses. "Piatigorsky, are you trying to make a fool out of me? I do not understand." He shook his head. "And I certainly can't teach you. Go home. I don't want you in my class anymore."

* * *

Shutkin's store had few customers. Who needed old tools or wanted a dented samovar? No one dared insinuate he sold junk, but few parted with their rubles or kopeks when they entered the low doorway. Ivan had to drop his head when he came to visit and so did Gregor. Shutkin was so bent he moved in and out with ease.

The landlord often came by to inquire about the health of Shutkin's business. "Will you pay the rent or shall I throw this worthless junk into the street?" he asked each time he appeared.

Shutkin would shuffle to the cabinet where he counted out enough rubles to satisfy the landlord for a few weeks. "I'll polish this old samovar," Shutkin said one afternoon after the landlord had left. "It's silver. I think I can sell it to the fellow who has a tea shop near Saint Basil's cathedral."

And so they survived on a few rubles here and a few kopeks there. Gregor continued to sleep on the table. He was too long for the sofa and sleeping on the floor gave him a chill. Every day he practiced. Shutkin's friends and neighbors stopped by, sometimes listening to him play, more often to seek the old man's advice.

"You shouldn't be so stubborn," Shutkin said one evening as they ate their dinner of bread cooked in sour milk. "Perhaps if you apologized to your teacher, he would let you return."

"No. That man's a fool. He doesn't care what I do as long as I don't embarrass him."

"And did you embarrass him?" said Shutkin, a slight smile on his wrinkled face.

"I did. He thought I was the worst student in class. That's why he made me perform before all the others."

"And you showed him he was wrong?"

"I did."

"How was that?"

Gregor stared across the table at Shutkin. The old man's blue eyes were laughing at him. With one question Shutkin could turn everything around. Papa, with his big booming voice and waving hands, never made his point as well.

"Never mind," Shutkin said, handing Gregor the remainder of his bread. "Your music would be no different in a cathedral."

Gregor looked down at the food and felt his stomach growl. This was the last of the bread.

"Tomorrow I must find work." He swallowed the last drops of thick milk. "We need money to buy food."

"You are a stubborn fellow." Shutkin moved to the washbasin. "I'd better agree with you before you run away again."

"I'll look for work in the cinema. I've worked in one before."

"Really. That's a fine job for a young man. Why did you leave?"

Gregor hesitated. The old man looked at him with raised eyebrows. Gregor could never lie to Shutkin. "I broke a chair over the conductor's head."

"Ahhh, a good reason to leave." Shutkin rinsed his bowl. "I have a better idea. I know a place that might hire you. But remember. Always carry your identity papers. The Provost is snatching up young men like you and sending them to the front lines."

* * *

The crooked signboard over the red door read TRAKTIR-THIRD CLASS. Broken vodka bottles littered the gutter and a feral cat crawled over a nearby garbage barrel. A crude drawing of a horse was scrawled beneath the word TRAKTIR with an arrow pointing toward the alley.

"Here it is," Shutkin said. "I used to come here when I was young. Only sixty I was then and still drove a troika." He wheezed as he spoke and for a moment had to steady himself with a hand on the doorframe. Gregor took his arm but the old man waved him off. "The owner put up a wall, but it still smells of animals." He sniffed the air as if to confirm the presence of horses. "It's filthy. I wouldn't eat anything they serve, but their tea and vodka is no worse than anywhere else."

Inside, the low ceiling and dirty windows made the place gloomy even at midday. A dozen tables sat at odd angles on the uneven floor and the copper samovar was dented. A few sleepy looking patrons were scattered along the walls, leaving enough room in the center to dance, but no one seemed inclined to merrymaking at noon.

"*Gospodin* Shutkin, my friend." The owner, a greasy man in dirty peasant clothes and a military hat, greeted them then motioned to a table. "I haven't seen you in years, but you're still as ugly as ever." They both laughed at the insult.

"I've been busy eating good food and drinking fine wine." Shutkin grinned.

"And making love to beautiful women no doubt," the owner said and wiped his hands on a gray apron.

"That too." Shutkin lowered himself into a chair.

"What brings you and your young friend here today? Would you like to taste the goulash? It is still new. I made it yesterday."

Gregor would have loved a big bowl of goulash, but Shutkin waved his hand. "Tea, just tea will meet our needs."

The owner looked disappointed but returned from the kitchen with two glasses and a steaming pot. While they drank hot sweet tea, an accordion player began to squeeze his instrument for the benefit of the customers.

"This is Gregor," Shutkin said. "He's a musician and looking for employment."

"As you can see, I already have a musician." The owner gestured to the short moustached man who continued to squeeze his asthmatic instrument.

"But my friend has played in many important dance clubs and at the cinema," Shutkin said. "People will come to dance. When they're thirsty from dancing they'll spend money buying your food and drink."

"Hmmmm." The owner rubbed his hand along a meaty jaw. "Why don't you come back this evening? It's payday at the tin factory. We'll see if your music increases sales."

The accordion player overheard them. "What about me? Your customers love my music."

"I can accompany you," Gregor offered. "I'll follow your lead."

The accordion player scowled, but the owner shrugged. "Be here by six, that's when the factory lets out."

When the whistle blew at six, signaling an end to the workday, men, women and children poured from the textile mill and the tin works. It was already dark, the air chill and damp. Women pulled their shawls and scarves tight around their heads as they hurried for home. The tired children had no energy for fun and games. They moved in little groups, like schools of fish, stumbling and whimpering in their fatigue. The adults paid them no mind. The men and older boys called out to one another, "*Pasha*, where will you drink tonight? *Natanchik*, come join us at the Traktir." Few mothers and wives would see their men that night.

"What is that thing?" exclaimed the Traktir owner, when Gregor and Shutkin arrived after dark.

"It's a musical instrument, a cello," Shutkin said.

"I know what it is, but can he play dance music? My customers don't want to hear Tchaikovsky."

Gregor pulled up a chair next to the accordion player who eyed him with distrust.

"Do you know "Dark Eyes?" he said to the stocky mustached man.

"Of course." The accordionist filled his instrument with air and began to squeeze out the tune. Gregor managed to follow. As they finished the first round, the accordion wheezed to a stop, but Gregor continued with a variation he improvised. When he was done, the crowd, factory workers, prostitutes and a few soldiers broke into applause.

"Hey, keep the boy," someone called out. "Get rid of the accordion."

"Will you give him a job?" Shutkin said.

"It seems I must." The man pounded Gregor on the back. "One ruble a night if sales increase."

Everyone was happy except the accordion player, but Gregor let him take the lead in choosing songs. Only when the man had exhausted his repertoire and went to the latrine, which he seemed to do quite often, did Gregor play alone.

Shutkin accompanied him every night to the Traktir. He always sat at the table closest to Gregor, sharing tea with a few very old men, discussing in great detail events Gregor had never heard of before, Tsar Alexander and the night of the assassination, socialists, zionists and something called the Bund. They argued and waved their hands at one another, but they always left the Traktir smiling, patting each other on the back.

With an income of one ruble a night, Gregor and Shutkin's standard of living improved. Shutkin traded the silver samovar for a new bed frame and Gregor inherited the sofa, though it was so short he had to lay his feet on a stool when he slept.

On payday the number of women who frequented the Traktir increased. They were exotic looking creatures, mostly whores with bright red lips and darkened eyes, each one hoping to separate the men from their hard-earned pay. One woman, a Tartar, peddled opium, which she kept stuffed down the front of her blouse. Some of the women offered their services to Gregor, but Shutkin always pushed them away.

"He is just a boy. Take your wares to someone old enough to appreciate your tricks."

"I know what they do," Gregor whispered to Shutkin when an Armenian woman grabbed his elbow and tried to pull him onto the dance floor. Shutkin reached out a bony hand and pushed her away.

"I will show him *pleeeaasssuuure*," the woman hissed through the space in her teeth.

"You'll give him the clap or worse. And still expect him to pay you for the gift."

By midnight the prostitutes had all found customers and left the café for darker haunts in the alley. The Traktir owner charged a woman ten kopeks if she wanted to use an empty horse stall for her business, twenty kopeks if she wanted clean straw. By closing time the drunks were broke and the opium users asleep on the floor. Gregor packed up his cello and helped Shutkin to his feet.

After spending hours in the smoky overheated room, the cold air felt good on Gregor's face, but it made Shutkin's cough worse. With every breath, he wheezed like an accordion with a leak. Each night the trip home became slower and Gregor had to help the old man up the steps when they reached the shop.

"You should stay here and keep warm," Gregor said one rainy April night. "Don't come with me tonight. I can go alone."

"What? And stare at the dirty ceiling? It's lonely here without you. Besides, the military police will never stop you if you're walking with me." He was right. The police were everywhere. They rounded up army deserters and anyone else who looked healthy enough or stupid enough to be sent to the front lines.

Late into the night Gregor and the accordion player performed the usual round of dance tunes for the disinterested crowd. The prostitutes plied their trade and when the accordion player headed for the latrine, a voice called out from across the room. "Can you play Bach?"

Gregor could hardly believe his ears. "I can," he called back as he peered into the darkness, unable to see the requester. "I know many Bach pieces."

"Play something good."

Sitting up straight, he closed his eyes and imagined he was in the conservatory concert hall. He needed something fast and loud, something to cut through the noise of the crowd. "Prelude in C major." He memorized it long ago. After playing nothing but gypsy tunes night after night, playing Bach was like breathing fresh air. His fingers moved easily over the strings and the sound of music filled his head.

"Hey, stop torturing that cat," called a drunken voice.

Gregor ignored the jeers and continued playing, moving onto a variation of the melody in G.

"Did you hear me?" A drunken soldier staggered across the dance floor, a vodka bottle swinging in his hand. "I said stop that noise. I can't sleep." Without warning the man raised the bottle like a club and aimed it at Gregor's head. The assault was so unexpected it threw Gregor off balance. He pulled back, tipping sideways on the chair. His foot slipped and he landed on the floor, the cello tangled beneath the leg of the chair and his knee. The sound of wood splintering nearly stopped his heart.

Above him the attacker kept swinging the vodka bottle, spewing cheap liquor on Gregor's face. As he struggled to regain his footing, the bottle arced toward him and he raised an arm. The impact of the glass on his elbow shattered the bottle and he ducked as pieces rained down on him. Too late, he watched the soldier's boot snap the fingerboard.

"No, no." Shutkin struggled to pull the soldier away.

"Who's attacking me?" the drunk roared. He staggered away, knocking Shutkin to the floor.

In a moment Gregor was on his feet. Fists ready, he swung, missed and swung again. Shutkin tried to right himself and, ignoring his own safety, reached for the remains of the cello. But he couldn't move fast enough. Again the boot struck, landing in the middle of the old man's back.

As patrons joined in the fight, Gregor slid his arms around Shutkin's chest and dragged him off the dance floor. Fearful of missing all the fun, the drunken patrons cursed and the women screamed as a brawl ensued. Holding the old man around the waist, Gregor headed toward the front door. The screaming and grunting behind him grew louder.

"Kill the son of a bitch!" Gregor heard someone cry. He staggered into the street, half dragging Shutkin.

Outside, the rain had frozen on the cobblestones, creating a slick glaze that made standing difficult.

"Wait," a voice called from the doorway. Gregor turned and saw a slim young man dressed in European clothes. a style that made him look out of place. But he recognized the voice. It was the man who had requested Bach at the Traktir.

"I'm so sorry." He held out the remains of the shattered instrument. "I did love your Bach. Those ignorant *mujiks* have no idea what good music is." He managed to shove the remnants of the cello into the canvas case.

"I can't... I don't know..." Gregor stammered, at a loss for words. He took the cello case and felt the shards of the broken instrument inside like broken bones. If he tried to say more he would surely cry. Turning away from the stranger, he slung the case over his shoulder and wrapped his arm around Shutkin's shoulders. The old man wheezed and every few steps he paused as a spasm of coughing shook his frail body. Beneath the light of a butcher shop lamp, Gregor saw blood on the old man's lips.

"You can do it. Here, let me help you walk," Gregor said taking more of the man's weight. "We only have to get home. I'll get Ivan. He'll know what to do."

Inside the dark shop he lowered Shutkin onto the bed, lit the oil lamp and knelt beside him. Shutkin's head seemed too far back, so he pushed a pillow under his neck. With his coat, Gregor tried to wipe the blood from the old man's lips.

"I'll tell Ivan to bring the doctor." He tried to sound confident. "He'll know what to do."

Sounds gurgled from Shutkin's mouth but it was all mumble and cough. Dried blood still caked his chin. His eyes fluttered open, but remained glassy and unfocused.

"I'll be right back." Gregor pushed to standing. "I promise." He ran out the front door and into the dark empty alley. Ivan had to be home, he had to save Shutkin. There was no one else to turn to.

Running toward Leventova Street, Gregor's foot hit an ice covered cobblestone and he fell flat, hitting his hands and knees. Ignoring the pain, he ran again. He would not let Shutkin die.

* * *

"He's been sick for a long time," the doctor said. "Bad lungs." The sour looking man raised his head and sniffed the air. "What can he expect at his age. He should know better than to drink so much vodka."

"He only drinks tea," Gregor said.

"Don't lie. I can smell it." The stethoscope went back into his black bag. "I can do nothing for him. He needs a hospital." The doctor turned and ducked his head as he passed through the low doorway. "And for God's sake, don't carry him. Get a carriage."

But carriages cost money. Instead, Ivan borrowed a two-wheeled grocer's cart and they put Shutkin on sacks of straw used to cushion eggs on their way to market. Gregor climbed in back and wrapped a blanket around the old man.

"I'm going to hold this over your head to keep the rain off," he said. He made a tent from a second blanket and held onto Shutkin as the wagon lumbered along the cobbled streets. "I don't want you to die." He stroked Shutkin's hand. "Please, you have to live."

The charity hospital, run by an order of nuns, loomed dark and dirty at the end of the narrow street. Ivan carried Shutkin up the steps while Gregor ran ahead to find help.

"You have to pay extra if you want a bed near the stove," said a young skinny orderly in a dirty white coat. Ivan carried Shutkin and Gregor followed down the corridor into a crowded room.

"There's an empty one," said the boy. Ivan laid Shutkin on the cot. All around them a dozen cots were lined in tidy rows. The nearest one held a man with sparse whiskers who coughed incessantly, groaning and spitting into a cloth.

"I helped your grandfather." The orderly held out his hand. "Give me twenty kopeks."

"I have no money." Gregor held out his equally empty hands.

"I guess you spent it on vodka," the boy sniffed and turned to leave. "I won't help you."

"Wait," Ivan said. "Here are ten kopeks. I have another twenty for the doctor if you can find him."

"Doctors won't work for twenty kopeks. Besides, it's late. The doctor doesn't come until morning."

"My friend is very ill," Ivan said in a slow, measured voice as if he were talking to an idiot. "What kind of help can he have for twenty kopeks?"

"I'll try and wake the nurse, but give me half the money now."

"I'll give you my boot on your rump if you don't move."

The boy disappeared and Ivan turned to Gregor. "Here's all the money I have." He dropped the coins in Gregor's hand. "Get what help you can. I have to return the grocer's wagon then go to work. I'll come again tomorrow."

Gregor watched Ivan make his way around the rows of cots and disappear down the hall. Don't leave, he wanted to cry. Instead, he stood and waited until he saw the door swing shut. Someone coughed, a long wet rattling sound that seemed to go on forever. Gregor pressed his hands to his ears and squeezed his eyes shut. If Mama were here, she would know what to do.

He sank down on the floor beside Shutkin's cot. The old man lay still, his wrinkled skin the color of ashes. Only the faint rasping of his breath passing his parched lips gave indication he was still alive. Gregor tucked the damp blankets around the man's thin shoulders. It had been a mistake to bring him here. At least in the shop he would have been warm.

He removed his own coat and felt the chill from the stone walls and damp floors penetrate his body. Rolling the garment, he made a pillow and slid it under Shutkin's head. The coughing patient in the next bed motioned to him.

"What is it?" Gregor kept his voice low.

"The pan, give me the pan or I'll wet myself." The man's voice was no more than a hoarse whisper. "It's underneath, on the floor." The man motioned with a stick-thin arm.

Gregor got up, retrieved the rusty dish and handed it to him.

"The nurse never comes," he whispered. The man slipped the container under his blanket. "Don't leave your grandfather alone."

Talking sent the man into a round of consumptive coughing. Gregor backed away, moving around a column into the midst of the great cot-filled room. He inhaled the stench of unwashed bodies, urine and vomit. A few oil lamps high up on the walls gave the room a yellow glow. All around him the sick and the dying coughed, groaned and whimpered. A few family members tended their kin, speaking in hushed voices, but there wasn't a doctor or a nurse in sight.

Dropping onto the floor beside Shutkin's bed, Gregor folded his arms and rested his head on the edge of the mattress. If it weren't for Shutkin he would have fled this house of death. If it weren't for Shutkin he would be dead. He closed his eyes and slept.

"Your music lives not in your hands but in your heart." Shutkin *said and smiled at him from his place on the sagging sofa.*

"But I can't play without my hands." Gregor *stared down at his frozen fingers. They were as white as bone marrow. "My fingers are made of ice. I can't move them."*

"They are your hands. You must use them or you, too, will die."

Gregor *stretched his fingers and saw them turn from white to pink growing warmer with each movement. Running his hand up the strings of the cello, he felt the familiar vibration of the instrument as he plucked each note.*

"You see," Shutkin *said. "They're your hands if you use them. If you don't they will grow cold and wither away."*

A rough hand shook his shoulder then shook it again.

Gregor pulled away, covering his face with his arm to block the light.

"Wake up. Your grandfather needs you." A nurse with a hard-etched face stood over him holding a pitcher and cup.

"Your grandfather must drink this broth."

Gregor pushed up on numb legs, disoriented and confused. "He's not my grandfather."

"Whoever he is, you'd better get him to drink." The woman poured half a glass of warm brown liquid and handed it to him. "The doctor will make rounds soon."

As she moved past the next cot, where the coughing man had been, Gregor saw it was empty. "Wait." He pointed at the empty bed. "What happened to him?"

"Gone this morning to the morgue." She moved on, the keys hanging from her belt tinkling as she moved through the rows of sick.

"Please, Shutkin." Gregor knelt beside the bed. "Wake up." He held the glass of broth to the old man's lips. Brown liquid dribbled down staining the white stubble. "You must drink."

Shutkin's eyelids fluttered and a low moan escaped his lips, nothing more. A shadow fell over the cot and Gregor looked up.

"Let me examine him." The man was stern, his gray suit spotless. "I am the doctor."

"Can you help him?" Gregor stepped out of the doctor's way.

"Hmmmph." The doctor sat his bag on the foot of the cot and removed a small carpet. Spreading it on the concrete floor, he knelt on the carpet square and listened to Shutkin's chest with a stethoscope. "Hmmmph." He ran his hand inside Shutkin's shirt then rolled him on his side. "He can't breathe. His ribs are broken. How did it happen?"

"There was a fight. He got kicked."

The doctor returned the stethoscope to his bag and shook his head. "He won't live much longer. He doesn't even know you're here."

"He knows I'm here. He talks to me."

"Hmmmph." The doctor shook his head, returned the carpet to his bag, straightened his jacket and moved onto the next patient.

Gregor sank to the floor and took Shutkin's thin hand in his own. "Remember when you did this for me?" He rubbed the bony fingers. "Open your eyes. Please?"

For a moment it seemed the old man's hand tightened slightly, but then the pressure was gone.

Gregor gave the last of Ivan's kopeks to the errand boy in exchange for a heavier blanket, which he wrapped around Shutkin. Late in the afternoon Ivan appeared with half a loaf of bread.

"I'm on my way to the factory, but I brought you two something to eat."

"Thank you," Gregor said and bit off a chunk of bread. It was hard and dry, but he felt his stomach growl in anticipation.

"Is he awake? Did he speak to you?"

"No." Gregor wiped crumbs from his lips. "But I know he can hear me. He squeezed my hand."

"What does the doctor say?"

Gregor swallowed hard and looked up at Ivan, but he couldn't bring himself to repeat the doctor's grim words.

The doctor came again, but didn't even open his bag. "You should go home."

"No," Gregor said. "He wouldn't abandon me."

He sat on the floor beside Shutkin all night, getting up only to relieve himself and warm his hands at the big tile stove in the hall. When his belly growled again he slept but dreamed of bread and cheese and hot tea.

* * *

"You can go home now."

Gregor opened his eyes and saw the orderly standing over him. A hunchbacked man knelt on the other side of the cot. Gregor watched as the man pulled the wool blanket off Shutkin and handed it to the boy. Then from a canvas sack he removed a dirty sheet and wrapped it around Shutkin.

"What are you doing?" Gregor scrambled to his feet and tried to grab back the blanket. "He needs it to stay warm."

"Your grandfather's dead." The boy held the blanket above his head, out of Gregor's reach. "He doesn't need it anymore."

"No!" Gregor lunged at the hunchback, pushing his gnarled hands away. "He's not dead. Please, Shutkin, tell them."

Shutkin didn't move. His mouth hung open, cheeks sunken hollow below his eyes, lashes white against gray skin. For a moment Gregor couldn't take his eyes off the lashes. Life had left the body.

"I'm taking him to the morgue." The hunchback pulled the sheet back over the corpse. "Tell your family to send a coffin or he'll be buried in the river plot."

Gregor tried to move, nearly falling, his legs numb, more wood than flesh. They lifted the swaddled body onto a rickety cart and the hunchback pushed it down the hall, the broken wheel clacking against the floor.

He should have been awake, should have been there for Shutkin, should have said good-bye. Squeezing his eyes shut, he fought back tears. Papa was right. He was a terrible, worthless son.

"Will you pay to bury him?" The skinny boy folded the blanket and tucked it under his arm.

Gregor couldn't reply. Shutkin would be buried in the mud by the riverbank. No funeral, no one to sit Shiva for him, no stone to mark his place. He pressed his fist against his mouth and shook his head. Beside him, a patient coughed. It sounded like the death rattle. At any moment the hand of death would reach out and grab him too.

Turning, he dodged the occupied cots and ran down the corridor to the front door, down the steps and into the street. He sucked in great gulps of cold wet air then doubled and dropped to his knees. His stomach heaved but nothing came up. Holding his belly he struggled to his feet. If he didn't distance himself from this house of death, he would be next.

The morning light had brought people into the street. Troikas filled with passengers rolled past him, bells jingling. Everywhere noblemen and peasants went about their lives, oblivious of death, pretending they didn't know.

Without a glance back at the hospital, he ran over the cobblestones, tripping, falling, getting back up. He crossed the footbridge over the canal where the smell of morning latrines filled the air. His side ached, his lungs were ready to burst, but he didn't stop. Sokolniki Park was the only place of safety. In the dark green forest, among the paper white birches, death would not find him.

Chapter Thirteen

It was dusk when Gregor saw the walls of the Moscow Conservatory looming ahead. The statue of Tchaikovsky guarded the front entrance keeping out those who were less worthy. The windows of the pale yellow building stared at him with blank dark eyes. Of course, it was Friday. The students and teachers had gone home. At this hour they would be warming themselves in front of a hot fire, eating potato dumplings and crispy fried herring. He wished, more than anything else in the world, he could be one of those boys, someone who had a family and a home.

"What are you doing here?" The voice came from the side of the building. Gregor turned and saw the custodian standing in the end of the narrow alley, a broom and ash bucket in his hands.

"I went to the park, but the policeman…" It was pointless to try and explain. The policeman that patrolled Sokolniki Park hadn't listened either.

"Did you forget your instrument?" the man said.

"No— I don't have mine — it's gone."

The custodian stepped closer, peering into Gregor's face. "You don't look so good. Do you want to come inside?"

"Yes—please." Gregor followed the man through the side door.

"I've seen you here before. Aren't you one of the string students?"

"Yes. I play cello."

"Why aren't you at home with your family?"

"They live in Ekaterinoslav. I have nowhere to stay."

"Ahhhh," said the custodian as if he understood. "Why don't you spend the night in the classroom down the hall, the one near the woodstove. There's a bench in there with a cushion. It's better than the street."

"Thank you very much," Gregor said. "I'll work for you tomorrow, anything you ask."

"We'll see," the custodian said. He went back to sweeping the floor. "There's a coal bin downstairs that needs filling. But that can wait until morning."

* * *

"Hey, get up. The director wants to see you."

Only half awake, Gregor rolled in the direction of the voice, fell off the bench and landed face down on the floor.

"What?" He scrambled to his feet. "Who wants me?"

"Director Ivanov. He wants to see you right now." The custodian stood over him, mop in hand. "I told him you were sleeping here."

"I'm sorry. I'll leave."

"No, he wants to talk to you. I told him you were helping me."

The director's office was on the first floor near the Great Concert Hall. Before Gregor knocked he tried to brush the wrinkles out of his jacket and wipe the sleep from his eyes. He knocked, once then twice.

"Enter," called a deep voice. Director Ivanov was a short man whose head seemed too big for his stubby body. Gregor felt awkward, towering over him. He stood at attention, hands clasped behind his back, waiting for the man to speak.

"Piatigorsky?" The director said the name slowly, exaggerating each syllable. "I have heard you frequent some very strange places, nightclubs and other disreputable establishments. Is it true?" His tone was stern, but Gregor found it difficult to be frightened by such a little man.

"I had a job in a dance club. I needed money to pay my rent and buy food."

"This is very distressing. The Moscow Conservatory must maintain the highest standards. Do you understand?"

"Yes sir."

The director rose and began pacing in front of his desk. "You also insulted your professor and have performed poorly in class. I've reviewed your academic record. It is terrible." He stopped in front of Gregor and looked up. "You must be punished."

"Yes, sir." He would take whatever penalty was coming.

"Where is your instrument?"

"I don't have one."

"Why? What happened to it?"

"It was broken— in a fight." For a moment the memory made him wince.

The director shook his head, walked to a side room and returned with a small cello.

"Are you still able to play?" Without waiting for an answer, he pulled up a chair. "Convince me that you should be allowed to rejoin the conservatory."

Gregor took the unfamiliar instrument in his hands. It was small and lightweight, an instrument for a girl. But this was no time to complain. Taking a deep breath, he tried to still his trembling hands. "What do you want me to play?"

"Do you know the melody from "Fiameta" by Minkus?"

"I think so."

"Play it for me."

Gregor closed his eyes and tried to remember the tune he had played long, long ago. If only his hands were warmer and the cello bigger. *They're your hands. Use them.* Shutkin's words came back to him. Setting the bow on the strings, he started softly. He didn't dare open his eyes for fear the melody inside his head would disappear. Only when the last note died away did he open his eyes and look at the director. The man sat as his desk holding his big head in his pudgy hands.

"Sir?"

The man rose and without a word walked around his desk. He took the cello and laid it aside. Gregor watched, not knowing what he had done wrong. The director stood before him. They were almost eye to eye. He reached out and took Gregor's hands in his own.

"Your hands look no different than others I have seen." He sighed and began gently rubbing Gregor's fingers. It felt uncomfortable to have the director touch him this way. Still, he knew better than to object.

"God knows why some talented young men dig ditches instead of growing wings." He continued stroking as he spoke.

"Sir?" Gregor said, hoping to make him stop. "Was my performance acceptable?"

"Acceptable?" The man's eyebrows shot up. "How old are you?"

"Fourteen."

The director sighed. "So young, so young. You didn't believe I would take you back?" His voice had a tenderness Gregor had never heard from a man. He tried pulling his hand back, but the director's grip hardened. "You should be more grateful."

"I am grateful, sir. Thank you for taking me back."

"You haven't eaten today, have you?" He let go of Gregor's hands and returned to his desk.

"No, sir."

The director opened the top drawer and retrieved a handful of coins. "I want you to go back to your classes." He handed Gregor the money. "Here, rent a room from Babushka Lubish and get something to eat." He handed Gregor the little cello. "And stay out of those wretched nightclubs."

"I will, sir."

The director handed him a slip of paper. "Stop at the commissary and get a new uniform."

"Thank you, sir," Gregor said. "You won't be sorry. I promise."

* * *

Moscow Conservatory
April 1916

Dear Nadja,

Please write to me and tell me you received my letters. When I write to Mama, I get no answer. Surely you must hear from her. Tell her I am well and back at the conservatory. I have a room only one block from school. Babushka Lubish rents to twelve students, only two rubles a week. I give lessons at night to new students and also sometimes play at the cinema, so I have enough money.

I miss you very much and would like to come see you, but I'm afraid. Please tell me you are well. Give me news of the others. Do you need anything? If I have it, I will give to you, only please answer me. Write to me at 24 Gatvianisk Street. Love, Grisha

"Piatigorsky," someone called from outside the practice room. Gregor opened the door and saw the custodian leaning against the wall, his broom in the crook of his elbow. "Do you know Mr. Kachouk?" he asked as he picked his teeth with a bit of broom straw.

"No." Gregor slid the small cello into its case. "Should I?"

"I'm sure you know Fyodor Chaliapin."

"Chaliapin? The opera singer? Everyone's heard of him."

"Mr. Kachouk is Chaliapin's manager. Right now he has a problem. The regular stopgap is sick. He needs a replacement."

"Stopgap?"

"Someone to entertain the audience before the performance and again during intermission. I told Kachouk that you and Professor Keneman at the piano are the ones for the job, so I made the arrangements."

"Arrangements?"

"Kachouk will pay you for three performances. He gave me a deposit. Half now and the rest later." The custodian held out a handful of coins then quickly slid the money back in his pocket. "I knew you could use work." He handed Gregor a slip of paper.

Piatigorsky: Rehearsal with Keneman. Thursday, Four o'clock in the Great Concert Hall. Wear a dark suit and clean shirt. Kachouk

Gregor shook the custodian's hand. "Thank you."

Running back to the practice hall, he searched for Joseph. The chance to play for Chaliapin was incredible. For that he needed the best cello in the conservatory, and Joseph had an Italian instrument.

Gregor arrived for rehearsal early, anxious to begin. Keneman was already there, leaning on the stage door, a cigarette dangling from his lips. "Have one," he said, holding out his pouch of tobacco and rolling papers. "Let me warm my fingers." The pianist took a long drag from his cigarette then coughed.

Gregor shook tobacco onto the paper square then rolled it up and carefully slid the cigarette into his jacket pocket for later. Tobacco was a luxury he could rarely afford.

The rehearsal turned out to be short and easy. Keneman hardly spoke except to nod and say *da* or *nyet*. They ran through a set number of pieces, none of them very challenging. Keneman began with the *Polonaise* by Popper. The piece started with a brief piano introduction then the cello solo, which Gregor knew by heart.

"The performance is tomorrow at eight." Keneman lit another cigarette. "We'll play a fifteen-minute opening and a twenty-minute intermission. Be here on time."

When Gregor entered the Great Concert Hall the next night, the rehearsal room beneath the stage was dark. He stood alone, listening to the murmur of the audience above. Though he knew the music, he felt the knot grip his empty belly. Rehearsals were easy, but one day of practice on the borrowed cello wasn't enough.

"Where—have—you been?" A short man grabbed Gregor's arm. "I'm Kachouk. Come with me."

"I'm ready. Where is Professor Keneman?"

"He's already here. Tonight is Chaliapin's opening. Keneman is waiting with him in the wings."

They passed through a narrow doorway, up the stairs and into the wings. The bright electric stage lights nearly blinded Gregor. The noise of the crowd grew louder, but it wasn't applause. The audience was enormous, filling the Great Concert Hall, overflowing the aisles and the balcony.

"Go, now. You're on." Kachouk pushed him toward the stage.

No one in the audience seemed to notice either Gregor or Keneman as they walked across the stage. Instead, people greeted each other, laughing gaily. Surely they would quiet down when the music began, Gregor thought.

The professor sat down at the grand piano and started the *Polonaise*. He played with gusto, louder than he had during rehearsal. The audience didn't seem to notice. While Gregor waited to begin his solo, he surveyed the hall. In the back row a cluster of his conservatory friends waited to hear what he had promised would be the biggest performance of his life.

At the appropriate moment Gregor began, playing with as much energy as he could create. Instead of quieting the audience, the crowd grew louder. How could they be so rude, he wondered? Why didn't they listen? He continued to play despite the fact that no one seemed to be listening.

Halfway through the second piece, a movement from the Peer Gynt Suite, Gregor felt a hand on his shoulder and glanced up to see Kachouk standing beside him.

"Enough. Chaliapin is ready," the manager muttered. Gregor stopped playing, but Keneman, unaware the performance had been interrupted, continued unaccompanied. Finally, when the pianist saw Kachouk walk off, he stopped. Embarrassed and confused, Gregor picked up his instrument and followed the two men off the stage.

Near the stage door hovered a young man who paced back and forth studying the music. "Forte … Forte… Adagio… Piano… Forte," he muttered to no one.

"His accompanist," Keneman said. His lip curled up. "I taught him myself, though I doubt he remembers me."

They passed Fyodor Chaliapin standing in the wings, a massive man made even larger by a full-length fur coat. It was sable, the same color as the opera singer's beard, a trimmed dark line that defined his angular jaw. He was formidable, a mountain of a man big enough to make Gregor feel small. A shiver of excitement ran down his spine. Gregor passed so close to Chaliapin he could have reached out and touched him, if he had dared. For a moment he forgot the embarrassing performance and wished he could think of something to say. Nothing clever enough came to mind, so he remained mute.

Chaliapin ignored Gregor as he ignored everyone else around him. Then he called out, his voice booming. "Kachouk! Tell them to flash the lights, off then on. That should quiet the mob."

"Yes— yes sir," stammered the manager. "I—will."

While the lights flashed, Chaliapin cleared his throat and sang a few deep notes. The sound made the air around Gregor's ears tingle.

"The devil," Chaliapin complained to no one. "My throat's good for spitting, not singing." He made the sign of the cross over his massive chest, motioned his pianist forward and stepped into the bright lights. At the sight of him the frantic crowd roared approval.

Gregor watched in awe as Chaliapin captivated his audience. Each round of applause was more enthusiastic than the one before. He moved like an animal and the fur of the sable glistened under the stage lights. Only Professor Keneman looked bored with the whole affair. The pianist sat near the back door smoking one cigarette after another, crushing out the butts with his heel.

Gregor crouched beside him. "What will we play during intermission?"

"What does it matter?" Keneman took a long drag and blew smoke into the air. "No one will notice us. We are fleas on the back of an elephant."

He was right. No sooner had Chaliapin walked offstage for intermission than most of the audience rose and headed for the lobby.

"Go on," urged Kachouk. "Play something. Anything. No one will notice." He was right. The audience was there to hear the greatest opera singer in all Russia, not a conservatory student and his cello.

* * *

The heat of humiliation burned Gregor's face as he left the concert hall. His friends gathered near the door, slapping him on the back as he stepped into the street.

"You certainly pleased the crowd with that performance," Ivan teased. The others broke into peals of laughter.

"Tomorrow night Chaliapin will ask you to play solo," Sergei said. "The audience will love it. They'll demand an encore."

"It's not my fault," Gregor said. "The manager wouldn't let me finish."

"Lucky for you," Ivan said. The group headed toward the café without him.

"It will be different tomorrow night," Gregor called after them. "I swear it will."

Back in his little room in Babushka Lubish's boarding house, he lay the cello on his cot then lit the oil lamp. The cracked mirror over the washstand reflected the light, making the room almost bright. He stared at the face in the mirror. It was the image the audience had seen. His dark hair, badly in need of a cut, was combed to one side. A long face made him look older than fourteen, he thought. He glared into the mirror, trying to make his eyes fierce, eyes that would demand attention. Instead, he just looked silly. Maybe it was his clothes that made him invisible.

He had worn a clean white shirt, brushed his black jacket and smoothed his pants, though they were a bit short and his socks showed. But his shoes were polished with lampblack and his tie was nearly new. The borrowed cello was the right size.

As he stood before the mirror, the figure in the glass stared back. He pulled his shoulders up and stood tall. "Tomorrow night will be different," he said in a loud voice. "Tomorrow they will listen to me. I swear it."

The next evening Gregor waited in the wings watching Chaliapin pace back and forth, muttering all the while to himself. The man was oblivious of those around him. Keneman arrived late, a cigarette dangling from his mouth. Gregor took a long slow breath, trying to calm the butterflies in his stomach. He waited. His performance tonight would change everything. If it didn't he would never go back on stage again.

Kachouk motioned them forward, but Gregor let the pianist go first. While Keneman settled himself at his instrument, he hung back. Then, at the right moment, he marched across the stage holding the cello high above his head.

Facing the crowd he cried, "Silence," as loud as he could. No one in the audience seemed to notice. Jumping onto the chair, he again stretched himself to his full height and screamed. "Silence! Now!"

A few heads turned and some people pointed. Keneman began the "Polonaise", but it sounded pitiful, lost in the chatter of the crowd. Still standing on the chair, Gregor threw his bow into the air, jumped down and caught it in his right hand. Then with a swing of his arm, he spun the cello on the pin and started in on the solo, as loud and as fast as he could.

A hush fell over the crowd. Keneman struggled to keep up with the tempo, as Gregor played faster, creating flourishes and variations as he went along. By the time he reached the end of the piece he was soaked with sweat.

"Peer Gynt!" Gregor cried, then tried to catch his breath. Keneman pounded out "Hall of the Mountain King" and Gregor played the refrain, stomping his foot to the beat of the music. The audience began to clap, keeping time with the music. When the piece ended, Gregor stepped forward to the edge of the stage and took a deep bow. With head down, his damp hair hanging in his eyes, he listened to the thunderous applause.

"Bravo! Bravo! Bravo," the audience chanted. He lifted his head and strands of hair stuck to his dripping brow. With a flourish, he brushed them aside and glanced at Keneman. The older man stared at him, a helpless look on his face.

"Play it again," Gregor said. "Play Grieg from the beginning."

Keneman pounded out the introduction and the sound of the piano reverberated through the quiet hall. In the wings, out of sight of the audience, Gregor noticed frantic movement. He glanced right and saw Kachouk waving his arms in desperation, a look of panic on his weasel like face. Next to him Chaliapin's figure filled the stage door. The opera singer looked like a volcano ready to explode. He shook his fists at Gregor then drew a finger knife-like across his throat. There was no escape. The only way off the stage was through the doorway where Chaliapin stood.

With a crashing chord as a signal, Gregor realized it was his turn to play. He began as hard, as fast and as loud as he could. Now, the only safe place was on the stage, in front of a thousand eyes.

"*Biis. Biis,*" screamed the audience wanting more. Gregor obliged them with more musical acrobatics. Chaliapin disappeared from view and in the middle of the piece Gregor threw his bow in the air, caught it, then ran for the exit. In an instant he was through the door, out of the lobby and into the street. Kachouk followed him, red faced and breathing so hard he sounded like he was choking.

"How—could—you—do this?" His face was inches from Gregor's. "You and your cheap circus tricks! Chaliapin will never forgive you and I will never forgive you!" He shook his fist in the air. "You will never work in Moscow again."

Chapter Fourteen

Moscow
March 1917

Dear Leo, I can hardly speak of what I see every day. Soldiers hunt for
Whites and Reds. They don't care who gets in their way. I saw a man run down
the street with his insides hanging out. His eyes were open ,but he was already
dead. Bodies lie like firewood, stripped of their clothes, frozen solid.
     Gregor paused to rub his icy fingers. With no heat in the room, his hands
were already numb. He tucked them under his armpits to restore some feeling.
His breath clouded the cold air and the tiny window barely gave him enough light
to see the paper before him. It was a far cry from the luxury of the tiny room at
Babushka Lubish's boarding house.
     When his fingers regained some feeling, he continued writing.
     I hear crying outside my window, but in the bread lines no one hears a thing,
not screams or gunshots. You must not lose your place or you will starve.
Everyone wants revenge. No one cares about innocence. People fight over scraps
in garbage piles. I heard shots this morning. If I had a gun, I would fight too, but
against what? I don't know which party is right. Someone pushed a piano out a
window. Those who caused it to fall cared nothing for the people in the street that
were hurt. In the marketplace a princess traded diamonds for bread. Typhus is
everywhere. I'm hungry. I'm afraid.
     He crammed the last words in small script at the bottom, then turned the
sheet over.
     I want to be part of everything. I hear guns firing and screaming. It's a
volcano, all blood and convulsions. Yesterday a soldier told me that God was
dead and the House of Romanov had fallen. It's so cold and we have little wood,
no oil for lamps. I live behind the house of a seamstress. She makes dresses from
rags and trades them for cabbage and bread. I gave her my extra socks to trade
and she let me eat yesterday. Now I have nothing to trade.

There was a tap at the door and the seamstress peeked in. "I have a guest coming for dinner. He wants to meet you."

"I have nothing for your table." Gregor held out his empty hands.

"We have good fortune." She smiled showing broken teeth. "Tonight there is meat in our ragout. That alone is reason to celebrate."

She disappeared and Gregor looked back at the letter. Should he say more? Should he tell Leo the truth? Maybe just part of the truth.

The shops are empty. The conservatory is closed. My A string broke and the D has a knot below the bridge. I have no job and no money. I can't practice because I can't think. I miss all of you. Give my love to Mama, but don't tell her what I write. Kisses, Grisha. P.S. If I had money I would buy a rail ticket home. Would Papa let me stay?

He folded the letter and slid it in an envelope, but didn't address it. Postal service had stopped months ago. The only chance of it reaching home was if he found someone traveling that way and paid them to deliver it.

The last of the afternoon sunlight disappeared behind dark buildings and the air grew cold. In the gloom, Gregor crossed the muddy kitchen yard to the main house. His room, an unheated storage shed, was hardly worth the one ruble a week the seamstress charged. Still, she hadn't asked for money in over a month. She must be afraid he would report her to the Cheka as a bourgeoisie landlord. Making a profit was now a crime.

Inside the house steamy heat billowed up from the cook stove in the corner of the kitchen. Gregor helped himself to weak tea from the old samovar, warming his fingers on the hot glass. The place reminded him so much of home he could close his eyes and imagine Mama at the stove. Nadja would be playing the piano, Leo the violin and Alex would be crying. If only he could wish himself there.

He opened his eyes and moved through the low doorway into the cluttered dining room. Two men sat at the table. In animated conversation, neither one noticed him.

"Do you actually think the Bolsheviks will kill them?" the tall stranger said.

"*Nyet, nyet.* They will hold them for ransom." Gregor recognized the short bearded man as the seamstress' husband. "The Romanovs have plenty of gold. They will pay."

For political reasons the husband, a Bolshevik official, lived in another section of the city, though Gregor often saw him in the kitchen at suppertime. The tall man, thin and clean-shaven, looked familiar.

"Professor Zeitlin?" The seamstress wiped wet hands on her apron. "This is Grisha. He studied cello at the conservatory until it closed."

The stranger rose and memories of that disastrous night at the Traktir came flooding back. This was the man who had requested Bach, then helped him salvage the pieces of his broken instrument when he and Shutkin were thrown into the street.

"An excellent cellist, if memory serves me," he said. "I wondered what became of you."

Gregor smiled and they shook hands. "I went back to my studies. I'd still be at the conservatory, but no one studies now."

"And Gregor is the wise one who stays away from trouble," the seamstress said. "Let's eat while the food is still here. You never know when someone might break in and take what little we have. Better that we hide it in our bellies."

They crowded around the table and she dished out thin soup. Then she sliced half a loaf of hard black bread, but it crumbled when she cut the pieces too thin.

"When I learned the professor was coming for a visit I made something special," she said proudly. "Tonight our ragout has meat."

Gregor spooned the warm food into his mouth, grateful for every bite. He was able to identify a small piece of potato, maybe an onion and for certain a turnip. All were overcooked but delicious enough for a king, or at least a commissar. The unidentified meat was stringy and sparse, but no one complained.

"Perhaps it is fate we meet again," said the professor between bites. "I belong to one of the best string quartets in all Russia. I and one other play violin. We have an excellent viola, but our cellist," he paused and shook his head. "A very talented young man, but he got involved with politics. No matter what side you take there are always risks. Enemies within and enemies without. His death was an untimely loss. Do you have an instrument?"

"Yes, I traded my coat for a cello at the vegetable market. The owner was happy to be warm and I was happy to be able to play."

"Would you consider joining us in rehearsal?"

Gregor could hardly believe his ears. "I would be honored to play with you. When should I come?"

"Monday would be good, but I warn you, our rehearsals are long and a young fellow like you might grow weary."

"I never grow weary of playing, I promise—."

At that moment the kitchen door burst open. The seamstress let out a gasp. Instead of soldiers or police, an elderly woman stood in the doorway. Dressed in a thick quilted coat and *babushka*, her face was twisted with anguish as she wrung her hands.

"My kitty, have you seen my dear kitty? I let her out this morning and she hasn't returned."

Gregor recognized the woman. She lived alone in the house next door, the calico cat her only companion.

"Dear, dear," fussed the seamstress. "You should never let precious kitty out all alone. How many times have I told you, no animal is safe on the street these days?"

"But she so loves to catch mice in the alley."

"I'm sure she'll come back." The seamstress put a gentle hand on the older woman's shoulder. "You should go home in case she returns. Here, take some bread for your own supper." She handed her the hard end of a loaf.

The old woman's attention focused on the ragout pot. "What are you having for supper? It smells so good."

"Just the same old ragout we had yesterday. I added some pepper."

The neighbor left with the bread clutched in her hands. The seamstress returned to the table. Everyone was silent. Gregor stared down into his bowl at the stringy piece of meat floating in the broth.

"God bless kitty," said Professor Zeitlin.

* * *

"Grisha," Professor Zeitlin said one morning before the daily rehearsal. "There's going to be a competition for the Bolshoi Orchestra."

"The Bolshoi?" Gregor looked up from the Bolshevik Party newspaper he had found lying in the gutter. "What position?" The thought of even auditioning for the country's greatest orchestra was only a dream.

"First cello. The competition will be furious." The professor flipped through a folder of dog-eared scores. "Cellists from all over Russia will come to Moscow. I think you should try out."

"I'm not good enough for the Bolshoi." Gregor shook his head. "My instrument is no good. It needs new strings."

"Maybe not, but competing against the country's best will be a good experience. All young musicians need to be challenged."

"But why first cello? Aren't there members of the orchestra who will be promoted?"

"Not so. Every seat in the Bolshoi must be won. Even members of the orchestra compete. That way every performer is always the best. In any case, I've already submitted your name. The competition is in two weeks."

The next fourteen days were torture, both mentally and physically. Fear of failure gripped Gregor. He could hardly eat, which was fortunate since there was nothing to put in his belly. At night, he lay awake thinking of all the things that could go wrong. Still, he pushed himself, practicing every piece he knew, over and over until his back ached and his head throbbed. Unwilling to rely on written music, he memorized each phrase and nuance of a dozen pieces.

When the day of the audition arrived he rose before dawn. The seamstress trimmed his hair. He wiped his jacket with a damp rag but couldn't press his pants. No one wasted coal on something as trivial as heating a flatiron. His shirt was almost clean and he blackened his shoes with chimney soot. He didn't eat breakfast. There was no food.

Walking up the steps between the tall columns that graced the front of the Bolshoi Theater, he thought only of failure. Could this audition be worse than any other? Yes, it was ten times worse than any he had ever done. The weight of the giant portico bore down on him, crushing him. Maybe the building would collapse. If it did, he would be spared this torture. Better to be dead under tons of stone.

But the building remained standing. He pulled the door open and entered the hall of doom. Inside the lobby, an usher in black uniform directed him down a long hallway. Sitting in chairs along the corridor an army of cellists eyed each other with suspicion. These were his competitors, some middle-aged, some young, all nervous, all eager.

Gregor took the empty chair at the end of the row and studied his adversaries. Most had music stands that held scores of well-known pieces. All practiced frantically and the noise in the narrow space was deafening.

When the door at the end of the corridor opened, everyone's bow arm stopped. There was a moment of silence then the next name was called and the noise began again. There seemed to be no order to who was called. As one applicant entered the audition room, another exited. Gregor saw the look of anxiety on each face and knew it spelled disaster for the next one.

He slumped in his chair and closed his eyes. No amount of practicing would make any difference. The air in the narrow hall grew too warm. His shirt dampened and wilted under his jacket. A trickle of sweat ran down his neck. He tried to block the cacophony around him by taking deep breaths. By the time he heard his name called, his head ached. He wanted to vomit. Too late.

"Gregor Piatigorsky? You're next."

He glanced at the faces of those who remained. No one spoke. Some averted their eyes. The atmosphere was of an impending execution.

The audition area was set up in the concert hall. A pianist sat to the left of the stage and a group of six judges was arrayed in a half circle. In the center of the group sat a lone chair and an empty music stand. Giving the judges a slight bow, Gregor took the seat and faced the six somber old men, all of whom had to be over forty.

"What did you bring to play?" said the judge with a long narrow face and down-turned mouth. He had a commanding voice and seemed to be in charge.

"I didn't bring any music," Gregor replied with a sinking heart. "Only my cello."

Turning to the pianist the judge asked, "What do you have that he could play?"

"The Dvorak Cello Concerto," replied the man at the keyboard. "But I have only one copy of the score."

The judge looked at Gregor and raised his eyebrow. "Can you play it without music?"

"Yes."

"Begin two bars before the solo," the judge said. The pianist began mid-phrase.

"Stop," Gregor shouted. "Start from the beginning. I need the lead in." He turned to the panel of judges. "Please?"

There was an uncomfortable silence. "It's not customary to waste time on a long piano introduction," said the hoarse voice of the oldest judge. "Begin again, two bars before the solo."

The pianist began. Gregor had no choice but to jump in, completely off balance and disoriented. Closing his eyes, he forced his mind to go blank and let the music take over. It flowed through him like the blood pulsing though his veins. The judges were gone. There was no competition. He was alone in the room, just he and the cello.

At the conclusion of the Allegro, the accompanist stopped and Gregor opened his eyes. It was like waking from a dream. All around him the room was silent. He scanned the faces of the men before him. They looked like stone.

The man in charge turned to the second judge and whispered something in his ear. A few hurried exchanges among the judges, the first one motioned to him. "Play the second movement. There is no hurry." He nodded to the pianist. "Start at the beginning of the Adagio."

He exhaled a sigh of relief and gently laid the bow on the strings. This time the music flowed from the cello as if the instrument were alive. His heart no longer pounded. At the conclusion of the piece, he stood, made a slight bow then waited.

Sweat ran down the side of his cheek and he fought the urge to tear off his jacket and free himself of the intense heat inside him. There were more whispers between the judges and long silences. Why didn't they just tell him to go so he could get out of this damned jacket?

The first judge rose and the others followed him. "Let me congratulate you on winning the position as first cello of the Imperial Orchestra," said the judge, extending his hand.

Gregor couldn't speak. He willed his legs to move and stepped forward. As each judge shook his hand, he watched their lips move and knew they were congratulating him, but their words didn't penetrate his skull.

"Piatigorsky?" said the first judge. The deep voice broke through the fog that surrounded him. "How old are you?"

"I'm—I'm fifteen."

The judge shook his head. "So young and so talented. You have a great future ahead of you."

"Thank you, sir."

At that moment he noticed faces crowding the doorway. They belonged to the other contestants, his rivals. The young ones wore looks of amazement, but the older artists didn't look happy. No matter what he did, he would never be able to appease them.

Chapter Fifteen

Moscow
October 1918

Dear Leo,
I write to you again, but you don't write back. Why? Did you get my letters?
Do you know I play with the Bolshoi Orchestra. It's good that you aren't here.
The Party turned everything upside down. Class and money mean nothing. Party
means everything. Mujiks and factory workers fill the streets. They chant Peace.
Land. Bread. But most would be happy with bread. I pray that you have food. I
hear rumors that the hungry in Siberia eat human flesh. That has not happened
in Moscow. The whores work for matches and bread. There is no money, so
everyone trades.
The Party loves musicians, actors and dancers. We are children of the
Revolution, they tell us, and we march first in parades. We also get extra food
rations, while starving bankers and merchants shovel snow and ice from the
streets. Only the Cheka police carry rifles. I saw one shoot a priest. No one
protested.
Do you have food enough? I put my extra ration coupons in this letter so
Mama can buy bread. Write to me, Leo. I dream at night that Mama is crying.
Don't forget me, Grisha.
P.S. Does Papa ask about me?

"We will no longer play decadent bourgeois music." The conductor stood
before the orchestra members who had been ordered to assemble in the empty
rehearsal hall. There weren't enough chairs, so the percussionists huddled in the
back smoking homemade cigarettes.

The room was so cold Gregor saw a cloud of condensed breath hover in
front of the man's face as he spoke. "Capitalist music will be removed from the
repertoire." He paused to push his glasses up, then blew his nose loudly in a dirty

handkerchief. "This is the time of the New Order. Our music now belongs to the workers."

Gregor leaned left and whispered to Mischa Mischakoff, the first violin. "What is bourgeois music?"

"I don't know," Mischa said under his breath, never taking his eyes off the conductor. "Don't ask."

"Sir?" Gregor stood and raised his hand. "What is bourgeois music?"

Beside him Mischa inhaled sharply. The conductor stared over his glasses and the room fell silent, as if everyone had held his breath. Feeling their eyes, Gregor sank back into his chair. Mischa ran a finger around the inside of his collar, as if it was too tight, then glanced in the direction of the uniformed men standing at the door.

"Music by German composers is forbidden," the conductor continued. There was a murmur of disbelief and Gregor shot up out of his seat again. "Do you mean Mozart and Bach? What about Beethoven?"

"Those composers worked for the elite. Their music represents everything the Revolution rejects."

Mischa's shoe hit Gregor's ankle and he sank back down. "Shut your mouth, stupid." His friend's whisper was barely audible.

"You will be assigned to performance groups," said the conductor. "Each group will visit factories, collective farms and army barracks. From this time forward great music will belong to the workers, not performed for the wealthy." The conductor's gaze passed over each musician. No one spoke.

"You will be issued Party identity cards and ration books." The conductor turned to the two uniformed men who moved to the front of the room. They were both young and on the collars of their ill-fitting coats they wore a red pin with a hammer and sickle stitched in yellow. The taller of the two, who looked not much older than Gregor, spoke first.

"This is the time of the New Order." His voice was high-pitched and boyish. "All power to the Soviets." He raised a clenched fist above his head. "From this time forward The Beethoven String Quartet will be known as The National String Quartet in the Name of Lenin. The Imperial Bolshoi Orchestra will be known as The National People's State Orchestra. You will greet everyone as Comrade. All people are equal."

"Why should you name the quartet in honor of Lenin?" Gregor said as he raised his hand. This time he remained seated. "What does Lenin know about music?"

The room was as silent as a funeral. What was going on? Why had asking questions become so terribly wrong?

"Everyone must belong to the Party." The first Comrade ignored Gregor's question while the second man scribbled notes in his ledger. "Musicians who are not Party members cannot belong to the Orchestra." His gaze bored into Gregor.

"You will also be assigned to an army unit. All orchestra members must serve the Party."

Then the Comrade moved to a small table at the side of the rehearsal room. He opened a valise and spread a thick pile of documents across the table.

"Line up," he directed. "All of you." He pointed his finger at Gregor. "You first."

Gregor started to open his mouth in protest, but saw the cowering looks on his colleagues' faces. He moved forward while the rest of the musicians hung back.

"What's your name?" the man asked.

"Gregor Piatigorsky."

"Age?"

"Sixteen."

The man frowned. "You don't look sixteen. It says here on the roll that you are first cello?"

"I am," Gregor said.

"Hmphhhh." The man scribbled in his ledger. "Are you Red or White?"

"Neither."

The man glared up at him. "If you're not Red, then you must be White. All Whites will be dismissed."

Dismissed and probably killed, Gregor thought. "I am Red."

"Good. Here's your Party identity card. Keep it with you at all times." Looking down at his list, the man added. "Because of your age you will also receive a children's ration allotment."

"I'm not a child."

"You're younger than eighteen so you'll get a child's ration book. You'll also receive milk and chocolate on the first of each month."

"I don't want it. Give me the adult ration."

"That is not possible." He handed Gregor the light pink ration book instead of the darker red one. "Next."

As Gregor walked past the line of his fellow musicians, he heard someone snicker. "There goes chocolate baby."

He pretended not to hear, but he felt the heat of humiliation flood his face.

The second Comrade sat on the piano bench with a ledger book on his lap. "Piatigorsky?" He ran his finger down the list of orchestra members. "You're first cello in the orchestra? You'll be assigned to the Second Brigade, Fifth Unit." He scribbled a name on the military identity card. Gregor studied the card, which was emblazoned with the yellow hammer and sickle. *Comrade Private, G. Piatigorsky 2nd BR, 5th U.*

"Will I be given a uniform?"

"You'll have to ask your commander."

As he turned to leave, the comrade called him back. "Wait. You're also a member of the string quartet?"

"Yes, I'm the cellist."

"Then you are also a member of the Fourth Brigade, First Unit." The man scribbled out a second card and handed it to him. *Comrade G. Piatigorsky 4th BR, 1st U.*

"I am a soldier twice?"

"You must serve the Party by any means necessary." He waved forward the next man in line.

* * *

Gregor found a new home near the concert hall, a tiny room in an old house that looked onto a dirt yard, surrounded by a high board fence. A Red Ukrainian family occupied the front of the house. Like good Bolsheviks they charged him no rent, but were happy to accept his duplicate ration cards.

In early June the new comrade conductor announced the Orchestra would perform Strauss's "Don Quixote" for the first time. The rule against German music was temporarily suspended because "Don Quixote" was not a bourgeoisie capitalist, but a peasant. The performance would be free for the workers, but the best seats were saved for Party leaders. In the workers' paradise some comrades were worthier than others.

The conductor had expressed doubts about Gregor's ability to handle the new, complicated solo passages. Gregor intended to prove him wrong.

A timid knock at his door interrupted his evening practice. Gregor paused, not sure if he had really heard the sound. The knock came again, a hesitant request. Before he could unlatch the door, he heard footsteps receding down the hall.

"Wait," he called and pulled the door open. A woman stood at the end of the dark corridor, a shawl over her head and shoulders. "What do you want?"

Her eyes dropped to the floor and she turned away.

"I have no money for whores," he said and started to close the door.

"I'm no whore." There was edginess in her voice, like it might crack. "I'm looking for—." She paused and he saw her frail body tremble. "For Gregor Piatigorsky."

"What do you want with him?" He stepped into the corridor and she retreated. With her shawl pulled across her mouth, she leaned against the wall as if for support. Her face looked ghost-like, deeply sunken eyes and hollow cheeks. She doesn't get enough to eat, he thought. But no one had eaten well for a very long time.

"I'm Gregor," he said. "What do you want with me?"

"Grisha?" Her voice dropped to a whisper. "It's me, Nadja."

A mixture of horror and joy overwhelmed him. "Nadja!" He threw his arms around her, hugging her thin frame. Then stepped back, he slid the shawl off her face She was a shadow of the beautiful girl he remembered. Pulling her into his tiny room, a hundred questions spilled from his lips. "Did you get my letters? I wrote a dozen times, but you never answered. Have you seen Mama and Papa? Are they well? What about Leo and Alex?"

"Grisha." Nadja's voice trembled. "I don't know where to begin." Tears filled her eyes as she sank onto the edge of the bed.

He sat beside her, his arm around her shoulders. For a moment she didn't speak and he pulled her close. The sight of her pain was more than he could bear. She rested her head on his chest and he held her, mumbling nonsense words, trying to comfort. "I'm so happy to see you— I'm glad you came. It's been hard. I wrote you and Leo, but the post is so bad— I didn't know if my letters ever arrived."

"I saw your letters only two weeks ago. Dimitri kept them hidden from me. I found them in the cupboard."

"I went back to our old apartment twice," Gregor said. "I wanted to see someone, but everyone was gone. I haven't been there in almost five years." He paused and took a deep breath, remembering that spring afternoon. "I even went to your apartment and stood by the door. I listened. I wanted to hear something, like you playing the piano."

"I had no idea you were there," Nadja raised her head and wiped her eyes with her sleeve. "Why didn't you knock?"

"I ran away. I was afraid. I didn't want Papa to see me."

He rose and dampened a cloth with water from the pitcher then handed it to her. "And I didn't want to see Dimitri."

She wiped her face with the cloth, sniffled and blew her nose. Finally she gave him a weak smile and for the first time he saw something of the girl he once knew. She was sixteen when he left home. Now, at twenty-one, she looked old and haggard.

"What about your baby?" he said, as he pulled his practice chair close to the bed.

She nodded but he saw overwhelming sadness in her eyes. "I named him Gregory Pavelovich." She hung her head and wiped away a tear. "But there was something wrong with him when he was born. He lived only a few weeks. He was a pretty baby but he couldn't eat."

She drew a photo from her pocket and handed it to him. It was her wedding picture and she wore the bridal dress that had been Mama's. Even in the weak light of the oil lamp, he could see how beautiful she had been. To her left stood Dimitri, a smirk on his face. For a moment Gregor felt his hand tighten into a fist. On Nadja's right stood Mama and Papa, and the sight of them made his heart ache. "Nadja, you were beautiful."

"Grisha, did you ever see Papa cry?"

"No. Papa would never cry."

"He did. I saw it. He cried the day you left and he cried the day I married Dimitri. After the wedding he couldn't stay in Moscow." She shook her head. "He said he had failed at everything."

"Not everything. He never played with the Bolshoi, but I was chosen. I'm first cello now."

"Oh, Grisha." She grabbed his hand. "Papa would be so proud."

"What about you and Dimitri?"

"I was young and foolish. I thought Dimitri loved me, but he only wanted a slave. I'm never allowed any money. I have to cook and care for Dimitri's mother. She can no longer walk or keep herself clean. His father comes home drunk and..." Her hand went to her mouth and he saw her fingers tremble.

"What happened? What did he do to you?"

She turned away and covered her face with her hands. "He used me as his wife," she whispered.

In an instant the anger was back, clawing up inside him. "I swear." He hit his fist in his palm. "I'll kill him."

"No, Grisha. I didn't want to tell you because I was afraid. Not afraid for me, but for you. I knew how angry you'd get. I don't want you to get into trouble on my account."

He stood and began pacing, but the room was too small. "You'll stay here with me. I have enough food rations."

"Please, sit down. Let me hear you play." Just like that she changed the subject. "I miss hearing your music."

"For you, I'll play anything." He forced a smile.

"Blue Danube." She picked at the hem of her shawl. Her fingers looked like white bones, old and scaly. "It's my favorite."

Gregor picked up his cello and pulled the chair closer to the bed. Nadja stretched out, cradling her head on her arms. Before he finished the melody, her eyes closed. He continued, playing softer with each refrain until he saw the lines on her face soften. In sleep at least, she was at peace.

Early the next morning Gregor rose from the pallet of blankets he had made on the floor. While Nadja slept, he drafted a letter of divorce. With the crude document in his pocket, he headed across the city to the apartment house that had once been his home. Moscow had not yet wakened from the short summer night. The alleys and stairwells still held the sleeping bodies of orphans and whores. He paid hardly any notice to the occasional rat that scurried out from beneath piles of rubbish. Most of the streets were empty.

He walked then ran, glancing left then right on the lookout for the Cheka. This time of the morning they would be bored and might take interest in a lone pedestrian. The knot in his stomach grew with each step. By the time he reached his old neighborhood he was sweating and out of breath.

Vodka shops were shuttered and the streets empty of Tartar children. The houses, which a decade earlier had been shabby and rundown, now appeared vacant. They loomed over him like corpses with hollow eyes. The familiar apartment building that had once been home now looked grim and foreboding. He slipped through the open gate, which hung crooked on a single rusty hinge. From somewhere in the distance a rooster crowed.

This time he didn't go upstairs, but stood before the ground floor apartment, the one where Dimitri lived.

"Open up." He pounded on the door. "Open or I'll kick it in." He hit the door again and again.

Finally a quivering voice called through from the other side. "Go away. Leave us alone."

Gregor halted his attack, breathless from the assault on the door. The side of his hand ached from the blows. Stepping back, he kicked, bringing the heel of his boot down hard against the latch. The wood didn't budge so he hit it again. As he backed up, ready to kick the latch a third time, the door swung open. Standing there, with a stove shovel in his hand, was Dimitri. He was older and more slovenly than Gregor remembered, but the unshaven face had the same unforgettable sneer.

"Who the hell—?"

Before he could finish, Gregor reached out and caught Dimitri by the neck, sinking his fingers into the soft flesh. Dimitri's stove shovel came down toward Gregor's head, but he caught it with his left hand, twisting the weapon away.

"You stinking piece of filth." Gregor punctuated each word with a snap of Dimitri's head.

"Let –me—go," he squawked as he staggered back into the apartment

"Only when you and your parents sign this divorce paper." He pushed Dimitri into a kitchen chair then slapped the letter on the table. "Nadja is no longer your wife."

"What's all the noise?" a voice called from the hall and Gregor looked up to see an old man with broken teeth lumbering toward him. At the sight of Dimitri's father and the memory of Nadja's words, he went insane. Lunging, he grabbed the old man by the arm and shoved him against the wall.

"Leave me alone." The old man waved his identity card. "I'm a Party member. You can't do this."

"And you will be publicly hung for the crime of rape." Gregor knocked the card from his hand. With his forearm pressed against the old man's throat, he pinned him against the wall. "You will sign this divorce letter or I will drag you and your son to the Party police myself."

The man's eyes narrowed and Gregor smelled the sour stench of fermented *bragha* on his breath. "Your sister is a useless Jewish whore." The man spit at Gregor's face, but the glob of phlegm landed on the floor. "She's no good in the kitchen and barren as well. Her Jewish blood made her child weak. My son's next wife will be Christian."

Gregor pulled his arm back, a fist ready to smash the ugly sneer off the man's face. But he hesitated. If he killed this disgusting pig he would never get the necessary signatures on the divorce petition. With every bit of self-restraint he possessed, he lowered his fist. Dimitri sat quivering at the table, unable or unwilling to defend his own father.

Gregor released the old man and backed away. The document was the most important thing, not his rage. Pulling a pencil from his pocket, he shoved it across the table to Dimitri.

"Sign and I'll leave."

Dimitri was almost crying. He grabbed the pencil and scribbled his name to the document without even reading it.

"Now you." Gregor grabbed the father by the arm.

"I'll report you to my Party captain," the old man said. "I have friends in high places."

"There are no high places anymore," Gregor snarled. "No one will help you."

The man screwed up his wrinkled lips and spit at Gregor's feet. "Dirty *Zhyd.*"

"Sign it!" Gregor pushed him toward the table.

"This will never be accepted by the Party."

"Do it. Now!"

Muttering obscenities, the old man took the pencil and scribbled his name to the paper.

Gregor ignored the man's profanity. With two out of the three names, he wanted to end this insanity. "And your wife, she must sign as well."

The father shrugged and waved toward the rear bedroom. "In there, unless you fear the cholera."

Keeping his eye on the two of them, Gregor backed into the tiny room. The smell of sickness and defecation was overpowering. A gray-haired woman lay on the bed, a dirty blanket covering her skeletal frame. The sliver of light coming from the curtained window only illuminated the filth of the place.

"Get out." Her voice sounded more animal than human. She pulled the blanket over her scabby arms and shoulders.

"Sign this." He shoved the paper in her face.

The woman's claw-like hand grabbed the document, crumpled it, then threw it at him. He stepped back and caught the missile. Opening it, he smoothed out the wrinkles against his thigh.

"You will sign." He grabbed her bony wrist. "If you don't, I'll drag you naked into the street."

"Dimitri!" Her voice quivered. "Help me."

"Your son's a coward. You'll get no help from him. Sign and I'll be gone."

The absence of any aid from family must have convinced her. Without looking at the document, she scrawled her signature. "Get out. Leave us alone."

With the paper safe in his pocket, Gregor made a hasty retreat. Outside in the bright morning sun, he sucked in deep gulps of fresh air. The stench of the cesspool that had once been his sister's home permeated his clothes. He wanted to wash the filth of their evilness from his body, but none of that mattered now. With this signed confession, Nadja was free. Once he showed the document to Party officials, they would have to grant her a divorce.

* * *

All summer Nadja stayed with him and he was happier than he had been in years. He slept on the floor and shared his meager rations with her. With each passing day and each bite of bread or cabbage, she grew stronger. The color returned to her face and the dark circles under her eyes faded. When she smiled, his heart felt warm.

They often stayed awake late into the night, talking of the old days in Ekaterinoslav, reliving the funny moments, laughing together. But he could tell by the catch in her voice when she was about to cry. Then he changed the subject.

After rehearsals, he took her to parties and introduced her to his friends. In the concert hall she played the piano while he and the others practiced. He even took her to his former landlady, the one who made dresses. With money borrowed from his friend Mischa, he bought Nadja a pretty blue gown to wear to concerts and the theater. Everyone loved Nadja and some of his friends would have loved her too much if he had let them.

"She's your sister, not your betrothed," Mischa said. "You can trust me. I want to take her to the festival tomorrow. I told her I'd teach her how to dance like a gypsy."

"Mischa, I would trust you with my life, but not my sister's reputation."

"Why don't you let her decide?"

Gregor thought for a moment. "I'll ask Nadja if she would like to go. If she says yes, I'll let you take her."

"Wonderful. I promise you—."

"But," Gregor warned. He leaned closer and pointed a finger at Mischa nose. "Leave your violin and bow with me." He took pleasure at the look of distress on his friend's face. "If I'm to trust you with my sister, then you must trust me with your instrument."

"You wouldn't —"

"I'll make kindling wood of it if she comes back with one hair out of place."

* * *

The summer sun finally set and for a few hours darkness returned to Moscow. The air was less sooty and laundry, when hung out to dry, was still clean when Nadja brought it back inside.

"Grisha," Nadja said, as she lifted the last of his shirts from the wash bucket. "I want to go home."

"But this is home." He took the wet shirt and draped it over the high board fence.

"No, Grisha," she said softly. "This is your home. I want to see Mama and Papa. Little Alex is almost eight and he hardly knows who I am."

"You can go for a visit while I'm on tour. You'd come back to Moscow, wouldn't you?"

She turned to him and took his hands in hers. They were warm and damp. "No, Grisha, I won't come back. You should come home to Ekaterinoslav with me. That's where we belong."

He felt his heart sink. "I can't. I'm first cello in the Bolshoi." He pulled his hands away and began pacing in the small back yard. "Nadja, I'm seventeen. Last month I applied for permission to go to Berlin. If I get a chance to study abroad I might even make it to America." He stopped and held out his open hands. "What would I do in Ekaterinoslav?"

"I know, but you must understand my situation. I can never remarry. No man would have me. I can't have any more children, so what's left?" Despite the warm summer breeze, she hugged her arms as if she were cold. "Living with you has been wonderful, but I must leave before you go on your next tour. I couldn't bear it here alone."

Nadja was right and he knew it. She had to have her own life. Keeping him company was not enough.

"I'll buy you a railway ticket," he said. "I'll get it tomorrow."

* * *

They stood side by side on the platform as the line of peasants with baskets and bundles pushed and shoved to board the train to Kiev. Nadja's only luggage was the canvas valise Gregor had given her.

"I wrote this last night," he said as he handed her a folded note. "Give my love to all of them." He paused. "And to Papa."

"Grisha, he doesn't hate you."

"I think he must."

She reached into her pocket and withdrew a silver watch, Papa's watch. "Take this," she said, pressing it into his hand. "Papa gave it to me when I married Dimitri. He said if I ever needed money I should sell it." She squeezed Gregor's finger around it. "I couldn't bring myself to part with it, but I want you to have it." She stood on tiptoe and kissed his cheek. "Come see us when you can."

"I will. I promise."

He stood alone on the platform as the train belched a cloud of smoke, then pulled out of the station. Nadja waved to him from the window as the car moved away. His feet were frozen to the platform and he was unable to move until the train was out of sight. He felt empty, as if all the blood and all the air had been sucked out of his body.

Back in his room, Gregor sat in the evening twilight staring out the window. He should be practicing. He should be studying the new score with all the changes the conductor wanted, but he couldn't bring himself to play. The room seemed empty without Nadja.

Leaning his cello in the corner, Gregor stretched out on the bed he hadn't slept on in two months. Maybe he should have asked the director for time off so he could go home and see Mama and Papa. But he had no more money. He had used it all buying things for Nadja. He had even borrowed money from Mischa for her train ticket. There was no way he could afford to leave Moscow now. Besides, the Second Brigade commander demanded four concerts a month for the troops. That and orchestra rehearsals had already put him behind schedule with the Fourth Brigade.

He rolled onto his side and felt the hard lump of Papa's watch in his pocket. Sitting up, he pulled the watch from his pocket and held it in his palm. The sight of it brought back a flood of memories. Carefully, just the way Papa had taught him, he wound the stem then held the watch to his ear. With his eyes closed he listened to the *tick, tick, tick* of seconds passing. Papa's voice counted quarter time. *One, two, three, four. One, two, three, four. Play for me, Grisha. Let me hear you make beautiful music.*

With Papa's words ringing in his ears, he picked up his cello and sat straight in the chair. But he didn't touch the bow to the strings. All he could do was wrap his arms around the instrument and rest his cheek against the scroll. The cello was all he had.

Chapter Sixteen

November 1918

The thick smoke made the café seem warmer, or maybe it was the *bragha*. Gregor drained the last of the sour beer from his glass then reached across the table and plucked the cigarette from Mischa's fingers.

"That's my last one," his friend said.

"I need it." Gregor sucked hard on the hand-rolled stub. It tasted worse than the *bragha*. "Agghhh." He spit tobacco crumbs on the floor. "What the hell did you put in these things?"

"Whatever I can find." Mischa took the cigarette back and smoked it until his fingers were singed. "Beggars cannot choose."

"I'm hungry," Gregor said.

"So tell the waiter you want some *kasha*. It's the cheapest thing they have."

"I have no money. That *bragha* took my last kopek."

"Don't forget you owe me five rubles." Mischa ground the cigarette out on the scarred tabletop but rescued the last crumbs of tobacco and returned them to his empty wallet. "You should have taken that dance hall job with me last week. I was paid three loaves of bread and a cabbage, all for a few dance tunes. I traded the cabbage for this tobacco and paid my rent with the bread."

"I had to play for the Second Brigade," Gregor said. "The commander says I'm behind on my military obligations. They always want me on Friday and then they pay me nothing." He slumped in the chair, leaned his head back against the wall and closed his eyes.

"You shouldn't have let Nadja go home. You've been a miserable bastard ever since she left."

"I don't want to talk about it." Gregor leaned back in the chair and rested his head on the wall. "You should be thinking about the Kremlin recital next Tuesday."

"Why should I worry?" Mischa sneezed then wiped his nose on his sleeve. "I've played the Kremlin before. It's no different than the Bolshoi, only the acoustics are worse."

"This time we play for Lenin, not some Party committee."

"Then nothing too long? We don't want to bore him. He'd have us shot."

"Do you really think he'll be there?" Gregor was glad Mischa had forgotten about Nadja.

"He loves music, at least I've heard he does." Mischa leaned his elbow on the table and rested his chin in his palm. "After all, we are the National String Quartet in the Name of Lenin."

A waiter approached their table. "If you aren't spending any more money in my shop, then you can find some place else to warm your bones."

They looked up at the one-armed man wearing a greasy apron. "I have no more money." Gregor held out his empty hands.

"Then out you go."

Reluctantly, they headed for the street. "See you tomorrow," Gregor said and waved good-bye. Lucky Mischa. At least he roomed with a family that had kinfolk in the country. Sometimes he even ate sausage and potatoes.

Gregor felt weak and his stomach hurt. *Bragha*, even watered down, was no good on an empty stomach. As he made his way down the narrow alley toward the boulevard, he veered left to avoid the legs of a boy stretched out behind a rubbish bin.

"Bread?" The boy called to him, extending an arm with a stump where his hand should have been. Gregor shivered and turned away, avoiding the pleading eyes. The damp wind blew leaves and bits of trash into the gutter and he hunched against the blowing spits of rain. The boulevard was empty except for a large wagon rumbling toward Red Square. Chains clanked against the undercarriage as the vehicle came to a sudden stop.

"You there," called a loud voice. "Halt."

Gregor turned into the wind and saw three soldiers jump off the wagon. With a sinking heart he read the words People's Police painted on the side. Stepping back against a shop wall, he held up his empty hands. "I've done nothing wrong."

Two uniformed men with rifles moved to either side, blocking any hope of escape. The third man, an officer by the insignia on his collar, stood with legs spread wide, tapping a wooden truncheon on the palm of his hand.

"Are you a soldier?" The officer poked Gregor's chest with the stick.

"Yes, but—."

"You're out of uniform and it's past curfew."

"I don't have a uniform."

"A deserter," said the man. "Into the wagon."

"I have my identity card," Gregor protested. "It's in my pocket." He tried to pull it out, but they grabbed his elbows and shoved him toward the wagon.

"Stop. I'm a Party member. I'll show you my card."

"Search him," said the officer. Rough hands moved inside his coat and down his legs.

"He's got quite a few cards." The soldier handed the identity papers to the officer. Under the light of the street lamp the man held up the card.

"Are you Gregor Piatigorsky?"

"Yes."

"Liar." The stick struck the side of his jaw, forcing teeth into his lip. Excruciating pain shot up the side of his face. The blow knocked him backward. Instinctively, his hands turned to fists, but the soldiers caught his arms.

"This is a child's identity card," the officer screamed as he shook the documents in Gregor's face. "And a child's ration book. You have betrayed the Revolution. You are a liar and a thief."

"I am—no—liar," Gregor said. Already his lip had swollen and he tasted blood. "Those are my papers."

"These cards are forgeries. You'll be shot." Turning to the two soldiers he said. "Tie his hands. We'll take him before Commissar Shokoff. He can decide what to do with this traitorous dog."

* * *

"Get out of my way, you Bolshevik pig." The new prisoner was a giant of a man with a black curly beard that covered his chest like a bib. He spit, just missing Gregor's face.

"I was here first." Gregor held his ground. "Find your own place."

The man started to turn away then spun back and with a heavy boot slammed his foot into Gregor's leg. "I want this bench."

Gregor looked at his fellow cellmates. No one met his eye. He pushed his shoulder against the wall, rose and tried to make a fist but couldn't. His wrists still ached where the ropes had cut into his flesh during the long wagon ride. Now his fingers looked like boiled sausage.

Dropping his eyes, he stepped sideways past a sleeping boy, until he found a space beneath the only window and leaned against the wall. Cold air seeped down his neck, but it helped lessen the smell of filthy bodies and the overflowing chamber pot.

"There's a wise fellow," the big man said as he settled onto the bench. "Bend over for the Cheka and you might yet live." The man laughed loudly at his own humor.

How long had he been in the cell? It felt like eternity. More prisoners arrived. The Cheka were busy. He tried to rub feeling back into his fingers. What if they never returned to normal, what if he got gangrene and ended up with no hands. Better that they shoot him now.

The door opened and a small balding man joined them. The light from the gas lamp in the corridor shone off his pate. The cell now held six.

"Maxim?" The newcomer squatted in front of the giant. "I'm glad to see the Cheka hate Whites as much as Reds. What brings you here?"

"No doubt the same that brings you." The big man leaned his head back and laughed, showing yellow teeth the size of dice. "The Cheka are Cossack pigs no matter who pays them."

"And you?" The man looked at Gregor. "Which side are you on?"

"Why?" Gregor nearly stepped on a dark bundle wedged against the wall. It moved and a hand swatted his ankle. The cell held seven prisoners, not six.

"This swine is Rubonovich," Maxim said. "Rudi the Red. Be careful what you say. He reports all to the Party." Maxim spit again. "He's a Bolshevik spy."

"I'm a socialist and a zionist."

"I'm a musician, a cellist." Gregor held out his hands. "But they tied my hands. Now I can't move my fingers."

"If the Cheka put a bullet in your brain." Maxim laughed. "You won't be able to play well either."

"It's all a misunderstanding," Gregor said. "I'm a member of the Bolshoi Orchestra."

"The last fellow who had a misunderstanding with the Cheka ate six bullets." Maxim coughed then pressed a finger against his nostril and blew a white glob of mucus on the floor.

"Don't listen to him." Rudi sank onto the other end of the bench but stayed out of Maxim's reach. "I'm loyal to the Party. All Jews are."

"Then why are you here?" Gregor squatted beside Rudi, his back against the cold wall.

"Like you, it's a misunderstanding over the price of bread." Rudi sounded apologetic.

"Got caught making a profit? You blood-sucking capitalist," Maxim said. "If we lived in the west, you could sell bread at any price you wanted."

"What do you know about the West?" Rudi buttoned the collar of his dingy shirt and smoothed the few strands of long hair that ringed his head like fringe. "You've never been west."

"I know that a man is free to do what he wishes. No Cheka, no Party, no questions asked."

"Where is west?" Gregor said. "Do you mean America?"

"Berlin, America, even Warsaw. It's all west. No Bolsheviks or police."

"He's a liar." Rudi scraped his teeth with a dirty fingernail.

"I know about America." Gregor leaned forward taking some of the weight off his heels. "My Aunt Julia lives in America. She said everyone is happy there. The sun always shines, even in winter."

"She's a liar." Rudi took out a dirty handkerchief, blew his nose, folded it neatly and returned it to his pocket. "My cousin lives in America. Wisconsin. Hates it. Snows worse than Moscow. Wants to come home."

"So he can freeze to death in beautiful sunny Moscow?" Maxim folded his arms across his chest and leaned back against the wall. "I'll trade places with him. He can even have this bench."

"So he can live here in a worker's paradise?" Rudi pointed a finger at Maxim. "The Party will never make slaves of the people the way capitalists like you do."

"I'm not the one in jail for making a profit."

"No, you're here because you support the Tsar and his monarchist friends." Rudi's voice grew shrill.

"And you're a Red cock-sucking pig who sleeps with anarchist dogs." Maxim's voice echoed off the stone walls.

A sleeping prisoner in the far corner sat up. "Shut up, you Trotskyite. Let a man sleep."

"You'll be sleeping for eternity soon enough." Maxim stretched his foot out and kicked the complainer's leg.

The man lunged forward, his arms and legs entangling with Maxim's. Rudi squealed and ran for the door, pounding it with his fists. Gregor rolled out of the way as Maxim rose, his thick arm circling the attacker's neck.

The cell door opened and two Cheka guards, clubs in hand, started swinging. "Back to the corners, you dogs."

"Save me," Rudi cried. "I'm a loyal Party member. Don't leave me here with these Tsarist swine."

The Cheka guard pushed Rudi into the corridor and the door clanged shut. Maxim sank back on his bench, holding his bloodied head in his hands. Gregor pressed himself into the corner, wishing he could make himself invisible. The other prisoners grumbled and repositioned themselves. The cell grew quiet. No one spoke.

Minutes later the silence was broken by the sharp one-two crack of a rifle.

"That was Rudi," Maxim said with a touch of sadness in his voice. "Party members get two bullets. Socialists four. But it takes six bullets to kill a loyal Monarchist."

It was dawn before the guards took Gregor from the cell. With hands again tied behind his back, the guard pushed him forward into a low, smoky room. Behind a low table sat a little man. He wore the same army uniform as the other soldiers, but his jacket was cleaner and he had a red button on his collar. This was the man that gave orders to shoot prisoners.

"Untie him," he said. The guards removed the ropes. As blood flowed back into his fingers, he felt the burn.

"Who is Gregor Piatigorsky?" The Commissar slid the ration book and identity cards across the table.

"I am." He tried to massage feeling back into his fingers.

The man stood and glared up at him. "According to these papers, Gregor Piatigorsky is a sixteen-year-old Jew." The man jabbed a stubby finger at him. "Don't lie. You're neither sixteen nor a Jew."

"I was born April 17, 1903. I am sixteen." He hesitated then added. "I am a Jew."

The man's eyes narrowed. "Why do you have two military identity cards?"

"I'm first cellist in the state orchestra so I belong to the Second Brigade, Fifth Army Unit." He searched the Commissar's face for some sign that the man believed him. "I'm also cellist for *the National String Quartet in Name of Lenin*, so I'm assigned to the Fourth Brigade, First Army Unit."

"You are a musician?" the man said, skepticism apparent in his voice.

"Yes, sir."

"If you're lying —." The threat did not need to be spoken.

"I'm telling the truth."

The man frowned then opened the door. "Send Comrade Nebakov to me." There was an awkward silence as the Commissar lit a cigarette and blew smoke into the already sour air. His eyes never dropped their piercing gaze. Gregor kept his eyes fixed on an irregular stain on the wall just above the man's head. Finally another soldier appeared at the door. The Commissar turned his gaze to the new arrival. The soldier glanced back and forth, fear in his eyes.

"Comrade Nebakov," said the Commissar. "This man says his name is Gregor Piatigorsky. He says that he's assigned to your unit. Have you ever seen him before?"

"No, he's not one of my men." Nebakov's eyes moved between Gregor's face and the Commissar's.

"Comrade," Gregor pleaded. "I played at your barracks last Friday. I am a cellist with the State Orchestra."

With that the man's eyes grew wide. "Yes, yes," he nodded. "The People's State Orchestra did come to our post. Yes, you are the tall one who carries his fiddle over his head."

"Yes, that was me." Gregor exhaled.

The Commissar took a long drag on the cigarette, his eyes narrowing as he blew out a long stream of smoke. "Comrade Nebakov, was he any good?"

"Yes, sir. He played an excellent piece from *Swan Lake*."

"Good." The Commissar dropped his cigarette and ground it out with his heel. "Then today we will not shoot him."

Chapter Seventeen

On the occasion of a command performance, the National String Quartet in the Name of Lenin was issued Fourth Brigade uniforms. The sleeves of the gray, poorly fitted jacket didn't even cover Gregor's wrists. The pants were much too short for his long legs and he had only one day to get them altered. Thankfully, his former landlady made do with scraps of fabric and adjusted them so Gregor didn't feel like a fool when he walked across Red Square to the Kremlin gate.

Gregor saw Professor Zeitlin standing by the guard box. "How long have you been waiting?"

"Too long. They won't let us in until everyone's here." Zeitlin lit a cigarette. "Where are Pulver and Senofsky?"

"I hope they get here soon." Gregor pulled the watch from his pocket. What would Papa think of him now, playing at the Kremlin and for Lenin himself?

Finally, the others arrived and the militiaman escorted them through the gate in the Kremlin wall and across the courtyard to a smaller door that opened onto a staircase. Gregor followed, staring up at the walls and parapets. He was inside the Kremlin, where a thousand years of Tsars had fought all manner of holy wars. The great and the not so great had all been here. Now it was his turn.

Making their way through long quiet corridors, only the sound of the their footsteps echoed off the walls. At the door of a second floor chamber, a small bearded man greeted them. He bore little resemblance to the legendary figure that had led the overthrow of the Romanov dynasty. Lenin stepped aside and welcomed the quartet into his parlor.

"Would you like tea?" Before any of them could reply, he motioned to the comrade who stood outside the door. "Please bring us tea and the little chocolate cakes."

His manner made Gregor feel like he was visiting an elderly uncle, not the leader of the Union of Soviet Socialist Republics.

"I heard you play at the opera." Lenin took a sip of tea. "I'm quite impressed by the talent of your group."

"Thank you." Gregor realized he had become the spokesperson for the quartet, the others having fallen mute. When they finished their refreshments Lenin called for the tea to be removed.

"Would you play something for me now?" Lenin folded his hands in his lap and waited.

"Yes, sir." Gregor felt sweat dampen the tight collar of his uniform. "What would you like to hear?"

"Do you know anything by Edvard Grieg?"

"Yes, sir."

"You should call me comrade, not sir," said Lenin with a slight smile. "All such titles are useless now."

"Yes—c-comrade." The words felt unnatural on his tongue.

They played the first movement from the Grieg quartet then waited. Did Lenin want more? The Premier smiled and seemed satisfied. He stood, extended his hand and they each shook it.

"Thank you for coming," he said. "You're a credit to our new nation."

"We're pleased that we could come," Gregor said. Professor Zeitlin put his instrument away while Gregor loosened his bow and retracted the endpin.

Lenin placed a hand on Gregor's arm. "You stay."

Gregor felt like he had been kicked. He looked at Zeitlin, whose eyes grew wide. Gregor silently mouthed, "Wait for me, please."

Zeitlin nodded, then opened the door and followed the others out of the room.

"Come with me," said Lenin. Gregor had no choice but to follow. They moved along a narrow carpeted corridor to a small study. One window provided light in the book-lined room. Gregor kept a firm grip on his cello and bow. For some absurd reason, he felt the instrument offered him protection from this little man.

"Sit down." Lenin motioned to a chair. Gregor obeyed but kept his cello close to his side. Lenin sat in a straight wooden chair across from him. He pointed at the cello. "Is it a good instrument?"

"Not very. I traded my coat for it."

"The finest instruments used to be in the hands of wealthy amateurs." Lenin spoke with a slight accent and Gregor felt himself relax, slightly. "Soon the best instruments will be in the hands of musicians rich only in talent."

"Yes. sir . . . comrade, sir."

Lenin ignored the blunder. "You're very young, but you have a responsible position." Lenin shook his head then abruptly changed the subject. "Is it true you objected to renaming the Quartet? That you think I know nothing of music?"

Gregor's heart skipped a beat. "I'm s-sorry."

"At your age one speaks first and thinks afterwards," Lenin said. There was no animosity in his tone. "It's true. I know very little about music, but I greatly admire the German composers. I know that there is no more fitting a name for a quartet than Beethoven."

"You aren't angry with me?"

"No." He smiled. "In time many things will change. The Lenin String Quartet will not survive, but Beethoven's name will be with us for the ages." He stood and Gregor rose. "But for now it is best to keep such opinions to yourself."

* * *

In late March, after the regular concert season ended, the orchestra was divided into small touring groups. Gregor's quartet was assigned to play in factories, worker clubs and collective farm villages. Sometimes there were as many as four programs a day. They traveled from place to place on trains, wagons and even big wooden sleds. The horses wore bells that rang, announcing the arrival of the entertainers. Ragged children ran into the streets and chased the sleds, while bony dogs, their ribs showing, barked at the commotion.

The conductor instructed them not to play anything too slow. No soft music or long works, just single pieces that could carry across large rooms with bad acoustics. Certainly nothing that might bore the audience or keep the peasants from their work. So Gregor again found himself playing popular dance music, folk tunes and simple melodies. Pieces by Brahms or Bach were once again allowed, but were not always well received in the countryside. Without a full orchestra, the music was lost inside the great factory spaces.

When there was no hall or stage to perform on, the orchestra used wooden benches set in the muddy village square. The cold air made playing more than one piece painful. His lips cracked and his fingers lost all feeling. He wore dirty wool gloves with the fingertips cut off the left hand and he traded his only dress jacket for a mangy fur coat with a tear in the right sleeve. It was long enough to cover his legs but he had, on Mischa's advice, left the damage unrepaired. Rip the label out, Mischa had said. You don't want to look too *bourgeois.*

Even his cello complained of the cold and damp. The precious strings became brittle and broke when the air grew too cold. He tried tying knots in them to make them last, but for one entire week he performed with only three strings.

On the collective farms, mothers wrapped in heavy quilted coats brought small children to hear the music. The little ones were so bundled up they could hardly move. Often, the youngest children wanted to climb onto the musicians laps and touch their instruments. The older ones danced and jumped if the tunes were lively, but when the music was soft or slow their attention waned and they would fall asleep on the frosty ground.

"Mama," said a boy who sat right in front of Gregor. "When that man finishes sawing his box in half, can we go home?"

For weeks the group traveled the countryside, sleeping in the worker's club or on factory floors. The local People's committees paid for their performances. In bigger cities it meant one ruble for each of them, but in small factories they were paid with pots, chocolate or mittens.

When they arrived in Kiev they were offered a real stage in the Grand Opera House on which to perform. Their accommodations, in a run-down old hotel, seemed positively luxurious. A hot bath and the chance to clean his clothes lifted Gregor's spirits.

"The State Opera is joining us for a week-long program," announced the director at the first rehearsal in the concert hall. "They will perform pieces from Bizet's "Carmen" and Mozart's "The Marriage of Figaro."

"Finally," whispered Mischa. "Something worth performing."

"I've forgotten how to play real music," Gregor whispered back.

There was a commotion in the wings as a group of people filed slowly onto the stage. Leading the group of opera singers was a dark bearded man in a fur coat.

"I'm dead," Gregor groaned as he slid down in his seat.

"Huh?" Mischa looked at Gregor, a puzzled frown on his face.

The man in the fur coat turned, his eyes scanning the pitifully small orchestra. His gaze settled on Gregor's face.

"YOU!" His voice boomed across the stage as he pointed at Gregor. Everyone turned and stared. "Cellist! I remember you." There was no hiding from Fyodor Chaliapin. Gregor stood and faced his nemesis. In the two years since they had last shared the stage, Gregor had grown tall enough to stand eye to eye with the opera singer.

"I am Gregor Piatigorsky."

"I will never forget who you are." He threw his big fur-covered arm around Gregor's shoulder and hugged him.

"Never in my life have I seen a performance such as yours." As Chaliapin spoke, he pounded Gregor on the back. "I am so happy that you are alive and not devoured by the monster." He stepped back and smiled a great dark grin. "Tonight. My room. Just you and me. Yes?"

All Gregor could do was nod.

                                    * * *

Chaliapin poured vodka from a silver flask and handed Gregor a small glass. "You are a Party member?" He poured himself a drink twice as large and downed it in one gulp.

Gregor stared down at the clear liquid and hesitated.

"You are Russian? Yes?" Chaliapin said, one eyebrow raised. "Then you must drink vodka." It was an order not a question.

As he raised the glass to his lips, Gregor inhaled the acrid smell that brought back a flood of memories. The North Star Klub, the Café Chantant and worst of all, the Traktir.

"Drink," said the opera star as he slapped Gregor's back. In one gulp he downed the fiery liquid and almost choked. "Of course," he gasped. "I am Russian." Then he sneezed.

"You like my vodka?" Chaliapin grinned. "I get it special, from a friend." He poured another glass for himself but didn't offer Gregor any more.

Gregor didn't answer, fearing he might be offered more. There was only one chair in the room, but he decided not to take it. Instead, he sat on the edge of the narrow bed.

"Hasn't the army found you?" Chaliapin said. He flung his great fur coat on the bed. Every move the great man made was dramatic, as if he were still on stage. "You look like you could carry a gun."

"I am enrolled in two army units." Gregor felt too hot, as if the vodka were smoldering inside him.

"We all serve the Party. More than we would like." Chaliapin dropped into the chair and stretched out his long legs. "The question is, what of your music? Are you studying with anyone?"

"There's no need to study. We play the same music for everyone. Besides, there is almost no printed music to work from."

Chaliapin leaped to his feet and Gregor pulled back, trying to leave enough room for the man and his enormous energy. He paced back and forth, two long steps, turned, then took two more long steps. While all other performers shared rooms and beds, Gregor knew why Chaliapin had this room to himself. Clearly, being a celebrity still counted for something.

"You must leave Russia," Chaliapin moved impatiently. Gregor had to pull his feet under the edge of the bed so as not to be trampled. "Go west to Berlin or Paris, even America. If you stay here you will be smothered." He poured a third drink and swallowed it. "As will I if I'm forced to perform like this much longer."

"I would love to go to America." Gregor set his empty glass on the floor, careful to tuck it under the bed. "I've applied to study abroad three times, but always, I am turned down."

"How much do they pay you?" Before Gregor could answer, Chaliapin continued. "Don't tell me. I know what you receive. We all receive the same salary no matter what our talents or responsibilities. That's how it is in this worker's paradise."

"Our conductor told us that our duty is to the Party, not ourselves."

"I disagree," Chaliapin said as he waved his hands. "Your duty is to your audience, but that means becoming the very best musician you can be." He threw his arms into the air. "An impossibility under these circumstances."

He dropped back into the single chair and pulled a valise out from under the bed. "Let me show you what I was paid for a performance of "Boris Godunov." He reached into the bag. "These—these—." He shook the offending objects then dropped them into Gregor's lap. "They paid me with these."

Gregor looked down at a pair of pink baby shoes. "Baby shoes?" He tried to hide his smile but the vodka worked against him.

"You laugh!" Chaliapin's eyes grew wide. He leaned forward, resting his big hands on his knees. "Before the Revolution," he said. "I was paid two hundred rubles for a concert of selected pieces from *"Godunov."* He snatched the shoes from Gregor's hand. "Now I perform an entire opera and I receive baby shoes."

Gregor expected to see smoke rise from the man's nostrils. Instead, the opera star doubled over and laughed out loud. "Someday I will gild these shoes and mount them on my wall."

"But if they won't let me leave, or study abroad. What can I do?"

"You must find a way." Chaliapin stuffed the baby shoes back into his valise and Gregor noticed the smile had disappeared from his dark face. "We all must leave. If we don't, we will perform at our own funerals. I will sing *The Miller's Daughter Milked the Cow* and you, my talented young friend, will accompany me."

* * *

After three performances to a packed house, the state opera left Kiev and headed east while the state orchestra traveled west. Unlike early May in Moscow, where piles of dirty snow still lingered in dark alleyways, spring in the Ukraine was mild.

At the farming collective of Khmel, the orchestra director divided the group in two. The string quartet, along with a tenor and soprano, went further west by horse cart to Farm Collective Number 7 near Volochisk. The chairman there had requested a performance for the workers. The rest of the orchestra traveled north to Lutsk, playing in villages and factories along the way. In ten days they would all meet at the rail station and return to Moscow for the summer concert season.

The muddy road to Volochisk pulled at the wooden wagon wheels. Six of them sat facing each other on two narrow benches, with instruments and luggage jammed between their feet. Gregor's cello took up the most room and everyone complained. They were all irritable and exhausted when the wagon finally arrived in the rundown farming commune.

"We're only a few kilometers from the border." Mischa kept his voice low. "This might be our only chance."

Gregor passed Mischa the battered leather satchel, then retrieved his own belongings before jumping down from the wagon bed. The other performers moved ahead, carrying their luggage into the collective barn, but Mischa hung back. Gregor balanced his cello on the toe of his boot, saving the case from the mud. Ahead he heard the chairman of the collective farm shouting directions to the new arrivals.

"How do you know where we are?" Gregor kept his eyes on the other musicians.

"Stupid," said Mischa. "I studied geography. The river we've been following is the Zbrunch. Poland is on the other side."

Gregor looked west toward the setting sun. Beyond the rooftops and farm buildings, past the open fields, he saw a line of trees. Was it possible? There, only a short distance away was the west, real Europe, cities with lights, people who ate hot food every night and wore beautiful clothes.

"Keep moving." Mischa waved him forward. "Don't look that way or they'll get suspicious."

Gregor picked up his bag and followed his friend into the barn, but he couldn't forget that across that river was a whole new world. What would happen if tonight, while everyone slept, he just walked across? Would the soldiers come after him? Could he run fast enough? What would happen if he were caught? Actually, he knew what would happen. It was too unpleasant to think about.

"You will perform tomorrow morning for the workers of North Farm," announced the chairman of the collective. "In the afternoon you'll perform for South Farm. You can sleep in the dining hall tonight after everyone has eaten. If you need to practice, you may use the school building. Do not play in the barn during morning and evening milking. The cows may object."

Gregor studied the lopsided platform, which occupied one end of the building. It was only slightly better than playing in the cow stalls that filled the other end of the structure. This was, without a doubt, the worst place they had ever performed.

"This is a damned barn," Sergei Vesilovsky, the tenor, said as he stood in the middle of the platform. "How can I sing in a barn?" He sniffed the air, which reeked of manure. "I can't compete with cows." He sank down onto his suitcase and held his head in his hands. "This is insane. I can't go on any longer."

Late in the evening, after an abysmal rehearsal in the schoolhouse, Gregor and Mischa stood outside under the overhanging roof. A light rain, almost a mist, had started to fall. The only light came from an oil lamp hanging inside the schoolhouse window. Mischa rolled a cigarette then handed the nearly empty pouch of tobacco to Gregor. "Grisha?" He lit his cigarette and exhaled a long plume of blue smoke into the night. "How much money do you have?"

"Why?" Gregor shook the last crumbs of tobacco onto the square of rolling paper. "There's nothing to buy in this town."

"Did you see that farmer, the one with the tall black boots?" Mischa re-twisted the ends of the cigarette paper. "He said there's a German who can get us across the river if we pay."

"Why should we pay? We can walk across after dark for free."

"Because stupid, there are guards on both sides of the river and they'll shoot us."

Gregor paused and touched the tip of his cigarette to Mischa's then inhaled the acrid smoke. "How much does he want?"

"Probably more than we have, but Madame and Sergei want to go too."

"I have fifty-seven of the new Party rubles."

"That's not enough. He wants two hundred to take the four of us over."

"That's all I have." Gregor paused and wiped the beads of water off his sleeve. "I could give him my coat, it's wool."

"I think that would look suspicious." Mischa held his hand out. "Give me your money and I'll see what I can do."

"How do you know he won't keep our money then refuse to help us?"

"Because if he doesn't take us to the smuggler I'll tell the chairman that he talked to us about joining the Trotskyites. That should get him the rope."

Gregor inhaled and held the smoke in his lungs. Escaping was treasonous. The punishment for treason was death by hanging if you were lucky, something far more painful if you weren't.

The burning embers singed Gregor's fingertips and he dropped the remains of the cigarette, grinding it into the dirt with the toe of his boot. He would give all the money he had to escape, but should he risk his life? Was music or being the best cellist in the world worth the risk? But if Chaliapin was right, if he stayed here chances were he would disappear into a deep hole, full of Party mud and Party propaganda. This might be his only chance.

He reached in his pocket and drew out a handful of coins. "Here."

"Wait here. Don't talk to anyone," Mischa whispered. "And for once, Grisha, keep your big mouth shut."

* * *

He waited for the command, the word that could end or begin his life. Let's go. Let's go, he thought as he crouched in the dark. Why is it taking so long? He wasn't cold. He wasn't hungry. Only the thought of a cigarette appealed to him.

"Why can't we—" He poked Mischa in the back.

"Shhhh," his friend whispered.

More waiting.

He shifted to the other knee and felt his cello slide off his shoulder. All he had left was his instrument. The smuggler had taken everything else.

He closed his eyes and prayed. "God, let us make it across."

As if answering him, the smuggler whispered, "Go. Run!"

The words were electric. Gregor's feet came alive. Beside him boots pounded the bridge planks. Madame's short legs couldn't keep up and she cried, "Wait, please wait."

Sergei passed her, but Gregor's long legs outran them all. One, two, three, four steps and he reached the center of the bridge.

The crack of gunshots split the night air. Return shots from behind them answered the first. The darkness was punctuated with flashes of bright light. Gregor knew instantly that he could not survive the gunfire. Despite the smuggler's warning, he moved to the left and stepped off the edge of the bridge. Dropping into the absolute blackness, he held his breath.

The water was cold, but his feet hit the soggy bottom before his shoulders went under. Miraculously, he kept his cello above his head. He struggled to keep his balance as the current tugged on his chest and thighs. For a moment it almost pulled him downstream. He struggled to remain upright. Turning right so the current had less to push, he spread his feet wide. There was no way he could run. Beside him something splashed, then twice more. Madame screamed but water filled her mouth and her voice became a gurgle.

The river only reached his armpits, but it was over Madame's head. Holding the cello above him with his left hand, Gregor reached to the right and found long hair floating on the water. Wet tendrils slipped through his fingers, but he got enough to pull her to the surface. In the next instant Madame's fingers locked onto his arm. She crawled up his back, choking and gasping for air. Her weight tipped Gregor backward, his foot slipped and he started to fall. Water gurgled up his nose. He snorted, regained his balance in the muck and leaned forward, shifting Madame's weight onto his back.

More gunshots split the darkness. A bullet whizzed past his head and splashed on his right. More shots rang out but they seemed to be targeted at the far end of the bridge.

"Downstream!" Mischa sputtered and flailed, splashing water in all directions.

Gregor pressed forward, his feet sinking with each step. He couldn't see anything. Running was impossible. Madame still clung to his back, her fingers digging into his neck, her panicked breathing loud in his ear. The current pushed them farther from the bridge and the gunshots grew distant. Finally the water level dropped from his chest to his waist, then to his knees.

Still dragging the sobbing Madame, Gregor staggered up the bank and fell, his knees sinking into muddy shoreline. The cello case was wet but hadn't gone under water. He pushed it against a bush then rolled over and tried to disengage Madame from his back. "Let go." He pried her fingers loose from his collar.

She crawled forward over his outstretched legs, her long black coat dragging behind her. "I can't—I can't—." She gasped, then dropped face down on the muddy bank.

Mischa staggered out of the river, fell beside them, breathing hard, spitting and snorting water from his nose and mouth. "We crossed. We're free."

"We did more than that." Gregor dropped back on the mud and stared up at the star-filled sky. "We can never go home again."

Gregor Piatigorsky and friends in Europe about 1922,
shortly after he left Russia.

1930s Studio publicity photo taken for Arthur Judson Management

Gregor Piatigorsky: Berlin about 1930

PART III

Chapter Eighteen

"You have taught your cello to sing.
Now you must teach it to speak."
Fyodor Chaliapin

Polish Border
April 1921

It took only a few minutes for the Polish border guards to find them. The barking came first, then a big snarling dog crashed down the bank and tried to sink his teeth into Gregor's leg. He kicked back, first missing then landing his heel on the dog's snout. The animal yelped, retreating as Gregor struggled to his feet, his wet coat hanging heavy around him. Turning to an easier target, the dog sent Mischa scrambling back into the dark water. Madame followed, screaming and splashing as she tried to escape.

"Shut up," Mischa said. "They'll hear you."

Above them a lantern moved back and forth on the bank. Unintelligible voices called out and Gregor heard footsteps moving through the underbrush. There was no place to run and nowhere to hide. The soldiers could shoot him, drown him or imprison him. Worse yet they might send him back across the river. With a sinking heart he stood there, waiting.

"Halt," said a deep voice. "Raise hands."

"Please, please," Madame sobbed. "Don't send us back. They'll kill us for leaving."

The soldier's knowledge of Russian didn't extend beyond a few cursory commands and he switched to Polish. Gregor didn't know the language but understood his tone and gestures. He lifted the cello overhead, holding the instrument high enough to keep it out of the man's reach. One soldier held up a lantern and pointed to the instrument. Making wild gestures with his rifle, he uttered incomprehensible phrases. Gregor didn't move. A second soldier shoved the barrel of his gun into Gregor's back while two more escorted Mischa and Madame from the river. Together they all marched up the bank.

Prisoners and guards assembled on a rutted farm road. Two more soldiers joined the group, both carrying rifles. Now there were six of them guarding three.

"Please don't shoot." Madame's hat was missing and strands of her long blonde hair stuck to her face.

"What about Sergei?" Mischa whispered.

"Did he jump?" In the dim lantern light, Gregor saw one of the guards glare at him.

"What will they do to us?" Mischa didn't seem to care if he was heard.

"I don't think they'll hurt us if we do as they say," Gregor said softly. His arms ached and he lowered the cello, slinging the strap over his shoulder. The soldiers exchanged words then again pointed to the cello. One soldier pointed his gun at Gregor's middle and tried to grab the instrument.

"*Nyet*. It's only a cello."

Two more soldiers shoved rifle barrels into his gut and made menacing noises.

"Let me show you." Gregor slid the case off his shoulder and opened it. One man grabbed the instrument while another examined the contents of the case. The first shook the cello and peered inside the F holes then ran his fingers over the strings plucking a few notes. The second man removed the extra socks, underwear, a comb and a toothbrush Gregor had tucked in the bottom of the case. The man slid the socks and comb into his pocket but returned the underwear and toothbrush.

They seemed to lose interest in the cello and turned to Mischa's instrument. One soldier tucked the violin under his chin and made like he was going to play. Thank God, Gregor thought. The man must be a musician. But the soldier scowled when the bow produced only squeaks and scratches. Mischa had nothing worth stealing so the guard returned the violin to the case.

At that moment one of the soldiers pointed down the road and called out something that sounded like a question. A voice answered from the darkness and all the lanterns were raised. Out of the woods a seventh soldier appeared escorting the dripping wet Sergei. Gregor started to speak, but the gun barrel jammed in his ribs silenced him.

"*Pospiesz sei*," said the leader of the guards. "March."

Gregor slung the cello case over his shoulder and the entire group moved down the road. At least they hadn't been shot, he thought. Yet.

The Polish jail was a cell attached to the Provost's office. Wooden benches lined three walls and a heavy plank door with a small barred window let in enough light for Gregor to see his friends faces. If he looked as bad as Mischa, with wet hair and muddy clothes, he must indeed be a frightening sight.

Madame sank down on the bench and kicked off her wet shoes while Sergei tried to ring the water from his coat. Mischa had cradled his violin case but the leather covering had already started to pucker from the soaking it had taken. In the middle of the cell floor, he knelt and opened the instrument case.

"Please, please don't be ruined." Mischa spoke to his instrument like it was a child. Gently, he removed the violin and pulled it from the flannel inner bag.

"Is it damaged?" Gregor sank onto the bench. "Did it get wet?"

"I don't think so." Mischa leaned back against the wall with a sigh of relief. "The case is good. The bag is only damp on one end."

"Is that all you fools care about?" Sergei said. "You can buy a new violin when you get to Warsaw."

"Buy it with what?" Gregor said. "We gave all our money to the smuggler."

"You're a fool," Sergei said. He turned to the narrow barred window and called out foreign words in a loud voice.

"You speak Polish?" Gregor said.

"Of course. I spent five years in Warsaw when I was young." He motioned to Madame who gathered up her shoes and joined him at the door. "When the guard arrives I'll ask you a question. I want you to smile and say *Tak. Tak.* That means yes in Polish."

Gregor didn't like Sergei's attitude. Weren't they all in this together? "What are you doing? Can you get us out of here?"

"I'm working on it," said Sergei. Again he called out and pounded his fist on the heavy plank door. A moment later the guard appeared and opened the cell door. One kept his rifle pointed in Gregor's direction while Sergei engaged in a long Polish dialogue. Occasionally the tenor pointed to Madame and she nodded, repeating the syllable *Tak, tak.* But when the guard gestured toward Gregor and Mischa, Sergei shook his head.

"Wait!" Gregor cried jumping up from the bench. "We came together and-."

The guard used the butt of his rifle to push him back into the wall. "*Nyet! Nyet!*"

With a sinking heart, Gregor watched as Sergei and Madame were allowed to leave.

"Please Sergei," Mischa cried. "Don't forget us." The door clanged shut.

Gregor pushed past Mischa and screamed out the window, "Sergei, you are a stinking son of a whore!"

"He was our only hope." Mischa leaned into the wall then slid back to the floor. "He'll tell them to release us."

"Mischa, you're a fool." Gregor dropped onto the bunk. "We've been betrayed."

They waited in gloomy silence. Mischa fell asleep but Gregor was too angry. After a while he stood, took off his soggy coat and tried to wring the water out. Then he did the same with his boots, which were still caked with river mud. The hole in the sole of the right one had drained off most the water but the left one was still squishy wet. He tried slapping his boots against the cell wall and was able to knock off the worst of the mud. Mischa groaned and rolled over to face the wall, his hands over his ears.

Then Gregor turned to his cello case. First he removed the instrument, placing it carefully on the empty bunk. He ran his hands over the wood. A cursory examination, but the best he could do without proper light. The instrument seemed intact though two strings had come loose, so he tightened them. At the bottom of the case, where a thick block of hollow wood cushioned the instrument, Gregor located a snap. Opening it revealed a narrow compartment in which he kept the small things every cellist needed, a worn piece of rosin, an extra set of strings and a spare peg. Beneath that lay a bundle wrapped in a handkerchief.

Moving toward the window, which gave a little more light, he opened the cloth. In the palm of his hand lay Papa's watch and beside it the gold cross Papa had made him wear for so long. A dozen times he had wanted to throw it away, but something always prevented him from doing so. Had wearing it really saved him, or was it just another one of Papa's lies?

"What are you doing?" Mischa said. He had stretched out on his back and rested his head on his folded arm.

"Whatever I can." Gregor rewrapped the bundle and returned it to the case. Then he sat and peeled off his soggy socks, wringing the Zbrunch River out of them. "I think we might be here for a long time and I'd like my clothes to be dry."

It was late in the morning when the guards returned. Gregor had slept fitfully on the wooden bench, wearing only his shirt and undershorts. When he heard the key in the lock, he threw off the itchy wool blanket and hurriedly pulled on his cold damp pants. As the guard motioned them out of the cell, he grabbed his shoes, jacket and cello.

They were escorted down the hall to a door marked *Provost*. The guard motioned them to stand against the wall and Gregor managed to finish dressing while they waited. As he buttoned his damp jacket, he smelled something wonderful. A young woman walked toward them with a tray of sausage, eggs and bread. No girl he had ever seen looked as good as that food. His hand reached out for the tray, but before he could grab a piece of bread, the guard raised his gun.

"Grisha." Mischa pulled back Gregor's offending hand. "Don't be a fool."

The girl averted her eyes and waited while the guard knocked then opened the Provost's door. As the food disappeared from sight, Gregor sagged against the wall. It had been twenty-four hours since he had eaten the thin borscht at Farm Collective Number 7. Now the devils in his belly were furious. Only when the girl returned empty handed, were they escorted into the Provost's office.

"Where are your papers?" the officer demanded in accented Russian. The breakfast from heaven was spread before him. Gregor watched him as he took his time spreading butter on a thick roll.

"We have no papers." Gregor extended his empty hands.

"No papers?" the officer said, a scowl creasing his plump face. "Then you're spies."

"No, no," Gregor said. "We're musicians with the State Orchestra. These are our instruments."

"That is not what the other man said. He told me you were not to be trusted."

"He's a notorious liar." If he could have strangled Sergei at that moment, he wouldn't have hesitated.

"Be careful how you speak," the officer said. "Sergei Vesilovsky and his wife are well known in Warsaw. She is the daughter of a Prussian prince."

"He is a —." Mischa caught his eye, silently pleading with him to stop then interrupted.

"Please sir. Let us show you we really are musicians." Mischa opened the violin case. "We'll play for you."

"Very well." The officer cracked his hardboiled egg with the back of a spoon. "But it won't prove a thing."

As Gregor unpacked his cello, Mischa whispered, "Do you know any Polish music?"

"Schoen Rosemarin." Gregor quickly tuned the cello. "They should know that."

"Find them an audience." The officer sliced sausage into thick chucks and speared them with his fork.

Without a chair Gregor had to extend the pin and prop the cello on the toe of his boot to get it high enough. As the room filled with half a dozen uniformed men and the food bearing young lady, Mischa began to play the melody. Several of the soldiers smiled in recognition and when Gregor joined in with the harmony a few feet began to tap in time with the rhythm. One man moved his hands dramatically, as if conducting the duet.

"*Dobje, dobje!*" The uniformed conductor smiled as they finished. The only one who wasn't pleased was the well-fed Provost officer.

"So you're talented fiddle-playing spies. What better disguise for a Bolshevik?"

"Please." Gregor tried to keep his voice level. "We can't live under Bolshevik rule any longer. We want to go to Warsaw and study music."

"Poland doesn't need any more unemployed musicians." He pointed to one of the guards and said something, then turned back to Gregor. "You'll be taken back to the border and returned to your own country."

"I beg of you, don't send us back." Now he was willing to beg. "We will be imprisoned or killed."

"That's between you and your government." The officer waved to the guards who raised their guns and marched them out of the building.

"Save your breath," Mischa said, keeping his voice low. "They're stupid, ignorant animals."

In the courtyard they were forced into a rickety wagon, pulled by a single scrawny horse. Only one of the soldiers, the middle-aged man who had pretended to conduct their duet, drove. He settled onto the wagon seat and lifted the reins. A second armed soldier, who couldn't have been more than sixteen, climbed in the back with them. Gregor felt like a piece of freight.

As the cart lumbered through the middle of the town, Mischa whispered,. "I'll knock him off the seat. You take the one with the gun."

"Not a good idea," Gregor said. Neither guard seemed to understand Russian. "The driver is the only one who likes music. Maybe we can convince him to let us go."

At the far end of the street Gregor saw the red roof of the railway station. Yanking on the driver's jacket, he pointed to the platform filled with people. Then he pointed at his cello case and made a motion like he was playing. The guard smiled and made a gesture like he wanted something to drink. He pulled the wagon up to the freight dock. The boy with the gun slung it over his shoulder as he climbed out of the wagon. The four of them made their way through the crowd of waiting passengers.

In the middle of the platform Mischa unpacked his violin and Gregor set up his cello. People pointed and a few moved toward them, smiling and chattering. A crowd gathered and a food vendor moved through the group offering pastries and beer for sale. The guard bought himself and his partner lunch while Gregor started with a lively gypsy tune. Two small children began dancing and several people threw 5 groszy and 10 groszy coins in Mischa's empty violin case.

When they completed two rounds of "Festiva" the audience broke into applause. Out of the corner of his eye, Gregor caught sight of a train slowly pulling into the station. Some of the audience started moving toward the cars. Gregor continued to play, plucking the melody as Mischa played. At the same time he began inching his way toward the edge of the platform. Mischa glanced and began moving with the crowd in same direction. People climbed aboard as Gregor and Mischa began playing "Schoen Rosemarin". The engine puffed white clouds of steam as they finished the second encore and began to pull away.

Gregor finished the piece with a flourish, grabbed his cello case and jumped onto the platform of the last car. Mischa followed, his violin still tucked under his chin. Several members of the audience waved and Gregor waved back. From his slowly moving vantage point he saw the guards staring at him, pierogies and beer in their hands.

"We did it." Gregor threw back his head and laughed as the train picked up speed. For the first time in days he forgot his hunger, his wet clothes and his fear.

"Get inside before you fall off," Mischa called out over the sound of the train whistle. "I'm not going to rescue you."

They moved through the railcars looking for a place to hide. Gregor slid the cello into its case and stashed it in the luggage bin at the end of the first car. Then he walked to the end of the nearly empty car and slid into the last seat.

"Keep going," he said. Mischa moved past him and slid into a seat at the far end of the car. More passengers entered from the adjoining cars, but were too busy securing their own seats to pay attention to them. For the first time in days Gregor let himself relax. Closing his eyes, he leaned his head against the window. Every turn of the wheels took him farther from Russia and closer to some place else. Where that would be, he had no idea. But whatever, it had to be better than the life he had left behind.

Images of Nadja flooded his mind. Would he ever see her again? Would he ever see any of them again? In the excitement of the escape, he had never given his family a thought. The Party would make his family pay for his crime, punishing Mama for the sins of her son. Cold reality sank in. He really had burned his bridges behind him.

* * *

"Please. Just a moment," Gregor called through the lavatory door. The pounding continued. He had ducked into the tiny space when the conductor started through the railcar collecting tickets. He stood with his back pressed against the door, trying desperately to come up with an escape plan.

Metal wheels screeched as the train shuddered then began to slow. He peered out the tiny soot-covered window and saw the peaked roof of a station. A faded sign hanging from the roof read L'VOV.

Behind him he heard the conductor rattling the doorknob and saying something ominous in Polish. If he were going to get thrown off the train this was as good a place as any. He pulled open the lavatory door, grinned at the conductor then began speaking rapid fire Russian.

"I see that we have arrived in L'vov. This is a lovely city. I am so happy to be here." He pushed past the conductor and reached for his cello. "My good friend Mischa and I are here to audition for the symphony orchestra. You look like a man who enjoys good music."

The conductor protested in Polish as he waved his book of tickets in the air. Gregor kept speaking, smiling all the while, heading for the door. Safe on the platform, he hurried away from the train, the conductor's angry voice still ringing in his ears.

"Grisha, over here." Mischa waved to him from the waiting room.

"We made it. We're in Europe now, real Europe." He turned a full circle, soaking up the sights and sounds of everything around him. "Look at these people. Their clothes are fine and the women are beautiful."

"Let's go," Mischa said. "There may be soldiers nearby."

As they headed into the city Gregor remembered the excitement of his first days in Moscow. But L'vov was better than Moscow. There were more automobiles and streetlights shone on every corner as dusk began to fall. Store windows were filled with fine clothes and expensive looking shoes. Gregor had never seen such abundance.

Mischa seemed less impressed. "It's getting late," he said. "Soon it will be dark and we don't have a place to stay. We've got to find a room and something to eat."

"Where?" Gregor said. "We can't even ask for work. No one here will understand us."

They stopped in the town square near a fountain that spouted water from the mouths of big green fish. Above them a clock tower chimed six o'clock.

"I'll tell you what to do." Mischa seemed unimpressed by the glamour all around him. "You go in that direction and try to find some food or money. If you see any Russians, beg them for a few coins." He took Gregor's cello. "I'll take the instruments and look for lodging. Meet me here by the fountain in two hours. Mark this spot in your dreamy Russian head."

They parted, heading in opposite directions. For a while Gregor wandered the streets staring into shop windows, admiring the well-dressed men and women who stepped out of big automobiles. He stood on the curb watching as they entered fancy restaurants. What would it be like to feel so secure, so rich and so important that you could eat in a restaurant every night and ride there in an automobile driven by a chauffeur?

As darkness fell the streets came alive with people. Ahead of him a black car pulled to the curb and a man carrying a cello case stepped out. The sight of a fellow musician lifted his spirits. He called out to the man and waved, but a puzzled expression creased the man's face and he turned away.

"Wait," Gregor said. "Please." But the man picked up his instrument and hurried down the street. Gregor ran after him. The cellist glanced over his shoulder then hurried around the corner. "Stop, I only want to ask you—." Gregor called after him, but it was too late. The man disappeared into a crowd of people leaving a hotel.

Out of breath, Gregor stopped long enough to catch sight of himself in a shop window. No wonder the man had run. The image that stared back at him was hatless, with dirty hair plastered against his head. He hadn't shaven in days and his clothes were filthy. His worn sock protruded through the hole in his muddy boot.

He walked slowly back toward the Town Square. Looking this terrible, he would never be able to find work. The smell of fresh bread wafted out of a bakery and his stomach growled so loud that he was sure the sausage vendor on the corner heard it.

Ahead, he saw a black and gold sign hanging over a big glass door. Café de la Paix. A man in a dark blue uniform with brass buttons stood at attention, holding open the door for guests as they arrived or left. It looked like a wonderful place to spend the evening if you had money.

He stopped and tried to get a glimpse of what was going on inside, but all he saw was a carpeted staircase leading up to the second floor. From somewhere above him the sound of music drifted out an open window. It was a tune he had played in his nightclub days.

The doorman glared at him then said something. Gregor moved past the restaurant doorway, but as he reached the corner, a big black automobile pulled up to the curb. The doorman moved from his post to open the car door. Two women in stylish short dresses stepped out followed by a man in a long coat and top hat. The gentleman began conversing with the doorman. Gregor saw his chance.

In an instant he slipped behind the doorman's back and was through the big glass door, taking the stairs two at a time. It was a stupid thing to do, but desperation had taken control of his mind.

On the second floor, a room was filled with small tables where people laughed as they drank coffee and wine. At the far end of the room on a stage, a string quartet entertained the crowd. From behind Gregor heard pounding footsteps that could only be the doorman.

"Psst, psst." Gregor tried to get the cellist's attention. "Please let me play." He spoke in Russian while pointing at the cello then himself.

"You want to play?" The man answered in perfect Russian. He smiled and beckoned Gregor to join him.

Gregor took the man's cello and joined the others. The cellist stepped back and lit a cigarette. Out of the corner of his eye, Gregor saw the doorman enter the room. The man said something in Polish to the cellist and pointed at him. The cellist replied. The doorman shrugged and walked away.

Gregor played three short pieces, two of which he knew well and a third, which he faked. Then the group took a break. The other three musicians greeted him then disappeared into the back room.

"You look like you swam across the border," the cellist said when Gregor handed him back his instrument.

"Last night, four of us. We were caught and the police tried to send us back to Volochisk. My friend Mischa and I escaped by rail. We just arrived in this wonderful city."

"I came across last January, from St. Petersburg," the man said. "Where are you from?"

"Moscow. I was first cello with the state orchestra." He extended his hand. "I am Gregor Piatigorsky."

"You studied at the Moscow Conservatory, didn't you?" The man shook his hand. "I remember your name. I attended one year but left for more lucrative endeavors. I am Petr Ondov."

The man handed Gregor a cigarette. Not an ordinary hand rolled one, but a manufactured cigarette, twice the size of the ones Gregor was used to. "French," the man said. "The only ones better come from America."

"Thank you. I'll save it and share it with my friend."

"Here, take two." He handed him another cigarette. "There's not much work here in L'vov for a cellist. You should go to Warsaw. It's a bigger city and there are plenty of groups you can audition with."

"Then why do you stay here?" Gregor said. He lit the cigarette from Petr's match and inhaled the bitter tobacco smoke. It had been so long since he had smoked a cigarette this strong that it made him dizzy.

"Ahhh," said Petr. "I have a very beautiful reason for staying in L'vov. Her name is Lilly."

"You are a lucky man indeed," Gregor said. He coughed. "How far—is it to Warsaw? Can—can we walk there?"

"Heavens no. Go by rail."

"We have no money."

Petr smiled. "None of us had any money when we arrived. Look at me now. I have a job, plenty to eat and I sleep in a warm bed at night with a beautiful woman. What more could a man want?"

"You are indeed fortunate."

Petr reached into his pocket and produced a handful of paper money. "Here, this should get you to Warsaw if you ride third class. You can pay me back once you find work."

"I hardly know what to say," Gregor said. He grabbed Petr's hand and shook it. "I will pay you as soon as I find work. Thank you so very much. My friend Mischa thanks you as well."

"Do you know the conductor Gregor Fitelberg?" Petr picked up his cello.

"Quite well," Gregor said. "I almost played "Don Quixote" for him in Moscow."

"Almost?"

"I read the part." Gregor shrugged. It would do no good to let this man know his true feelings about the conductor. "The rest of the orchestra gave me an ovation, but the authorities liked Kubatzky. He was older than I was."

"Now Fitelberg teaches in Warsaw." Petr returned to the stage. "You would do well to look him up."

As Gregor headed for the town square and the green fish fountain, he toyed with the other French cigarette. It was calling him with a promise of easing the hunger pains. Instead of lighting it, he slid the cigarette back in his coat pocket.

"Grisha!" Mischa waved from the other side of the square. "I found a room and we don't have to pay until morning." He handed Gregor the cello. "Let's go before someone else takes it. The landlady said it's ours if we hurry. We only have to share it with a few others. Best bargain in the city."

The landlady was right. The big attic room under a sloping roof was filled with a dozen men, old and young. Most sat or lay on bare mattresses scattered around the floor. In a corner of the room under the lowest part of the ceiling sat a sagging iron bed. The only illumination in the room came from the streetlight that shone through the dormer window.

"Be careful." Mischa stepped over a snoring man. "How do you like it?"

"I adore it," Gregor said laughing at the absurdity of it all. He slid his cello under the bed. "Where's the bathroom?"

"It's no place," said Mischa. He removed his pants, lifted the mattress and lay the garment out flat on the planks that supported the bed. "I saw a slop bucket in the corner near the window."

Mischa crawled across the dirty sheet and lay facing the wall. Gregor hung his coat on the headboard, but he was too tired to do more than remove his boots. When stretched out on his side of the bed, his feet hung over the end. There was one thin blanket to share and no pillows, but at least he had a place to rest his head.

He laid there listening to the grunts and snores of his roommates. This was his second night in a foreign country, his second night in a country other than Russia. Compared to last night in a Polish jail cell, this was a big improvement. Something tickled his neck and he scratched at it. Then he ran his fingers through his dirty hair and felt something fall on his cheek. The last tenant must have left breadcrumbs in the bed, Gregor thought as he drifted off to sleep.

"Yeeeowww." Mischa clawed at the bed covers.

Gregor sat bolt upright and hit his head on the low ceiling. "Owww," he cried as he fell back on the bed, rubbing the dent on his forehead.

"Get off me," Mischa crawled over Gregor's legs, tumbling onto the floor. Gregor tried to stand, but the two of them became entangled. His foot landed on something soft. The snoring tenant beside them on the floor groaned and rolled off his mattress.

"What are you doing?" Gregor struggled to free himself from both Mischa and their neighbor.

"They're all over me." Mischa slapped his neck and arms. "Bed bugs. They're crawling in my ears and up my nose."

"I thought it was crumbs on the sheets." Gregor tried to find a steady footing that was not part of someone's body.

"Shut up you two," a voice barked from the darkness. "I'm trying to sleep."

"I'm not staying in that bed." Mischa pulled his pants from under the mattress and gathered up the rest of his belongings. "It's crawling. It's alive." He continued to slap at bugs as he stepped over sleeping bodies. Gregor retrieved his boots and cello from beneath the bed then carefully picked his way across the room. In the darkness they managed to feel their way down the stairs and into the street.

It was still the middle of the night, but the streetlights showed a disheveled Mischa standing there in his underwear. "And I thought that place was such a bargain." He balanced on one foot, trying to put on his pants. "At least we didn't have to pay for it."

Gregor sat at the curb and pulled his boots on. "I think we should go to the railway station and take the next train to Warsaw."

"How are we going to do that? We have no money." He balanced on one foot as he pulled on his pants.

"I have some," Gregor said with a smile. He produced Petr's money.

"Where in the hell—," said Mischa, almost losing his balance.

"I met a Russian from St. Petersburg. He plays cello in a quartet at the "Café de la Paix." He pulled on his coat and picked up his instrument. "He gave me money and said we could find work in Warsaw."

"This is wonderful." Mischa finished dressing. "Fortune is with us. Let's buy two tickets and if there's any money left we can eat."

They headed toward the railway station. Gregor pulled the second French cigarette from his pocket. "Here." He offered it to Mischa. "This will fill your belly for a while."

Chapter Nineteen

Warsaw, Poland
July 1921

Dearest Nadja,
I now live in Warsaw. It's more beautiful than any city I have ever seen. The street lamps are electric and glow all night. The railcars are clean and the food, Nadja, you would not believe the food. I'm eating and growing fat like the bear. In Poland everyone smiles and no one cares if you're Red or White. If the Cheka ask about me, tell them I have disgraced the family and you never want to see me again. Or tell them I am dead, but tell Mama not to worry.
Mischa and I share a room above a shoe shop and I have a job. I play for the Warsaw Opera Summer Orchestra. It's only for two months and we must tour every week, but the pay is good. I must tell you the best news. I have met an American Jew named Mr. Held. He is rich and speaks no Russian, but he knows German and Mischa told him that I wanted to study in Germany. When Mr. Held comes back to Warsaw in September, I will play for him. If he finds me worthy he'll pay for my studies in Berlin with Hugo Becker. He does this for many students because the Polish government does not allow Jews to study at the Conservatory.
Nadja, do you know what this means? Never before have I studied with a teacher so important. Tell Leo to write to me. I'm sure if he came to Warsaw I could help him find a position. I miss you all. Please write to me. You can send a letter to Adamyzk: Shoe Maker, 23 Plyskyiack Street, Warsaw.
Love ,Grisha. P.S. Does Papa ever ask about me?

The Sunday after their last concert, Mischa had his twentieth birthday. Gregor and the rest of the string quartet joined Mischa to celebrate at Barbaraks. They drank toast after toast to their collective good fortunes, making speeches and promises that none of them could hope to keep.

"I'm going to spend the summer in Rome," said Alfred, an Armenian pianist. "My father took a job there with a textile firm. I will offer my services as a piano teacher." He grinned and stroked the thick black moustache that made him look older than nineteen. "And I will accept only female students younger than eighteen."

"Then I am afraid you'll be unemployed." Gregor laughed.

"Grisha." Alfred punched him in the shoulder. "You're the best cellist in all of Europe, but I hear that there is a better one in China." He paused in his praise to take a long swallow of beer.

"I'll go to China," Gregor said before downing his drink. "And find that cellist. We can play "Don Quixote," even if I have to play standing on my head."

"You'll be Gulliver among the Lilliputians," Tomas said. He was a violinist who desperately wanted to be a conductor but had never moved beyond third chair in the orchestra "And you'll have to learn to speak Chinese."

"Chinese will be easy. I've already learned Polish."

"Grisha, you speak Polish like a two year old. You'd better stay in Warsaw until you learn Chinese."

"Not Chinese. Now I must learn German," Gregor said. "Last night Mr. Held offered to send me to Berlin. He wants me to study with Hugo Becker."

"*Wunderbar.*" Tomas waved his beer glass in Gregor's direction. "You're one lucky Russian."

"What do you think?" Gregor turned to Mischa. "If I study with the greatest cellist in all of Europe, maybe someday I can take his job."

Mischa shook his head and pointed at Gregor. "I've heard Germans hate Russians and they certainly don't like Jews." He drained his glass then stood, leaning a bit too far left. "You have no papers or passport. You'd better learn to speak German and change your name to Luther Schmidt. Then you might stand a chance in Berlin." Grabbing an empty beer glass, Mischa pounded the table. "Listen to me. I also have good news."

The group grew quiet. Only Tomas's burping broke the silence.

"Let's hear your great announcement," Gregor said. "It can't be as good as my news."

"My brother wrote me from America." Mischa pulled an envelope from his pocket. "He has obtained a position for me as violinist in the Town Hall Symphony. Next week I leave for New York City."

There was a chorus of cheers and the clink of glasses in congratulations, all except Gregor's. "You're going to America? How is it possible? You've never auditioned. No one in America has heard you play."

"My brother is very persuasive." Mischa dropped into his chair and reached for the empty pitcher. "We need more beer."

"I wish I could go to America," Gregor said, forgetting all about Berlin.

"Mischa," Alfred said. "Can you speak English?"

"I don't need to speak English. My violin will speak for me." The waiter appeared and replaced the empty beer pitcher with a full one. "But my brother said that America wants no Bolsheviks and no Reds. All of you—you're all Reds. They would throw every one of you in jail. Then send you back to Russia. You'd be digging potatoes with your bare hands in Siberia."

"That's not possible," Gregor shook his head. "America welcomes everyone."

"Not true. My brother said that American police arrested ten thousand Bolsheviks in one night." He punctuated the number ten thousand with his finger. "They were all sent back to Russia in leaky boats."

"Mischa." Gregor still didn't believe him. "You were in the Red Army and so was I. And you have no passport. You're no better off than I am."

"My brother posted bond and guaranteed I would have work. He has American friends who helped him get me a visa."

The thrill of Berlin was gone. Gregor didn't want to believe Mischa's warnings about the American police. If it were true, he could never be able to go there. Without a passport, he was trapped. His employment certificate from the Warsaw Philharmonic was useless anywhere else.

By the time the party broke up, a cloud of gloom had settled over him.

Two weeks later autumn came to Warsaw and the summer tour ended. After more farewell drinks at Barbaraks, Alfred left for Rome and two violin players with legitimate Polish passports left for Paris. Mischa departed for America with a promise to keep in touch. Somehow they all knew he wouldn't. Gregor, the last one to leave, headed by rail for Berlin, uncertainty hanging over him like a dark cloud.

He carried his new cello, a suitcase full of clean clothes and a letter from Mr. Held to the agent in Berlin. Everything else would be handled, his benefactor assured him. Arrangements had been made for German language lessons and a room near the Hochschule Conservatory where Professor Hugo Becker taught cello. Of course Gregor would have to audition with the professor, but that wasn't what worried him.

As he sat in the second class seat and watched the Polish countryside roll by, he tried thinking happy thoughts. For the first time in his life he had the chance to study music without worrying where his next meal was coming from. He should feel grateful, excited, even happy. But he wasn't happy and he didn't know why.

"The situation has changed," Professor Becker said after four weeks of instruction.

Gregor waited patiently for Nicholas Ochi-Albi, the only student at the conservatory who spoke both languages, to translate the professor's words from German to Russian.

"*The professor says you hold your bow quite well.*"

"Tell Professor Becker that I'm ready to learn everything I can from him." Gregor smiled and tried to look polite.

"*You are no longer a pupil,*" said the professor. "*You are ready to play the greatest music in the world. You and I are equals.*"

"Tell him that I am honored by his confidence in me," Gregor said.

"*We have to be frank. I expect you to express your opinions freely and honestly,*" Professor Becker said, then picked up his own cello and settled into the chair. "*I will play the beginning of the Dvorak Concerto, just the beginning. After I have played the first few phrases you will do the same. Then we will discuss the merits of each.*"

Gregor nodded. "Tell him I am anxious to hear him play."

Becker began playing without even checking the cello's strings. As his bow hit the center of the strings, a gust of rosin flew off, spraying in all directions. Playing with wild abandon, Becker let the bow knock loudly against the sides of the instrument. At times he pressed so hard the hairs separated from the bow.

As he continued to play, Becker thumped loudly on the fingerboard creating his own discordant tempo. The spectacle was hideous. Ochi-Albi, a pianist, didn't appear to notice or care. He covered a yawn with the back of his hand.

When the professor reached the conclusion of the first phrase of the Dvorak Cello Concerto, he dropped his bow arm and exhaled deeply. He was actually sweating from the effort of that one brief performance. But as he spoke his voice sounded happy and a wide smile spread across his face.

"The professor wants to know how you liked his performance," said Ochi-Albi.

For a moment Gregor hesitated. Surely this was some sort of test. Should he lie or tell the truth? "Tell the professor it was terrible."

"What?" Ochi-Albi's eyebrows shot up. "You want me to say that?"

"Tell him what I said."

Ochi-Albi spoke and Gregor watched Becker's face change from smile to a frown. He looked down at his watch and with an angry wave of his hand shouted, "*Finis!*"

Gregor stood and picked up his cello. Bowing slightly he said, "*Gott sei Dank.*"

"*Heraus!*" Becker cried as Gregor and Ochi-Albi retreated from the room. In the hall, even with the door closed, they could still hear the professor screaming.

"What did he say?" Gregor asked, glad to be out of that little room.

"He said, '*Get out of here. You are an ignorant, conceited idiot'.*"
"But he told me to be honest with him."
"You didn't think he really meant it, did you?" Ochi-Albi shook his head as they hurried out of the school. "Why did you say *Gott sei Dank* when he told you the lesson was over?"
"I thought it was the polite thing to say."
"You are an ignorant Russian *mujik.*" Ochi-Albi shook his head. "It means 'Thank God!'"

* * *

Leipzig, Germany
December 1921

Professor Klengel was old. He smoked cigars and his beard was stained with tobacco juice. He was smoking a short wet cigar when Gregor entered the studio at the Leipzig Conservatory.
"You want to study cello?" Klengel said in German. The man's eyes twinkled, but the big cigar stuck in his mouth made it hard to tell if he was laughing. At least he didn't ask about Hugo Becker. Hopefully word of Gregor's disaster in Berlin hadn't spread to Leipzig.
"*Bitte,*" Gregor replied. "Please. Yes."
"Why?"
"I must learn." He paused as he formulated the next sentence. He didn't want to offend. "You are the best teacher in Germany."
"Hmmphh," Klengel muttered, then went to his piano and began playing the Haydn Cello Concerto. With such music, no interpreter was necessary. As the professor played, Gregor moved quickly to set up his instrument. After listening to a few bars, he started on the cello solo, playing as best he could from memory.
"*Sehr gut,*" Klengel said when they finished.
With that simple audition, Gregor was a student again. He moved into the Hartung boarding house where he joined a half dozen other Klengel students. Fortunately Frau Hartung was almost totally deaf, otherwise she could not have tolerated the cacophonous noise of late night and early morning practice.

* * *

Leipzig, Germany
January 1922

Lieber Herr Held,
   You must know by now that I am no longer studying in Berlin. I am a student at the Leipzig Conservatory. I study with the Great Master, Julius Klengel. My lessons go well and I work with the younger boys to assist the professor, so my costs are very little. I will write to you through your agent in Berlin and give you a full accounting of my expenses. I hope to see you the next time you are in Germany.
   Your dearest friend, Gregor Piatigorsky

Gregor looked over the letter to Mr. Held. Hans, a first year cello student, had helped him write it. His German was getting better, but for such a letter he wanted it to be perfect.

By living frugally, he was able to pay Frau Hartung for his room and board and even have his clothes cleaned regularly. For the first time since accepting Mr. Held's patronage, he felt relief. Lying in bed at night, he thought about how to make extra money. If he could convince even two or three of the new students to pay him for private lessons, he would have enough to support himself.

* * *

"Do you want to meet the Madame tonight?" Henri asked one Saturday morning after breakfast. At sixteen, Henri was the oldest of Gregor's level one students. Though the boy had only recently given up the violin for the cello, he was already quite good.

"Is she also a cellist?" Gregor said, intrigued by the thought of a woman playing the instrument.

Henri doubled over laughing as he slapped his hand on the table. Paul, who at fifteen looked more like twelve, snickered. "Madame and her girls certainly know how to make music. You should hear them sing at night."

"They belong to the opera?" Gregor asked, confused by their laughter. His comprehension of German had improved as a result of lessons with Professor Bruchen, but he still struggled to converse with the boys and he never understood their jokes.

"They have their own opera house called the Blue Monkey," said Alex Cores, the violin teacher. At nineteen he and Gregor were the youngest teachers in the conservatory. But Alex preferred the company of cellists to that of his own students, at least in the off hours. "It's a bordello, just a block from the river. Do you want to go?"

"It must be very expensive," Gregor said, wondering if they were teasing him.

"No, not for us. Besides, who has money anymore? No one wants Deutsche marks. Bring your instrument. You can let it work for you."

"This is our new friend," Alex said that evening when he introduced Gregor to Madame. "He's a doctor and a musician. He instructs us in all things important."

"Herr Doctor?" Madame's eyebrows went up. She was a small woman with a silky French accent. "You are indeed a big one. What do you have for me?"

"I have my cello. Would you like me to play?"

"Certainly, and if you play well enough to keep my customers satisfied while they are waiting, I will reward you."

She led Gregor to an overheated parlor where two elderly men sat stiffly on red brocade chairs. Both men glanced at him and one, with a florid face and sagging jowls, scowled. "I was here first. You will have to wait your turn."

"Don't worry, Herr Schmidt. This is Herr Doctor. He will keep you entertained until Trude is ready for you."

"Can you play a polka?" asked the second man. "None of these girls here can play a note. Not even on that piano."

"I can play dance music on my cello," Gregor said as he took a seat on the end of the piano bench.

"These are crazy times," muttered Madame. "Last Saturday we sat here playing cards. I thought all the men in town had been castrated. Today the girls don't have time for a meal."

As she spoke, the curtained doorway moved aside and a dark haired girl, dressed only in a loose fitting robe, looked around the room. She smiled when her eyes settled on Gregor.

"Who's next?" As she spoke Gregor saw the gleam of gold on two teeth.

"I am," said the man with the sagging face. The girl nodded and motioned for him to follow her down the hall.

"That's Trude," said Madame. "But you should see Halina." She laughed with a high squeaky voice. "She is firm, like a new apple, good to bite into. How are your teeth?"

"My teeth are fine," Gregor replied trying to keep a straight face.

She leaned over and whispered in his ear. "Play for the customers, talk to them, keep them distracted until the girls are ready. You will be well rewarded."

* * *

"I heard you playing your fiddle in the parlor," Halina said, her blue eyes twinkling as she smiled. She stood in the doorway of her room, her bare arm stretched up the wall. The floral smell of her perfume spilled into the hall, enticing him to come closer.

"It's not a fiddle," Gregor replied. "It's a cello."

"It's a very big fiddle," she said. "Just like you."

She took his much larger hand in her tiny one and drew him into the room. "Madame said you are the best musician of all the students who come here. I love hearing you play in the parlor." As she spoke she removed the pink silk robe that covered her lacy white undergarments.

"You don't have to do anything for me," Gregor said, trying to keep his eyes focused on her face. "I'm happy to be invited to supper at Madame's table. I have heard her cooking is excellent."

"But I want to thank you personally." She loosened a hairpin and golden curls tumbled over her bare shoulders. "I'm so tired of all those old men." She mimicked Madame's high-pitched voice. "Make them happy. Make them smile so they will come back and spend all their money."

"Money is not such a prized thing anymore," Gregor said as he jammed his useless hands in his pockets.

"Not with the inflation. No one wants Deutsche marks anymore. Now the men who bring us meat and soap are the ones we love."

"I have nothing so valuable," Gregor said, suddenly aware of how warm the room had become.

"But you make beautiful music. We have no phonograph. Madame traded it for schnapps and medicine for Judith." Halina motioned to her bed. "Sit here so I can see your face. You're so tall, I feel like I'm looking up at a tree."

Gregor sat and the bedsprings squeaked beneath him. Halina stood before him and slowly began unbuttoning his jacket. As her fingers worked, she moved closer, slipping her legs between his knees. When she finished with the buttons, she slid her hands behind his neck and a chill ran down his spine.

"Have you been with any of the other girls?" Her voice was soft and he was keenly aware of her chest rising and falling before his eyes.

"I have only been in Leipzig one month. I'm fortunate to be able to study with Professor Klengel."

"I'm glad you come to visit us. Some of the students who come here are so . . . young. It doesn't seem right." She began to rub his neck, her fingers massaging the muscles along the tops of his shoulders. He exhaled a long slow breath and swallowed hard.

"Are you from Poland?" he asked, wishing he knew what to do with his hands. "I can hear it in your voice."

"I grew up on a farm near Danzig," she said softly. "Do you know Danzig?"

"I performed there once. The audience was very . . ." He closed his eyes. "Very enthusiastic."

Her hand slid off his neck and she ran her fingertips down his arm until they reached his lap. "I can certainly understand why they loved you." She lifted his hands and placed them on her breasts. The thin fabric accentuated the warm softness beneath his fingers.

"It was a memorable experience," he said, but his voice sounded funny, like his tongue was too thick.

"I like your big cello," she said, as she moved both his hands from the roundness of her breasts, down to the flat of her belly then around her narrow waist. Beneath his palms he could feel the gentle rise and fall of her abdomen as she inhaled and exhaled.

"Do I remind you of your cello?" she said as she drew his hands over her hips and down the outside of her thighs. "Does touching me make you think of music?"

"Yes," he replied, his voice a whisper. "It does." Now his eyes were on the middle of her chest, but she was so close her breasts were out of focus. He pulled back a little and looked up at her.

"I want you to take your bow," she said softly as she slid her right hand between his legs. "And put it on my strings." Her left hand took his palm and placed it between her thighs. "I'd like to see just how good a cellist you really are."

Chapter Twenty

Berlin, Germany
November 1923

"Guten Tag Herr Held." Gregor reached out to shake Mr. Held's hand.

Instead of offering his hand, the little man threw his arms out and tried to embrace Gregor like a long-lost son. But he was too short and his hands only reached Gregor's shoulder. For a moment the nervousness Gregor had felt for days eased.

"It is good to see you again," Mr. Held said as he stepped back. "You have grown even taller than I remember and your German is fluent."

"I have you to thank for that. My lessons were excellent and I practice speaking every day."

Mr. Held led Gregor toward the elegant dining room of the Hotel Adlow. "I have just returned from New York. I want to hear about your studies with Herr Becker."

Gregor hesitated. Why hadn't Mr. Held's agent made a full report? It was clear his benefactor had no knowledge of his disaster with the professor. "Did you get the letter I sent?" Gregor said as the waiter seated them at a linen-covered table by the window. "I gave it to your agent and asked him to forward it to you."

"Oh, I have received regular monthly reports from my agent."

As he settled into his chair and unfolded his napkin, the happy expression on Mr. Held's face changed to a slight frown. "But I am curious. You don't drink alcohol do you?"

"Sometimes a glass of beer. Why?"

"I know the monetary situation here in Germany has been terrible," said Mr. Held as he shook his head. "The inflation is so extreme. That's why I always send American dollars. I sometimes feel guilty that I live so well when others are starving." The man paused. "Still, I never imagined that the life of a student would be so very costly."

"But it isn't. Since I moved to Leipzig, I've spent very little of your money. Prices are much cheaper there and Professor Klengel allows me to teach." It was apparent that Mr. Held had no idea what he had been doing for the past year. "I hope you understand. Professor Becker and I . . ." He paused not wanting to offend his benefactor. "The professor's teaching style and mine were in opposition. I left the Hochschule a year ago. Since then I've been studying with Professor Julius Klengel in Leipzig. He is an excellent instructor. I only left last week when I learned you were unable to assist me any longer."

"I don't understand. I have sent you a great deal of money for books and music. The tuition, your rent and food?" Mr. Held frowned. "How did you spend so much? I know the economy is bad, but my agent has always been very precise with his reports."

Gregor pulled back and his heart quickened. The man had just accused him of theft. "Here," Gregor said as he pulled the notebook from his pocket. "I've kept an account of everything I spent in Leipzig."

"But I've sent you much more than that." Mr. Held pushed the notebook aside. "I did not expect this kind of thing from you. I've transferred over a thousand American dollars to you in the past year. That is more support than any other student I sponsor."

A thousand dollars! Even without calculating Gregor knew it was an enormous sum. Now this American, a man who had treated him like a son, was accusing him of lying, stealing and cheating, even insinuating he was a drunk.

Gregor felt the heat of embarrassment flood his face. Slapping the account book on the table, he stood and felt his body shake. "I have never taken a penny that was not accounted for." His voice was too loud and patrons nearby turned to stare.

Totally mortified, he still couldn't control his rage. "I am not some poor wretch in need of your pity or charity. Your agent is a liar and a cheat."

He reached into his pocket and pulled out all the Deutsche marks he had and threw them on the table. "This is all the money I have." He snatched up the account book and shook it at Mr. Held. "And this is what I owe you. As soon as I am able, you will receive every penny of it back."

"Please, sit down. There is no need to be—."

"No! I don't need your help or anyone else's."

"Sir, is there a problem?" The waiter said. Several other waiters and the maitre d' gathered, ready to assist. Gregor saved them all the trouble and stormed out.

* * *

Gregor sat cross-legged in his room on the lumpy bed, his back against the wall. He should apologize to Mr. Held, but he couldn't even bring himself to write the word "sorry" on the blank paper. Was he wrong to feel anger at such a grievous accusation? The mistake all along had been taking charity, depending on someone else. He would never, ever do that again.

Rolling off the bed, he pulled on his boots and grabbed his coat. He needed to get out of this room. The small room with stale air and near darkness had suddenly grown too close.

"*Guten Tag, Frau Kulasch,*" he said as he descended the stairs and headed for the front door. The stout middle-aged woman carried a bowl, adorned with pink and blue cats, and filled to the rim with cream.

"*Guten Abend.*" She followed him into the narrow cobbled street. "Next week's rent is due tomorrow." She smiled as if she were bidding him good day.

"Of course. I'm going to the bank to withdraw funds."

"You'd better hurry. The bank closes in twenty minutes." Gregor detected something unsettling in her cheerful tone.

"Come, come, my Little Angel." She set the dish on the sidewalk. A fluffy orange cat appeared from under the hedge and meandered toward the food. "Good Little Angel." She knelt and stroked the animal.

Gregor hurried away toward Charlottenburg Strasse, anxious to put distance between himself and the landlady. When he reached the plaza he slowed. There was no reason to hurry to the bank. His account had been empty for a week. The rent he had paid in advance was the last of his money. Instead of heading downtown, he crossed the street and turned toward the park. The damp, autumn air made him shiver and he buttoned his coat.

The grassy area of the park surrounded a beautiful lake. Gray clouds tinged with the pink of the setting sun reflected in the still waters before him. He stood at the edge of the lake, not knowing what to do. He couldn't return to Leipzig and study with Professor Klengel without Mr. Held's financial support. Anyway, he didn't have enough money to buy the railway ticket to get there. By now the name Gregor Piatigorsky must be known all over Berlin. Professor Hugo Becker would have made sure of that.

* * *

Standing by the lake, Gregor remembered every word of that horrible encounter a year ago. There was certainly no future for him here in Berlin. In fact there was nothing for him anywhere. But he couldn't afford to leave and he couldn't afford to stay.

Gregor walked around the lake, moving slowly, afraid the path would come to an end too soon. Ahead, several people walked dogs. It was peaceful and quiet, even the dogs were well-mannered and orderly. Thoroughly German, he thought, so unlike the wild pack dogs of Ekaterinoslav.

As he walked, he thought about what it would feel like to be German, to know exactly where you belonged in the world. If he were a Berliner, he would have a warm house or flat, a cheery fire and a good meal on the table. There would be someone waiting there for him, happy to see him, anxious to hear how his day had been. He remembered Tuesday nights with Mr. and Mrs. Held and how secure he had felt, almost like he was home. One stupid outburst and he had destroyed it all.

He remembered Shutkin, the shop crowded with junk, bowls of potato soup and day-old bread. And so long ago, the wooden house at the foot of the little hill in Ekaterinoslav, Mama cooking borscht for supper and Nadja playing the piano. And even earlier than that, the sound of Papa reading aloud from Slatesky's History of the World.

The memory of it all brought tears to his eyes, but he angrily wiped them away. That was all gone now. He had no home, no family, no place to go. For a moment he considered going back to Ekaterinoslav and showing up at the door of the house where he had been born. Would they be happy to see him? Would Papa even let him in?

Perhaps he should take his cello and try to find work at a nightclub. But the thought of playing gypsy tunes and dance music was just too humiliating. He was twenty-one years old now. How could he go back to the place he had been when he was just eight? Images of Gelko and the North Star Klub played across his mind and he shuddered. He had sworn he would never again play silly music for pennies.

The darkness had long since fallen when he returned to Frau Kulasch's house. Her husband was home from his job at the municipal court and Gregor heard them chatting in the kitchen. As he tiptoed through the hallway and upstairs, the smell of cabbage and bratwurst cooking made his belly ache with desire. In his room, he undressed and crawled under the blankets. If he slept he wouldn't be hungry. If he slept, he wouldn't have to think.

"Do you have the rent money?" It was the voice of Frau Kulasch calling through the door. Gregor rolled over on the lumpy mattress at the sound of her voice.

"You will have it today," he called back. "I swear to you."

It was a stupid promise, one he could not fulfill. As he washed, shaved and dressed, he tried to think of some way to come up with the rent money.

Standing before the mirror, he parted his wet hair on the side then combed the rest straight back. His hair had grown much too long and already hung below his collar, but the cost of a barber was out of reach.

The face that returned his stare was gaunt. He needed to eat and that meant more money for food. But food was not what he wanted at that moment. What he needed was a cigarette to ease the craving for tobacco that gnawed at his insides.

On his way out the front door he passed Frau Kulasch. She held the obese orange cat in her chubby arms. "Here you are, Little Angel."

Placing the bowl on the sidewalk, she filled it with thin strips of pink meat, maybe chicken. The cat ate better than half the citizens of Berlin, Gregor thought. Certainly better than he did.

"I'm on my way to the bank," he offered. "It was closed when I got there yesterday."

Frau Kulasch gave him a look that said, "You had better get me the money".

As he walked toward Kurfursterdamm Strasse, Gregor felt the gold cross and Papa's watch in his jacket pocket. If he sold them he might have enough money to cover the rent for one week, maybe even two.

He passed a bakery just opening for business. The smell of warm bread filled him with desire. A sausage vendor set up his cart at the curb and the matron of a café swept the sidewalk in front of her shop. Why was it everything he saw looked and smelled of food?

On a side street near the Kaiser's Kirche he saw what he was looking for, a small shop tucked between a tobacconist and a bookstore. The place was hardly wider than the window and door that faced the street. The dusty gold lettering on the window said ROSENS, and the display of items in the window looked forlorn and unloved. A brass clock, a silver teapot and matching tray, a trumpet and a collection of pocket watches all seemed to beg for someone to want them, to love them, to take them home.

Gregor walked past the door, glancing into the shop to see if there was any sign of life. A small light glowed inside. At the end of the block, he stopped and took the watch from his pocket. It was silent, its hands marked 6:35. He wouldn't get much for it if it did run. Carefully, he wound it the way Papa had taught him. Above him, the clock tower on the church read 9:10. He set the black hands then closed the case and rubbed the silver cover against the sleeve of his jacket until it shone.

The watch went in his right pocket. What remained was the little gold cross and chain. He held it in the palm of his hand and remembered the Holy Father, his shoes full of pebbles. Why did he remember only that? He didn't bother polishing the cross but dropped it into his left pocket, turned and headed back to the pawnshop.

"You received this for your Bar Mitzvah—Pavel?" The elderly man with a yarmulke held open the watch as he peered at Gregor over his tiny glasses.

"Uhhh, no. I have not been Bar Mitzvahed. Pavel is my father."

"And you want to sell your father's watch?" The man's white eyebrows went up. "What kind of son are you?"

A terrible, stubborn, worthless son, he thought as he fought off the urge to grab the watch and run from the shop. Instead, he lied. "My father has a much better watch now. He doesn't mind that I sell his old one."

"There's not much demand for watches with Hebrew inscriptions." The old man shook his head. "No one cares anymore." He held the watch to his ear and nodded. "I might be able to remove the letters. I'll give you four thousand marks."

"Give me six thousand."

"Hmmm, for your father I will give you five thousand." The man counted out five one thousand mark notes and fanned them temptingly across the glass counter. It was enough for almost two weeks' rent if he didn't eat. One week's if he decided not to starve to death. Gregor took the money.

"And this. What will you give me for this?" He slid the cross across the counter. "It's real gold. Worth a great deal."

The man pulled his hand back as if he didn't want to touch it. "Where did you get this?"

"From my—." He couldn't say it was from his father.

"Did you steal it from a Christian?"

"No. I found it on the street."

"No good Jew would pick up a cross, even if he saw it lying in the gutter. It is bad luck."

"I did. If you won't buy it, I'll take it to someone else."

The man wiped his hands on his dirty smock then picked up the cross. "This is not gold."

"Of course it's gold."

"Russian gold. You see here on the back, where it lay against the skin." He turned the cross over and pointed to a dull spot. "It is only gold plated and a poor job at that. The finish has already worn off."

"You won't buy it?"

"I have no customers for such a poorly made thing." He pushed it back across the counter.

* * *

Back at Frau Kulasch's, he paid for the week's lodging, then locked the door to his room and feasted on the supply of hardboiled eggs, cheese and bread he had bought with the remainder of the money. Undressing, he hung his black wool suit in the empty closet and put on an old shirt and worn pants. With food in his belly the dark cloud that hung over him lifted.

Again he sat cross-legged on the bed, his back against the wall. With the stub of a pencil, he drafted an apology to Mr. Held. He wrote slowly, his command of spoken German far exceeding his knowledge of the written language.

Liebe Herr Held,
I am sorry for my anger. I will not be so much angry at you but at the man you paid money to give me. He is a thief and has not spoken true words. All of this is wrong and I am always thankful to you for help I receive in my music. I play wonderful music in Leipzig and will play here in Berlin some day, soon maybe, all because you help me. I will not forget. Please look for me in the concert hall and come to hear me play.
Always your friend, Gregor Piatigorsky

When he finished the note, he slid it in an envelope, but didn't address it. He would leave the letter at the Hotel Adlow and ask the manager to give it to Mr. Held the next time he came to Berlin.

On a second sheet of paper he addressed Professor Klengel in Leipzig.

Liebe Herr Professor,
I have found a good place in Berlin and will not return to Leipzig this year. Berlin is a wonderful city and I know I can work here with my cello. All that I learned in Leipzig I will not forget. Now I wish you to give me a letter to show, so that I can be hired at the orchestra. I will speak well of your conservatoire to any students I meet. You may reach to me at 45 Klienwirth, Charlottenburg, Berlin.
Respectfully, your student, Gregor Piatigorsky

He had just enough money left to buy a stamp. How long would it take Klengel to write him back? Without some kind of reference in hand, applying for an orchestra position would be difficult.

Sliding to the edge of the bed, he laid his cello across his knees. With eyes closed and head turned, he plucked each string, listening carefully to the sound. If it were out of tune, he turned the peg a little. Not enough. The A string refused to comply. He gripped the wooden peg in his fist and turned too hard. There was a loud snap and the A string broke near the top of the fingerboard. Cursing, he loosened the peg and managed to tie a tiny knot in the end of the string then reattach it inside the scroll. He wasn't about to use his last set of good strings just to practice.

For the remainder of the afternoon he played. With eyes closed, he ran through Dvorak's Cello Concerto. It was the piece that had won him first chair in the Bolshoi orchestra, and the same piece that had cost him his career in Berlin. Then he moved on to the Schumann, a tougher piece but one that took every bit of energy and attention.

Practice, eat and sleep. That was his life. When he couldn't stand being in his room one more minute, he walked, never wasting his pfennings on the streetcar. *Why pay to ride when feet are free?*

On the east side of Berlin the River Spree ran dark and sluggish through the industrial side of the city. A highway of commerce, it curved past gray warehouses and smoky steel factories. From the Oster Strasse Bridge, Gregor stood above the oily water, watching the factory wastes spill from rusty pipes, adding an orange stain to the river. Beneath him a boot floated by upside down, swirling and bobbing as if caught in a manic dance.

For a moment he closed his eyes and remembered the Dnieper sparkling in the sun. He remembered the way water splashed over the rocks above the quays. He remembered the high banks above the shoreline where Papa once took him and Leo to fish, and he remembered the great squiggling eels they scooped up in a net. How long had it been since he and Papa had been happy? Ten, no twelve years had passed since they had played in the Dnieper. Did Papa ever remember those times? Did Leo? Did any of them even remember him?

In the bottom of his pocket his fingers found the cross, the one that was not gold and was worth nothing. For a moment he held it in his hand, the sight of it so ordinary, the feel so familiar. Leaning against the bent railing, he let the cross dangle at the end of the chain over the churning water. For a moment it swung back and forth in a graceful arc. Then his fingers parted and the cross fell. It hit the water without so much as a splash and was gone.

He was no better than the little cross. An unemployed Russian Jew without papers, no work permit and no money. He could fall into the River Spree and without so much as a splash, he would disappear. No one would know and no one would care. He would never even be missed.

That night he fell into bed, exhausted and hungry. If he slept, he saved money. He could always eat in the morning. But dreams of water, bright and dark, haunted him. He saw the bloated face of the dead man he had pulled from the Volga, his white skin spongy and soft. The dream woke him and he couldn't return to sleep. Instead, he pulled one of the three Russian books he still had left from under his bed. Not Gorky, not when life seemed hopeless. Instead, he read Alexander Blok's poems about a beautiful woman who filled men with passion and desire. Passion and desire? He had even less chance of finding a woman like that than he did of finding food.

A week later he was back at the pawnshop. In one arm he carried his good black wool suit and in the other his three books.

"You are a very sad young man," Rosen said, after examining the goods. "You will be sadder still when I tell you I can only give you two thousand marks for that suit and another four hundred for these Russian books."

"They are worth twice that." Gregor started to pull them back.

"Who do you think wants to read the love poems of Alexander Blok or the gloomy tales of Maxim Gorky? Most of my customers want modern books in German, or traditional books in Yiddish."

"But I need more money than that. My rent's gone up to three thousand marks a week."

"All right, I'll give you two hundred marks more, but that's only because you're a Jew."

"Thank you," Gregor said. He took the bills but knew it wasn't enough.

"Lucky for you the government just issued new currency." The old man hung the suit on a hook with other pawned garments. "What will you offer me next week, your soul?"

"If you would pay me for it," Gregor said. "I would gladly sell you my soul."

"You shouldn't say that." The man frowned and shook his head. "Haven't you read Goethe?"

"No, who's that?"

"Some say he was the greatest German writer that ever lived. His book, *Faust,* is the story of someone like you. A man who trades his soul to the devil for wealth and fame."

"I don't believe in the devil." Gregor counted the money. "Do you?"

"I'm a Jew. We have the Christians to contend with. Why should we make up an imaginary devil when we live with real ones every day?"

Back in Charlottenburg, Gregor handed over two thousand and four hundred marks to Frau Kulasch. "Here's the rent money I promised you. My word is good."

"A week's rent is three thousand marks." She pocketed the money then held her hand out for more.

"That is all I have."

"Then I'll turn off the electricity and the heat to your room," she said. "This will only cover your rent until Thursday."

"I can live without heat."

The room grew cold and he slept in his clothes. In the morning he nibbled at the hard cheese and bread he had stockpiled. Then he went to the Tiergarten, but couldn't afford the entrance fee to the zoological park. In the afternoon he practiced his cello, again tying a knot at the end of the D string which broke halfway through a Beethoven sonata. By evening he had played all the printed music he owned or could remember.

On Tuesday he ate the last of the cheese and bread, practiced some more then walked in the park until dark.

Wednesday he woke to no food. Outside, it was still dark but he heard the sound of the milk wagon on the cobblestone street, followed by the clink of glass bottles being left at the front door. For a moment the urge to run downstairs and steal one of those bottles was overwhelming. But the sound of Frau Kulasch's footsteps in the hall reached his ears and he knew his opportunity was gone. By noon he felt faint and tried to fill his empty belly by drinking water. It didn't help. One day left. One day before the rent was due.

On Thursday morning he woke with such pain in his belly, he thought he would surely die. Curled on his side, he watched as early morning light filled the room. He tried counting the leaf pattern on the wallpaper. When he got to fifty-five, the cramps subsided. Outside his window, he heard Frau Kulasch's shuffling footsteps.

"Come here, my Little Angel," she cooed. "Look at what I have for your breakfast."

Gregor climbed onto a chair and looked down at the courtyard from the little side window. The landlady stooped and placed a plate on the ground then poured milk from a bottle into a small bowl.

"Come, Little Angel," she called again then waited with thick hands on wide hips. The cat was nowhere in sight. "Very well." She turned toward the door. "You shall have no company for breakfast."

By the time the landlady's footsteps had receded to the kitchen, Gregor had his pants and socks on. Shoeless, he tiptoed down the staircase. No sounds came from the kitchen. Little Angel was out of luck this day. It took Gregor only seconds to scoop up the cat food with one hand while grabbing the bowl of milk with the other. Some spilled down his chin but he managed to swallow most of it. The milk tasted like glue, but brought instant relief to his belly.

Back in his room he examined his plunder. Little Angel's breakfast consisted of strips of raw chicken. He tried eating a piece but couldn't chew the cold, slimy strips. From the recesses of his suitcase he found a box of matches. The box was still half full, since he had been too poor to buy cigarettes for weeks.

Crouched on the floor, he lit match after match, holding the meat above each one until the flames nearly burned his fingers. When the last match had burned down, he examined his repast. The meat was scorched but being warm, it went down easier.

That day he managed to avoid Frau Kulasch and her demand for the rent money, but there was no getting away with it again. It was time to take his meager belongings and leave. The only thing left to do was to find a café or nightclub where he might play before he became too weak from hunger to even work. This would be his last night in a bed with a roof over his head. Tomorrow it would be the streets again.

He closed his eyes and allowed himself to drift away. To Warsaw where he sat at a table filled with sausage, potatoes and warm bread. To Mama's kitchen, borscht simmering on the stove and finally Shutkin's cottage where the smell of sweet tea and cabbage filled the air.

"Wake up!" Lights blinded him and he sat straight up in bed, unable to breathe, his heart pounding. Two policemen in dark uniforms stood over him. One carried a menacing-looking wooden stick, the other held a pistol.

"You are under arrest." The man with the gun pulled the blankets down. "Put on your shoes. Come with us."

Gregor stumbled to his feet, then knelt and slid his hand under the bed searching for his shoes. "I have not committed a crime," he cried. "Why are you doing this?"

"You will be informed of the charges at the police station."

They escorted him down the stairs, one policeman in front, the other behind. With each step the officer behind propelled him forward with the stick in the back. When they reached the front door, Gregor saw the moonlike faces of Herr and Frau Kulasch staring at him through a half-opened kitchen door.

At the police station his pockets were emptied. They held very little. His wallet contained only his expired student card and the addresses of friends in Russia and Poland. All attempts to learn what crime he was charged with went unanswered.

Without explanation, he was shoved into a narrow cell that smelled of urine and mildew. The cramped space contained two iron cots covered with damp blankets. He sank down on one and leaned back against the cold wall. Above him a single light bulb glared down from the ceiling. Someone had wisely enclosed the bulb in a wire basket. No doubt to prevent prisoners as despondent as he was from ending their misery with a broken shard of glass.

Why? He kept asking himself. Was all this about not paying the rent? Did Mr. Held think he was a thief? Had that lying agent falsified some incredible charge? Who could he turn to for help? There was no one. Suddenly his life of bread and cheese at the Kulaschs' seemed luxurious compared to the future he now faced.

During the night two angry drunks joined him in the cell. One man screamed obscenities through the barred door while the other urinated in the corner. The night dragged on and Gregor tried his best to stay away from the newcomers. Toward dawn both of his cellmates passed out on the floor.

When feeble daylight shone through the small high window, Gregor stepped over the prostrate bodies and peered through the barred door. All he saw was an empty corridor. After an interminable time, a guard appeared carrying a bowl.

"Wake up, you drunken oafs." The man hit the bars with a leather strap. The drunks stirred slowly from their sleep, coughing and moaning as they sat up.

Gregor stepped back from the door and the guard slid the bowl of greasy potatoes through the opening near the floor. It was followed by a bucket of water with a dipper. Never before had Gregor been so happy to eat repulsive food with his hands. Though he hardly tasted it, the feeling of pure pleasure it brought to his stomach lifted his spirits.

"You pig," said the younger of the two prisoners. "You can't have it all." He was shorter than Gregor but much heavier. In the confines of the small cell, it seemed unwise to argue. Gregor let the man grab the bowl. The drunk retreated to the cot where he began eating with gusto. The other prisoner had no interest in the food but climbed on the other cot and lay there moaning.

Some immeasurable time later the guard returned and opened the door. Gregor was led from the cell and escorted to a small room. The proceeding was in the hands of a gray-haired officer who sat behind a high bench. Gregor's expired student card lay before him.

"This card is no good." He tapped his finger on the document. "Where is your passport?"

"I have none."

"Then how did you gain admittance to our country?" The commander shook his head and his jowls jiggled. "Are you here illegally?"

"I was studying music in Leipzig with Professor Klengel. Then I came to Berlin to find work."

"A student card does not allow you to work. You will have to go back to your own country. We have too many unemployed Germans looking for work. We don't need foreigners taking jobs."

"I have no country to go back to."

"Then you can't be here."

"But I am here."

"I can see that." Turning to the policeman who had carried out the arrest, the man said. "I can't deport him if he has no passport. No country will take him back. Why in heaven did you bring him in?"

"Herr Kulasch is a clerk in the court." The policeman produced Gregor's signed contract and placed it in front of the officer. "He said this Russian signed and now won't pay his rent."

"A contract? You waste my time on a Russian who doesn't pay?" The man's frustration showed on his plump face. "Is this true?" He pointed his finger at Gregor. "You made a contract but now won't pay?"

"I have no money. I will collect my things and leave the house."

"The contract calls for you to pay a ten thousand mark penalty or forfeit your goods."

"Ten thousand marks? It might as well be a million. I have no goods to forfeit."

"He had a large fiddle," said the policeman. "It may be worth that much."

"No!" Gregor cried. "You can't take my cello."

"Herr Kulasch can hold it until you pay the money owed in this contract." The officer folded the contract and handed it back to the policeman. "Take him to the house and let him get his other belongings. The fiddle and anything else of value stays until the rent is paid. If he doesn't pay, the landlord can sell his goods in one month."

Chapter Twenty-one

Herr and Frau Kulasch watched from the hall as Gregor made a bundle by wrapping his extra shirt around his underwear, socks and toiletries.

"Remember," said the policeman. He pointed to the cello and suitcase Gregor had left behind. "You must hold his property for thirty days. If he comes back and pays what he owes, then you must return these things to him."

"Not much chance of that," said Frau Kulasch.

With nowhere to go, Gregor took his little bundle and headed for the park. Any chance of earning a few marks playing in a café was now gone. He carried the bundle under his arm and despite the fine drizzle, didn't hurry. He passed the lake, stopping on the other side at a kiosk that in summer sold ice cream. It was closed and faded pictures of treats flapped in the wind.

At the edge of the park he saw a brightly lit theater marquee. Drawn to it, he stared at the poster of a beautiful dark-skinned woman crouching on her knees in an animal like pose. She had smooth skin and almond eyes. She was face to face with a leopard. *Josephine Baker. Direct from New York and Paris*, read the caption. If only he could see this exotic woman from America. But with tickets starting at five thousand marks a seat, all he could do was dream about her.

On the next block the soft lights of the public library beckoned him. At least it was warm and dry inside. By the look of some of his fellow patrons, he was not the only person seeking shelter among the books. He joined three other men at a big table and tried reading the daily newspaper. The headline announced yet another devaluation of the Deutsche mark and the government's attempts to stabilize the economy.

The rest of the news, at least the part he could read, seemed mostly unpleasant. Next he tried a copy of *Faust* that the librarian located for him, but soon realized that with his limited command of written German, the newspaper was easier to read.

"It is closing time," the librarian said.

Gregor and his fellow readers obediently filed out. Back outside in the afternoon drizzle, Gregor walked without purpose. Near the Brandenburg Gate he saw people lining up for an automobile exhibition. It was free, so he joined the queue and was again glad to get out of the rain. All the automobiles on display were either American or French. The ones from America were big and sleek with names like Ford, Oldsmobile and Buick. They had long gleaming engines and leather upholstery. Beside them the French cars looked small and pitiful.

By the time darkness fell he found himself in the Tiergarten at the entrance to the zoo. Exhausted, he sank onto a park bench and stared down at his hands. Of what use were they without his cello? Maybe he could become a carpenter like Pradid, or a bookseller like Grandfather Piatigorsky? No. He had no talent except making music. A cellist was all he ever wanted to be. Not just an ordinary musician, but the best cellist a human could become. Now, that was impossible.

Folding his bundle of clothes into a pillow, he stretched out on the hard bench. Sleep beckoned him and he dreamed of a banquet table filled with every imaginable kind of food. Roast duck and fried fish, pierogi, thick goulash with warm bread drenched in butter, and huge round circles of cheese. Yet every time he reached for it, the food evaporated, leaving him hungrier than before.

Daylight came abruptly and the sound of the street traffic woke him. He stretched and looked up at the bare limbs of the tree that arced over the bench. Sitting up, he ran his hands over his face and rubbed the grit from his eyes. His jacket and pants were rain soaked and his fingers and feet were numb from the cold. He had to find something to eat and soon. Picking up his bundle, he headed for the public restroom near the Tiergarten gate.

When he emerged from the lavatory a policeman approached him. Unlike the officers who had arrested him, this man was young and had a smile on his face.

"I saw you sleeping on that bench."

"Is it forbidden?" Gregor asked, worried that he might be arrested again.

"More likely it is unwise." The policeman shook his head. He had the smooth face of an adolescent, too young to shave. "Last night a man stabbed a woman over there." He pointed past the bench where Gregor had slept. "Some bastards can't decide whether to make love to a women or kill her."

"I had no idea. I heard nothing."

"You are either very lucky, very foolish or both. Why do you sleep in the park? You don't look like a drunk."

"I'm a musician. This was my first night here."

"I'm going for coffee. Come join me and tell me your hard-luck story."

It turned out Gregor never had a chance to tell the young policeman anything. The officer did all the talking. His name was Gerhard Heinz, he was twenty-five years old, single, and had come to Berlin from Hamburg after the war. Gregor sensed the man was lonely, but since the policeman was willing to provide coffee and rolls, Gregor was willing to be his audience.

"At night this part of the park is the workplace for a half dozen whores," said Heinz. "The bench you slept on is one of their places of business. If I don't bother them they can make quite a bit of money there under the trees. During the day they sometimes use the bushes to hide what they do, but after dark they don't mind working in the open."

Gregor listened, all the while devouring bread, butter and coffee.

"Some of the women charge the perverts extra to watch their lovemaking from behind the hedgerow. But of course, money is so inflated that the girls prefer to be paid with cigarettes, schnapps or soap. Last night I chased them all away, but they'll be back tonight."

Gregor nodded, acknowledging every word the man said, as he slid another roll into his pocket. "Thanks for the warning. I'll find another place to sleep tonight."

"I was like you two years ago," Heinz said. They left the café and walked back to the Tiergarten. "I came to Berlin from Mecklenburg after the war. I slept without a roof over my head and begged for food. I wanted to study law, but patrolling the Tiergarten is as close as I'll ever get. Now I have a room in the police barracks and free food from the shopkeepers who like my presence. But there is never any money to take a girl to the cinema or a concert."

"If I ever get my cello back and find employment, I'll see that you get tickets to my first concert."

"What became of your instrument?"

"My landlady kept it because I didn't pay the rent. Now she wants to charge me even more money to get it back."

"Would you call your cello the tools of your trade?"

"Yes, I suppose so. Without my cello I can't work."

"Then it must be returned to you," said the policeman with a grin on his face and a gleam in his eye. "It is the law. A man's tools may not be seized in payment for a debt. How can you be expected to pay what you owe if you cannot work?"

"But what can I do? The police officer told my landlord she could keep the cello and my suitcase for thirty days. If I don't pay her, she will sell it."

"I know a man, a Russian like you. He can speak for you."

"Why would he help me?"

"Because," said Heinz. "He owes me a few favors."

When they reached the little police shelter box near the Tiergarten gate, Heinz stepped inside and a moment later returned with a blanket and a slip of paper.

"Here, take this. One of the whores left it in the bushes. You might as well use it if you have to sleep outside again." He scribbled a name and address on the slip of paper. "Go to the Brandenburg Gate then follow the alley between the bakery and the shoe store. At the end is a small hotel. Ask for Tols. He's the man you want to talk to."

* * *

"You don't need to tell me about your landlord," said Tols in a cheerful voice. "Bastards! I know that kind, but they will soon meet their match. I am the crusader for impoverished tenants." He was a short, well-dressed Russian aristocrat, and he readily shared his French cigarettes with Gregor.

"I only want my cello and my suitcase back," said Gregor. "I don't want a fight."

"When I'm done, your former landlady will pay you to take your goods away."

"What will you say to her?" Gregor's curiosity was piqued.

"Leave that to me. I'll need a half an hour, maybe a little more."

Gregor waited outside the bakery around the corner from the Kulaschs' house. He didn't want the landlady to see him, but he couldn't sit still either. Pacing back and forth, he wondered how Tols was doing and whether he really could persuade Frau Kulasch to give up the cello.

"Success," Tols announced when he appeared an hour later. He carried the cello in its case and the satchel that held the rest of Gregor's possessions. "Frau Kulasch was difficult. I much prefer dealing with men, but when I described the unsanitary conditions she would face in the penitentiary she weakened." He smiled broadly as he handed over the instrument. "When I told her that her cat would be taken and fed to the police dogs, she capitulated."

"I don't know how I can ever thank you," Gregor said as he took his instrument and opened the case, checking for damage. "I am so grateful. How can I repay you?"

"I have fulfilled one of my several debts to our friend Heinz." Tols grinned and patted his coat pocket. "I also collected the one thousand mark fine Frau Kulasch was willing to pay to cover the court appearance I saved her from having to make."

With the cello under his arm and the remainder of his belongings in his bag, Gregor felt liberated. He walked from the Charlottenburg district toward the center of Berlin, done forever with the Kulasch family and the Tiergarten. The rain, which had almost stopped during the morning, began again, harder than before. This time the wind picked up, bending trees and chilling him to the bone.

At the central railroad station he ducked inside and dropped exhausted into an empty seat in the waiting room.

On the shiny black tile floor a lone cigarette butt lay like an offering. For a moment he imagined the feel of smoke in his lungs and nicotine coursing through his veins. He saw his hand reach for it just as a woman in a fur coat walked in front of him. The look on her face was one of pure disgust.

Pulling back, he retrieved the abandoned newspaper from the adjacent seat and pretended to read. How far had he fallen to lust after a discarded cigarette?

All around him people moved back and forth, boarding and exiting the trains. They had places to go and things to do. He had nowhere to go and nothing to do. His feet throbbed and his legs ached. As he slumped on the bench, he broke pieces off the roll he had saved from breakfast, grateful to have it. He ate it slowly, making the meal last.

Across the room he noticed the walls were covered with posters. One was of Josephine Baker, again staring down the leopard. The next was a poster for the Berlin Philharmonic showing Conductor Wilhelm Furtwangler with his arms outstretched, ready to give the downbeat. If only he could listen to music, Gregor thought, he would forget his troubles, if only for a moment.

He sat up straight. Why not go to the symphony? With his cello in hand, he might be able to sneak in through the musicians' entrance. Excited at the thought, he left the station and headed back into the rain, hurrying down a narrow side street toward Symphony Hall.

Getting through the back stage door was easy. His cello was as good as a ticket. A sign directed him up a flight of stairs toward the musician's quarters. With an air of casualness he climbed the stairs, unnoticed by anyone. At the top he passed a dressing room where a man balanced on one foot as he pulled on his dress trousers.

The next room contained storage spaces for instruments and music stands. Slipping his cello and suitcase onto an empty shelf, he paused by the door to check himself in the mirror. He needed a shave and his jacket was wrinkled and damp. He used his fingers to comb down his hair, then tried to brush his clothes smooth.

From far below, he heard the muted sound of the orchestra beginning its performance. Standing alone in the corridor, he listened. They were playing a Haydn symphony. Hearing it was like food to a man dying of hunger. He wanted to take it in, absorb it and feel every note.

He waited until the piece ended, then, as the audience applauded, he opened the side door and slipped into the great hall. The obstructed seat behind a column was empty and he took it. "Beethoven's Eighth" symphony was just beginning and despite the faster than usual tempo, every note was food for his soul. He applauded wildly when the piece ended, then along with the rest of the audience, demanded an encore.

Gregor was the last to leave the hall. As the concertgoers slowly filed out, he waited unseen in the alcove of the stairwell. He stayed until he was sure the last member of the orchestra had come down from upstairs, then ran upstairs to retrieve his cello. It was after nine o'clock when he stepped out the side door. An icy blast of air hit his face and he shivered.

Where should he go? What should he do? If he slept outside again, he might freeze to death. Looking down at his hands, he remembered the pain of frostbite that had nearly cost him his fingers.

Stepping back inside, Gregor pulled the door shut. He had to stay in the concert hall, at least for the night. But chances were a guard would come by and lock this door. Not wanting to get caught, he headed back down the hall toward the lobby. Somewhere far off he heard the sound of voices, but they gradually faded away. Standing by the coatroom, he waited. But for what? He didn't want to leave but he couldn't stand there in the lobby all night.

Then someone, somewhere, turned off the lights. Everything around him was instantly black. He closed his eyes, hoping they would grow accustomed to the sudden darkness. He counted to sixty. Slowly. When he opened his eyes it made no difference.

For an eternity he stood there listening. The only sound was his pounding heart. Panic crept up inside him. The muscles in his legs tensed, ready to run. Where? If he cried for help, who would hear him? Who would care?

Shrugging his cello case over his shoulder, he picked up his suitcase and began groping along the wall. Every few steps he paused, trying to see something in the inky blackness. Nothing. His fingers touched doorknobs that would not open, then the rough texture of wallpaper and spaces where the wall was recessed.

Finally, he came to an opening and cautiously stepped through it. His knee hit something hard and he gasped. Dropping the suitcase, his hands explored the obstacle until he realized it was the back of a seat. He felt another, then another. This was the main floor of the concert hall. As he worked his way down the aisle, his eyes began to notice faint shapes.

From somewhere an unknown source of light gave just enough illumination to see the opening of a private box. His hand found the knob and the door opened inward. As his eyes grew accustomed to the near darkness, he recognized the window that looked out on the concert stage. He explored the room with his hands and discovered a long upholstered couch and several chairs. A room at the Hotel Adlow could hardly have been more comfortable.

His fear vanished as he made himself at home. First he opened his suitcase and shook out his blanket. Everything he wore was wet and this was a chance to dry his clothes. Stripping to the skin, he hung each damp item over the backs of the chairs.

With that done, he wrapped himself in the blanket and stretched out on the couch. The velvet cushions were so soft, he felt like he was lying on a cloud, certainly a huge improvement over the park bench in the Tiergarten.

Perhaps this private box could become his new residence. As he lay there staring into the darkness, he thought about home. But where was home? Was it Moscow or Ekaterinoslav? If he went back to Russia he would be sent to a labor camp in Siberia. Maybe the Party would just shoot him.

Was his home in Warsaw? No, he didn't know anyone there anymore. Most of his friends had left Poland for America, Paris or Rome. Maybe he could go to America. If he found Mischa he could ask him for help, but he had no idea how to contact him. Would the Americans even let him into their country? Probably not without a legal passport. In the end there was never going to be a place he could call home.

As thoughts whirled through his mind, he tossed and turned. He was afraid to sleep. If he slept the night would pass too quickly. Morning would come and he wasn't ready to face tomorrow.

This place, this concert hall, was the closest thing he had to a home. He was overcome by an urge to play. Rolling off the couch, he crawled around the box until his hand touched his cello. In the dark he couldn't see it, but his fingers traced the smooth graceful lines of the instrument. Its very presence made him feel less alone. Standing, he pulled the blanket off the couch and made his way out of the box. The air of the great hall was cool on his naked skin. Even when he used the blanket as a cape, he still shivered.

Above the stage a faint glow from a skylight gave Gregor enough light to see the conductor's platform, but he couldn't find the staircase to get onto the stage. Dropping the blanket, he carefully laid his cello on the edge of the stage, then used the strength of his arms to pull himself up. Grabbing the closest chair, he pulled it to the front of the orchestra. Before him the ghosts of empty chairs made up his audience.

In the darkness of the hall the sound of his cello was eerie, yet strangely human, like the voice of something alive. The music flowed from his instrument and the audience received it all. Time seemed to stop and he played as if morning would never come. Every piece he had ever learned poured out of him. Concertos, sonatas, dance tunes, even something that sounded like jazz. What he was missing in an orchestra, he made up in his head. He played to the limits of his endurance, until his muscles ached and his fingers couldn't move.

Exhausted but no longer cold, he stood naked before his audience of chairs and took a bow. In his heart he heard the thunderous applause. Bravo! Bravo! the silent voices cried.

Stretching out his arms, he stood and raised the cello over his head, stretching to his full height. This is what he really was. Not a criminal. No longer a stateless person without papers. Never again a pauper stealing food. No matter what country or what nation he found himself in, this was where he belonged. Even in an empty concert hall, he knew he had found a home.

Gregor woke to the sound of a Schumann symphony. It had to be midmorning and the rehearsal below was a gift. He lay there warm and dry on his velvet couch. Furtwangler chided and goaded the Berlin Philharmonic Orchestra into perfection. When the conductor finally gave the musicians a break, the orchestra members headed for the lobby.

He stood naked in the corner of his little room. The thick velvet drapes shielded him from view as he dressed in dry but somewhat stiff clothes. When the hallway was clear, he slipped out and visited the men's room. With comb, toothbrush and razor, he attended to his appearance. All he needed now was breakfast and life would be good again.

Below him, he heard the orchestra returning to the stage. He tried to remain inconspicuous, hiding in the alcove under the stairs. Finally, the lobby was empty and he slipped out the side door. The morning air was cool and damp, but the sun was starting to break through the clouds. Gregor's stomach reminded him it wanted to be fed. Halfway down the front steps a voice called out.

"Hello. Wait. You there."

Gregor pretended he hadn't heard it and continued walking.

"Piatigorsky? Is that you?"

That stopped him. He turned to see a man running toward him.

"Aren't you Gregor Piatigorsky?" the man said, his voice nervous, his body seeming to vibrate.

"Yes?"

"*Wunderbar!*" He threw his hands in the air. "Alex Cores said you were here in Berlin."

"Alex? Here?" Gregor pulled back a little. "Who are you?"

"I'm Paul Bose, flutist for the Philharmonic." He fluttered his fingers to the right as if he were playing an imaginary instrument. "I saw Alex last night at the Ruscho Café. He said Professor Klengel told him you were here. I've been asking everyone. Where do you live?"

"I . . . uhh, I just returned today from holiday in the Alps," Gregor lied, too embarrassed to admit his poverty. "I haven't found a room yet."

"No wonder I couldn't find you." Bose looked at his watch. "I only have a few minutes before Furtwangler calls us back. Do you know the music of Arnold Schoenberg?"

"I've heard "Verklarte Nacht," Gregor said wondering what this nervous little man could possibly want with him.

"Do you know his piece *"Pierrot Lunaire?"*

"I've heard of it. It's modern."

"Very. And it's never been performed in Berlin. A group of us will present it in three weeks. We started with a cellist but he quit. He didn't want twenty rehearsals without being paid."

"Maybe he needed to eat." Gregor rested the cello on the toe of his shoe. His stomach growled at the mere thought of food. He hoped Bose couldn't hear it.

"Food is no problem. Artur Schnabel is our pianist and we meet at his apartment. He serves tea and cake every afternoon. Will you join us?"

"I would love to play, but will I be paid?"

"If Schnabel can sell enough tickets to fill the great hall at the music academy for two nights, we'll all be paid."

"Then I'd be happy to join you. Do you know where I can find Alex?"

"Good." Bose found a crumpled piece of paper in his pocket and scribbled on it. "He has a room on the other side of the Spree. Here, I think this is it, and Schnabel's address too."

"Thank you." Gregor slid the paper into his pocket.

"Be there at two o'clock tomorrow afternoon. *Puncto*. We have a rehearsal. *Gott im himmel*, will they be surprised when you show up." Bose turned and headed back toward the concert hall, skipping as he went.

Chapter Twenty-two

Gregor stood before the forbidding door, hesitated then pulled the scrap of paper from his pocket. Bose's handwriting was almost illegible. It looked like 27 Hauptmann Strasse, but it could be 17. In the darkness he wasn't sure. He looked again at the heavy iron knocker. This was his last chance. Bose had said Alex Cores rented a room on Hauptmann Strasse. If this wasn't the place, he would spend another night on the park bench. Making a silent wish, he knocked.

"*Guten Abend?*" The slender young man who answered the door looked older than the poor violin student in Leipzig he remembered. Now Cores wore a modern dark gray suit, black tie and his hair was freshly combed with oil. "Is that you, Grisha?"

"Yes. I'm so glad I found the right address."

"Come in, come in." He stepped aside and Gregor squeezed past him into the narrow hall.

"Thank you. I heard you were in Berlin." Gregor set his suitcase down and they shook hands.

"I thought you were still in Leipzig." Cores surveyed Gregor and he lifted one eyebrow. "You look like you've slept in the street. Where are you staying?"

"I don't have a room tonight." He hoped he didn't sound too pathetic. "But if you have a lady, I mean . . ." He held out his open hands. "I understand it would be an imposition if I stayed."

"No, no." Alex pushed open the door at the end of the hall. "Of course you can stay here."

The room was tiny, a single bed, a chest and a faded upholstered chair beneath a curtained window that looked onto the alley.

"I can sleep in the chair." Gregor leaned the cello case in the corner. "I'll not inconvenience you."

"Grisha, you worry too much. We can share the bed, back to back."

"Alex." Gregor sank into the chair. "I'm so grateful." For a moment he closed his eyes and let his body wilt into the cushions.

"Where have you been?" Cores said as he slipped off his suit coat and hung it in the closet. "What have you been doing?"

"I've had trouble finding work, but today I met Paul Bose. Do you know him?"

"Of course. He was at the Café Ruscho just last night." Cores sat at the foot of the bed.

"He's playing Schoenberg with Artur Schnabel. I'm going to join them tomorrow."

"Lucky you. I have five private students here in the city, but I hope to have two more by the end of the month. They're all foreigners and pay with real currency, not marks."

Gregor pushed himself upright in the chair, but as he moved to stand the room began to spin. He grabbed the chair for support and dropped back into the seat.

"What's wrong? You don't look so good." Cores retrieved a cup from beneath the small sink and filled it with water. "Here, drink. Are you ill?"

"I haven't eaten since yesterday."

"Why didn't you say so." Cores moved to the window, opened it and returned with a metal bread tin. "Here, I have a salami. Would you like some?"

"Like it?" Gregor's hands trembled as he took the meat, a good thick German sausage. "I can't thank you enough." He didn't bother removing the casing but attacked the food like a wolf on its prey. It was pure heaven, salty, greasy and delicious. As he ate, Cores smoked.

"I have some cheese too if you'd like."

"Cheese?" Gregor looked up, hardly believing his good fortune. "I'd love some. If you don't mind."

Cores returned with the slab of white cheese, almost fresh with only a little blue mold on the rind. Gregor ate this a little more slowly, the salami already bringing relief to his emptiness.

"Do you have a lady friend here in the city?" Cores stretched out on the bed and propped his head on his hand. "I haven't had much luck. All the women want foreign men, at least men with hard currency. Even the whores want American dollars or British pounds. None of them will work for Deutsche marks."

"I think I should first find a room before I try entertaining a lady for the evening."

"Even a room is not enough. This place is a good boarding house and the landlady serves tea and rolls every morning, but it's not *Sturmfrei*."

"Not what?"

"You can't bring women home. The landlady is very religious."

"I have no money so I doubt a lady would want to spend the evening with me." The thought of a woman, any woman wanting to share his bed was too absurd. "Perhaps when I finish playing with Schnabel my situation will improve."

"You jackass! You kicked me out of bed." Cores struggled off the floor, disheveled, the blanket hanging from his shoulders. It was dawn in the gray room.

Gregor swung his bare legs over the edge of the bed and sat up. "I told you I should have slept in the chair."

"I have never had such a wretched night in my life." Cores staggered to the sink and turned on the water. "You snore and you kick." He cupped his hands and drank loudly from the tap. "And you took all the blankets for yourself."

"I'm sorry," was all Gregor could say, stepping into his pants, "I'll take the floor tonight."

"Oh no, you won't." Cores plunged his face into the bowl full of water, making bubbling sounds as he exhaled. When he surfaced he sucked in a deep breath, then shook his wet head like a dog. "I think the landlady has another room. I'll convince her to let you have it. Maybe you can pay the rent in full after the concert."

"Wonderful," Gregor said as he dug through his suitcase looking for a razor and soap. "I'll be happy to take any space she has."

* * *

"Bravo!" Bose greeted him at the door of Schnabel's apartment house. "You're on time."

Gregor followed him upstairs to a large sunny room. A grand piano dominated the space with two violinists and a violist arranged in a semicircle to the right.

"I am so sick of the orchestra," said Bose. "My little flute gets lost among all those brass and timpani. Chamber music, that's where a real artist can shine." He pulled another chair into the circle then whispered, "Here is Schnabel, a very courageous man." Then louder, he pointed to Gregor with an exaggerated flourish. "Herr Schnabel, I found you a cellist."

"I'm thrilled you've joined us." The older man settled his wide bottom on the piano bench. He was a box of a man, thick-bodied with a square head centered on the middle of wide shoulders. "But we have no part for cello." He motioned Gregor to his side and handed him the printed music. "Can you play from the score?" Without waiting for an answer, he continued. "Of course you can. Have a seat. We're discussing the personality of a sixteenth note. It is utterly impersonal. No emotion whatsoever. Don't you agree?"

Gregor didn't even try to respond to such a bizarre question. He was saved by the violist who began offering his interpretation of the character traits of the notes. Instead, he took a seat and paged through the music. Schoenberg's "Pierrot Lunaire" was modern, but looking over the score Gregor realized just how unusual it was. There was a speaking part that called for a narrator whose voice had to follow a particular pitch. Who would do it? A singer? The conductor? The pianist? The thought of Schnabel playing two roles, one facing the piano and one facing the audience made him smile.

"What do you think is so funny, cellist?" Schnabel demanded. The room fell silent and Gregor felt all eyes measuring him.

"I just thought of . . . nothing. I'm sorry." He certainly didn't want to offend Schnabel and get thrown back on the street. His stomach already ached and he didn't want to face another day without food.

"We will continue," Schnabel said.

As they played, Gregor pushed hunger from his mind. He studied every part of the composition. Contemporary music was radically different from the classical harmonic repertoire he was used to. He had to sight read every unpredictable note. The melody, if it existed at all, was elusive, but the rest of the group seemed satisfied with his efforts, especially Schnabel.

"We will rest," Schnabel said. "It's almost four o'clock. Tea is waiting for us in the next room."

Gregor was out of his seat before the others and heading for the door. But instead of recessing, the other musicians gathered in little groups, arguing about the meaning of modern music in general and "Pierrot Lunaire" in particular. This evolved into a discourse on the politics of communism and modernism.

"The Bolsheviks promise equality for all," he said. "No one ever goes hungry or homeless in the new Soviet State. Modern music is the future. It will feed the soul of the masses. The old repertoire will fade away."

Gregor suppressed a smile at hearing such rot. The right to starve to death equally was what the Bolshviks promised. Music would never fill the void in anyone's belly.

As the others debated, he edged his way to the back of the room. No one but him seemed interested in eating. Slipping around the corner into the parlor, he stared in awe at the feast laid out before him. Breads, meats and cheeses were all neatly arranged on trays. At the end of the table lay an assortment of cakes and pastries, all decorated with fruit. From a large samovar came the heavenly aroma of coffee, beside it sat a steaming pot of tea. It was like leaving a baby lamb in the care of a wolf.

He worked fast, starting with the meat and cheese. His hands trembled as he scooped up as much as he could hold. The hunger, which he had kept in check for so long, was now unleashed. Taste meant nothing. Only the feeling of pure pleasure the food brought to his stomach mattered.

In minutes all the real food was gone and he turned to the desserts. Though sweets had never appealed to him, this time he didn't care. Only when everything had been devoured and his stomach ached with fullness did he realize what he had done. Mortified, he quickly brushed all vestiges of food from his face and clothes. Then, as discreetly as he had exited, he returned to the rehearsal room. His absence seemed to have gone unnoticed.

"We are riding the crest of a new era in music," Schnabel said. "Our performance will mark the beginning of a new dawn."

Everyone listened intently and some nodded. "But for now," Schnabel said with a wave of his hand. "Let us adjourn to the next room. The refreshments await us."

*　*　*

Gregor's new room turned out to be the maid's quarters on the third floor under the slope of the roof. It was so low he had to be careful not to hit his head on the ceiling. But the window gave him a great view of the city and the sheets were clean. Each morning the landlady served breakfast, one roll and a cup of tea for each guest. By four o'clock Gregor's stomach was growling again. Fortunately, Schnabel's afternoon tea provided enough food to get him through until the next day. When hardboiled eggs were served, he always pocketed one for his supper.

With a warm bed, food in his belly and music to occupy his day, Gregor felt like a great weight had been lifted. In the morning Bose and the other orchestra musicians rehearsed with the Philharmonic. Gregor either stayed in his room and practiced, or wandered the streets in search of a library or bookstore. Several times a week the Philharmonic gave evening performances and Gregor's new friends left the back door ajar so he could attend.

The three weeks of afternoon rehearsals at Schnabel's passed quickly and the first performance of "Pierrot Lunaire" received an enthusiastic reception among the young music lovers of Berlin. But the older, more traditional attendees were upset and some of them even protested in the lobby of the Singing Academy on the first night. The objectors' cries and boos were heard all the way to the stage.

Maria, the singer-speaker Schnabel had hired to do the narrative parts, was so confused by the ruckus, she seemed to lose her voice. Schnabel tried to distract the audience from the noise in the lobby by ordering his group to play a circus polka. It was loud enough to draw the young crowd back inside. With order restored, "Pierrot Lunaire" was presented without interruption.

After the confusion of opening night, the second performance went better. The newspaper reviews praised Schnabel's effort in presenting such a controversial work. Best of all Gregor collected enough money to pay his rent.

But there was no money left over and the delicious afternoon teas at Schnabel's ended. Gregor needed to find work and if he were lucky his employer would pay him in salami and cheese. The fifty thousand Deutsche marks he received for his performance were nearly worthless.

* * *

"Grisha, can you play jazz?" violinist Boris Kroyt asked. Like most of Schnabel's avant-garde musicians, Kroyt was a displaced Russian and now desperate for work. Gregor, Kroyt and several others gathered on Monday morning in Der Sturm Club. The owner, a retired pianist, had agreed to let them practice in the empty café before opening at noon.

"I can play a little, but only by ear," Gregor said as he tuned the cello.

"I have a job at the Ruscho Café on Sunday and at the Der Tariffa mid-week." Kroyt tucked his violin under his chin and ran through a series of flourishes. "Most of the customers are foreigners and all they want is American jazz."

"How do you play it? I've never seen a score."

"That's because Americans can't read or write music." Kroyt laughed. "But we could use a good cellist. Want to join us?"

"Does the job pay? I have to work for money. I can't afford not to eat."

"The owner of Der Tariffa has a farm near Potsdam. His son brings in fresh food every week. If we're good, he said he'd pay us in cheese and eggs. Your landlady will be happy to get her rent in something she can use instead of worthless currency."

"For cheese and eggs I'd work anywhere," Gregor said. "With currency like that farmers must live like kings while the bankers are paupers."

"And well they should be," said Kroyt. "I hear that whores only work for food. Lucky is the farmer who comes to town with a truckload of cabbage."

"I'll be there," said Gregor. "Can I start tonight?"

The food Gregor received in payment for his nightly work tended to be more along the lines of pastries and cake, and none too fresh. He saved the best of the baked goods for his landlady and bartered the rest for an occasional pierogi or wedge of cheese.

It was the nouveau riche foreigners, the ones with plenty of hard currency, who frequented the nightclubs. They were often loud and demanding. As the night wore on they became so drunk they fell on the floor when they tried to dance. Most seemed less interested in music than they did in the beer and the prostitutes.

Mostly, Gregor had to play tangos, impromptu jazz and popular dance tunes. It embarrassed him to play such stuff. It was worse when other musicians and well-known writers came to the club. The evening that the renowned cellist

Emanuel Feuermann came in, Gregor wanted to hide in the lavatory. Still, life was better than it had been during his tenure in the Tiergarten, sleeping on a park bench. He reminded himself of that when the snow fell in January.

"Grisha?" said Paul Bose as he and Gregor sat across from one another at the Café Ruscho eating stale bread dipped in tea. "Maestro Furtwangler said I should bring you by after rehearsal tomorrow."

Gregor almost choked on his drink. "Fur—Furtwangler? You're joking."

"I'm not. I mentioned you to him and he heard you last week at the café. I think it was the night you and Kroyt played that piece from "Carmen."

"Oh, no." Gregor dropped his head into his hands. "It was a disaster."

"It must not have been too bad." Bose spooned more sugar into his tea. "The concert season's already started and all the regular jobs are taken, but he still wants to hear you. Will you come?"

"Of . . . of course." The thought of playing for Maestro Wilhelm Furtwangler made Gregor's heart pound.

"Be here at two o'clock," Bose said. "We should be done with rehearsal then."

* * *

Gregor practiced all morning. Sitting alone in his cramped attic room, he played with his eyes closed, one phrase at a time, over and over again. Weighing the bow in his hand, letting it touch the string, drawing it gently, creating just a breath of sound. But there wasn't enough time to prepare, not enough time to perfect the sound. At exactly one thirty, he packed the cello in the case. No matter how much he practiced, he knew it wasn't enough.

"Come up here." Bose waved to him from the stage as the rest of the orchestra left for the afternoon. "Let me introduce you."

Furtwangler stepped down from his platform. "I am glad to finally meet you," the conductor said. Gregor shook the man's hand and noticed how bony the conductor's long fingers were.

"Grisha was first cello in the Bolshoi," Bose said. "Then he played with the Warsaw Symphony. He's even studied with Hugo Becker and Julius Klengel."

Gregor winced at the mention of Becker's name, but Bose didn't seem to notice. Furtwangler listened, nodding without changing expression on his narrow face.

As Bose went on explaining how the two of them had performed together with Artur Schnabel, Gregor's eyes wandered across the concert hall to the private box he had once called home. It was hard to believe he had slept there, lay there naked while Furtwangler and the Berlin Philharmonic rehearsed. His eyes fell to the chair nearest him, probably the same chair he sat on when he played like a madman that night. What would Furtwangler think if he knew?

"What's the matter with him?" It was Furtwangler's voice and the tone of it snapped Gregor out of his daydream.

"What would you like me to play?" he asked, hoping it was the right thing to say.

"You choose," said the conductor. "I'll listen from down there." He turned and walked off the stage then reappeared in the audience where he sat halfway back in the empty center section.

Gregor took the chair closest to the front of the stage and faced the concert hall. His last performance had been in this very same hall. Now, with an audience of one, he couldn't afford to make a mistake. First he played the solo from Schumann's "Cello Concerto," then a movement from Dvorak's "Cello Concerto." Finally, he played the opening from Strauss's "Don Quixote".

Furtwangler remained motionless and Gregor continued, wondering how long the man would let him go on. He played "Kol Nidrei", then Saint-Saens, "Concerto No 1." After weeks of playing jazz and polkas, the music was cleansing.

Finally he played part of Brahms "Double Concerto." When the last note drifted across the great empty room, he lifted the bow from the strings and stood. For the first time, he made eye contact with Furtwangler. The man rubbed his long hand across his chin then slowly rose and walked to the door at the foot of the hall. Gregor waited. He heard footsteps behind him but didn't move as the conductor came up behind him.

When Furtwangler's bony hand came down on his shoulder, Gregor turned to face him. Up close he saw how old the conductor really was, probably forty. He had a long neck like a bird, but his sharp light blue eyes caught everything.

"Would you sign a one-year contract and play with us?" The man's face was expressionless. "I am willing to offer you the first cello seat."

"It—It would be an honor to play for you," Gregor managed to say.

"Good," Furtwangler said and a slight smile lifted his face. "But it won't be just for me that you will play." As he led Gregor off the stage, the conductor's hand still rested on his shoulder. "I want you to meet my assistant. He'll take care of all necessary paperwork and explain the rehearsal schedule."

The contract was written in German and Gregor didn't even try to read it. The sheer joy of having a job made him reluctant to ask questions. The manager was an intense beady-eyed man who appeared to be wearing a wig.

"You will need a proper three button black suit, white shirt and…" The man's right eyebrow went up as he looked down at Gregor's shoes. "And a new pair of shoes. Black socks only." He opened a steel box and extracted a handful of new Deutsche marks. "While you are at it, get a haircut, nothing below midear, preferably higher."

"Yes, sir." Gregor took the money but didn't have the nerve to count it. "Thank you, sir."

"At twenty-one Sudenstrasse you will find a photographer. Tell him we will need at least six photographs as soon as possible. New posters must be made ready for the next concert series. In the meantime, I will have to make do with adding your name at the end of the program."

The man hardly seemed to take a breath before continuing. "Here is the rehearsal and performance schedule." The manager handed him two sheets of paper. "This covers only the next two weeks' worth of performances. I will have the remainder of the month's schedule by Friday."

One look at the list and Gregor wondered how he would have time to eat or sleep. There were two rehearsals daily, one at eight in the morning, another at one in the afternoon. Five days a week there were evening performances. Furtwangler conducted some of them, but people he had never heard of conducted other performances such as the Volks Konzerts at the Singing Academy.

"Your first program will be on Friday night."

"I can't play these," Gregor said pointing to the first two pieces. "I've never even seen the scores, much less heard them played. Can't I substitute something else?"

"No." The man shook his head and Gregor was sure his wig would fall off at any moment. "The programs are already printed and the newspaper reviews have been written."

"How can they be written? We haven't even performed yet."

"That's the way it's done. The reporters have heard the repertoire before."

"But I don't have a copy of the cello score."

"You can play from the violin score. Our last cellist did and the audience loved it."

Gregor was speechless. The memory of an entire month of rehearsals for a single performance now seemed positively extravagant. He studied the schedule and decided that the best chance of playing well would be Friday night when they performed the Dvorak "Cello Concerto." At least he knew that one.

"I'll need two tickets for Friday's performance," he said hoping Officer Heinz liked Dvorak.

"We don't give out free tickets, not even to orchestra members."

"Then take the cost from my salary," Gregor said and smiled. "I know you want me to show up for rehearsal on time."

"You wouldn't dare be late on your first day."

"I will tell Furtwangler that the schedule was too confusing. My German is very poor."

"Very well," grumbled the manager "You'll have your two tickets, but get used to our schedule. I'm sure in time you'll learn to love it."

The man was wrong. Gregor never got used to cramming thirty hours of work into twenty-four. But he did learn to keep his mouth shut and show up on time.

He was now a contract musician, but not a tenured member of the orchestra. Older players tolerated him but kept their distance. They were accustomed to young performers dropping in for a single season then moving on.

When changes in the schedule were necessary, the permanent members of the orchestra met privately with the conductor and the manager. Gregor and the other contract performers were shut out of these meetings. After all, the orchestra was not a democracy, Furtwangler informed him when he complained. It was a dictatorship and Gregor had better get used to it.

Chapter Twenty-three

Berlin, Germany
1927

"Grisha? That's what people call you, isn't it?" Alexander Merovitch said.

"My friends do," Gregor replied, still wary about the man sitting across from him at the street-side table in Café Kurfursterdamm.

"I am confident that we will become close friends." The man smiled but his eyes never wavered. "You can call me Sacha. Tell me. What kind of papers do you have?"

"Papers?" Gregor set his beer glass on the table and stared at the aristocratic Russian. "I don't know what you mean."

"Identity papers. Do you have a passport?"

"No." The word passport always made him nervous. "I don't have a passport, but I have a German labor card. That's all I need."

"That's true if all you want to do is stay here in Berlin. If you want to travel as a soloist, if you want to achieve your full potential, you will need a passport. Especially if you travel off the continent."

"Why would I travel outside of Europe?"

"Because you're talented enough to do so," Merovitch said. His eyes burned with intensity in his otherwise ordinary face. Gregor was reminded of the portrait of Rasputin he had once seen.

"What makes you think I could be that successful?"

"Because I know these things. I recognize in you a talent missing in many others."

He was certainly persuasive, Gregor thought as he studied the man across the table. "The Germans won't give me a passport. I have tried twice. They always turn me down. Even Furtwangler cannot convince them to make me a citizen."

"Then I recommend you make application for a Nansen passport."

"A what?"

"A Nansen. It's a document for stateless persons like you. The League of Nations has authorized it for travel. In theory all signatory nations have agreed to accept it for entry."

"Even the Americans?" Gregor felt a moment of hope.

"No. The United States never ratified the Treaty of Versailles, so they don't consider the Nansen authentic. However, that doesn't mean you can't perform in America. It just takes a little more effort to obtain the correct entry documents."

"And you can do that?"

"I have taken it upon myself to guide the careers of several great musicians, none of whom have passports. Two years ago Vladimir Horowitz debuted at Carnegie Hall in New York. Nathan Milstein has traveled throughout South America without a passport. Perhaps you've heard of them?"

"Of course. I know Nathanchik and I played with Volodya in Hamburg, but how can I..."

"I know," said Merovitch. "I know." With a wave of his hand he appeared to dismiss Gregor's concerns. "Let me explain. Horowitz and Milstein have entrusted their careers to me. Unconditionally. As their manager, my obligation is to protect their unique gifts from the pitfalls of the artistic profession. Do you know what those pitfalls are?"

"I've worked with agents before." Gregor folded his arms and leaned back in his chair. "The first one took all the concert receipts and left me in Riga with nothing but a third-class railway ticket home."

"That was very unfortunate, but I'm not surprised."

"The second agent wanted to book me for a vaudeville tour with a circus. I declined. Then he convinced me that I could make easy money performing with a dance band. Also a big mistake. I later found my name displayed on billboards selling obscene recordings."

Merovitch's face cracked a smile. "You see what I mean about pitfalls."

"And working with you would be different?" Gregor studied the man's face looking for some evidence of his honesty.

"Come to my apartment tomorrow. You can ask Horowitz yourself."

* * *

Vladimir Horowitz looked fragile. "I hate Germany." He spoke in Russian, as he paced back and forth across the parlor floor, his shiny leather shoes sliding a bit each time he turned around. "In Kiev my professor told us stories about the Germans." He rubbed his knuckles. "I swore I would never come back. Now I'm supposed to perform in Berlin? I would much rather be in Paris."

"Volodya," Gregor said, trying to reassure the frail young man. "Berlin is a good city and the people here love music. You will have no trouble finding an audience."

"But do they love Jews?" Horowitz held out his open hands, as if he could grasp reassurance with his long white fingers. "I have heard Hebrews are not welcome in Berlin."

"Those ideas come from a disgruntled minority," Merovitch said as he poured three glasses of Scotch. "Don't pay any attention to German politicians and their hot air. I want to talk about your future."

"What about Milstein?" Gregor settled into a comfortable chair with his glass of Scotch.

"Nathanchik wired me yesterday from Spain. He's met a young lady in Madrid and she's teaching him Spanish. He will no doubt be fluent by the time he returns."

"Will you be joining us?" Horowitz asked as he sat at the piano and ran his fingers lightly over the keys. The mere act of touching the piano seemed to soothe him.

"I can't," replied Gregor as he accepted the Scotch. "I have a contract with the Berlin Philharmonic."

"The season is almost over and there is no reason for you to renew a contract for another year," said Merovitch. The man certainly seemed to have an answer for everything, Gregor thought.

"He wants Milstein, you and me to tour the world," said Horowitz.

"Actually, we will start with expanding your horizons," Merovitch said settling into a big upholstered chair. "First I want each of you to become well known as soloists. You must develop a following and stand out above all others who play your particular instrument."

Merovitch threw back the glass of Scotch, swallowing it in one gulp. Gregor did the same, but Horowitz only sipped his then set the glass aside.

"Grisha, as long as you play with the Philharmonic, you'll always be overshadowed," continued Merovitch

"But I can't afford to leave my job," he protested. "I have rent to pay and bills that are due."

"You can still perform as a guest soloist with Furtwangler, but I think your appearances should stand out. I also want to introduce you to audiences in Italy, Austria, England and France."

"You mean leave Berlin?"

"You will spend at least nine months of every year on tour. The entire world will eventually become your home."

Gregor was at a loss for words. Should he abandon everything he had accomplished in the past four years on the chance that he might make it as a soloist? Horowitz picked out a melody on the piano while Merovitch waited for Gregor's reply.

"I want to talk to Horowitz alone," Gregor said as he moved toward the piano.

"Certainly." Merovitch rose from his chair "I'm all out of cigarettes. I'll just go down to the tobacconist on the corner and buy some. You can take all the time you need." He picked up his hat and left.

Gregor couldn't sit still. He began pacing and Horowitz looked up at him, a worried expression on his narrow face. "What's wrong? Did something happen?"

"Do you know what he's asking me to do?" Before Horowitz could reply, Gregor answered his own question. "I have a secure position with the Philharmonic. I receive a salary every month and I make extra money teaching three students at the Scharwenka Conservatory. I have a comfortable flat just around the corner. Every night I eat a good supper and sleep in a clean bed."

He ran his hand over his face and felt perspiration on his brow. "He's asking me to give up everything I've achieved. For that I am to go on tours to places where no one has even heard the name Piatigorsky."

"What are you afraid of?" Horowitz asked as he continued to pluck at the piano keys.

"I'm afraid of—." Gregor stopped. What was he afraid of? Failure? Humiliation? The possibility of disappearing, of being forgotten?

"Our hotels are always clean," said Horowitz. "I travel first class rail, except of course when I went to America. Then I went by ship, but I did have a first-deck cabin." He continued to pick out a Chopin melody as he spoke. "Finding kosher food is difficult in Spain and Portugal, but in New York I had no problem." Horowitz looked up at Gregor but his fingers kept moving as he ran through a series of scales. "There is nothing you need to worry about. Let Merovitch take care of you. He takes good care of me."

Gregor stood there and stared at the pianist. The two of them were about the same age, but he knew Horowitz had never gone hungry, never been cold or slept in the street. Never been broke or imprisoned. Horowitz trusted his talent, his piano and his manager completely. Gregor, on the other hand, couldn't imagine allowing someone else, much less a total stranger, to control his life. Still, there were things he wanted and this might be the only way he could achieve them.

"Do you think Merovitch could get me a tour of America?"

"I don't see why not. Arthur Judson is a very important New York music promoter. When he heard me play last year in Paris he contacted Merovitch and *voila!*" Horowitz's fingers flew over the keys, finishing the melody with a flourish. "I was performing in Carnegie Hall. The audience loved me and my bank account grew by almost three thousand American dollars."

Gregor sank onto the edge of the piano bench and exhaled a long slow breath. "Three thousand dollars? That is an enormous sum."

"Don't worry," said Horowitz as he removed a silver case from his jacket pocket. "You will be a big success." He removed and lit a thin cigarette. "Merovitch will see to it."

The parlor door opened as if on cue and Merovitch stepped inside. Gregor wondered if the man had been listening outside the door. "I am back. Are we ready to talk business?"

Gregor slowly stood and faced the agent, towering over him, yet feeling slightly intimidated. "I will agree to let you represent me if you can guarantee me a tour of America."

"In time, in time," said Merovitch as he stubbed out the cigarette in a marble ashtray. "America is the land of opportunity, but when you arrive it should be with a fanfare, not a whimper."

"How long must I wait before I can go?"

"Give me one year. I want your name to stand for something." He moved to the desk in the corner. "Let me show you the schedule I have in mind." A broad smile lit up the man's face. "It's all European and the dates have already been confirmed."

* * *

Before Gregor left on tour there were numerous sessions with a photographer. He could still see the bright light of flash bulbs when he closed his eyes at night. There were posters printed and sent out in advance, news releases written and wired to the papers. Merovitch even hired a local man to have the posters displayed throughout each city prior to Gregor's arrival.

"This is necessary," Merovitch said. "If you are going to be a star you had better get used to public attention and bright lights."

Between his concert in Milan and one in Venice, Merovitch arranged for Gregor to visit an Italian tailor. Not one, but two custom-made suits and a formal tuxedo were fitted to his six-foot-three-inch frame.

"You are tall like a mountain." The Italian looked up at Gregor. "I will make you look even taller." With pins pressed between his lips, the tailor began pulling down on the trouser cuff.

Gregor studied his reflection in the mirror. Never before had he worn clothes that fit so well. He smiled at the reflection and the image smiled back. What would women think of him now? He certainly looked the part of a star. But why didn't he feel like one? At any moment this bubble of success could burst leaving him destitute again. He'd better not get too comfortable with his new-found celebrity status.

Two weeks later at the end of the Italian tour, Gregor returned to Berlin exhausted but excited by success. The Italian women, especially the young ones with their black hair and gypsy eyes, were his favorites. Much more enthusiastic than German girls.

"Let's go over your accounts." Merovitch opened a black ledger book.

Gregor took a seat at the dining room table in the agent's apartment and tried to read the numbers upside down.

"This is your income based on the receipts from the entire tour." Merovitch pointed to the first column. "Here, in this column I've listed your expenses."

"It looks very good." Gregor tried to add the numbers in his head but quickly lost count.

"I've used Italian lira," Merovitch said. "Since that's what the Italians paid you in. Don't worry, I'll convert everything to marks."

The numbers were enormous. "This is wonderful." Gregor tried to calculate lira into a number that made sense. "I had no idea I made so much."

"Of course you were successful. Now let me go over the cost of the tour." He pointed to the second long list of numbers. "I get twenty percent commission. Then there's the cost of railway and hotels."

As Merovitch reeled off figures, Gregor felt his heart sink. "Here's the cost of food and drink, publicity photos, local agent's fee, bribes paid to local officials—."

"Bribes?" Gregor jumped up and leaned across the table, pulling the book from Merovitch's hands. "What do you mean bribes? I never paid a bribe to anyone."

"In Italy everyone must be bribed. It's the custom. Think of it as a gratuity. Why do you think you were allowed entry into the country with nothing more than your German labor card?"

Merovitch leaned back in his chair. "Do you remember the young man who met you at the Milan train station? He paid the border guards in advance so they would ignore the fact that you have no nationality. Such services do not come cheap."

"I had no idea." Gregor sank back into his chair.

"Of course you didn't. You don't need to worry about such things. That's what you pay me for." Merovitch pointed to a third set of numbers. "Here's the cost of two new suits and the cleaning bill for the rest of your clothes. There is also the shipping charge for your cello."

"But I carried my cello with me. I never let the porters touch it."

"Nevertheless, the Italian railway charges a shipping fee for instruments. The price is the same, even for a piccolo."

Gregor exhaled and ran his finger through his hair. "So how much money do I have left?"

"Actually, none." Merovitch waved a hand as if dismissing such an inconsequential thing. "You are in debt to me two hundred Deutsche marks."

"What?" Gregor pushed back his chair and stood, looking down at Merovitch. "You are a fraud and a cheat. I made more money teaching music to the crippled and maimed at the State Music School."

Merovitch lit a cigarette then motioned to the chair. "Sit down, sit down. There is nothing to be concerned about. I will deduct the debt from the receipts of your next tour."

"Next tour?" Gregor shouted. "This is a disaster. I am firing you as my manager."

"Calm yourself. This is the cost of starting a business. You went to Italy as an unknown, but look at these reviews." Merovitch pulled several newspaper clippings from a large envelope.

"I can't read Italian." Gregor scanned the clippings that Merovitch pushed across the table. The only words he recognized, besides his own name, were Bach, Beethoven and Dvorak.

"It says you were a huge success. The reviews are glorious. Trust me."

Gregor had no choice and he knew it. For the next several nights, he lay awake wondering why he had let Merovitch take control of his life. Trusting a manager, any manager with his career was a big mistake, but he was already in too deep. Merovitch had committed him to a tour of the Balkans. Backing out now was not an option.

*   *   *

In July the four of them took a month-long vacation in the Swiss Alps. In a chalet that Merovitch rented in the resort village of Crans sur Sierre, the agent spent most of his time plotting strategy. Horowitz and Milstein slept late, but not Gregor. Each morning he rose with the sun and strolled into the little village at the foot of the hill. And every day he saw something new and interesting. The woodcutter unloading fuel for the bakery ovens, the milk boy delivering bottles of fresh cream to the shops, even a housewife feeding her chickens. He stopped and spoke to each of them, inquiring about what they did and how they did it.

The only man he avoided was the farmer he saw pulling a newborn calf along a pathway. Only a few days old, the animal wobbled on unsteady legs. When the calf balked at the gate of the village butcher shop, the man hit the animal with a stick. Gregor was sure that the creature knew what was coming.

Some of the Swiss people were friendly, especially the women and children, but the baker scowled and said he was too busy to chat. Gregor discovered that if he bought a hot roll, the man suddenly became gracious. With the warm bread for breakfast, he continued his tour until the village clock chimed eight.

In the afternoon Merovitch worked at planning their lives while Gregor, Milstein and Horowitz practiced, playing duets and trios, testing their own compositions on each other.

"I've chosen the programs I want you to play," Merovitch said over lunch. He handed each of them a sheet of paper. "Remember this, the public's attention is short. Your pieces must be likewise."

"But the critics will think I am lazy if I don't play anything over five minutes." Gregor stared at the sheet.

"Russian works are never less than ten, even fifteen minutes," said Horowitz. "I've been working on Stravinsky's "Petrushka" and Prokofiev's "Third Sonata."

"No, no," Merovitch waved his hand. "Those works are unforgiving. I want you to concentrate on the pieces that have the most effect. Remember, short is better. Fast is best. For you Milstein, Vivaldi is perfect."

"What will the critics say?" Gregor pointed to the Rimsky–Korsakov. "They cannot take this seriously."

"Critics don't buy tickets. In fact they are admitted gratis. But the paying public loves "Flight of the Bumble Bee." In the end Merovitch got his way.

After lunch Milstein always took a siesta, a habit he acquired while touring in Spain. Horowitz practiced alone and Gregor, feeling restless, hiked in the hills above the chalet. He discovered the burrows of the little creatures that inhabited the highland meadows. Insects, butterflies and flowers abounded. Sometimes he lay on the ground watching the little creatures live out their lives oblivious to the rest of the world.

One morning he borrowed a bicycle from a neighbor and tried riding to another village, but the hills were too steep. An afternoon rainstorm drenched him and the wet gravel caused the bicycle's back wheel to skid out of control. In an instant he found himself lying in a heap along the side of the road, muddy and wet.

At night, after supper, the four of them talked of the future and Merovitch laid out his plans.

"Milstein, you will take your violin and leave for Cuba in August. I've booked you on the White Star Line leaving the twentieth. My contact in Havana has arranged excellent accommodations. You'll have several days after your performances to visit the rest of the island. Maybe you can find a pretty senorita for a guide."

"If my hotel room is that good, my guide won't have to travel far." Milstein grinned and ran his hand over his black hair. He had taken to wearing a pompadour and affecting a poor Spanish accent.

"On September fifteenth you'll sail to Baranquilla, Colombia and begin your South American tour. You'll finish by November first in San Juan, Puerto Rico. It should be a good tour with an opportunity for you to practice your Spanish. We'll see you back here for New Year's."

"I hope you don't send me to Iceland," Gregor said and they all laughed.

"I would if there were an audience, but Reykjavik has no concert hall." Merovitch slid a sheet of paper across the table. "Horowitz, you're going to concentrate on France, Germany and the Balkans. I've got you scheduled in major cities in those countries and I made sure your performances weren't competing with Artur Rubinstein."

"Thank you for that gift." Horowitz said and turned to Gregor. "You have no idea what it means to play Tchaikovsky's Concerto in B flat in a city where Rubinstein has just performed the very same piece the week before. Ughhhh." Horowitz grimaced and rolled his eyes. "I was totally humiliated. The hall was half empty."

"You see," Merovitch said. "A good agent would never allow that to happen."

"You do earn your twenty percent." Milstein slid another veal cutlet onto his plate. Gregor, remembering the calf he had seen on the way to slaughter, declined his portion.

"Grisha, your tour begins in London. You have two performances with the London Philharmonic, then you'll go to Edinburgh, Leeds, Birmingham and Bristol."

"A steady income would be good," Gregor spread fresh butter on his bread. "I could pay off my debts."

"Grisha," said Milstein. "You worry too much about money. As an artist you should not let thoughts of money fill your head. It will rob you of spontaneity."

"Have either of you ever tasted bone soup?" Gregor refilled his glass from the bottle of Burgundy. "It's all I lived on in 1918. That and the taste of cat. Something I'd rather not eat again."

"Forget hunger," Merovitch said. "None of you will ever have to worry about money. You're young, talented and have great futures ahead of you. Now, pay attention, Grisha." He slid a sheet of paper across the table. "You will have three free days in London before you leave for your tour of Baltic States. Once in Riga, you'll be the soloist with the Latvia Philharmonic, then on to Estonia and finally Danzig. If you do well I promise you New York next season."

"Ah, Grisha, I will be thinking warm thoughts of you while I lie on a beach in Cuba," said Milstein, laughing. "There's nothing like a late autumn tour of the Baltic to chill a man's bones."

"He'll be greeted warmly, especially in Danzig," said Merovitch. "I'll have posters distributed announcing the return of Poland's own *Gregrz Piazniczki*."

"But I'm not Polish." Gregor pointed his fork in the agent's direction. "I do not want to end up in a Polish jail cell."

"You know you're not Polish," said the agent, a smile wrinkling his face. "And I know it. But do you think the Poles know it?"

Chapter Twenty-four

North Atlantic
October 1929

"Is this your first trip to America?" The woman spoke German, but her words were almost drowned out by the crash of a wave against the ship's bow. Salt spray rose like a white cloud and Gregor pulled back from the railing. So did the heavyset woman in a long fur coat who had come up behind him. She was almost as tall as he was and carried herself like royalty. The ship rolled left and she reached out, grabbing his arm to steady herself.

"Yes." He smiled but noticed she hadn't let go of his arm. "I've dreamed of America. My friend Mischa is there and so is my father's sister."

"You're a musician, aren't you?" The woman let go of his arm and extended her hand. Each finger was adorned with a glittering jewel.

"Yes." He accepted the woman's hand and shook it. It was as cold as ice. "I'm a cellist. My name is Gregor Piatigorsky."

"You performed in Warsaw last year with the symphony, didn't you?"

"Yes. Were you there?"

"No, but I sang on the same stage two days later. I am Madame Sophia."

"The opera singer?" Gregor felt suddenly awed.

"I will be performing *Carmen* and the *Marriage of Figaro* in New York then onto Chicago and San Francisco." She stroked the fur of her coat with her long fingers then turned her collar up against the damp wind. "And yourself?"

"In December I play at Carnegie Hall, but first I must go to Ohio then Philadelphia. Do you know any of these places?"

"Ohio. A flat land filled with farmers and merchants." She moved closer, leaning against the rail, her fur coat brushing his shoulder. Gregor saw the line of black that exaggerated her eyelashes and the rouge on her cheeks. He caught himself staring, fascinated by a face more artificial than real. If she were going to play Carmen, he thought, she would need a lot more make-up to look the part of a young woman.

"Have you seen my performances?" Her left hand touched his arm. "I am quite good, at least all the critics say so."

"Unfortunately, no." Gregor inched his arm away. Not wanting to offend her, he reached inside his jacket and removed a silver case. "Would you like a cigarette?" He held open his offering.

"My dear young man." She pulled her hand back, a look of disgust on her face. "My career and my life are in my voice. Would you leave your cello to lie in the mud? Would you expose it to the elements?"

"I'm sorry." He closed the cigarette case.

"Smoking is a nasty, filthy habit. It ruins the voice and stains the teeth. Someday it will probably kill you." With that dire warning, she turned and headed down the deck. Just past the lifeboat stand, she sank onto a lounge chair next to a young man dressed in a military officer's uniform. "Have you ever been to America?" he heard her say as she laid her jeweled hand on the officer's arm.

Gregor climbed the narrow metal staircase to the upper deck, relieved to have escaped Madame Sophia. He had been at sea for nine days and according to the cabin boy, New York would soon be in sight. The voyage had been uneventful which to Gregor meant boring. On the first day at sea he had explored every possible part of the ship. He tried talking to the crew, but only a few spoke German. After reading every newspaper he could beg or borrow, he tried practicing his limited broken English on the American passengers.

The adults were polite, but their odd way of speaking English made the language even harder to understand. The American children spent much of the voyage running up and down the decks. When he attempted to communicate with them, they laughed and ran away. He wished Horowitz or Milstein had come on this tour. Perhaps it was the idea of going to a new country so far away, without even a friend to share the excitement, that made him feel lonelier than ever.

"Look, look," cried the Americans crowding the rail. They pointed and waved at the irregular objects on the horizon.

"What is it?" Gregor said to the steward who was gathering empty dishes from the deck tables. "What are they looking at?"

"It's the Statue of Liberty," the waiter said in Bavarian accented German. "Those Americans." He shook his head. "Every time we arrive in New York it's the same thing. They've seen it a dozen times, but they always act as if it were new."

"Why?" Gregor scanned the horizon. "What does it mean?"

"Liberty? Freedom? Democracy?" The waiter wiped up spilled coffee. "If you ask me, it means chaos and anarchy."

Gregor joined the crowd on the fore deck, but he couldn't see anything that looked like the magazine picture of the lady holding a torch. Why did Americans get so excited about a statue? Berlin was filled with statues and so was Paris. Even Ekaterinoslav had its statue of Empress Katerina.

As the New York skyline began to gradually take shape, Gregor noticed a small boat moving toward the S.S. RELIANCE. It looked like the pilot boat that had escorted the vessel out of the dock at Hamburg. The excitement on deck increased as the boat pulled alongside the ship. A half dozen men climbed the ladder and fanned out over the deck.

"Mail's here," a man in a dark uniform cried and people moved like a school of fish toward the forward deck lounge. A tall boy followed carrying a huge canvas bag filled with newspapers.

"Big crash! Read all about it," the boy shouted. "New York Times. Just five cents."

Some passengers, hungry for fresh news, showered the boy with money and he quickly sold all his papers.

"Are you the famous Russian cellist?" said a man with the camera.

"I am cellist," Gregor said trying to use his English.

"Let me get your picture." Before Gregor could say more several flashes went off nearly blinding him. "I'm from the New York Times," shouted another man. "What do you think of America?"

"I not yet arrived." Gregor shrugged. "I do not know." He smiled again for the camera as the reporters scribbled notes.

"Are you famous all over Europe? How long will you be here?" The questions came from all sides faster than he could answer. "I happy —I say that—."

He couldn't finish before someone else called out. "Do you plan to stay here? Will you apply for citizenship?"

"Citizenship?" He recognized the word but before he could answer, the man with the camera turned away, aiming his lens at Madame Sophia.

"Look, it's that famous opera star from Berlin. Hey! Let me get your picture." Just like that the reporters were gone, clearly excited to find a more talkative subject. Madame Sophia obliged and Gregor saw her jeweled fingers stroking her fur coat as the cameras flashed.

Ignored, Gregor wandered back into the lounge, ordered a beer and leaned against the bar.

"Better enjoy it while you can," said the German bartender. "You won't be tasting anything like it for a long time."

"Dortmunder beer?" Gregor took another sip.

"Any kind of beer," the bartender said. "I will certainly never visit America. No alcohol of any kind allowed."

"You are making a joke."

"It is no joking matter. The American government has forbidden beer, wine and anything else worth drinking."

"I don't believe it."

"You'd better get used to drinking milk," said the man, then he moved down the bar to wait on another thirsty passenger.

No beer, no vodka, no wine? Why would the Americans do this? He finished his drink, wishing he had hidden a bottle of Scotch in his suitcase.

On the other side of the room the mailman was still calling names, but the crowd had thinned out. Some lucky people tore open their envelopes and eagerly devoured news from family and friends. It must be nice to get mail, Gregor thought. He had tried writing home to Ekaterinoslav, but no matter how many times he wrote, his pleas for a reply went unanswered.

"Pee-att-gor-ski." The mailman called his name. "Gregory Pee-att-gor-ski?"

He had a letter? From all the way across the ocean? Who could it be? He reached over the heads of a family of short statured Americans and retrieved his letter. The envelope bore a seal *Arthur Judson Company-Concert Management Inc.*

Opening it, he felt keen disappointment. The letter was brief and the only part he understood was the address, 113 West 57th St. and the name at the bottom, Arthur Judson.

Gregor folded the letter and slid it into his pocket. Americans certainly seemed to be all business. What would it be like working for Arthur Judson? More important, what would the American audiences be like? Would they enjoy his music or would they grow impatient, even bored? Maybe short pieces would be better received. Perhaps they were no different than the people he had played for back home in Russia.

After finishing the last of his beer, he headed back on deck. From the port side he heard the sound of the tugboat horn. The ship responded with three blasts from its tower, loud enough to drown out all other sound. As he headed to his usual spot at the rail, Gregor lit a long cigarette. Holding his hands around the match, it took three tries before he could get it lit. Inhaling the first puff of acrid smoke, his eyes moved up. Then he saw her.

The sight of her body draped in long, flowing fabric stopped him. He slowly removed the cigarette from his lips as his eyes traveled up her form. Her bare arm reached skyward toward the heavens. As the ship moved past the base of the statue, Gregor tilted his head back and stared at Lady Liberty. She was overwhelming, enormous and unforgettable. For a moment, all he could think of were the first chords of Beethoven's Fifth Symphony. It was the only thing fitting for such a sight.

* * *

"All persons holding United States passports gather at table one with your papers. You will be processed for entry at this time." The uniformed officer stood at the gangway to the terminal building. "Those persons holding French, German, or British passports gather at table two. All other passport holders meet at the rear of the terminal room." The man repeated the announcement in passable French then in German.

At the sound of the word passport, Gregor slipped his hand inside his jacket pocket and felt for his documents. Merovitch had sworn that the Nansen passport was all he needed to get into the United States. He removed the small brown booklet and held it open. The small black and white photo of his own face stared back at him, a somber looking individual. The line designating the place of his birth was filled with an illegible scrawl, as was his birth date. Even his signature was smudged. Intentionally.

Most officials will just glance at it, Merovitch had said. After all, it's just a formality. But the American immigration officer didn't look like a man who believed in mere formalities.

"*Sprechen Sie Deutche?*" Gregor said when he reached the table at the back of the terminal. "*Bitte.* Please. My English . . . not good."

"German citizens must go to table two," the man said, speaking slowly like Gregor were a child.

"I am not German citizen."

"To what country do you belong?"

Gregor felt a knot form in his belly. "I have passport." He slid the Nansen document across the table.

The officer shook his head and muttered something Gregor couldn't understand as he peered at the document with its illegible scrawl. "This is not a passport. I can't even read it." He pushed the document back across the table.

"In Hamburg this acceptable."

"Of course, they told you that. All they want to do is sell you a ticket and take your money. You must apply for a tourist visa at the American Consulate in Berlin."

"I go back Germany? *Nyet!* I have concert. One week."

"Then I would advise you to cancel it." The officer motioned Gregor aside and a porter picked up the cello case.

"No! Do not touch!" Gregor pulled the cello from the man's hands. It was the wrong thing to do. Two uniformed officers appeared and the next thing Gregor knew he and his belongings were pushed back up the gangway and onto the ship.

"No," he said. "I must go."

A ship's officer, wearing a black uniform liberally decorated with gold buttons, appeared and began arguing with the immigration official in rapid fire English. Gregor tried to step between the two men and explain the unexplainable.

They ignored him as they continued their animated and completely unintelligible conversation.

If the argument hadn't involved his uncertain future, the situation might have been humorous. Instead it was infuriating. Even without knowing much English, Gregor deduced that the ship's officer did not want to take a stateless person back to Hamburg without being paid.

The American immigration official, on the other hand, did not want to let a stateless person enter the United States. Gregor sank onto his trunk and waited while the rest of the passengers disembarked. The only other person detained was an old woman who babbled incoherently and picked at imaginary insects she seemed to think were crawling up her arms. When a nurse appeared carrying the old woman's handbag and passport, she too was allowed to disembark.

After much hand waving and finger pointing the two officers came to an agreement regarding Gregor's fate. The first officer pointed to Gregor's luggage. The two porters, who had been standing nearby smoking, began loading the bags on a handcart.

When one of them tried to take his cello, Gregor waved them off and carried the instrument himself. The porters shrugged, exchanged words that didn't even sound like English, then rolled the rest of his possessions off the boat.

The little caravan of men and luggage snaked its way through the cavernous terminal building, then out to a waiting automobile. Gregor slid into the backseat with his cello tucked between his knees. The two officers rode in the front, silent.

They rode past docks and warehouses, railway cars and empty lots, finally stopping at a shabby building. Inside the small dusty room he waited alone on an uncomfortable wooden bench. When he grew tired of sitting, he paced around the little room, glancing out the dirty, wire-covered window. The only thing to look at was the street map of New York City nailed to the wall.

"*Guten tag,*" said the stern red-faced man who finally entered the room.

"*Guten abend,*" Gregor said, relieved to be speaking German. "I am glad to meet you." He extended his hand and the man shook it.

"I'm William Krautz from the U.S. Office of Immigration."

"You are German?" Gregor said. Maybe this man would understand his dilemma.

"My parents were from Munich." Krautz continued to speak German. "I understand you have no passport."

"I have a Nansen passport." He handed the man the little brown booklet. "It is legal for travel. I am a cellist. I have engagements in New York and Chicago."

"Do you have German citizenship?"

"No. I have a German labor card."

"What is your nationality?"

"I was born in Russia, but I have no citizenship."

Krautz studied the smudged writing on the passport. The only thing clear was the title, *"League of Nations, Paris, France."* "The American government didn't sign the Treaty of Versailles and it does not allow entry to persons without nationality. Congress passed a law to keep out Reds, Bolsheviks and anarchists."

"But I am none of those. I have the right to enter."

"Do you have return passage, already paid for?"

"No." Gregor tried to control his growing anxiety. "I will buy a ticket when it is time to return."

"How much money do you have in your possession?"

"Do you think I am a beggar?" Gregor said. His tone came out all wrong. Taking a deep breath, he tried to control his mounting frustration. "I have a draft for one thousand Deutsche marks from the Bundes Bank and I have twenty British pounds."

"That should be enough to get you back home."

"I will earn more than that while I am here and —"

Krautz raised his open hand. "I'll pretend I didn't hear that. We have more unemployed in America than we can take care of right now."

"What must I say to gain entry?"

"Are you willing to sign a document that states you're a tourist and will leave the United States after thirty days?"

"But my agent has scheduled me for three months-worth of concerts."

"When your thirty day visa expires you may apply for an extension, but I must warn you this is not a work visa, only a tourist visa. You may not work while you are in the United States."

"But I must perform. That is my work."

The man shook his head as he pulled a small black book off a shelf. "It says here on page. . ." He flipped through the book. "On page thirteen it states that sports competitions, musical performances, magic acts, dancing and painting do not constitute work."

He closed the book and Gregor noticed a peculiar expression on the man's face, as if he were suppressing a smile. "You may engage in any of these allowable activities while you are a tourist, but you may not work." He returned the book to the shelf. "So, you see, all you have to do is sign a document that states you are here for thirty days as a tourist and that you promise not to work. Then you are free to enter the country."

"That's all I have to do?" It seemed too easy, too simple.

"Yes." Krautz pulled a sheet of paper from a folder on the top shelf. "Will you sign this document?"

"Of course, I will."

"I'm glad to hear that, Mr. Piatigorsky." The man's face broke into a genuine smile. "Because my wife and I have tickets for your concert at Carnegie Hall. We wouldn't want to miss hearing you play."

Chapter Twenty-five

New York City
November 1929

"Forty floors," said Dorle Jarmel in slow, clearly enunciated English. "Our office is on thirty-one."

Gregor looked down at the top of her head. Even in high-heeled shoes, she came only to his shoulder. "I not see such place."

"Is this your first trip to New York?" She looked up at him and smiled. Her dark brown eyes contrasted nicely with her blonde hair.

"Yes. Tall building, only Eiffel Tower in Paris. New York is *wunderbar!*"

"I'm afraid you won't have much time to be a tourist." She laughed. Then, just as quickly, the smile left her face. "Mr. Judson is not—uhhh— very happy today, so be careful what you say."

"He is *krank*?" Gregor struggled to remember the correct words. "Sick?" What else could possibly go wrong?

"Not sick but . . " She paused and pressed her perfectly red lips together. "Did you hear about the crash last Thursday?"

"Crash?"

"The stock market took a terrible drop." She stared up at the needle ticking off each floor as they ascended. "Mr. Judson lost . . well, I don't know how much he lost. No one is talking about it, but he is worried."

"My tour?"

"Probably not. Your performances have been booked for over a month. Yesterday's Times said that J.P. Morgan and the other big-wigs won't let the market drop any further."

None of what she said made much sense to Gregor, but it didn't sound good. They both grew silent as the elevator carried them up, the floors ticking by with regularity. In the corner of the cramped car a rotund Negro woman silently operated the controls. Gregor focused on the roll of flesh at the back of the woman's neck, topped by tiny black ringlets. He had an urge to reach out and touch her hair, just to see how it felt.

"Thirty-one." She spoke in a monotone, opening the elevator door in a single motion that was both fluid and languid. Gregor followed Miss Jarmel as they passed room after room. He tried to decipher the names and was able to make out, Transportation. Community Concerts. Theater and Opera. Business Office. The last door had the name *Arthur Judson* painted on the frosted glass window in black and gold letters.

He followed Miss Carmel into the office and when she stopped he almost ran into her from behind. Mr. Judson sat before a large window that looked over New York City. Gregor's first impulse was to walk past Miss Jarmel and look at the view of the city below him. But Mr. Judson might find that rude, so instead, he waited for a proper introduction. Mr. Judson, however, seemed preoccupied.

"Absolutely not!" Judson shouted into the phone that was pressed to his ear. As he spoke, he puffed furiously on a cigarette. "There are no cancellations and no refunds. The concert will go on. I can sell twice as many tickets if Horowitz performs than I can with Rubinstein." As he spoke, he smashed his half-smoked cigarette into the overflowing ashtray.

Gregor glanced at Miss Jarmel. She stood very still, almost like a wax figure at Madame Tussaud's in London. Not even her perfect, black eyelashes moved.

"The market will recover." Judson's voice dropped as he tried to soothe his listener. "Trust me. This reversal will have no major effect on the economy. The bankers will put a stop to it. I have it on good authority that prices rose when the market opened this morning. Besides, people will always spend their money on entertainment. I know, I know. Good-bye."

When he hung up the phone, Judson noticed he had company. A smile spread across his broad face. "Mr. Piatigorsky." He emerged from behind the desk, his hand already extended. "I was afraid something had gone wrong. My man couldn't find you at the port."

"I am sorry." Gregor shook Judson's hand. Carefully, he tried to form his next sentence using correct English. "I was alt—stopped— but all good now." He knew this was not the time to discuss passport difficulties with a new manager.

"Don't tell me. Did immigration give you the runaround about a visa?"

"I sign paper." Gregor hoped this was the correct response.

"Those bastards. I swear I am going to call the commissioner. We've forwarded the names of all our artists to the immigration office. Miss Jarmel, will you see to it that his tourist visa is properly extended until April."

"Yes, sir, I'll get the papers in order and he can sign them all ahead of time."

"Good, and get me a copy of Mr. Piatigorsky's concert schedule."

As she hurried off, Judson retrieved a newspaper from the leather sofa. "I see you've already been noticed by the press. That's good, very good."

Gregor looked down at the folded page. He saw his own face staring back at him. Except for his name, the English words meant nothing. "What is this?"

"It says 'Russian cellist here for first tour. Not sure if he likes America'." Judson slapped the paper in the palm of his hand. "Great interview. You've got the press eating out of your hand."

"Eating? I not say…"

"Probably not." The reporters make up most of what they print. Still, it's an eye grabber and that's what counts.

"What? I not…"

Judson waved his hand. "If you're controversial then your name will stay in the papers and we can sell more tickets."

"I . . . con-tro-versial?"

"Let them take all the pictures they want. Never turn down an interview. If you get the chance, have your picture taken with a pretty girl. And smile. Always smile. No matter how you feel or what you think. Smile."

"But music? I must tell them about music?"

"Don't waste your breath. Symphony, sonata, serenade. They all sound the same. The important thing is that the public remembers your name and your face. That's what sells."

"I not know." He felt overwhelmed. Everything seemed so different, so unreal here in America.

Judson moved to a large map hanging on the wall beside his desk. "Let me show you what I've got in mind." He pointed to a red pin stuck in the heart of the words, New York City. "We're here. Next week, on November fifth, you'll perform at Oberlin College in Ohio."

"Yes." Gregor nodded. "I know—flat place."

"I don't know about that. I've never been to Ohio, but my sales people have sold three hundred tickets already. A dollar a seat. Fifty cents more for the front rows. They've got one hundred seats left and we're hoping for a sellout crowd."

"Oberlin *mit* farmers *und* merchants?" Gregor tried to imagine what the audience would look like. "I play with orchestra?"

"No orchestra. Your agent Merovitch said you can play chamber music, so all you'll need is a pianist."

"Pianist? With orchestra?"

"You'll have an orchestra in Chicago, Philadelphia and New York, but there aren't any orchestras in the small towns."

"Who pianist?"

"Don't worry. I have auditions scheduled for tomorrow and Wednesday. We'll find you one."

"We rehearse together. It is marriage."

"Don't worry. You have three, maybe even four days to get acquainted. The train to Oberlin is an overnight car and you don't have to play until next Tuesday afternoon."

Gregor was speechless. Locate and rehearse with a brand new accompanist, a complete stranger, then travel to Ohio, all in less than a week? What was it about Americans that made them move so fast?

"From Oberlin you'll travel to Madison, Wisconsin, then on to Milwaukee," Judson said. "The brewery owners there once supported two orchestras." Judson pointed to the little blue pins. "But not since Prohibition. Now there's only one, paid for by a meatpacking plant."

He moved his finger to another spot on the map. "Then you'll come back through Chicago, Pittsburgh and Philadelphia. There's a big performance scheduled in Philly with the symphony. Leopold Stokowski is conducting. That should really pull them in."

He tapped the red pin covering New York again. "You'll be back here by Christmas in time for your December twenty-seventh debut at Carnegie Hall."

Gregor stared at the map in awe. The size of America was huge, much more like Russia than anyplace he had been in Europe. "I play six concerts?"

"That's six big ones, though in Chicago, Philadelphia and, of course New York, you'll play two concerts on consecutive nights."

Judson extracted a cigarette from a silver case and offered one to Gregor. "My organization, Community Concerts, has afternoon programs scheduled in smaller towns. That way you can arrive on the morning train, perform and leave on the late train. Those only draw a hundred or so people, but we can squeeze in three or four a week between the big gigs."

"How will I pay?"

"Don't worry. We'll deposit your money in the Hanover Bank. You can write checks on the deposits."

Gregor took a deep breath. "I like very much to see America? Not only railway cars."

"You'll have a few days off before and after your Carnegie Hall engagement," said Judson as he returned to his desk. "Then we've got you heading out again on the fifth of January. You'll play all across the Midwest then on to Texas, California and Oregon. You'll see the entire country before you're back here on March fifteenth."

The piano in the audition room was a Steinway Grand. Miss Jarmel, wearing an attractive yellow dress that hugged her figure nicely, opened a portfolio and spread a dozen pages of music across the top of the closed piano lid.

"You should pick one of these for the accompanist to play."

Gregor looked over her shoulder. As he studied the selections, he couldn't help noticing the sweet fragrance of her perfume. He took his time making a choice. "Brahms good. Dvorak more good."

"I'll ask them to play both." She set the scores on the music rail.

While Gregor tuned his instrument, Miss Jarmel brought in the first pianist. He was a frail middle-aged man badly in need of a haircut. "Mr. Piatigorsky, this is Mr. Fein," Miss Jarmel said.

"Good morning," Gregor said and reached out to shake the man's hand. Mr. Fein looked at Gregor's offering with suspicion as he rubbed his own knuckles.

"I'm sorry but I don't shake hands." He smiled nervously and Gregor noticed most of the man's teeth were black or missing.

Gregor retracted his hand and turned away so not to see the man's pained expression. "We play Dvorak Cello Concerto. Do you know it?"

"Ahhh, I know it well."

"*Gut, sehr good.*" Gregor sat and opened the music.

"But I have never accompanied a cellist before," said Fein. "Only a violin."

Gregor's heart sank. He didn't want to waste any more time with this man who was clearly unsuited for the job. But he didn't have the heart to dismiss him without giving him a chance. "Play," he said, resigned to suffer in silence.

Mr. Fein began. His opening was so soft, so timid that Gregor could hardly hear him. The concerto dragged on interminably, the tempo slow and hesitant. Gregor's cello drowned out the piano.

"Thank you, thank you, Herr Fein," Gregor said at the end of the first movement.

"I have your number," said Miss Jarmel, her voice as sweet as honey. "I'll be in touch when all of our auditions are finished." Mr. Fein was shown to the door.

Gregor loosened his shirt collar. Already the room was too warm. How could he ever manage three months on the road with a man like Fein?

"This is Mr. Philpot," said Miss Jarmel motioning in the next applicant.

Gregor studied the well-dressed young man. His suit was stylish and neatly pressed. His hair was combed back from his high forehead and his long fingers had the look of a fresh manicure. A much more presentable musician than Fein. The only thing out of the ordinary was the fact that Philpot wore not one but two ties. One red and the other gray.

"*Guten Morgen* . . . Good morning," offered Gregor, trying hard not to stare at the man's strange attire. He extended his hand and Mr. Philpot shook it with a firm grip. A good sign, Gregor thought.

"Thank you," said Philpot. "But I must warn you that I cannot play today. I never play on Sunday."

"Today is Tuesday," Gregor said. He looked past Philpot to Miss Jarmel who only shrugged and looked helpless.

"No," said Philpot. "Today is Sunday and I do not play on Sunday."

"Why are you here?"

"I want the job but I will have to return on Monday and play for you then. Good-bye." With that he turned and headed out the door. Gregor stood with his cello in hand, staring after the man.

"I'm so sorry," Miss Jarmel said. She looked as confused as Gregor felt.

"He is *krank*," Gregor said and touched the side of his head. "Not well?"

"I think so. There was one more applicant, but he hasn't arrived yet. Let me see if he's in the office."

She left and Gregor sat down on the piano bench. Absentmindedly, he flipped through a few pages of the score. There was no way he could perform solo music without a good accompanist. He should have insisted that Karol Szreter come along. With almost five years performing together, they knew each other's style. It was Merovitch who wanted him to hire an American accompanist. Less expensive and besides, Arthur Judson would know plenty of good ones, he had said. If this was the best America had to offer then his tour was doomed.

Unable to sit still, he laid the cello on top of the closed piano and walked to the big window that overlooked New York City. From this height he could see all the way to the harbor. In the distance the autumn sun gleamed off the river's surface and through the haze he could just make out Lady Liberty.

For so long he had wanted to come here, wanted to be here, knew that America was the answer to his prayers. Had all this been a mistake? In Berlin he had friends, audiences that loved his music and parties with pretty girls. He had a small flat and plenty to eat. Why wasn't that enough?

Standing above the city, he felt removed from humanity. Below him tiny automobiles moved like mice in a maze. He was no different, just one of those mice, running in search of food, turning back, never finding enough, never finding his way out.

Once, in Switzerland, when he had climbed to the top of the mountain overlooking Crans sur Sierre, he had looked down on the village and the people scurrying about. They were no different than people here in New York. Again he felt the overwhelming desire to be free from the frenetic activity below him. For that one clear moment he wanted nothing more than to push off from the earth, soar above everyone and everything and be free.

Only the window glass separated him from the birds that soared and dove a few yards away without a care in the world. They could fly anywhere, no restrictions, no fears and no border guards to stop them. This was America. He should have found that kind of freedom here. Instead, he found only frustration.

"*Zdrastvuytye.*" The greeting was in Russian and the voice carried a tone of confidence.

Gregor turned and saw Miss Jarmel standing beside a tall blond young man. His dark suit was perfectly tailored, definitely European cut and a cigarette hung casually from his lips.

"*Kak dela,*" Gregor replied in Russian, happy to be able to speak in his own language.

A confused look furrowed Miss Jarmel's brow. "Do you two know each other?"

"*Nyet*— No," replied Gregor. "Russians not strangers."

"Valentin Pavlovsky," said the young man switching to broken English as he shook Gregor's hand firmly. "I am arrived from Berlin, only one week. I will play for you. *Da?*" With that Pavlovsky settled himself at the Steinway and glanced at the scores. "Brahms first, then Dvorak?"

"*Da, da,*" said Gregor, quickly retrieving his instrument.

They performed together as if it had always been that way. From almost the first bar of Brahms, Gregor knew he had found a partner in music.

When they finished playing, Miss Jarmel stood by the door and applauded. "Bravo! Wonderful," she cried.

Pavlovsky stood and bowed then turned to Gregor and said in Russian, "Will you be taking her to dinner?"

"It hadn't occurred to me to ask," he replied in Russian. "Why?"

"I would not want to encroach on your territory, but if you are not contemplating such action, I would like to ask her to spend the evening with me."

Chapter Twenty-six

Oberlin, Ohio
December 1929

Gregor collapsed onto the rear-facing seat of the Pullman car, dropped his head back on the couch and closed his eyes. He had made it onto the last train with only minutes to spare. Now, a complete sense of relief came over him as the train pulled out of the Oberlin station. One concert done and only twenty-nine more to go.

He had played before his first American audience in a church. Finney Chapel they called it, with the piano beside the pulpit. He faced a congregation of students and faculty, feeling awkward and out of place. He wondered if Jesus inhabited this chapel during Tuesday evening concerts. If he did, would he be displeased at hearing him play "Hindu Song" by Rimsky-Korsakoff? Maybe it was sacrilege, but the audience seemed to enjoy it.

At the post performance reception in the university president's residence, Gregor had signed programs and struggled to understand their unintelligible American chatter. Through the dining room doorway he saw a table filled with sandwiches and cakes, but the crowd of people prevented him from getting even a single bite. Pavlovsky had disappeared with a group of young ladies, leaving the older faculty and music students for Gregor to entertain.

When he realized that he had only thirty minutes to make the last train, he offered apologies to his hostess. Graciously, she arranged for her driver to take him to the station, but Pavlovsky was nowhere in sight. If his accompanist didn't make the train, there wouldn't be another one until morning. That would spell disaster for their performance in Toledo the next afternoon.

"Hey, move your legs, you giant," said the familiar Russian voice. Gregor opened one eye and looked up at Pavlovsky's disheveled blond hair. His tie was askew, his jacket wrinkled and a smear of lipstick marked his shirt collar.

"I thought you'd missed the train." Gregor slid to the seat by the window and laid his head against the glass. The dark Ohio countryside slipped by as the train shuddered, groaned, then picked up speed.

"I wanted to get the young ladies' addresses in case we play Oberlin again." Pavlovsky slipped off his jacket and shook out the wrinkles.

"Ha! After tonight's performance, do you think Oberlin will want us to return?" Gregor said as he loosened his tie and kicked off his shoes. "I can't believe you turned three pages instead of one on the Feltzer piece." Now he could laugh about it but then he had panicked. "I believe by shortening it you did the composer a favor."

"And the audience will never know." Pavlovsky carefully hung his jacket on the back of the door then removed his tie.

"I think you're right. When we get to—to—." Gregor stopped and reached into his jacket pocket for their itinerary. "Toledo, we could play it again and shorten it at the same place."

"When do we arrive in Toooleeedooo?" Pavlovsky asked as he stretched out on the empty bench seat across from Gregor.

"We should be there by ten o'clock tonight," Gregor said. "According to Miss Jarmel, we must take a cab from the *bahnhof* to the Hotel Drake."

"Don't call it *bahnhof*," said Pavlovsky. "In America they say *train station*. Can you say *train station?*"

"Of course I can say *trrrain station*." Gregor repeated the phrase. "*Trrrain Station, trrrain station. I want to go to the trrrain station.*"

"You still sound like a Russian." Pavlovsky lit a cigarette and handed the pack to Gregor.

"And you don't?" He followed Pavlovsky's example, removing his jacket and draping it over the back of the seat. "Did you get all the young ladies' addresses?"

"Only one of them." Pavlovsky pulled a little red book from his pocket. "Her name is Betty Johnson, she is twenty-one years old, attends Oberlin College, studies music and art, plays the piano and saxophone." He paused, raising one eyebrow. "Yes, she did say saxophone." He kicked off his shoes and propped his feet on the armrest.

"You probably know more about her than her own mother knows."

"I certainly hope so." Pavlovsky grinned. "She offered to come to Toledo if we stayed for an extra day after the performance."

"And she would do all this just for the opportunity to be your page turner?"

"I would instruct her very thoroughly," Pavlovsky said, a lecherous grin on his face.

"Then she will be disappointed to learn we must be in Cleveland the following day." Gregor felt hunger reminding him he hadn't eaten since noon. "By the time we check into the Drake Hotel, all the restaurants will be closed."

"Maybe the porter can get us some food." Pavlovsky squirmed on the bench seat, trying to get comfortable. "Tell him I want bratwurst, fried potatoes with sauerkraut and a good bottle of German beer."

"Have you forgotten that there is no beer anywhere in this great country?" The very mention of beer made Gregor wish he were in Berlin. "Don't even think about it. Did you eat any of those little sandwiches at the reception?"

"I was not thinking of food at that time," said Pavlovsky. He raised his arm to shield his eyes from the ceiling light.

Gregor's empty stomach drove him from the car. In his socks, he headed down the corridor, looking for the Negro porter. At the far end of the car he spotted the gray-haired man in a neat black uniform. He was polishing the windows with a large white cloth.

"*Entschuldger Sei.*" Gregor realized too late he had spoken in German and switched to English. "Pardon. May I have food?" He gestured as if he were eating with an invisible spoon.

The porter shook his head. "I'm sorry, the dining car's closed. A great big crowd of people got on in Pittsburgh and they ate every speck of food. The cook can't restock 'til we get to Toledo."

"There is nothing?" Gregor felt his stomach protest. "No food?"

"You want some of my corn bread and mustard greens? My wife cooks it with a little salt pork," the man offered, a wide smile on his face. "She packs it for me 'most every day."

"*Nein. Danke,*" Gregor said momentarily forgetting his English. "Thank you."

"It's probably not something a foreigner like you would care for," called the porter as Gregor made his way back down the corridor. "Not unless you're from Alabama."

"Nothing to eat until we reach Toledo," Gregor said when he returned to the car.

"We may expire by then." Pavlovsky rolled off the bench seat. "I think I have something in my bag." Digging through his suitcase, he tossed out a pair of dirty socks and a soiled shirt. Buried beneath the clothes he located a half-eaten chocolate bar. The suitcase had apparently been sitting too close to a radiator because the chocolate had melted then re-hardened.

"A gift from an admirer." Pavlovsky triumphantly held up the candy. Putting it on the window ledge, he pulled back the sticky paper and used his thumbnail to divide the congealed mass in two.

"Ugh," Gregor groaned. "From now on I will remember to pack cheese and salami in my suitcase." Still, he took the chocolate. In one quick bite, he choked down the gooey mess and hoped it would quiet his belly. "I pray there is a good restaurant near our hotel." He lit a cigarette to rid his mouth of the foul sweet taste.

"Perhaps Toledo, Ohio, is like its Spanish cousin," said Pavlovsky. "Good wine, fine food and beautiful women."

"We can only hope." Gregor stretched out on the seat, his long legs hanging uncomfortably over the armrest. It was awkward lying there, tossing and turning. He covered his eyes with his arm and tried not to think about bratwurst and beer, salami and cheese, fried fish and potatoes. In the end he knew that the only remedy for unrequited hunger was sleep.

* * *

For the next two weeks they crisscrossed the snow-covered Midwest, sleeping in overheated hotels and missing meals. They performed in school auditoriums, town halls and civic centers. Arthur Judson's Community Concerts filled every seat at a dollar a head. In time Gregor began to realize that the audience would have come even if the stage had held a troupe of polka dancers, but when the audience left, they would never again ask, "Who is Gregor Piatigorsky?"

Arthur Judson allowed his performers one day a week to rest. Pavlovsky usually spent the entire morning sleeping, trying to recover from late nights of intensive training with the various young women he recruited as page-turners.

Gregor woke early each morning and went in search of breakfast. In some towns the hotel served a good meal for as little as twenty-five cents, but in the smaller settlements he would wander down Main Street looking for a restaurant that served a morning meal.

American small towns were depressing. Many stores were closed and even the businesses that were open were meagerly stocked. In Carbondale, Illinois, he spotted a sign in the dusty window of Tommy's Restaurant. Mush & Milk 5¢. Though he could afford better, Gregor sat down at an empty table and studied his fellow diners. Some were very young and wore ill-fitting suits. An old man dressed in farmer's clothes sipped a cup of coffee. The only woman present was the waitress.

"I like moosh und meelk," Gregor said slowly, trying to pronounce the words correctly.

The waitress, a skinny young girl with bad teeth, frowned and shook her head. "You want what?"

"Moosh und meelk," Gregor said pointing to the sign in the window.

"Oh! You want mush." The girl scribbled on her pad of paper.

"I never eat moosh."

"You want coffee with that?"

"Yes, coffee *bitte*." He caught himself then quickly added, "Please. Also newspaper."

"Coming right up."

When breakfast arrived, he stared down at the bowl of gruel. It looked watery.

"Put some sugar on it." The waitress poured steaming black coffee in a white cup. "You're not from around here, are you?"

"No. I am cellist. I play at university." He took a sip of the coffee and almost spit it out it was so hot.

"The boss says keep it boiling. You should've put some milk in it."

"I will remember." With his mouth burning he decided to try the mush, but not before he added enough milk to stop the steam from rising from the bowl. The mush was softer than the kasha his mother made, but it was filling.

"So what's a cellist anyway?" The waitress returned with a thin newspaper.

"I am musician." He mimicked the hand positions as if he were playing his instrument. "Also I perform with pianist."

"You got any records out?" She seemed interested. "My mom's got a phonograph. I like Rudy Valle and Guy Lombardo."

"I play Brahms, und Bach." He corrected himself. "And Debussy. Do you know these?"

"Never heard of 'em. They must not be too popular. Maybe you ought to get some American stuff. The kind of things people like to hear."

"I will try," was all Gregor could say.

"Here's your bill." She laid a scrap of paper on the table. "Twenty-five cents. The newspaper's a dime. You can still leave me a big tip if you want." After giving him a crooked smile, she moved to the next table with her pot of boiling coffee.

Gregor ate the mush and left the coffee to cool. While he ate he studied the front page of the *Chicago Tribune*. STOCK MARKET FALLS 66 POINTS. He recognized enough written English to know this was bad news, but the rest of the article was too difficult to read.

On the next page he studied clothing advertisements. Compared to German prices, American overcoats, hats and shoes were inexpensive. Before he left New York, he would have to buy a new suit and a pair of shoes.

On an inside page he saw a familiar sight, Fyodor Chaliapin. He deciphered enough words to learn his friend was performing "Don Quixote." Feeling suddenly homesick for a familiar face and Russian voice, he wished he could attend. While the citizens of Chicago enjoyed listening to the greatest opera star Russia ever had, he would be performing Debussy at the Southfield, Illinois grange hall to an audience of farmers.

Inside the rattling coach car Gregor tried to shuffle the deck of cards on the vibrating tabletop. "I win." He scooped up the cards. "You must remember not to show your hand."

"I think these card games are your own invention." Pavlovsky picked up the cards that had fallen to the floor. "Let's eat. The dining car should be open by now."

Gregor returned the cards to his briefcase and retrieved a newspaper from the overhead luggage rack. "You can read the reviews of our performance," he said as they headed to the back of the train. "What is the name of this newspaper?"

Pavlovsky took it and peered at the masthead "It says *The Dess Moi—ness Rrre—gis—ter.*"

"A terrible name for a newspaper." Gregor took a seat by the window.

Outside, flat, frozen farmland stretched as far as he could see. Only a lone farmhouse broke the monotony of the landscape.

A young Negro porter in a starched white jacket appeared and handed them menus.

"Do you have fish?" Gregor ignored the undecipherable paper.

"No sir. This is the Midwest Limited from Kansas City to Cleveland. There's no fish around here for five hundred miles."

"What *fleich*—meat?" Pavlovsky said.

"We've got pork, chicken and beef. Mighty nice pork chops, if I do say so."

"Good." Pavlovsky nodded. "We eat pork chops."

The porter smiled. "Yes, sir. Two pork chop dinners coming right up."

"What did you order?" Gregor said when the man was gone.

"I have no idea, but I'm sure it will be good."

Gregor unfolded *The Des Moines Register* and turned to the back page where the Americans always hid the music reviews. "You read it," he said, passing it across the table.

Pavlovsky opened the paper and studied it, his brow furrowed with effort.

"*Yesterday's performance*," he read, slowly translating into Russian. "*of the Cello Sonata in D minor by Caporale and the full-bodied tempo for cello was a rare performance for concert goers in Des Moines. Gregor Piatigorsky and his pianist Valentin Pavlovsky were inspiring but,*" he stopped.

"What is it?" Gregor tried to decipher the words upside down.

"You see this little word?" Valentin pointed to the word *but*. "When a newspaper uses this word, all things that follow it are bad. I will not read any more." He folded the paper and started to slide it back across the table.

"No, read the other news," Gregor pushed the paper back. "Your English is better. I want to know what is happening in the world."

"Let me see," Pavlovsky turned to the front page. "Hmmm, hmmm. . A man... an important New York banker was shot. . . . No. He shot himself."

"Why?"

"I'm not certain, but it appears he lost a great deal of money. Also a bird... no, no. The American Admiral Byrd is trying to fly his airplane over the South Pole."

"That is not possible," Gregor said. "Perhaps it is some sort of joke."

"To fly an airplane to the bottom of the earth?" Pavlovsky laughed. "I wouldn't think so. He will probably crash into the sea."

"How far away is the South Pole?" Gregor tried to imagine flying that far. It must be terrifying to leave the earth.

"I have no idea. I was not paying attention when that lesson was taught."

The pork chops arrived surrounded by a mound of soft white potatoes and bright orange, overcooked carrots. In just a few weeks Gregor had already learned that while Americans had plenty of inexpensive food, none of the chefs seemed to know how to cook. Pavlovsky didn't seem to mind. He ate every morsel, wiping his plate clean with a thick slice of bread.

The waiter appeared and refilled their coffee cups.

"I want beer," Pavlovsky pushed away his empty plate.

"No beer," said the waiter. "It's the Prohibition, you know."

Gregor noticed a slight smile turn the corners of the young man's lips. Gregor reached into his pocket and removed his wallet. Extracting a one-dollar bill, he held it out. "Perhaps . . . ?"

"Yes sir," said the waiter, his smile growing bigger. "There is a private lounge car at the end of the train. Some of the men go back there to smoke big cigars after dinner." The young man reached down and slid his hand over the bill. "I don't know what else they do down there. It's private, but my friend Cecil, he cleans up in the morning. I'll ask him if you two can join the others for a cigar."

"*Danke*—Thank you," said Gregor. He turned to Pavlovsky and said in Russian, "I think our lives have been saved."

Chapter Twenty-seven

New York City

Gregor glanced at the program. Carnegie Hall, December 27, 1929. This day would mark the beginning or the end of his career. It was the only performance that really mattered. He slid the program into the music pocket of his cello case. If he succeeded he would save the program forever. If he failed, he'd light a match to it.

He sat in the empty rehearsal room tuning the cello, adjusting the pegs a fraction. First he played pizzicato, listening to the ring. Then he drew the bow over each string, listening. Finally he ran through two scales, adjusted the A string with the fine tuner and tightened the bow a quarter turn. When he played he hunted for any flaw that might spoil the tone of even a single note. Then he sat, eyes closed, counting each breath, exhaling as slowly as possible. He wished he could vomit, purge himself of doubt, of fear, of despair.

Here in New York City, in Carnegie Hall, his career could be destroyed by any one of the music critics from a half dozen newspapers. They would sit in the audience waiting for him to fail. Their reviews would be read all over America. His fate rested entirely on Conductor Wilhelm Mengelberg, a heavyset Dutchman with an enormous head.

The schedule allowed for only one rehearsal with the New York Philharmonic. The very idea of playing with a new conductor and a new orchestra robbed him of sleep the night before. Images of every conceivable disaster swirled through his mind. Broken strings, untuned violins, obnoxious brass and squeaky woodwinds, illness. What if he felt dizzy and fainted? At two in the morning he paced the floor of his hotel room unable to sleep. He tried staring out the window at the city lights. They never went off in New York. It was never really night. He lay in bed listening to the *pinging* of the steam radiators. He was hungry and nauseated at the same time.

He wished Pavlovsky were here instead of entertaining the ladies of St. Louis. If he had had someone to talk to, someone who would understand what he faced, he might have been able to sleep. But he was alone and sleep would not come.

At ten minutes after nine, he and the other musicians waited for Mengelberg to start the rehearsal. "Do you admire Maestro?" Gregor said as he stood beside Alfred Wallenstein, both men smoking in a cloud of blue. "Is he a good conductor?" Gregor tapped out another Lucky Strike and offered it to the cellist.

"He's a man who doesn't like to rush the music," Wallenstein said, exhaled and coughed. "Never gets here on time either. Don't be in a hurry with this old bear."

Another fifteen minutes and several cigarettes passed before Mengelberg appeared from behind the curtain and stepped on the podium. The orchestra members wandered to their seats and Gregor tried to make eye contact with the conductor while he took the solo chair. There was no indication that the man had noticed him. Still, Gregor waited for the customary announcement from Mengelberg that would introduce him to the rest of the musicians. It didn't happen.

"*Ve vill* begin the Dvorak Concerto," Mengelberg said in thick, accented English. "And you *vill* play it in accordance with the composer's wishes, not your own." He tapped the baton as if scolding a disobedient child. "You *vill* follow my directions exactly."

He raised his arms and with a downward stroke set a tempo so slow and heavy that Gregor wondered if he were looking at the wrong score. The violins came in late, playing louder than necessary, as if volume would make up for speed. When the brass section entered they tried to pick up the tempo.

"*Nein, nein,*" thundered Mengelberg. "Stop playing. You go too fast. Follow me."

Gregor looked over his shoulder at Wallenstein. The man's eyes never left his music stand. If they played at Mengelberg's tempo, the audience would fall asleep before Gregor could begin his solo.

"You *vill* follow me," the conductor shouted. "Look at me. Get your noses out of the music." His loose jowls and thick neck shook as he pointed to the concertmaster. "Are you in a hurry to relieve yourself?"

The young man's face turned red.

"*Ve vill* begin again." Mengelberg tapped his baton. "These Americans," Gregor heard him mumble. "Nothing but farmers."

The orchestra members were silent as tension hung heavy in the air. When Mengelberg raised his arms they began again, playing ponderously, like an old man carrying a heavy burden.

"No, no. You must follow me," Mengelberg cried as he stopped then restarted the piece at the same place. Gregor felt like he was sinking into a quagmire. His debut would be a disaster and there was nothing he could do. The music critics would skewer him if he played according to Mengelberg's instructions.

Ten minutes. Twenty. He hadn't played a single note. The three-minute introduction stretched interminably. The tension in his belly increased. His palms grew damp and he wiped them on his pants. Each time the orchestra neared the point where Gregor was to enter, the conductor waved his arms and they stopped.

"It is clear that many of you wish to be elsewhere," Mengelberg said. He stepped from the podium. "If you are unwilling to follow me then go relieve yourselves."

Gregor stood along with the others, some of whom muttered and shook their heads. He had to speak with Mengelberg, to explain that the *tempo* needed to move faster. Surely the man would understand.

While most of the others moved away from the conductor, Gregor followed Mengelberg through the curtain backstage. "Excuse me, sir," he kept his voice low.

"What is it? What do you want?"

"I played this concerto many times. I performed with Mlynarski in Warsaw. Also Furtwangler in Berlin. Always much faster. You should—,"

"I don't care what you think!" Mengelberg screamed. Orchestra members standing near the stage door turned and stared. "I conducted this concerto when Dvorak himself was present. The tempo I am taking is the one he wanted. All of you . . . you . . . idiots are wrong!"

Gregor stepped back, embarrassed by the man's outburst and the attention it caused.

"Please, I want to tell you that—."

"I don't care what you or anyone else wants." With that Mengelberg turned, pushed his way past the others and left, slamming the door behind him.

"When he gets like this it does no good to point out the obvious," said the concertmaster. He tucked his violin under his arm. "The slower his tempo, the louder we play."

Twenty minutes later the torture began again. The notes and rests hung in the air as if weighted by stones. When time came for Gregor's solo entrance he focused on Mengelberg's face and took the opening bars at almost twice the conductor's tempo.

"Halt. Halt," Mengelberg waved his arms in the air. "You are playing too fast."

"No." Gregor stared at the conductor. "Your tempo is too slow."

"It must be played as I conduct it. You will follow me."

"No." Gregor rose from his chair and closed his score. "I will not follow you." With his cello and bow in hand, he turned and walked off the stage. Absolute silence followed him. All Gregor could hear was the pounding of his own heart. Then behind him he heard the orchestra break into applause as he ran for the restroom.

Alone in the men's room, he soaked a hand towel with water and pressed it to his face. The cold cloth on his overheated skin sent a chill down his spine.

"I don't believe I did it," he muttered inside the fabric. "Please. No. I didn't do it." He lowered the cloth and stared at the idiot in the mirror. The idiot stared back. "You are ruined," the image said.

"Grisha?" The voice was American.

Gregor turned and saw the orchestra manager peering through the restroom door. "I've been looking all over for you." The grim faced man entered the room then locked the door behind him. "You can't walk out on this program." His voice reminded Gregor of Papa. It had been years since he had heard that tone.

"I will not play," he heard himself say. "I cannot do what he asks."

"Need I remind you," the man said, a frown creasing his face. "That you have a contract to fulfill?"

"I will not play badly. I will not let him destroy Dvorak. It is injustice to the composer and—"

"You don't understand Mengelberg." The manager lit a cigarette and began pacing the small room. "This is Mengelberg's last season with the Philharmonic. He's old and tired. Can't you be charitable?"

Gregor stood with his back against the wall, arms folded across his chest. "It is better if newspapers say I did not play at all, than say I played badly."

"Listen to me," the man pointed the glowing cigarette at Gregor's face. "When Mengelberg was young he studied with all the great composers. He knew Schumann, Brahms, Wagner and Dvorak. He says that he has their absolute authority when he conducts."

"The audience and newspapers will not care. They will remember only bad performance and my name."

"Will you play if I can convince him to increase the tempo?"

"I will consider it. But I believe his answer will be, *nyet.*"

"Let me talk to him." The manager ground out his cigarette on the edge of the sink. "I'll try and make him understand."

* * *

Gregor wore his black tuxedo, crisp white shirt and white silk tie. With an hour to go before the performance, he and the other orchestra members milled about behind the curtain. There was much whispering and several musicians glanced in his direction.

"Are you going to play?" The French horn player said as he removed his instrument from its case.

"I do not know." Beneath his jacket Gregor was already sweating. He felt the starched fabric sticking to the skin of his neck. It would only get worse when he walked on stage.

"You were very brave to leave like that," Wallenstein said. "I've wanted to do it but never dared."

"Many of us have wanted to protest his abuse of the music," said the tall, sad-faced bass player. "But if we did we would be dismissed. This is no time for a man with a family to risk unemployment."

At that moment the rear stage door opened. The concertmaster entered followed by the orchestra manager.

"Unfortunately, Maestro Mengelberg is not feeling well," the manager announced. "The concertmaster will replace him and the second violin will take the first chair."

A buzz arose from the assembled orchestra as they all moved toward their seats. Gregor felt a hand on his arm and turned to see the bass player. "You did it," the man said in a low voice. "You drove him out."

Gregor felt suddenly weak. Was it really his fault? Was he responsible? He sank onto his chair and stared at the floor. He had to regain his focus and stop thinking about Mengelberg. This was his premiere and he was in Carnegie Hall. He had to play his absolute best.

Closing his eyes, he ran the fingers of his left hand up the neck and felt the familiar tingle. He let the bow touch the strings. The note was drowned out by the chaos of sound around him. Exhaling slowly several times, he opened his eyes.

The concertmaster, a man much smaller than Mengelberg, tapped his baton on the podium. He looked pale and Gregor noticed the man's hand tremble. I won't let him down, he thought. I won't let any of them down.

December 27, 1929

Dear Leo, This is the greatest night of my life. I played Dvorak with the New York Philharmonic in Carnegie Hall. Mengelberg was to conduct but the concertmaster took his place. I was happy. The Maestro took the tempo too slow. Even the orchestra members complained. But all went well and the reviews were excellent, at least those that I could read. Leo, I know Papa would have been proud. I wish you and he could have been there, and Mama too. I have enclosed a clipping from the New York Times. You see the photograph? It was taken in Berlin last year and now all of New York knows the name Piatigorsky. Show Mama my letter, please. And tell little Alex that his brother has not forgotten him. I know he is not so little anymore, but that is all I know. Please send me pictures. I have nothing but my memories.

Love always, your brother Grisha.

Gregor folded the letter and sealed it inside the envelope. Tomorrow he would mail it, but tonight he needed to celebrate. A soloist should be applauded. Toasts should be made. But how could he make a toast alone? He wished he had a pretty woman, any woman who would go dancing with him. He would buy her drinks and they would laugh. Well, maybe not drinks, not here in America where people couldn't even buy beer except in hiding. How could a man celebrate an important occasion without a drink?

On the bedside table lay a copy of the New York Times. *WORST SINCE 1892* screamed the headline. JOBLESS RATE 20% HIGHER FOR NEGROS. The text of the articles was too difficult to read.

He had purchased the paper hoping to locate news of the concert, announcements, predictions or at least a photo. Something he could mail back home to prove he had really played Carnegie Hall.

The overheated hotel room made him sweat. He dropped the newspaper on the bed then pulled off his shoes and stripped to his shorts. The steam radiator beneath the window hissed and popped as if it was trying to compensate for his undressing by cranking out even more heat.

He felt the sudden need for fresh air and studied the window latch. After a few tries he figured out how to open it, but the sash only went up six inches. Probably to prevent those inflicted with melancholy from ending their sorrows. How different from Moscow or Berlin where no hotel owner would think of interfering with someone's personal desire to destroy himself.

Returning to the bed, he stretched out and folded the small pillow under his neck. As he scanned each page of the newspaper, he looked for the word *music* or *Carnegie Hall*. Easily recognizable were the photos of the British King and Queen flanking a map of England. There was a long article about a murder and another account of Admiral Byrd's exploits. He flipped past the pages that described sports, which meant nothing to him.

A picture of Rudolph Valentino made him stop, but he couldn't understand the movie review. On the following page he saw *MUSICAL NOTES by Olin Downes*, the Times most important music critic. As he swallowed hard his heart beat a little faster. A cursory scan of the column turned up his name, though misspelled. Farther down he saw the word *cellist*.

Line by line he deciphered the article, picking out the words he knew or thought he understood. *Virtuoso. Brilliant* and *magnificent*. Thankfully he saw no sign of the dreaded *but*. Only after rereading it twice did he finally breathe a sigh of relief.

Using the thin blade of his pocketknife, he cut out the article then tucked the clipping in his briefcase. Through the hole he had made in the newspaper, he saw another familiar picture. *Jamblin Joe and his New Orleans jazz Quartet!! Just back from Europe. See them in Harlem at Le Cirque Bistro*. Four smiling dark brown faces stared at him from the page. Real Negro jazz right here in New York. Where else could he hear such a wonderful modern sound?

Leaping to his feet, he discarded the newspapers and grabbed his suit from the closet. There would be plenty of time to read reviews tomorrow. Tonight he was going to Harlem.

"Harlem?" said the cab driver. "That's way uptown, Amsterdam and hundred and twenty. You want to go to Nigger town?"

Gregor slid into the back seat and nodded. "Yes, I want to see Jamblin Joe." He held up the newspaper clipping. "You know this music?"

"Never heard of 'em, probably just a hole in the wall speakeasy. Bet they don't let whites in. What the hell, I'll drop you at a hundred and ten. That should be close enough."

The cab moved into traffic, heading north past the hotels with glittering lights and uniformed doormen, through a huge square crowded with people and up along a dark, tree-lined park. As they passed big three-story homes with carved balconies and railings, the traffic lessened. Gregor sat in back, his face pressing against the window. So many cars, so many lights, so many people and it was almost midnight. This was the most exciting place he had ever seen.

When they reached the intersection of 110th Street and Amsterdam Avenue the cab slowed then pulled to the curb. "Here you go." The driver got out and opened the back door. "Welcome to Harlem. You're probably the only white man west of Amsterdam Avenue." He held out his hand. "That'll be seventy-five cents."

Gregor slid out of the back seat and handed the man a dollar.

"You want change?"

Gregor recognized the sound of a man hoping for a tip. "Thank you—much for bringing me to Harlem." He shook the man's hand.

"Anytime." The cabby pocketed the bill.

The cab pulled away, making a fast U turn in front of oncoming traffic, leaving him alone on the sidewalk, staring at Harlem. Three and four story buildings cluttered with signs lined the avenue. On the upper floors blank windows stared down at him. Despite the damp December weather, music spilled from several open doorways along the street. Two little Negro boys carrying huge newspaper sacks ran toward him.

"Wanna paper? Wanna Post?" said one boy.

"Not him. Me, me," said the other boy.

"You see." Gregor held out the clipping. "Joe Jamblin. You know this?"

The taller boy turned the picture so he could see it by the light of the street lamp. "They play up at one twenty fifth, over from Amsterdam."

"That way," said the smaller boy, pointing north. "See the sign."

Gregor couldn't understand a word the boys said, but at least he knew which way to go. He reached into his pocket and gave each boy a five-cent piece. Their smiles and chatter continued as they again tried to shove newspapers at him. When he shook his head no, the boys scurried away toward the cab that had pulled up to the curb. Before the passengers could disembark, the boys were already hawking their wares.

Gregor headed north along Amsterdam Avenue. How strange, he thought. The street was named for a Dutch city but there were no signs that a single Dutchman lived here. All the faces he saw were various shades of brown.

Some buildings had doors and windows boarded up while others looked freshly painted and occupied. The window of a grocery shop was filled with a pyramid of canned goods. Next to it a meat market displayed de-feathered chickens and great glistening hams. He heard voices calling out and looked up. The yellow streetlight illuminated the tiny brown faces of children peering down at him, their noses pressed flat against the glass.

A dog wandered out of an alley and sniffed at his feet, but when he tried to pet the animal it growled and ran away. Ahead he saw a windowless door open as bright light spilled onto the sidewalk. A group of people emerged from an establishment, Savannah's Silver Dollar Lounge. They were laughing and in good spirits.

The two Negro men wore stylish suits and fedora hats. Each one also had a woman on his arm. The young ladies were dark-skinned and dressed in the latest fashion. One had a skirt so short the fringed hem just touched the top of her knees. The other girl wore a long coat with a fur collar, which she hugged to her cheek as she laughed. Both of the women reminded Gregor of the pictures he had seen in Paris of Josephine Baker.

"*Pardon, monsieur.*" He approached the group, "I must find Jamblin Joe."

"What'd he say?" the tall man said.

His companion shrugged. "Got me. You think he's lost?"

"Sure enough," said the fur-coated woman. "But he's mighty big to be lost."

"Jamblin Joe," Gregor said, this time more slowly. "Jazz?" He held out the newspaper clipping. The woman in the short dress studied it. "He's looking for Jamblin Joe and the Peppers."

"Jamblin Joe is cookin' up the tunes on a hundred and twenty fifth and 'dam Avenue," said the tall man. "There's a crowd up there now."

The tall man waved to an oncoming taxi. "Listen to me, my man. You keep heading up Amsterdam Avenue for two more blocks then turn left." He motioned with gloved hands. "That's where Joe's playing."

"A hundred n' twenty five" Gregor repeated while he walked. At each intersection he studied the street signs until he saw one that read 125th Street. Crossing over Amsterdam Avenue, he found himself on a side street in total darkness. The warm yellow glow of the street lamps did not extend into the dirty, cluttered alley. Above him lights shone from a few apartment windows, but their rays didn't penetrate the street level darkness. He hesitated. How could he find a jazz club when he could hardly see his hand in front of his face?

The faint sound of a tinny piano reached his ears, but it was coming from below the street. With a rough iron fence as a guide, he moved forward until the sound grew louder. A few steps down below street level, a door flew open and laughter competed with the sound of a saxophone. A man staggered up the steps followed by a woman. The light from inside the club held them in silhouette for a moment.

"Jamblin Joe?" Gregor asked. "Is he here?"

"Who's askin'?" said the man.

"I am musician. I am here for jazz."

"Then you got it. This place is the best damn jazz club in town."

The woman hung on the man's arm as if she would fall without his support. "You're going to love him," she said. "Joe has the best horn in Harlem."

"*Danke*," Gregor said. He tipped his hat as the couple headed toward brightly-lit Amsterdam Avenue, still laughing. Never before had he heard people so happy. Harlem must be a wonderful place to live, possibly the best place in all of America.

Le Cirque Bistro was crowded with people, all Negro. A layer of blue smoke hung near the low ceiling and the room smelled of sweat. In the front of the room sat a group of musicians, all dressed in identical white suits. The contrast between the fabric and their skin made their faces appear even darker. On a low stage stood a narrow upright piano and beside it a drummer and two men holding two unusual woodwind instruments. A double bass stood in the back. The dog-faced trumpeter occupied center stage. Jamblin Joe.

The little round tables scattered around the room held assorted bottles and glasses but few people sat. In the middle of the dance floor couples were locked arm in arm and hip to hip, moving to the beat of the music. The crowd standing around the wall watched the activity on the dance floor, snapping their fingers and clapping their hands. No one seemed to notice Gregor.

The drummer tapped out on the rim of his instrument, then the pianist started the next number with a low rumbling chord. A moment later the trumpet pierced the air with a shrill high C note that slid down an octave. As the music grew louder the tempo grew faster. The throbbing beat of the drum synchronized with the plucked strings of the bass.

"Go man. Go!" Someone shouted. Others took up the chant. The trumpeter played louder until his cheeks bulged and his eyes were ready to pop. The sound drew the remaining people to the dance floor like a magnetic force. Twisting, turning bodies swallowed up the floor space that remained. The expressions on the dancers' faces were ecstatic, unlike anything Gregor had ever seen. Even the waiters discarded their trays and joined in the dance.

He stood, his back pressed against the wall, watching this strange and exotic ritual. But the rhythm was infectious. An irresistible force pulled at him, drawing him toward the dance floor. No longer hidden in shadow, people began to notice him. One slim woman in a tight red dress pointed, then said something to her companion. The short, muscular Negro man turned and stared. So did others. For a moment he considered fleeing. Then a smile stretched across the man's broad black face.

"Welcome." He pushed his way through the crowd and extended his hand. Gregor shook it. The grip was strong. "Just tell me you ain't no revenue agent," he said. His smile grew as the grip tightened.

"I do not... understand English," Gregor stammered. "I musician—cellist."

"Ha! You hear that talk?" He motioned to a tall man in a dark double-breasted suit. "He's no Fed. Come on in. I'm Henry and this is my place." He escorted Gregor through the crush of people. "Netty." He motioned to the woman in the red dress. "Teach this man some moves. Show him how it's done."

"My, oh my." Netty moved toward Gregor, looking up at him with soft brown eyes. "You are a big one." Her dark skin glistened with perspiration. "You want to dance with me?"

Without waiting for an answer, she took him by the hand and pulled him onto the floor. Her feet moved rhythmically forward, back then side to side. He tried to mimic her steps but his feet felt like boxes.

"Put some hip into it." She placed one firm hand on his backside as she gyrated. The long string of white beads hanging from her neck swung like a pendulum. "Don't look at your feet, look at me."

He dragged his eyes off his feet and focused on her face. It was a warm pleasant face, not beautiful like a movie star but interesting and sensual. She smiled and her teeth were as white as her beads.

The pulse of the music vibrated through the floor, into Gregor's feet, up his legs and into his groin. He abandoned any pretense of control. With arms flapping and legs churning, he let the rhythm swallow him. The music was intoxicating, surrounding him in a sea of flesh and sweat. The air, overheated with smoke and sound, was as thick as seawater. No longer an alien among strangers, he was part of the group, one of the whole, part of a great human heartbeat.

"Go baby, GO!" Netty cried, pushing her hips toward him

With wild abandon he grabbed Netty's hand and spun her around. She laughed and slid her arms around his waist. Together they danced to one song, then another and another. The crowd parted as she pulled him toward the stage. Sweat poured from his every pore as he sucked in great gulps of smoky air.

Netty's energy was boundless and the crowd roared with approval as Gregor caught the small of her back with his arm. She arched over it, her hips pressed against his thighs, her head nearly touching the floor. If the band hadn't finally stopped, he would have danced until he collapsed. When Jamblin Joe hit the last shrill note the musicians and the dancers dropped to the floor. Gregor staggered toward the open door gasping for fresh air, dripping with sweat.

"Hey, man, you coming back for more?" Henry cried.

Gregor didn't have the energy to speak. Outside, the cold December air was refreshing. He loosened his tie and pulled off his jacket. Staggering toward Amsterdam Avenue, he kept his eye on the street lamp just ahead. When he reached the corner, he stopped and ran his fingers through his damp hair. Anyone seeing him would think he was drunk and indeed he felt intoxicated. Never before had Gregor behaved with such abandon. Feeling both exhilarated and exhausted, he wiped his brow with his handkerchief and looked for a cab. The street was empty, but for a lopsided truck moving slowly along the curb as invisible hands tossed bundles of newspapers to the curb.

By the time he walked three blocks, his teeth chattered and he was sure his wet shirt was freezing to his body. Headlights glowed from behind a rusty car, its side door marked with hand-painted letters, cruised slowly past. He waved and the car pulled to the curb. The Negro driver leaned over the passenger seat and rolled down the window.

"Need a ride, mister?"

"*Da*, Carlyle Hotel," he said as he slid into the back seat.

"Yes, sir," said the man. "Your first time in Harlem?"

"*Da*," Gregor said as he closed his eyes and dropped his head back onto the seat. "It is wonderful!"

"What's that?"

"Wonderful." He took a deep breath. "Everything is wonderful. I love America."

"If you say so." The man shook his head. "I can tell for sure you ain't been in this country long."

Chapter Twenty-eight

Berlin, Germany
May 1932

National Socialists win 23 more seats in the Reichstag.
Hitler demands audience with Hindenburg!
Nazis and Communists clash in streets.
Two shot dead, dozens more injured.
Police make no arrests.

The driver slammed the brakes and the cab slid on wet pavement almost plunging into the crowd. "Damn those Bavarians." He put the vehicle in reverse. "They should go back to Munich or burn in hell."

"What are they doing?" Gregor said, leaning forward from the back seat.

"Doing? Haven't you heard about these troublemakers?"

"I've been in Paris and Rome for the past two months."

The cab's back wheel bumped onto the sidewalk as the driver executed a tight U turn. "Ever since Hitler lost the election to Hindenburg, the Nazis have been causing trouble."

"But this is the second time Hitler has lost. Why does he persist?"

"He wants to take over the Reichstag. If he does, he'll expel all the Communists and the Jews."

Gregor sank back into the seat and stared out the side window. He had been gone two months, but in that short time things in Berlin had gone from uncomfortable to chaotic. Though he didn't care much about politics, he couldn't help but pay attention to the April elections. A month ago it seemed the Nazis would accept defeat and return to Munich. The brown-shirted bullies had few friends in Berlin. Now the marching, chanting Nazis were everywhere.

The cab driver maneuvered down a narrow side street. On the corner, the window of a kosher butcher shop was smashed, a freshly painted yellow Star of

David dripped down the door. The next two shops were also smeared with graffiti.

"If the Jews left," said the cabdriver as he looked left before turning toward the center of the city. "Everyone would calm down. These Nazis don't know how to run a country." He punctuated the air with his finger as he spoke. "Now take the Communists. They know how to take care of people. Look at Russia. No one goes hungry with Papa Stalin in charge."

For an instant Gregor imagined putting his hands around the German's thick neck and strangling him. A stupid urge that he shook off. "Have you ever been to Russia?"

"No, but my brother took me to a communist party meeting. They know what they're talking about. I'm thinking of joining if my wife doesn't object."

Disgusting. How could this well-fed German possibly know what hunger felt like? He had to get out of the cab.

"Stop."

The cab pulled to the curb. Before them the Brandenburg Gate rose like a Roman monument against the gray sky. Ahead, more people marched. Red flags with black swastikas waved gaily in the breeze above the heads of Hitler Youth.

"Let me out," Gregor said. "I'll walk the rest of the way."

"What about your luggage?" The cab driver opened the back door. Gregor grabbed his cello and briefcase as the driver exited the car.

"Take the rest of my belongings to Sudwestor Strasse, number seven." He extracted a five-mark note from his wallet. It was all the German currency he had.

"The fare is seven marks," said the cabdriver. "I can hardly feed my family as it is." He extended his hand for more money.

"I have no more Deutche marks." Gregor held open his empty wallet. "All my money is in the Bundes Bank."

The cab driver put his hand on the trunk lid. "Two more marks or I won't deliver the luggage."

Gregor reached into his pocket. "I have two packs of American cigarettes. Will you take them instead?"

The man took the cigarettes, studied the red and white package as he rubbed his chin with a meaty hand.

"You see," Gregor explained. "Lucky Strike. They are very popular in America. The finest tobaccos in the world come from America."

The driver slid the cigarettes into his coat pocket. "Stay away from those bastards." The cabby motioned to the crowd of Nazis. "I've seen them attack people on the street for no reason. The police won't do anything to help."

With his cello in one hand and his briefcase in the other hand, Gregor walked down Telle Strasse toward Sasha Merovitch's apartment. Behind him the pounding drums of the parade grew louder. Before he could cross the street an army of boys carrying a National Socialist Youth banner passed in front of him. They looked as innocent as children on an outing, but these boys didn't smile. Instead, with hands raised in salute, they sang, *"Ein Volk, ein Reich, ein Fuhrer. Heil Hitler. Blood must flow. Only Hitler can save us. Join now and be free."*

Along the sidewalk proud mothers and fathers cheered their children. But the boys didn't cast an eye toward their parents.

Gregor stood at the corner, the sight of the children so much like the Communist Youth Brigade, he trembled with the memory. It was all he could do not to grab the arm of the nearest father and scream at him to save his child. Instead, he said nothing, waiting for the marching boys to pass and the pounding drums to recede. Only when they turned the corner did he step from the curb and cross the wide boulevard.

"You there!" He felt a tug on his sleeve. "Wait, I want to talk to you." A middle-aged man, dressed in the starched Nazi brown shirt and canvas sack slung from one shoulder, pulled at Gregor's arm. "I can tell you're an intelligent man." He reached into his bag and extracted a small brown pamphlet. "This volume will tell you everything about the enemy and it is only three Deutche marks."

Gregor set the cello case on the curb as the man pressed <u>Handbuch fur Judenfrage</u> into his hand.

"Nein!" Gregor pushed the man's hand away.

The little Nazi persisted. "Come. You look like our kind of fellow. *Der Fuhrer* wants you to read this. Join us and we will rid our nation of Bolsheviks, Jews and all manner of foreign vermin."

"You are an idiot. I don't want your filthy book." Gregor dropped his briefcase and with both hands shoved the little man back toward the street. "I am Russian and a Jew. Where can I find an organization that will help rid the city of vermin like you?"

"Jew!" The man gasped as if he had been burned. He turned and ran down the street toward his fellow Nazis, crying. "Communist! Swine! Jew!"

Gregor didn't wait to see what would happen next. At a near run, he headed in the opposite direction, down the tree-lined avenue, glancing only once over his shoulder. But the quiet residential street remained empty. By the time he climbed the stairs to Merovitch's apartment he was soaked with sweat and gasping for breath.

"Let me in." He clenched his fist and pounded on the door.

"Grisha, you're back," Merovitch said when he opened the door, a surprised look on his round face. "Grisha, you're back. Why didn't you call? Where are your bags?" He led Gregor into the dining room. "You look like you need a drink."

"I need two. Scotch." He stood his cello in the corner then sank into the overstuffed chair. "The Nazis are marching in Brandenburgerplatz. One of them tried to sell me a filthy book."

"The brown shirts are peddling that book all over the city." Merovitch chuckled. "I bought one. Was surprised it didn't have my name in it."

"What is it?"

"A silly thing. Garbage. It lists people they think are enemies of the nation. Each edition gets thicker. Soon everyone of importance will be listed." He opened the Scotch and poured a generous glass. "Even you. The last edition listed all the great soloists. Horowitz and Menuhin too ."

"But Menuhin's American and he's a child."

"You see what I mean. The Nazis are afraid of children."

"Most of them are children."

"They're idiots. I'm surprised you didn't read about it in the Paris papers."

"I knew Hitler had lost the election, but I had no idea things had gotten this bad." He accepted the glass of Scotch and downed it in two gulps. Exhaling slowly, he waited for the fiery liquor to course its way through his body. "The Paris newspapers are not interested in politics." He extended the empty glass and Merovitch refilled it. "The Parisians care only about wine, the price of ripe cheese and the cinema."

"Then they are wise." Merovitch took the chair across from Gregor and lit a cigarette. "And we are the fools. Don't be concerned. This unrest will soon pass. The Nazis don't have enough supporters here in Berlin. In every election they are defeated. No one takes Hitler seriously any more."

"The people in the street seem to." Gregor loosened his tie. "Everyone worries about money and jobs, even the cab drivers."

"Forget that. In a few months you'll be in New York and no one will care about a Bavarian corporal and his brown pests."

"Things are no better in America." Gregor closed his eyes and let his arms hang down the sides of the chair. "The audiences are small. Judson dropped ticket prices so he can fill the halls."

"If the communists had their way, admission to all concerts would be free." Merovitch blew smoke toward the ceiling.

"Yes, and artists would be paid in bread and shoes." Gregor pointed a finger at Merovitch. "And there would be no need for agents or managers."

"What a horrible thought." Merovitch grinned. "Thankfully, that will never happen here. By the way, your friends came by yesterday. Horowitz thinks we should all relocate to Paris but Milstein says Spain."

"Paris?" Gregor said, studying Merovitch's bland face. "You said all this craziness would soon pass."

"I am sure it will." He blew another cloud of smoke into the air. "But in the meantime it creates a distraction. Paris is an ideal place and the French are so appreciative of good music. I think it would be wise to take an apartment there as soon as possible."

"You mean move? Now?"

"Find yourself comfortable lodgings. Nothing permanent, of course. Just until things settle down here. When Herr Hitler and his friends get tired of losing and return to Munich, we can all come home."

"Moving is not that easy. The French police require me to re-apply for a work visa every thirty days."

"Then do it. It is only a formality."

"Easy for you to say. You have a passport."

"Why don't you get one from Haiti, like Milstein did."

"Haiti?" Gregor laughed at the absurdity of it. "The Haitian government has an immigration quota. Only one Russian Jew a year and Milstein has already filled it. I think American papers would be better."

"I have a friend in Paris who is already helping Horowitz find an apartment." Merovitch waved his hand as if dismissing Gregor's concern. "I'm sure he can assist you. I've also arranged for the usual August lodging in Switzerland." He stood and took Gregor's empty glass. "Do you have anyone you'd like to bring along? A lady perhaps."

"I wish I knew one who likes the Alps." Gregor exhaled and stared at his hands. After four years touring America and Europe he knew he was the best cellist in the world, but with beautiful women he felt like a clumsy oaf.

"Maybe," Merovitch grinned, "Milstein will have a spare he could loan you."

* * *

Gregor hesitated, his hand lingering on the doorknob. There was no nameplate on the plain wooden door. Nothing indicated that this little room at the end of the hall was the official sanctum of Conductor Wilhelm Furtwangler. He knocked and waited.

"Come in."

Gregor took a deep breath and entered. Every surface in the narrow room was piled with music scores, opened books and newspapers.

"Come, come, Grisha." Furtwangler motioned him to the only other chair, an uncomfortable straight back piece of furniture that matched the one Furtwangler's lanky frame was slouched in. "We have no time to waste. You're leaving soon. When?"

"Today." Gregor removed a copy of the score for Wagner's *Gotterdammerung* from the chair before sitting. "I have to take the train to Bremen at three. My ship leaves tomorrow morning for New York."

"Milstein is going with you?"

"Yes, and Horowitz. Judson has us playing a benefit for American musicians at Town Hall in ten days." Out of habit, Gregor pulled a cigarette from the thin case that fit inside his jacket pocket. Without thinking, he lit it. The match burned toward his fingers and he blew it out, but there was no place to put the matchstick. Furtwangler didn't seem to notice as he thumbed through a stack of papers.

"The Brahms Festival. You'll be back in time for that." It wasn't a question.

"I'll return in late March, certainly by April first." He slid the burnt matchstick into his pocket. With the first drag he felt the nicotine course through his body, pushing away the edginess he had felt all morning. Nothing to worry about now.

"Good. I want you to play the "Don Quixote" for me in late April and the Schumann Concerto in May before the Festival." For a moment Furtwangler sounded just like Papa. No discussion, no room for questions.

"Of course, I want very much to play for you," he said. The ash on his cigarette grew longer, dangerously close to falling. Gregor looked around the room for something to deposit it in. The nearby trash can, filled with paper, was useless.

He cupped his left hand under the cigarette, catching the ashes as they fell. Furtwangler looked over his glasses. "I must have you play—." A deep furrow formed between the man's gray eyebrows. "Are you trying to burn down the Concert Hall?" Without waiting for a reply, he pushed aside a pile of newspapers and retrieved a coffee cup. "Here, for God's sake. Use this."

Gregor grabbed the cup and managed to get most of the ash in it with only a small amount falling on the carpet.

"I'm sorry." He stubbed the cigarette out in the sticky brown residue of old coffee.

"I don't care if you smoke," Furtwangler said. "But the last time I used the waste basket, I nearly burned down the building." He ran his hand over the long gray hair that circled only the back of his head. "Now I only smoke in the lavatory."

"I can wait." Gregor tried not to smile at the thought of Maestro puffing while sitting on the toilet.

Furtwangler pulled a calendar from the pile. "April fifteenth. Quixote," he said as he penciled in Piatigorsky. "May second, Schumann."

"May I send you a cable from New York if I'm free on those dates?"

"Why?" Furtwangler's eyebrows went up. "Do you anticipate a problem?"

"Sasha Merovitch mentioned a possible engagement in Argentina for May."

Furtwangler turned to face him, his black eyes the only dark spots in his otherwise pale face. "Grisha, I know the orchestra cannot reward you in the way you deserve. But before all others, I come to you."

"Maestro, Berlin is my home. When I am here, playing with you is my greatest pleasure."

"I'm pleased to hear that." Furtwangler relaxed back in his chair and smiled. "Four months in America is long enough for anyone. How long can you survive in a country where it is a crime to drink beer?"

"The Americans have a way. If you're willing to pay, a man can find beer, whiskey or anything else he desires."

"But it is still a savage country full of—."

"Cowboys and Indians?" Gregor said. "You warned me about them three years ago. You said they'd cut the hair from my head and pierce my body with arrows." He laughed. "The only Indians I saw were in Hollywood."

"You were lucky," Furtwangler said while pointing his fountain pen at Gregor. "But I was right about the Indians. I've seen them in the cinema."

"You should return to America," Gregor offered. "It's a wonderful country."

"And full of communists!" Furtwangler shook his head. "If Roosevelt wins the election, all America will become Red."

"You think Roosevelt is a communist?" Gregor again reached for the cigarette case then caught himself. "I think Americans hate communists."

"I read in *Zeitungvaterland*." Furtwangler rubbed the side of his temple with his fingers. "If Roosevelt is elected, Stalin will personally attend the inauguration."

Gregor couldn't tell if Furtwangler was joking or serious. "That's a Nazi paper. Merovitch says they always lie." As soon as he spoke, he regretted it. It was rumored among orchestra members, especially Jews, that Furtwangler was a secret Nazi, or at least a sympathizer. Gregor didn't believe it. He knew the man too well.

"Isn't your next American engagement a benefit for the unemployed? How much will you be paid?"

"Nothing. We're donating the proceeds to the musicians fund."

"You see." Furtwangler tapped his forefinger on a pile of old programs. "That's the way it is with the communists. Everything for the poor and nothing for the artist. You should know that. Have you forgotten Moscow?"

He had a point. Gregor had never thought about the political implications of the engagements Judson arranged. The man said a benefit concert was good for business and Gregor believed him.

"But what of the Nazis?" Gregor argued. "Do they care about music?"

"I have assurances from Herr Goebbels that, if the Nazis control the Reichstag, all artists will be exempt from any new restrictions."

"You believe him?"

"Of course. He is no communist."

Gregor felt the growing urge for a cigarette. He glanced at his watch and realized that if he didn't leave soon he would miss the train. "I promise that I'll contact you as soon as I reach New York." He rose and reached for the door.

Furtwangler paid no attention to Gregor leaving. "I don't expect to hear from you," Furtwangler said as he turned back to his pile of music. "Tell Merovitch he must be flexible and postpone your trip to Argentina until June. Then you can spend all summer in Rio if you want."

Cleveland, Ohio
February 1, 1933

Dear Maestro:

News came today of Hitler's appointment as Chancellor. I am in despair that such a thing has happened. When we last met I hardly thought it possible. Now I know I was too naïve, or too hopeful. Many colleagues have told me they will not return to Berlin as long as the Nazis hold power. It saddens me, but I must agree. As a Jew, I cannot betray those who suffer for nothing more than the accident of their birth. This situation cannot last. It makes my heart weak to tell you that I will not play the Don Quixote or the Schumann with you in May. But while this dark cloud hangs over Germany, I dare not return. Please tell me that you understand and forgive me for my fears. I know that you would do all that you could to protect me, but I cannot return. Your fear of Bolshevism in America is without cause. It's true that Roosevelt gives jobs to the poor. The government in every town and city feeds the hungry, but there are no Party meetings and no red flags. Artists are still paid, though much less than before. I know that we will meet again soon, perhaps in Paris or New York. When you come, please know that you have many friends in America and in France. You will be welcome wherever you go.

Always, Your friend, Grisha

Jacqueline and Gregor Piatigorsky returning to France 1937

Jacqueline and Gregor Piatigorsky: US Customs Inspection 1938

September 1939. Gregor, Jephta and Jacqueline Piatigorsky
arrive at Windy Cliff in New Russia, New York.

Windy Cliff, New Russia, New York about 1940

Piatigorsky taken in Elizabethtown by Carl Huttig, 1940s

Jacqueline, Joram, Gregor, Jephta Piatigorsky
with Baron and Baroness de Rothschild at Windy Cliff, June 1940

Gregor Piatigorsky American Citizenship application,
Essex County, New York Courthouse

Jacqueline and Jephta ice skating February 1, 1940 in Elizabethtown, NY

Photo of Gregor Piatigorsky in front of the Essex County Courthouse in
Elizabethtown on the day of his citizenship

PART IV

Chapter Twenty-nine

"In oceans of splendor I was alone,
Mud and laughter were for me unknown."
Jacqueline de Rothschild

Avenue Foch, Paris
June 1935

It sounded wrong. No matter how many times Jacqueline tried, she couldn't get the tempo right. She drooped on the piano bench, defeated. The piece by Debussy wasn't difficult. Alfred Cortot often played it as a warm-up.

"Jacqueline?" Ania peeked through the music salon doorway. "Is that you playing?"

"It's awful, isn't it?" Jacqueline said. She folded her arms and rested them along the music rail. "I practice and practice, but I never get any better."

Ania crossed the room and slid onto the bench beside her. She wore a filmy yellow summer dress with a matching cloche hat. At thirty-three, her friend was more than a decade older, but Jacqueline envied Ania's sense of style. Next to Ania, she always felt invisible.

"Why didn't you come to my tennis party last week?" Ania ran her fingers up and down the keyboard. For Ania everything seemed easy. "We had fabulous fun."

"I wanted to, really." Jacqueline felt herself blush with embarrassment. "But I was just too busy."

"Really?" Ania raised her perfect eyebrows in mock surprise. "Doing what? Mooning over that old man?" She picked up the silver-framed photo of Alfred Cortot that sat on the grand piano. "Jacqueline, he's almost as old as your father. Why are you wasting your time crying over him? He cares not a whit for you."

"That's not true. He and I have an understanding. We share the same love of music."

"He certainly doesn't love *your* music." Ania paused and her tone dropped. "I heard he left yesterday for London and that young Spanish beauty went with him."

Ania's words hit Jacqueline like a blow. She squeezed her eyes shut, trying to hide her disappointment. "He told me he would call before he left—." Of course he had lied to her. It wasn't the first time.

"I'm sorry," Ania said. Jacqueline felt her friend's hand on her shoulder. "But no amount of practice is going to make him love you."

Ania was right. The great Alfred Cortot would never love her. She straightened up and brushed a stray wisp of hair from her face. "If I were Catholic, I'd join a convent and spend the rest of my days counting rosary beads." She tried to force a smile, but failed.

"Oh, silly, don't say that." Ania turned the picture of Cortot face down. "You'll meet the right man. But your prince is not going to come knocking at your door. Of that I'm sure."

"I'll never meet the right man, or any man for that matter." She closed the music score and moved toward the tall windows that overlooked the gardens. "How can I trust them? A dishonest man says he loves me, but what he really wants is my money."

"A rich man won't care about your money."

"They all care about money," she said with a sigh. "Being a Rothschild is a curse. How I envy ordinary people. Their lives are so uncomplicated."

"You don't mean that."

"Even if I met a decent man, he would run the other way when he finds out I'm divorced."

"You were so young. Marrying Robert shouldn't count against you." Ania crossed the room to the window. "It was no marriage at all and no one faults you for leaving him."

"Mother did, at least at first. She said I should ignore his little indiscretions."

"Like bringing his mistress along on your honeymoon?"

"I didn't know that's who she was. I believed him when he said she was his secretary."

"Have you forgotten that he threatened to shoot you, then turned the gun on himself? Too bad the bullet missed. If his aim had been better, you'd be a widow now instead of a divorcee."

Jacqueline noticed the hint of a smile on Ania's face. Now, a year after the fact, the incident with Robert seemed overly dramatic.

"It wasn't the loss of my affection that upset Robert. It was not being able to get his hands on my bank accounts that bothered him most."

"Well, it doesn't mean you have to spend the rest of your life alone."

"I'm not alone, I have Renee. She's with me every day."

"Jacqueline! Renee is your maid. The next thing you'll be telling me is that the concierge is your best friend and the chauffeur is your suitor."

"You might be right. My concierge is the only man I trust."

"My dear Jacqueline, I see that I must take charge of your social life." Ania was already in full control. "Under the circumstances, you are quite incapable of taking care of it yourself."

"I'm afraid you've got an impossible task," Jacqueline said, shaking her head. "I'm too tall and I just don't know how to talk to men. You're much better at conversation than I am."

Ania took Jacqueline's arm and steered her toward the dressing room that adjoined the salon.

"Listen to me. On Thursday I'm giving a little birthday party at the Riviera Club for Josette. I want you to come and wear that light blue dress, the one you wore in May to Cortot's recital."

"Ania, I don't really like parties. I never know what to say."

"You don't have to say anything. Just be there. I've engaged a fabulous trio for the occasion. I heard them last month at the Du Guerre Salon. They're all Russians." Ania giggled. "The pianist is named Valentin. I want you to meet him. There's also a very handsome cellist."

"What should I say?"

"Just tell them you love their music. That should do."

"All right," she said, already thinking of some polite way to bow out. "I'll try to come."

"You promise?" Ania must have read her face. "No changing your mind?"

"Very well, but only if you stay today and have lunch with me. I hate eating alone."

"Of course." Ania headed for the garden patio. "By the way, have you ever played golf?"

"I had lessons when I was young," Jacqueline replied. "But I'm not very good."

"We'll take some lessons together. It's lots of fun. Besides, the golf course is filled with men."

* * *

The chauffeur dropped Jacqueline in front of the Riviera Club. A crowd of partygoers gathered at the door. She hesitated, a tingle of panic in her chest.

"I don't think I'll be long," she told the driver as he held open the door. "Can you wait nearby?"

"Of course." His face was expressionless. "I'll be in the car park near the river. Tell the doorman to call me when you're ready to leave."

Entering the club alone, Jacqueline instantly felt conspicuous. The other women had escorts, handsomely dressed men at their elbows. If she hadn't made that promise to Ania, she'd have turned and gone home.

"I'm here for the birthday party," she said to the maitre d'.

"Of course," he said as he took her coat. "And your escort?"

"I'm alone," she said. The heat of embarrassment flooded her face.

"Oui, Mademoiselle."

He pities me, she thought.

The elegant room was crowded and she scanned the clusters of chatting guests looking for Ania. Several faces seemed familiar from earlier parties, but Jacqueline didn't know anyone well. A waiter in a black tuxedo offered her a drink, but she declined. If she didn't find Ania soon, she would leave.

"There you are." Ania was suddenly at her elbow, steering her toward the guest of honor. "Josette, this is my dear friend, Jacqueline de Rothschild."

"Jacqueline de Rothschild?" A plump, middle-aged lady in an unflattering green dress took her hand. "You were married to my good friend's cousin, Robert Calman Levy. Such a shame. You seem like a very lovely young lady."

Jacqueline forced a smile. "I'm pleased to meet you."

The waiter offered Josette a glass of wine, immediately distracting her and allowing Ania to pull Jacqueline away. "Don't mind her, she's already had too much champagne."

"Do I have to stay long? I don't know anyone."

"You must. The musicians are setting up in the next room and I want you to hear them. They're wonderful."

The two of them made their way through the crowd to the small ballroom where the seats were already filling. A grand piano sat to one side with two chairs on the right.

"Who's performing?" Jacqueline whispered.

"A Russian trio." Ania leaned her head close. "The pianist is Valentin Pavlovsky. He's the one I told you about."

"And the others?"

"Gregor Piatigorsky, he's the tall one. He used to be first cello with the Berlin Philharmonic. When the Nazis took over, Goebbels decreed no Jewish musicians could perform. Maestro Furtwangler lost half his orchestra." Ania pointed to the side door. "There's also a violinist, but I can't pronounce his name."

From the side hall three men entered the salon. The tall one carried his cello above his head like a prizefighter. The other two musicians appeared small next to him. Jacqueline watched as the cellist crossed to the center chair, the others moving in his wake. His dark hair was combed to one side and his stylish suit fit his broad shoulders perfectly. As he turned to face the audience, a smile lit up his face. They all took a slight bow then settled in their seats.

"Isn't the pianist handsome?" Ania said, her voice a whisper..

"Pianist?" Jacqueline hadn't paid attention to the man at the piano. She glanced from the cellist to the piano and saw a fair-haired young man flipping pages of the score. He hardly looked more than a boy.

"When they're finished, I'll introduce you to him," Ania said.

Jacqueline had no interest in the pianist, but what could she say? Behind her a woman spoke in a loud voice. "Isn't that the cellist? Josette invited him up to her apartment after the concert. It is her birthday. I'm going too. Piatigorsky is totally fascinating. I hear women all over Paris are after him."

Jacqueline felt her heart sink. Of course, a man so talented and attractive could have any woman he wanted. Forget the cellist. Better keep her heart and her mind on Alfred Cortot, otherwise she would be competing with every ingénue in Paris. At least Alfred was kind to her during her weekly piano lesson.

Her mind wandered to thoughts of London and the concerts Alfred would play there. What would he say if she showed up at one of his performances? Only the thought of his beautiful Spanish page-turner spoiled the image.

She hardly heard most of the recital. When the program ended she couldn't remember the name of a single piece.

"Come, let me introduce you to the pianist," Ania said after the applause subsided.

"I'd really rather not."

"Oh no, I'm not letting you sneak out of here without meeting at least one man." Ania threaded her way through the crowd, Jacqueline in tow.

As she followed, Jacqueline glanced toward the cellist. A cluster of admirers, most of them women, already surrounded him. Someone must have said something funny and he laughed, a deep wonderful sound. She hesitated, unable to take her eyes off him. Handsome men like that were usually cads, they used women and then disposed of them. Worried her face would betray her thoughts, she turned away. Not fast enough. His eyes caught her gaze and he nodded ever so slightly. She felt her face grow hot.

"This is my dear friend Jacqueline de Rothschild," Ania said. "She's also a pianist."

Jacqueline quickly faced the boy and forced a smile. "I enjoyed your music very much."

"Jacqueline, I want you to meet Valentin Pavlovsky."

Valentin took her hand and gave her a grin. "It is my pleasure," he said in passable but Russian-accented French. Bowing, he kissed the tops of her fingers.

Jacqueline stiffened, caught off guard by his elegant behavior, but afraid to pull her hand back.

"Jacqueline's a very good pianist," Ania lied. "She studies with Alfred Cortot."

"My friend," came a deep voice from behind.

Startled, Jacqueline turned and saw the cellist standing beside her.

"I know you are hungry, Valentin," he continued. "But the lady will need that hand if she plays piano." His deep voice had a strong Russian accent, but his French was understandable.

Jacqueline pulled her hand back from Pavlovsky's grasp.

"I am Gregor Piatigorsky." The cellist extended his hand and shook hers, holding it a little longer than necessary. There was laughter in his eyes and she breathed a sigh of relief. He didn't seem quite so intimidating after all.

"I enjoyed your music very much," she said, praying he wouldn't ask which piece. Why couldn't she think of something witty or flirtatious to say?

"Mr. Piatigorsky?" The loud woman who had sat behind Jacqueline pushed her way through the crowd. "You are coming to Josette's little reception, aren't you?" The woman put her hand on his arm and tried to pull him away.

"I must go," he said and grinned. "Will you come?"

Attend Josette's private party? She froze, unable to come up with any response. Instead, she shook her head, no. With a shrug and a smile, Piatigorsky turned and was pulled back into the crowd.

Why had she panicked? Why couldn't she be bold and flirtatious like other women? He must think she was an idiot.

"Jacqueline?" Ania tugged at her elbow. "Valentin is looking for a page turner for his concert next week. I think you would be perfect."

"Yes," said Valentin, giving her a big smile. "I would like very much to have you assist me." He gave her a little bow. "A woman who can read music and follow the score is very valuable to me."

"Jacqueline would be perfect. She practices the piano every day."

"No!" Jacqueline said, suddenly feeling as if she were being auctioned off. "No, I couldn't possibly do that. I'm much too busy."

"But—?"

Before Ania could say more, Jacqueline put her hand on her friend's arm. "The party's wonderful but I'm sorry, I have to go." She turned and made her escape with the sound of Ania's protest ringing in her ears.

* * *

"Mademoiselle?"

Jacqueline looked up from her lunch and saw the concierge standing at the door that led from the salon to the balcony.

"Yes?" She spread marmalade on a croissant, then looked back up.

"This morning you said you did not want to be disturbed while you were practicing."

"Did someone call?" She cut two large strawberries in half as she spoke. "Was it Ania?"

"No. You received a telephone call from —." He looked at the slip of paper in his hand. "A Monsieur Pi-at-ti-gor-sky."

Jacqueline sat straight up. "When? Why didn't you call me?"

"I told him that you did not want to be disturbed." Now the man looked distressed. "That is what you requested."

Her hands trembled as she took the note. "What did he say? Did he ask that I call him back?"

"No, Mademoiselle. I told him you were busy and he asked when you might be available." He paused. "Was this incorrect?"

"No," she said, sighing. "You didn't know."

She returned to the table and sank back into the chair, her appetite gone. She twisted the linen napkin, then pushed the plate of cheese and fruit away. When she glanced up at the concierge, she saw a twinge of discomfort on his normally serene face.

"I suggested that he call back this afternoon," he offered.

"You did?" The gloom that had settled over her like a gray fog suddenly lifted. She threw the napkin on the marble table and ran from the patio into the house. "Make sure you put the call through to me," she said over her shoulder. "Renee? Renee? Where are you?"

The phone rang at quarter past four and Jacqueline's heart skipped a beat. She glanced at Renee, who was arranging fresh flowers in a vase.

"It's him," said Renee, her voice deferential.

"Should I—?"

"I think you should talk to him."

The phone rang a second time and Jacqueline picked it up, her hand trembling. "Hello?"

"This is Gregor Piatigorsky," said the deep voice. "Mademoiselle?"

"This is Jacqueline de Rothschild."

"I am sorry we could not speak last night. Your friend told me this is your name."

"Did you have a good time at Josette's party?" she asked, then immediately wished she hadn't.

"Yes, but too much chocolate."

"Chocolate?"

"Yes, too much chocolate served. I do not eat before I play. Chocolate does not fill my stomach."

Jacqueline laughed. "I'll be sure to remember that."

"Very good." There was a momentary pause. "I would like to see you again. We can . . ."

"Yes, I would like that," she replied, too quickly.

"When could that be?"

"Do you play golf?" It was the first thing that popped into her head.

"Yes—yes, I play golf."

"Then let's play on Friday. Eleven o'clock? At the golf ground near the river?"

"Very good. I see you then. *Au revoir ,mademoiselle.*"

Jacqueline hung up the phone. She pressed her still trembling hands over her mouth.

"Did he bite you?" Renee set the vase of flowers on a side table.

"Oh no, Renee. Gregor Piatigorsky wants to go out with *me*."

Chapter Thirty

"I called her and she has agreed to see me." Gregor dropped onto a chair in the corner of Valentin's hotel room.

"Who?" Valentin stretched out on the bed and lit a *Gauloise*. Blue smoke swirled toward the high ceiling.

"Jacqueline de Rothschild. I telephoned her and we have an engagement."

Valentin pulled one of the small pillows from behind his head and threw it at Gregor. "I saw her first. You had plenty of ladies to choose from at Josette's party."

"I liked her looks." Gregor lit his own cigarette. "She's taller than the others." He laughed. "And, she's taller than you." He exhaled smoke toward the ceiling. "She also doesn't giggle like a school girl."

"You're the storyteller. I thought you liked to make women laugh?"

"At the right time," Gregor grinned. "And in the right place."

"You should know Mademoiselle Rothschild is also a divorcee," Valentin said smugly.

"You're lying."

"Not at all."

Gregor leaned forward and stubbed his cigarette in the ashtray. "You mean she isn't a Rothschild?"

"Oh no, that is her name. She's the daughter of the Baron Edouard de Rothschild, richest banker in all of France."

"Then she can have any man she wants. She probably has a dozen suitors."

"But Grisha, my friend," Valentin said and laughed. "You see, I love a challenge."

"You only want to have a Rothschild girl as a prize. I don't think she's interested in being your new page turner."

"If you grow tired of her, please let me know." Valentin slid off the bed and went to the dresser where he uncorked a bottle of Canadian Club. "And where will you take the lovely Mademoiselle Rothschild? Not the Folies Bergère I hope." He handed Gregor a glass of whiskey then poured one for himself.

Gregor tossed back the liquor, savoring the fire as it burned its way down his throat. "She invited me to play golf."

Valentin almost choked on his drink as he burst out laughing. "Golf? What does a Russian bear like you know about golf?"

"Nothing, but I think today I will learn. It does not seem difficult. Children play it."

"You don't even have proper golf clothing. What will you wear?"

"Must I have special clothes?"

"Of course, and new shoes too." Valentin checked his profile in the mirror. "I would show you the best clothing stores in Paris, but I have an engagement with a young lady who wants to be my next page turner." He grinned and threw back a second shot of whiskey. "In one hour she and I will practice page turning in her apartment."

* * *

Jacqueline stood at the door of the clubhouse, her eyes scanning the long curving driveway. She had arrived at the golf course half an hour early, which meant now she had to wait and worry. What if he didn't show up? What if he changed his mind? What should she do?

"Will you need two sets of clubs today?" the manager asked.

"Yes—well —maybe. I'm not sure," she stammered. "I'm supposed to meet—meet someone, but I don't know if he'll make it."

"I'll get two sets for you." The manager disappeared into the back room and Jacqueline returned to the doorway. Now she was sure he had changed his mind. She walked out to the grassy lawn where the flag for the first tee fluttered in the warm breeze, then returned to the clubhouse. Humiliation was beginning to sink in. If she called for her driver now, she could avoid further embarrassment. But what if he came and she wasn't here? That would be worse.

At five minutes before eleven a black car turned into the driveway. Jacqueline stepped back from the doorway and held her breath. She didn't want to appear anxious. From inside the clubhouse she watched Gregor Piatigorsky climb out of the back seat. Her heart skipped a beat as she watched him cross the lawn. He wore a dark, charcoal gray suit, white shirt and deep blue tie. He looked strong and confident, attractive enough to take a woman's breath away.

But he didn't look like he was dressed for golf. In that instant, she suddenly realized he had lied. Gregor Piatigorsky had no idea how to play golf. He had probably never even been on a golf course before. Yet still, he had come. He was here because he had wanted to see her.

"Bonjour." He greeted her with an outstretched hand and a smile then ducked his head to get under the low doorframe. "It is a wonderful day for golf."

She looked up at him. "Yes," she replied, her nervousness and fear melting away. "It is a wonderful day."

* * *

She sat in the big chair at the foot of the silk-covered bed where Mother spent her mornings. "It was wonderful," Jacqueline said and sighed. "I taught him how to set up the golf ball and swing the club. If he took lessons he would be very good. He is tall and strong too."

"It's hard for me to believe that any man in this day and age doesn't know how to play golf." Mother nibbled an éclair then wiped her fingers with a linen napkin. "Where has he spent most of his life, in a cave?"

"Mother, he's Russian. I don't think there are any golf courses in Moscow, especially since the Bolsheviks took over."

"What do you know of his family? What does his father do? Where does he live?"

"I have no idea. I didn't inquire and he didn't tell me."

"Please, at least tell me he's Jewish."

"He is Jewish and he's very nice."

"But he's a foreigner, an immigrant. I want you to be careful."

"What do you mean? Careful about what?"

"You don't know him very well. It's not a good idea to encourage a stranger."

"But I've already invited him to come with me to Meautry. I want to take him to the country house and show him the horses. He told me he had no concerts scheduled for the next two weeks."

"You shouldn't have done that."

"But he's already agreed to come. I can't back out now."

"Of course you can. It's easy. Just write him a letter and tell him your plans have changed."

Jacqueline sagged in the chair. Maybe Mother was right. She was moving too fast, being too forward.

"Write the letter now," Mother said. "You'll feel a lot better."

"I suppose you are right," she said, feeling the old doubts return. "I don't want him to get the wrong idea."

"That's a good girl." Mother went back to reading her book. "And don't slouch, stand up straight. You'll look much more attractive if you keep your head high."

"Yes, Mother."

"You'll thank me for this later."

Jacqueline didn't reply.

* * *

"Bonjour Monsieur Piatigorsky," the hotel clerk said. He handed Gregor two envelopes and the newspaper.

Gregor glanced at the first envelope and recognized his manager's handwriting. Finally, his paycheck had arrived. "*Très bien,*" he said to the clerk. The letter informed him that the balance of money for the three-month tour he had just completed was on deposit at the Banque Centrale des Français.

He slid the letter inside his jacket pocket as he climbed the stairs. Glancing at the second envelope, he noticed the feminine handwriting and held off opening it. Inside his room, he tossed his hat on the dresser, unknotted his tie and changed into comfortable slacks and an open-collared shirt. He remained barefoot, resting his aching feet on the cool wooden floor. The stylish new shoes Valentin had talked him into buying for the golfing engagement had been too small. Now, even a day later, his feet were still sore. The discomfort had been a small price to pay for a wonderful afternoon with Jacqueline de Rothschild.

She was pretty and tall. He liked that in a woman. And she had a good head on her shoulders. Not silly like so many of the ladies he met. She also listened to what he had to say. The letter was from her and he wanted to savor it.

He poured himself a shot of whiskey, savored the burn of the alcohol as it slid down his throat then stretched out on the bed. His feet hung over the end. No hotel ever had a bed long enough for his six foot three inch frame.

His name and the hotel address on the front of the envelope were neatly written in a clear script, not a scrawl like his own illegible hand. Then he noticed there was no stamp. He frowned. Had she brought the letter to the hotel herself? More likely some employee had delivered it.

A tiny feeling of disquiet tickled at the edge of his consciousness and the uneasy knot made itself known in his middle. Why hadn't she mailed it? He slid his finger under the flap, noticing the expensive vellum paper.

Dear Gregor, I want to thank you for a lovely afternoon at the golf course yesterday. I'm sorry, but my plans to go to Meautry have changed. I will not be going to the country house as expected. Sincerely, Jacqueline de Rothschild.

It was short and to the point. He read the three lines, not quite believing what it said. She was brushing him off, discarding him like a used handkerchief. He read beyond her polite words. Her message was loud and clear. The rejection hit him harder than it should have. Why? At thirty-three, it wasn't as if he were inexperienced when it came to women.

"Why?" Crushing the letter into a ball, he threw it across the room. He searched for the answer in another shot of whiskey, but the question remained. Why? What had he done wrong?

The room was suddenly too small to contain his frustration. He needed air. Pushing his feet into his shoes, he headed downstairs for the lobby.

"Grisha?" He heard his name and saw Valentin standing at the clerk's desk. "Wait for me." His friend crossed the lobby then stopped short. "If you were not my friend I would be afraid for my life. What is wrong?"

Gregor turned away, frustrated that his emotions were so transparent. "Nothing of importance."

"You are a terrible liar, Grisha." Valentin held up an envelope. "Look, I have my payment for the tour. Let's go celebrate."

"I don't feel like celebrating."

"All the more reason to go," Valentin said, steering him toward the street.

* * *

"It's a woman, isn't it?" Valentin dug into the creamed chicken, then broke off a chunk of bread and sopped up the sauce.

Gregor had no appetite for food. "It's not important." He picked at his omelet.

"Grisha, Grisha, my friend. After all these years on tour you should know how to handle women." Valentin paused to wash down a mouthful of bread with a gulp of wine. "Listen to me. If someone dressed monkeys in suits then trained them to play good music, you and I would be out of a job. The women who come to hear us would love those monkeys just as much as they love us."

"That's absurd," Gregor said. He slid down in his chair and pushed the half-eaten food aside.

"No, no," Valentin said. "On the night of the performance we are everything these women dream of. If you take a woman back to your hotel as a souvenir, she will be happy until morning. But if you wait too long, the attraction fades. The problem with Mademoiselle Jacqueline de Rothschild is that you didn't play golf with her until three days after the concert. By that time you were as stale as three-day-old bread." He raised a forkful of chicken and pointed in Gregor's direction. "Next time you must move faster, then you will have all that you desire."

"At least I won't need those wretched golf shoes." Gregor forced a smile. No rejection or defeat ever bothered Valentin. "And I hope I never see another golf course again."

"Not to worry," Valentin refilled his wineglass. "In two weeks we leave for Venice and Barcelona. There are plenty of women in those cities and they all love music. Meanwhile, I will ask my new page-turner if she has a pretty friend."

Chapter Thirty-one

Jacqueline settled into the familiar softness of the patient's couch in Dr. Loewenstein's study. The clock outside chimed three times. Before the echo of the third chime ended, the door opened and the doctor walked in.

"Bonjour, Jacqueline." The doctor settled into his big leather chair.

"Bonjour," she said. They had begun the session like this every week for the past four years.

The doctor waited for her to speak.

"I'm afraid," she said.

"What are you afraid of?"

She almost said, "I'm afraid I'll be sitting here with you when I'm an old woman." But she didn't. "I don't know what I'm afraid of," was all that came out.

"Has anything happened since last week?"

"No, nothing has changed." That was the problem, nothing ever changed. "I hosted a recital for several young musicians from the Conservatoire."

"Did that cause you to be afraid?"

"No, it went very well."

"Will you do it again?"

"Yes, I've arranged for another recital tomorrow. It's good for the students, and Mother said I should busy myself with something useful."

"Do you like the idea of doing charity work?"

Jacqueline sighed. Sometimes talking to Dr. Loewenstein was like talking to herself.

* * *

The phone on her desk rang and she picked it up on the second ring. "*Allo?*"

"*Bonjour.*" She recognized Ania's cheerful voice. "Do you have everything ready for tonight?"

"The chairs are already set up in the salon," Jacqueline said. "You don't think we'll have more than a dozen guests, do you?"

"We may." Ania giggled.

"What's so funny?"

"Guess who just arrived in Paris?"

"Who?"

"Gregor Piatigorsky. Can I invite him?"

Jacqueline's heart skipped a beat. "Do you really think he would come?"

"I'll ask him."

"That—that would be wonderful."

Her hand was trembling when she hung up the phone. Would he remember her? It had been a whole year since their golfing date. Would he still be upset with her?

"Renee? Renee," she called. "Guess who's coming to the recital tonight?"

* * *

"He didn't want to come," Ania spoke lightly. "I'm sure he's tired."

Jacqueline felt as if she had been slapped. "You asked him and he said—no?"

"He and Valentin just got back from London. They took the ferry and had a car drive them in from the coast." Ania handed the concierge her jacket. "Gregor said he was tired and was going to bed."

He must hate me, Jacqueline thought. What a fool she had been to let Ania even mention her name to him. She felt totally humiliated.

The young musicians arrived, then the guests. Most of the people were her parents' friends. Jacqueline knew they were doing her and, more importantly, her parents a favor by coming at all. No doubt her mother had made a few discreet telephone calls on her behalf. *Poor Jacqueline could use your support. Thank you. You are such a dear for coming.*

While Renee silently served drinks and pastries, the young trio, a violin, viola and cello, set up in the salon. Jacqueline tried her best to smile and be sociable, but it was difficult.

"The students are really quite good," Ania said as she rearranged the fresh flowers in the Chinese vase. "I think the youngest is only fourteen."

And I feel like an ancient matron, Jacqueline thought as she greeted yet another of her mother's friends.

* * *

"So, what else do you have to do tonight?" Valentin leaned against the doorframe.

In less time than it took Gregor to bathe and shave, his friend had dressed and was ready to meet another new lady friend. The man was truly amazing.

When it came to dressing fast, Valentin was the best. For him it was probably the key to survival.

"I will lie here on my nice comfortable bed." Gregor rubbed a towel over his wet hair. "I'll drink a good bottle of wine and read the newspaper."

"You're a fool. Ania wouldn't have invited you if Jacqueline didn't want you to come."

"Why should I go? I don't need to be humiliated. Not again."

"Very well, I am off to see Mademoiselle Boichoit. I hope your evening is as pleasurable as mine." He tipped his hat and disappeared down the hall.

Gregor stretched out on the bed and propped several pillows behind his head. Spreading the newspaper open, he folded it so he could read the inside page.

Damn it. There was no way he was going to Jacqueline de Rothschild's house, to some fancy party and face her. Why should he? Even a year later, the rejection was still there. He didn't need her. He didn't need anyone. He had his music, his career, and a good manager. The audiences loved him, or, at the very least, they loved his music. Valentin was right. If you don't get them the first night there's no point in trying. After all, what decent woman would want to be involved with a traveling musician?

"*Chyort pobery!*" he swore. He had just read the first paragraph of an article and had no idea what it said.

His eyes ached and he ran his hands over his face. There she was again. In his mind he saw her, just as he had that first night a year ago. He couldn't remember whose party it was. There had been too many parties, too many women and too many countries since then. But he remembered Jacqueline. Why? He could still see her, slim figure, tall and pretty in a light blue dress, dark hair soft against her cheek. And he remembered her smiling at him on the golf course, her hands on his as she tried to teach a big clumsy Russian how to play golf. For the past year, as he had toured Europe and North America, he had pushed the memory of Jacqueline from his mind. But here, in Paris, it all came back, as fresh as if it had just happened. The joy and the pain.

"*Govno,*" he swore again. If he didn't go see her tonight, he'd never know why.

* * *

The concierge opened the polished wooden door of the elegant house on Avenue Foch. He peered out at Gregor, his eyebrow raised.

"I am here for recital," Gregor said, giving the man his best smile.

"Yes, monsieur. They have already started, upstairs in the salon. The second door on the right."

Gregor took the steps two at a time then stopped, his hand on the knob. He heard the sound of Bach, played a little too fast. The musicians must be nervous. So was he. This was his last chance to back out. He should turn around and leave before he made a bigger fool of himself. Instead, he took a deep breath and opened the door.

At first, no one noticed him. The audience had their backs to the door and the young trio was totally focused on their playing. As Gregor slid into the last row, he scanned the room and spotted Jacqueline sitting on the far left. Her hair was a little longer, but in profile she looked as pretty as he had remembered. And just like the first time, she was wearing light blue. She must have felt his eyes, because as the Bach piece ended she turned and looked right at him. He watched her eyes grow wide as recognition sank in.

The audience applauded politely and everyone stood, some moving forward to congratulate the performers. Jacqueline's eyes moved to the front of the room, then back to him. He gave her a big smile, joined in the applause then moved forward to speak to the young cellist.

"You will soon be a great musician." He shook the nervous young man's hand.

"Merci, Monsieur." The boy's face lit up. "You're Gregor Piatigorsky, aren't you? I heard you play with Mengelberg last summer."

"Someday you will play with them too." He leaned close to the boy and whispered. "You must not rush music. Sebastian Bach is best a little more slow."

"Yes, sir. Thank you for coming, sir." The boy blushed and turned to his friends. "Did you hear what he said?"

"That was very nice of you to say that." Gregor turned and saw Jacqueline standing behind him.

"They must be encouraged." Suddenly Gregor felt embarrassed and pushed his hand into his pocket. "Someday he may take my job. I hope he will be as kind."

"I'm glad you came." Jacqueline smiled. "It's good to see you again."

"I wanted to." He felt the nervousness melting away.

"Come." She touched his arm. "I'll introduce you to the other musicians. They'll be pleased to meet you."

"And I am happy to meet them." He smiled and nodded, and said all the right things, but he couldn't remember from one moment to the next whom he had met.

With the greeting done, she pointed to the table. "We also have refreshments." She smiled. "But there is no chocolate."

"Thank you." He gave her a little bow. "You make a musician very happy."

By half past seven the performers and the guests were gone. The maid moved silently through the salon, picking up wineglasses and dirty plates. Only Gregor remained.

"Can we go outside?" he asked, hoping she didn't have another engagement. "For fresh air?"

"Come with me." Again she touched his arm, but only for a moment. "This way."

He followed her from the room, down the hall and into a large ballroom. The setting sun cast a warm glow as it shone through the tall windows, its light catching the prisms of the chandeliers. Rainbows of color danced across the walls. From the size of the room, Gregor guessed it could hold two hundred people.

"What is this place?" He surveyed the cavernous space.

"Nothing. I've never furnished it. My great-aunt lived here before me. She was quite a hostess. When my mother was young there were parties here all the time."

"How is the sound?" He leaned back and looked up at the high ceiling.

"I have no idea."

"Hmmm, let me listen." He moved to the center of the empty room. Jacqueline waited a few yards away, watching him, a puzzled expression on her face. Turning slowly, he surveyed the walls. Polished wood, some were hung with drapes, mirrors filling the spaces where the windows should have been. The only real windows were at the far ends of the room.

He closed his eyes, hummed softly, then with a sharp clap of his hands, listened as the sound reverberated off the hard surfaces. The echoes continued for several seconds before dying away. Then he put his hand over his right ear and sang three notes: C, D and E in a warbled bass. He listened again until all vestiges of sound had faded away. "Never allow any artist to perform in this room." He shook his head as he looked up at the high ceiling. "Their efforts would be wasted. Everything here is too... too hard."

Jacqueline put her hand to her mouth but couldn't hide her smile.

"Why do you laugh?" he asked.

"It just sounds funny. The echo I mean."

He smiled then walked to her and held out his open hands. "My hands are better than my voice."

"I believe you." She reached out and touched the palm of his right hand. The warmth of her fingers sent a tingle though his body, but she pulled her hand back before he could close his fingers around hers. As they moved toward the back door, only the sound of their shoes on the polished wood floor broke the silence. Outside, a stone balcony stretched across the back of the house. They stood together, looking out over a neatly trimmed lawn bordered with flowers.

"Did you go to Meautry last summer?" He leaned on the railing. Out of the corner of his eye, he watched her face, trying to gauge her response.

"I went, but not until the first week of July." She stood with her back against the stone column, her eyes down. "I'm sorry," she said softly. "I shouldn't have written that letter."

"Why did you write it?" He turned to face her. "Did I offend you?"

"Oh no." She looked up at him, folding and unfolding her hands. Her nervousness surprised him. "I had a wonderful time with you. It's just that—." She hesitated.

"What is it?"

"My mother told me I was being—. That I should —. She said I was too— too—." Her voice dropped. "I'm sorry. I should never have listened to her."

Gregor could hardly believe his ears. The letter wasn't written because he had done anything wrong. Of course, a mother protects her young. A traveling musician was hardly the ideal suitor for an aristocratic young lady. But the important thing was she hadn't rejected him.

"I'm glad to hear you say that." He wanted to put her at ease. "I threw the letter away. Gone."

Smiling, she said softly, "I'm glad you did." As she turned, he stepped closer. The setting sun cast huge shadows across the lawn as they stood in silence. Strangely, he found the silence wasn't awkward the way it might have been with other women.

"How long will you be in Paris?" she said at last.

"Two weeks, then I go to London, Oslo and Stockholm." He laughed. "The Midnight Sun Concert, my manager says. We play at midnight, June twentieth."

"That sounds wonderful."

"It will not sound good. We must practice." He glanced at her out of the corner of his eye. "Do you know a good piano we can use?"

"I have a Bosendorfer Grand in the salon. Would you like to see it?"

"Very much." he said. "Your house is good. Our hotel is far from the rehearsal hall."

"Oh yes. It would be wonderful to hear you play." She smiled and he knew it was genuine.

The piano was concert quality. Of course the Rothschilds would have the very best. He sat on the bench and opened the keyboard cover. "Come, sit beside me." He slid over, making room on the bench. "I have no talent with the piano. Let me hear you play."

She hesitated and he saw her eyes move to the silver-framed picture sitting on the edge of the piano. He hadn't paid any attention to it before, but now his eyes focused on the photo of an older man.

"This is Alfred Cortot? He is your teacher?"

"Y-yes," she stammered. "I study with him every week, at least when he's not on tour." She sat down bedside him, but not too close.

"He is great musician." Gregor watched her face in profile.

"I'm afraid I'm not a very good pupil." She kept her eyes on the keys but didn't touch them.

"How long do you study piano?" He kept the question casual.

"Seven years." She ran her fingertips lightly over the polished surface of the ivories.

"You study very long time. He is master of the instrument. Please play for me?"

"Oh no, I couldn't." The mere request seemed to rattle her and she stood. "You and your friend can rehearse here any time you like. It won't be an inconvenience."

Her sudden shift from delight to nervousness confused him. Perhaps he had overstayed his welcome. "I will give you my photograph." He stood and started toward the door. "My manager says it is a good thing to give photographs."

"I'd love to have one." Again a smile lit up her face.

"I bring you tomorrow." He reached for the door handle. "May we practice, ten o'clock?"

"That would be fine." As she spoke she reached out and touched his hand. It was a small gesture and he felt the warmth of her fingers on his skin. "I'm glad you came tonight," she said.

"So am I," he said and smiled.

Chapter Thirty-two

"Jacqueline, have you lost your mind?" Mother sat before her vanity mirror, the pearl-handled brush smoothing her long silky hair. "Why are you encouraging this immigrant? You don't know anything about him."

"But I'm so lonely," Jacqueline pleaded. She stood at Mother's elbow, yet despite their closeness, only Mother's face reflected back in the mirror. Jacqueline didn't even exist. Mother continued brushing her hair, turning her head, admiring her beautiful reflection.

"Mother, why can't I ever be happy?" Jacqueline said to the image in the mirror. "Why can't I ever be loved?"

"Because," Mother said as she continued to admire herself. "You are a Rothschild. You can never be happy. Look at me. I've never been truly happy."

Jacqueline rolled over and opened her eyes. The high ceiling and the tall windows draped in crepe de Chine were real, but the faint light leaking under the bedroom door gave the room a ghostly appearance.

Almost every night she dreamed the same sad dream. Dr. Loewenstein said she would continue dreaming it until she discovered the cause of this dream. He always said the same thing and she always dreamed the same dream. Nothing ever changed.

That wasn't true. Something had changed. Gregor Piatigorsky had come into her life, like a prince in a fairy tale. Rolling onto her side, she closed her eyes. She needed to sleep or she wouldn't make it through the long night. The dream returned with a vengeance.

She turned away from the mirror that reflected nothing and crawled into bed, pulling the covers over her head.

"I know you're not sleeping." It was Robert's angry voice. "You're pretending to sleep, but you can't pretend you aren't my wife." Robert ripped the blankets back, exposing her to the full force of his wrath. "Wake up Jacqueline, wake up and look at me."

"No, I'm very tired. Let me sleep. I have a piano examination in the morning." She reached out and turned off the bedside lamp, hoping he would go

*away, but the darkness enraged him even more. Pushing her aside, he knelt on
the bed, grabbed her wrist and in the struggle knocked the lamp to the floor. With
strength that comes from rage, he ripped the cord from the wall and threw the
heavy lamp at her.*

"I will not let you humiliate me. Alfred Cortot is no more man than I."

"Leave me alone." She rolled away from him, but Robert moved faster.

*"I don't care about your damned piano exam." He grabbed her arm and
dragged her from the bed. As she struggled to regain her footing, he yanked her
arm hard, pulling her to her feet. "You are an imbecile!" He shook her,
punctuating each word. Then he made a fist and jammed it under her chin. "I
should smash in your face and break your nose. You deserve it." His lips were
tight across his clenched teeth.*

*"I will not talk to you while you are angry." Jacqueline tried to keep her own
voice low. "We can discuss this tomorrow."*

*The fist at her chin opened then his fingers closed around her neck. She
didn't move but kept her eyes locked on his. "I have never touched another man,"
she said, hoping the truth would appease him.*

*"You will not win," he said, his face red and contorted. "You will not defeat
me." He let go of her neck, and left the room, slamming the door behind him.*

*   *   *

Jacqueline was up before dawn, nervous and worried. Would everything go
well? Would it be perfect? Would he be disappointed?

At precisely ten o'clock there was a knock at the door and the concierge let
them in. Gregor wore the same stylish dark gray suit and blue tie she
remembered him wearing at the recital, his cello case tucked under his arm. He
looked wonderful.

Valentin swept off his hat as he took her hand and kissed it. Jacqueline felt
herself blush and looked at Gregor who tried unsuccessfully to repress a smile.
"Be careful," he said. "Valentin never eats breakfast and he has been known to
gnaw at people's fingers by this time of the morning."

"Not so," said Valentin. "My friend is jealous because I was introduced to
you first." The pianist tucked his hat under his arm and the two men followed her
up the stairs. "It's so generous of you to let us rehearse here," he said.

"I'm happy to offer my piano to such wonderful musicians." She opened the
big double doors. Valentin headed for the piano while Gregor unpacked his cello
and began to tune.

She stood just inside the doorway, hoping they wouldn't mind her presence.
But every minute or so Gregor looked up from his instrument and grinned. She
could have stayed there all morning and not grown tired of watching him. But
when Valentin pivoted on the piano bench and glanced in her direction, she knew

it was time to leave. She tiptoed from the room and headed down the stairs. As her hand followed the smooth curve of the banister, she heard the notes of the cello follow her all the way down the hall.

After the second day of rehearsal, Valentin left in a hurry, bowing in his usual courtly fashion as he headed out the door. "*Merci, mademoiselle. Merci.*"

Jacqueline sat down at the piano and waited while Gregor tucked his bow in the cello case. "It's a beautiful instrument," she said.

"It is Montagnana." He moved the cello closer to her. "It became mine only last year, a gift from my friend Ernest Dane. I name it Sleeping Beauty. For sixty years she lay in the English Castle, never touched by man."

"It must have cost a great deal."

"I do not know. One does not own such instruments. She has only come to live with me."

Jacqueline watched him run his fingers over the dark wood. Strong handsome fingers. "Someday it will live with another artist."

"Is it very old?"

"Two hundred years. Here, feel this." He lifted her hand and laid it on top of the instrument. Though she felt the delicate curves of scroll above the fingerboard and the silky softness of the wood, she was more aware of the warmth of his touch on her wrist "It is original," he said softly. "Carved by master's hand. Never replaced or repaired."

"You are very fortunate to have it—Gregor," she said. It suddenly felt awkward saying his name.

He let go of her hand, a little reluctantly it seemed. "You must call me Grisha. You see, now we are friends. Yes?"

She couldn't help smiling, "Yes, Grisha."

"Will you go to cinema with me today?" He loosened the bow, releasing tension on the hair.

"I can't." She stared down at the floor.

"You said no yesterday." He frowned.

"I have—another engagement," she stammered, not daring to tell him the truth.

Gregor said nothing as he returned his instrument to its case then reached for his jacket and hat. "Very well." His tone was both curt and dismissive. He was angry.

"It's just that. . ." She hesitated. How could she possibly explain her fear to someone so completely fearless?

"You owe me nothing," he said. "I thank you for our rehearsal here." He picked up his cello and headed for the door. "We won't need to come again."

"No." She started after him. "Please. Wait."

He paused, his hand on the doorknob. "Jacqueline, I do not understand." He glanced at the piano and her eyes followed his as they came to rest on the portrait of Alfred Cortot. "I will not stay if I am not wanted."

"It's not what you think."

She saw his eyes move to her trembling hands then back to her face. What was he thinking? Without a word, he walked past her and placed the cello case beneath the piano. She stood still, her eyes following his every movement. He looked over his shoulder at her then wordlessly reached out and turned the picture of Alfred Cortot face down.

"Come with me." He took her hand and gave it a little squeeze. "We will walk in park."

Beneath the canopy of trees, they moved in silence along a narrow path beside the brook. He held her hand in his, a big strong hand that wrapped around her cold fingers. Gradually, the trembling she felt inside lessened. Ahead of them a woman pushed a pram. In the distance children played, but along the path they were alone. He said nothing. Now his silence was not of anger. Instead it spoke of quiet acceptance.

When they came to the footbridge he stopped and released her hand. Ashamed of her own behavior, she couldn't face him. She kept her eyes down, staring into the water. Unlike her mother's empty mirror, the stream reflected back an image. It was her face, but warped and distorted by the current.

"Jacqueline?" His voice was gentle but firm. "*Ptichka. Kak Ptichka,*" he whispered and pulled her close. With eyes closed, she felt his kiss. For a moment she stopped breathing. As his hands moved down her back, the fear melted away. In all her life, in all the time she had been married to Robert, she had never felt a kiss like this. When his lips finally left hers, he still held her in his arms. "*Ptichka.* Like little bird," he said softly.

She looked up into his face. Despite his size and strength, she knew he would never hurt her.

"Alfred Cortot? You love him?" It was a simple, direct question, but it was more than that. He could read her mind.

"No. I don't think—not." She turned away, again feeling foolish. He reached out and touched her chin, lifting her face. Something about his touch soothed her and she regained her voice. "I thought I cared for him," she said. "But he wants nothing from me."

"Why you love him if he does not love you?"

"Because . . ." She hesitated and the trembling returned. "Because he never hit me." She meant to say *hurt me*, but the word *hit* had just come out.

A look of astonishment crossed Grisha's face and he stepped back. "Because he never hit you?" He repeated the words as if he couldn't understand them. "Is that what it takes? You love any man who does not hit you?"

"I didn't . . . I meant." It was all back again, the fear and the humiliation. Embarrassed, she turned away, but he wouldn't let her hide. Placing his hands on her shoulders, he turned her back to face him.

"Who hit you? Tell me."

"My . . . my husband Robert." She felt her voice drop to a whisper. Surely he must think it was her fault.

He waited.

She swallowed hard. "Robert tried to shoot me. He had a gun and wanted me to die. He threatened to shoot my mother then he tried to kill himself. It was my fault."

"Your fault? How can it be your fault?"

"I don't know." She shook her head. "Mother said I should talk to Doctor Loewenstein to learn what I did wrong." There it was. She had told him the truth. Now, steeling herself for his rejection, she said, "That's why I can't go to the cinema. I have to spend an hour each afternoon with the doctor."

She looked straight into his face. His dark brown eyes grew wide and his jaw dropped. Suddenly, he threw back his head and laughed.

"You have one hour each day with a psychiatrist?" He turned and took a few steps away as he shook his head. Then he looked back and threw his hands in the air. "Jacqueline, you do not need psychiatrist."

"But I do. The doctor said I will never stop having nightmares until I understand what I did wrong."

"*Nyet, nyet.*" He waved his hand in dismissal. "That doctor is liar. You must leave this crazy place."

She stared at him, confused. His reaction to her confession made no sense. "What place do you mean?"

"Come, *Ptichka*," he said, reaching out his hand. "I open the door to your cage."

"I don't understand. There's no place for me to go."

"Ahhh, but you are mistaken." As he spoke, a smile lit up his face. "Forget doctor. It is time you see the world without fear."

As his words sank in, she realized he wasn't rejecting her. Despite her failures, he hadn't turned away.

"Come," he said softly, taking her hand and pulling her close. "When you are with me," he whispered, pressing his lips close to her ear. "No one can hurt you. Come with me and you will learn to fly, *Ptichka*."

Chapter Thirty-three

"Let me hear you." Gregor pulled his chair up beside the piano bench. It was his turn to watch her play. "What is your favorite piece?"

"I don't have a favorite piece," Jacqueline said. She sounded apologetic. He saw lines of tension in her face and wished he could make them go away. "Do you remember the first piece you ever learned?"

"Not very well."

"Let me find something." He searched her portfolio until he located the score for the "Polonaise" by Popper. He knew it by heart. "I will start with the prelude, then you come in here." He pointed to the first bar on the second page. "Do not worry about keeping up. I will play slow for you."

Jacqueline placed her fingers on the keys then pulled them back. "I can't," she said.

"Try." Touching the bow to the strings, he played the first few bars. Still, she made no move to play.

He lifted the bow and tapped it on his knee. "I will count. One, two, three, four and you count with me." He started again and this time she touched the keyboard. As he played he saw her lips move, counting silently to herself. She managed the first two bars without difficulty but fumbled on the third. When she tried to correct herself, she failed.

"I'm sorry." She shook her head. "I can't do it. I'm never going to be a musician."

This was torture. He couldn't bear to see her struggle. Another ten years of piano lessons wouldn't make any difference. Setting the cello aside, he slid onto the bench beside her. Her hands lay in her lap, defeated. She didn't even look at him when he touched her arm.

"I believe your teacher is a criminal," he said, and took her hand in his.

"No. It's not his fault. I'm just not capable of learning."

"That is not true." He held her hand out as if to study it. "For every person there is a correct instrument, one that fits their personality and their talents. If my father had made me play the clarinet, I would have studied very hard, yet still I would have been a failure."

She turned to him, a hint of a smile on her face. "I can't imagine you playing clarinet."

"Of course not. It would not suit me. I see now that the piano does not suit you. It is the wrong instrument."

"How can I find the right one?"

He didn't answer but stood and walked around the piano until he was looking at her across the lid. Her eyes met his.

As he studied her, his mind ran through the entire ensemble of orchestra instruments. Percussion and brass were definitely out. He tried to imagine her holding various string instruments, but none seemed right. What he wanted was something that matched her quietness, her reserve and her strength.

"I have it," he said and moved back. Taking her hand, he led her away from the piano and closed the lid. "You are meant to play the bassoon. It has the same range as the cello but fewer notes so you will not need to play so fast."

"The bassoon? I've never even touched one."

"Then tomorrow I will bring one and you will play."

A little smile played across her face. "Can you teach me how?"

"I know nothing about the instrument, but you'll know if it is right for you."

There was a tap and the salon door opened. "Mademoiselle," Renee said. "You asked to be informed. Dinner is ready on the terrace."

"Please," said Jacqueline looking up at him, hope in her eyes. "Stay. Have dinner with me. I promise, there is no chocolate on the menu."

"I would never turn down an invitation from you." He slipped his arm around her waist. "Even if you were serving chocolate."

* * *

The evening light faded and only flickering candles lit the table. Renee moved silently, gathering up dishes, then slipped through the kitchen door and left them alone.

Jacqueline studied Grisha. On stage he was a towering presence, confident and sure of himself. In a crowded room he held everyone's attention, his good looks and social wit mesmerizing women, making men laugh.

But here, alone with her on the terrace, he seemed a little overwhelmed by everything around him. There was something childlike about the way he examined his surroundings, as if he wasn't sure what to do next.

"Would you like to drive down to Meautry on Saturday?" she asked. She did owe him a trip to the country after her last mangled invitation. "There's a thoroughbred race and the breeders will have their best horses on display."

"That sounds wonderful." His eyes twinkled as he grinned. "Is there an early train?"

"No, we'll have to drive. Do you have a car?"

He didn't reply but rubbed his hand over his chin. "I don't have an automobile."

"You can drive one of mine." She quickly offered, certain that she had embarrassed him in some way. "There are several in the garage."

"That is very kind." He leaned forward and took her hand. "But you see I have never learned to drive an automobile."

"Oh, I'm sorry," she said. "I just thought . . ." She stopped before any more foolish words could escape her mouth.

"But of course a man my age should be capable of driving an automobile. I wish it were true, but I never stayed any place long enough to own an automobile. I ride on ships and trains."

"I could teach you if you would like."

"And endanger your life?" He grinned then refilled his wine glass from the bottle of Chablis. "I value your friendship and your life too much to do that. It is best if I leave the operation of automobiles in the hands of those who understand such things."

"Then I will drive. I will even pick you up at your hotel, but we must leave early."

"I have never had a more beautiful chauffeur."

The door to the terrace opened and Renee appeared with a tray of fruit and sherbet. She silently removed the dinner plates then slipped back into the house.

"Do you have family here?" Jacqueline asked when they were alone again.

"Here?" He looked surprised. "In Paris?"

"Or in France?"

"My family . . . my parents are . . ." He hesitated and she saw a frown crease his brow. "I have not seen my family in many years."

"I'm sorry," she said, wishing she had never brought it up.

From somewhere across the lawn came the cooing sound of a dove, perhaps saying good-night to its young. Grisha drained the last of his wine then stood and stretched out his hand. She took it and he led her to the terrace rail.

"In two weeks I must leave." He sounded like he was apologizing. "My agent has arranged a concert tour which will take me around the world."

"Around the world?" She couldn't suppress a gasp. He spoke so casually, as if traveling around the world was an ordinary thing. "How long will you be gone?"

"Six months if my agent has done his job well, longer if he has not."

Six months? The words felt like a blow. The weeks of his summer tour had dragged on forever. Now, in less than two weeks, he was leaving again. The thought of being apart for six days, much less six months, was unbearable. Would he miss her as he visited exotic places and met adoring audiences? Would he even remember her in all that time?

"Six months is a long time," she said, trying to sound casual, but her fingers gripped the stone railing. She kept her eyes focused on the ground below. It would serve no purpose to let him see that she would miss him.

"It is a long time." He spoke with authority, as if he were condemning such an idea. "Look at me, Jacqueline."

She felt his hands on her shoulders as he turned her to face him. Her eyes moved up and she saw worry on his handsome face. "Six months is too long," he said. "I want you to come with me. Not next week, but when I get to Hawaii in two months."

"Hawaii. That's halfway around the world."

"Exactly. I will travel to Rome, Alexandria, Delhi then Bombay. We will play for Emperor in Tokyo. When we finish there, we will sail for Hawaii. Will you meet me there in November?"

"But I've never been that far from home." Even as she spoke, she knew she would do it. She would go anywhere he asked, no matter how far or how difficult the journey.

"Then it is time you see the world." He pulled her close.

* * *

"You did what?" Valentin's fork stopped midway to his mouth.

"She's coming on tour with us." Gregor watched his friend's face. He was not pleased..

Valentin dropped his fork and it clattered on the plate. "Grisha, this is a very bad idea. It will only cause you problems."

"She will be no trouble. It will be great fun."

"Oh, but you are wrong." Valentin retrieved his fork and attacked the potatoes. "First of all," he mumbled. "She will cost you a lot of money. No more sharing the cabin with me."

"I can afford it." Gregor broke off a piece of baguette.

"Very well, so it's not the money. What will you do with her while we rehearse?"

"I do not know. Perhaps she can tour the city or go shopping. I think all women love to shop."

"What about the receptions?"

"She can come to the parties. I will introduce her to all our friends."

Valentin shook his head and pushed the empty plate away. "There are so many beautiful women. Her presence will cool their interest."

"I have met hundreds of them before. I trust you can keep the adoring women of the world entertained."

"I will certainly try."

Gregor emptied his wineglass then refilled it. "Don't worry. She will not start the trip with us. Delhi, Hong Kong and Tokyo, these are no places to take a lady. She will join us in Hawaii."

Valentin waved to the waiter. "Another bottle of Pinot Noir," he said, then leaned back in his chair and pulled a Lucky Strike from a silver cigarette case. "What if she becomes bored or unhappy? Will you send her home?"

"She is free to come and go as she pleases," Gregor said. "Many years ago my sister Nadja spent the summer with me in Moscow. We had a wonderful time. She played the piano while I rehearsed. We went to concerts and the theater every night."

"I think Mademoiselle de Rothschild will expect more from you than your sister did."

Gregor smiled. "I will try not to disappoint her."

* * *

"Mademoiselle?" Renee stood in the middle of the bedroom, surrounded by open trunks and suitcases. "You must be prepared."

Jacqueline looked down at the three trunks open on the floor. "I may be going halfway around the world, but I can't take this much luggage. Grisha takes only one suitcase."

"Men don't need more." Renee took a lavender evening dress from the closet. "You'll need clothes for all occasions."

"I'm sure they sell frocks in America."

"American clothes?" Renee's eyebrow went up. "They're so . . . so common. Factory-made rags."

"Everyone there will wear the same. No one will notice what I have on." She shut the lid of the trunk. "What I need is one suitcase about this big." She held her hand just above her knee. "If there is no one to carry my bag, I'll do it myself. I won't be a burden."

"Mademoiselle, you are a lady, not a porter." Renee returned the clothes to the various closets. Jacqueline kept a herringbone wool suit and long black coat with matching hat. She would wear them on the crossing.

Comfortable shoes and a good pair for evening went into the pile along with undergarments, two blouses and two skirts. Renee found a large suitcase and Jacqueline spread it open on the bed.

"I'll take one dress and one robe."

Renee frowned. "You will be mistaken for an immigrant."

"An immigrant?" Jacqueline laughed at Renee's long face. "Are you afraid I won't return?"

"I will be happy if you come back just as you are."

"That's not possible." Jacqueline took three pairs of heavy hose from her dresser drawer. "Renee, after this trip, I will never be the same."

"Does Madame approve?"

Jacqueline took a deep breath then exhaled slowly. "Mother doesn't know, neither does father. I'll tell them tomorrow."

Renee shook her head as she slid her hand into her apron pocket. "A letter arrived this morning." Jacqueline took the envelope and her heart skipped a beat. Was it from Grisha? No. The stamp was French. The handwriting was definitely feminine, but with an odd backward slant. She turned it over. No return address. Inside, a plain white sheet of paper had been folded in half. There was no salutation, date or signature.

Beware!!! You are crazy to run after that adventurer. He is no good. If you take this journey you will regret it. You have been warned!!!

She reread the ominous words and felt a chill envelop her.

"Mademoiselle?" Renee touched her arm.

"Who could write such a thing?" She showed Renee the note. "Why would someone do this?"

Renee studied the letter and Jacqueline saw a frown crease her brow. Then she crumpled the paper. "Dirt. Disgusting cowardly trash."

"But why?" Jacqueline sank onto the edge of the bed.

"Jealousy. Some people can't bear to see happiness in others." Renee walked to the wastebasket and threw the paper away. "Ignore it. Take your journey. If you are ever going to find happiness you must leave."

"I hope so," said Jacqueline. But the threat was there and there was no erasing it. Was she making a mistake chasing after Grisha? There must be women in every city anxious to be with him. Doubt started to gnaw at her and she suddenly felt drained of all energy.

Covering her face with her hands, she tried to block out his image. It is time for you to see the world without fear. She saw his face, felt his hands on hers and heard his words ringing in her ears. *You will learn to fly, Ptichka, as far and as high as you want to go. And you won't be afraid anymore.*

* * *

Gregor peered over the railing at the huge pilings rising from the harbor floor. The *S.S. ASAMA MARU* pulled alongside the dock, the hull squeaking and groaning as it slid into place. Below him a dozen men ran back and forth under yellow lights, uncoiling arm thick ropes, securing them to huge metal stanchions. The ship's horn sounded three short blasts. Then the ever-present rumble of the engines fell silent.

He glanced at his watch. Quarter past six. The sun had started to turn the sky over San Francisco from black to milky gray. Surely she wouldn't be here this early. He should go to the dining room, have coffee and wait until he heard the announcement for disembarking. But he couldn't bear to sit inside if there was a chance that she might be waiting for him on the dock.

He scanned the pier again but saw only longshoremen pushing carts into place. His fingers touched the telegram in his jacket pocket and he pulled it out. By now he had memorized the cryptic message. *All US ships on strike. Will meet you in SF. Love, JR.*

Love, JR. That told him everything he wanted to know

Two months had passed since he had seen her. He closed his eyes and remembered their last evening together in the little café on the Champs-Elysee. He had forgotten the name, but the quiet smile on her face, the sound of her voice and the touch of her hand was still with him. He opened his eyes and scanned the pier below one more time. In an hour, maybe two, he would be ashore. His luggage was already packed.

He turned from the railing and headed for the dining room. Soon they would be together. This time he didn't intend to let distance separate them again.

Chapter Thirty-four

Ann Arbor, Michigan
January 27, 1937

Jacqueline signed her name for the second time in the Mrs Sink's guest book. Beneath the tight, cramped signature of yesterday, she now wrote *Jacqueline Piatigorsky*. This time her handwriting was larger and filled the space. She was not the same person she had been yesterday. Looking up at Grisha, she saw him smiling.

"A wonderful name." He gave her a little hug. "It fits you."

"Congratulations to both of you." Mrs. Sink held out two glasses of champagne. "I'm glad you were able to get the marriage license on such short notice."

"We are so glad you let us get married here at your home." Jacqueline took the glass but only sipped the champagne. "You have been very kind."

"It's the least we could do for an artist like Gregor Piatigorsky," Mr. Harold Sink said. "And I hope you'll accept an anniversary engagement with us next year. I know I can fill the university concert hall again."

"I will be happy to come back to Ann Arbor." Gregor lifted his glass. You are a wonderful host."

It was half past eleven in the morning and Jacqueline knew they didn't have much time. The train for Chicago left in an hour. If they didn't get on board, Grisha would miss his only rehearsal with the Chicago Symphony. This was certainly not the kind of wedding her mother would have wanted, but now she didn't care.

"Here's a toast to the new couple." Mr. Harold Sink raised his glass. The rest of them followed.

"May your lives be long and your children many," Valentin said before downing his drink in one gulp. "But no children until the tour ends."

"I will remember." Grisha grinned and extended his glass toward Valentin. "But we have a day of rest after the concert in Toronto."

Mr. and Mrs. Sink laughed and Jacqueline felt herself blush.

"I am thrilled you decided to do the honors in our home." Mrs. Sink said saving Jacqueline from further embarrassment. "I'm going to call the newspapers as soon as we drop you off at the train station. When the announcement appears I'll send you a clipping."

"Thank you." Jacqueline put the champagne glass on the dining room table. "But you must send it to my mother in Paris. There is no place we will stay long enough to receive mail."

Dearest Mama:

I don't know if you received any of my letters. I write and write, but you don't answer. Surely there must be a way I can hear from you. In the day I'm busy, rehearsals, recitals, concerts, always working but at night I think of you and home. My manager gives me one day each week to rest. So I think your letters must never find me because I'm never in one place. But now I want to tell you the best news. I have met a wonderful woman and we were married only yesterday here in America. Her name is Jacqueline and she is French. I know you are wondering how can I speak to her. But she speaks English and I learned English here in America. Still, I try to teach her some Russian. Mama, so many times I want to tell you all that I am doing and about my music. I pray that you will get my letters even if you are not able to reply. I have included a photograph of us taken in New York City. You see how happy we are. I would only be happier if you were here with me.

Love and kisses to you, Mama, Grisha

* * *

The sound of knocking was interrupted by Valentin's voice through the door. "The cab is here. Are you two ready?"

Gregor opened the door and slid his suitcase into the hall. Valentin's arms were full with an overcoat and two bags.

"We're ready." Gregor draped his coat over the cello case. "Where's the porter?"

"If you wait for the porter you'll miss the train." Valentin headed for the elevator.

"Jacqueline." Gregor called as he leaned back inside the room. "We must leave now."

"I'm coming." Jacqueline pulled on her heavy winter coat. Despite the Florida heat, it was easier to wear the garment than carry it. Gregor slipped into his own overcoat, leaving his hands free to carry his luggage and instrument.

"Go." She stuffed her cloth hat in her pocket. "I'll catch up."

Gregor nodded and headed for the elevator, hoping to catch it before the door closed.

"*Mach schnell!*" Valentin leaned past the elevator operator. "Hurry!"

Gregor dropped his luggage inside the elevator then turned to see Jacqueline push her suitcase into the corridor. "Wait," he said to the Negro woman. "Please."

"Yes, suh. I won't leave without your lady."

Standing with his shoulder against the elevator door, he watched Jacqueline pick up the heavy suitcase and hurry down the hall. During their first days together he had been a gentleman and helped her carry it, but she had quickly put an end to that.

"If it's too heavy for me to carry, I'll get a smaller one," she said. She had learned to move fast and keep up when they transferred between cabs and trains. "I'll not be a burden to you," she insisted. "If I become one, I'll go home."

He didn't want her to leave, but he knew better than to argue. Instead, he let her struggle with the luggage, glaring at Valentin when he grew impatient.

She squeezed into the elevator and the door closed at her back. The car creaked and shuddered down to the lobby. Gregor felt the tickle of perspiration inside his shirt. Four people plus luggage made the tiny space too warm. Wearing his coat only made it worse. The car stopped on the third floor and the metal door creaked open. A little man with a mustache pushed his way inside and stood in front of Gregor, face nearly pressing into his chest.

"Why are you wearing that wool coat?" the man asked. "It's not hot enough in Florida for you?"

"No." Gregor tried to keep a serious face. "It is cold this morning. I think tonight snow will fall."

"No kidding. You really think so?"

"Many people in Florida will freeze. But I am Russian. I love snow." He glanced at Jacqueline and saw the corners of her mouth turn up. "You see, my wife is prepared too."

The man's eyes turned right and Jacqueline nodded. "Thanks for the warning," he said as the door opened. "I'm going to buy a coat before everyone else catches on." The man hurried through the lobby past a forest of potted palms.

"You sure had him going there, mister." The elevator operator laughed.

"I think so." Gregor smiled. "You will be safe from snow. I am sure."

* * *

They were still struggling to get the luggage into overhead bins as the train pulled out of Tallahassee. Late passengers crowded the aisle while a woman at the end of the car complained loudly about the lack of good porters. A young

Negro in a crisp uniform carried her bags while a small gray man followed her, mute.

The sudden jolt of the engine snapping the cars into line nearly threw Gregor off his feet. Jacqueline, in the midst of pushing her wool coat onto an overhead shelf, was thrown off balance and fell against him. Getting tossed around on trains wasn't new. The American railway system, especially in the south was hardly better than the trains he remembered riding in Russia. Only the chickens and pigs were missing.

But this time, instead of catching herself and laughing at the silliness of it all, Jacqueline let out a gasp. The sound of it made him look down. He saw a wince of pain cross her face as she sank into the nearest seat.

"Jacqueline?" He slid into the seat beside her.

She didn't answer. Instead, she braced her arm on the back of the seat in front of her and rested her head on her elbow. "I need to lie down." Her voice was almost a whisper.

Gregor felt a sudden chill despite the Florida heat. Jacqueline never asked for anything and she never complained. "Are you ill?" he asked, feeling helpless.

She turned her head and he noticed how pale she had become. "Grisha?" she said, then closed her eyes and took a deep breath. "I'm bleeding." She opened her eyes and he saw fear. "I think I'm pregnant."

Pregnant. It took a moment for her words to sink in. Was it possible? Of course it was possible. But on tour? They had six more weeks before his final performance in New York. How was she going to make it? What should he do?

"We must find a doctor," was all he could think to say.

"No." She shook her head. "Not here. You need to be in Chicago by tomorrow night. If I lie down, I think I'll be all right."

"Yes, yes. You must lie down. I will find a porter and he will prepare a bed."

Where was he going to find a doctor? What if she bled too much? What if she died? *Nyet!* He couldn't allow himself to even think that. Pushing the door open, he made his way through two more cars before he saw the young Negro porter.

Gregor plucked at the porter's sleeve. "Please, my wife needs help."

"Yes sir."

"Thank you." Gregor headed back down the aisle. "My wife is ill. She must have a place to lie down."

"Yes sir, I'll get you fixed up right away."

Gregor led the way, pushing the door into the next car. He found himself face to face with Valentin.

"Grisha." He pulled Gregor's arm. "Let's get something to eat. They'll stop serving breakfast in a few minutes. Tell Jacqueline to hurry."

"I can't. She is not well. She is . . .is. . ." He couldn't bring himself to say the word. "She needs a doctor."

"Hmphhh." Valentin rolled his eyes with that 'I told you so' look. "I am not surprised. Nevertheless, I am starving." He headed for the dining car.

"*Govniuk! Cossack!*" Gregor shouted.

"Sir, come this way."

Gregor turned and saw the porter beckoning him. "I have a small single berth. You'll want to help the lady. Come with me."

The space allotted for sleeping was narrow, hardly big enough for one person to lie down. Jacqueline kicked off her shoes and crawled onto the bunk. The compartment had no place to sit, so he stood, bracing his hands against the wall as the train took another turn. Stale air made the room feel even smaller. There was a tapping and he opened the door. The porter offered a pillow and two blankets.

"Thank you," Gregor said.

"Would the lady like some hot tea or coffee?"

"Yes, I think so." Gregor turned and looked at Jacqueline.

"Some bread," Jacqueline said. She lay curled on her side, knees bent, her head cushioned on her arm.

Gregor knelt beside the bunk and slid the pillow under her head. "Are you cold? Do you want a blanket?" It was hard to imagine how anyone could be cold on this train. Sweat already dampened his shirt. He loosened his tie as he tried to breathe the thick air.

"Yes, I am cold." Jacqueline let him spread the thin cotton blanket over her legs. It was really only a lap robe and didn't even cover her feet. She smiled then closed her eyes, but just that smile made him feel better. Surely everything would be all right.

He sat across from her on the floor, cross-legged, his back against the vibrating wall. The little window to his right let in light but no air. If she hadn't said she was cold he would have opened it. Outside little pink and white houses nestled beneath palm trees and pine trees slipped by as the train moved north.

"Grisha?"

He looked back and saw her watching him. "Do you really think—?" he stumbled over his words. "I mean— is it really possible that —?"

"I don't know," she said. "But I'm three weeks late. And I haven't felt—well not quite the same. This morning it was even worse."

He suddenly remembered her struggling with the heavy suitcase while he stood waiting at the elevator. He could not allow her to do that again. Not now. Not with the possibility she might be carrying a baby. Instinctively, he pressed the heels of his hands against his eyes. Still, the image was there and Papa's words. *She couldn't run fast enough. She was carrying a baby. Nyet!* He must not allow the memory of Aunt Rosie to fill his mind.

* * *

Valentin sat alone in the dinner car, a plate of steaming eggs and biscuits piled before him.

"Grisha." He tried to speak with his mouth full of food. "Call the waiter and tell him you want to eat."

Gregor sat across from Valentin and stared at the mountain of food.

"What is that?" He pointed to a sticky-looking white gruel.

"I don't know. The waiter named it grits. Help yourself." He pushed a spoon across the table.

"I am not hungry. Besides, it is too hot to eat."

"Where is Jacqueline?"

"Resting. She asked for bread and tea."

Valentin looked up from his plate. "Bread and tea? Do you know what this means?"

"It means she is hungry."

"No, you idiot." He tapped his fork on the table. "It means she has a baby in her belly. That is what babies eat. Bread and tea." He pushed the half-eaten plate of food back and sighed. "This changes everything. Are you going to tell Judson?"

"Why? What does it change?"

"A woman carrying a baby cannot tour. She'll cry all the time and beg you to stay with her in the hotel."

"How do you know such things? You've never been married."

"I have known plenty of women and some of them have become—become indisposed."

"And what did you do?" Gregor rested his chin on his hand. "I know nothing of these things."

"In Moscow there was a gypsy woman, very old." Valentin smeared butter on a biscuit. "She was wise and always found a way to make the young ladies feel better."

"And here in America? What have you done here?"

"Fortunately, Judson keeps me moving so fast that if the problem arises, I have already left town."

"I will not leave Jacqueline. Soon, I will have a son and we will be a family."

"That will end our tour. I'll have to find some other, more serious musician to play with me."

"Why? A child does not mean my life will change." Gregor didn't like the way this conversation was going.

"Ha! What do you know about babies?"

"I have seen them in the park with their nurses." He leaned back in the uncomfortable bench seat, reached for his cigarette case, then realized he had left it in his jacket. "They seem content and happy. Sometimes the babies even smile."

"As I thought, you know nothing about women and even less about their offspring."

"And where have you learned so much?" His unmet need for a cigarette made him edgy.

"I have talked to men who have children. Musicians are the worst. Their careers suffer and their performances are drained of all energy. Worst of all, the young ladies stop asking for autographs."

"You're a liar." He stood, looking down at Valentin. "You only say that because you never wanted her to come with us. She is a beautiful woman, and a good and loyal wife."

"That she is, but beautiful women are like fine pianos." He pointed his fork. "They're lovely at home, but a man shouldn't drag a piano with him on tour. Not when there are perfectly good instruments to be found in every town."

Paris, France
October 9, 1937

Dearest Mama,

Now you are Babushka, here you would be called grandmother. We have a baby girl and we are a family. Jephta Marie Germaine Piatigorsky. You see, I do not forget. I live in a fine house here in Paris, one of many owned by Jacqueline's family. There is room enough for all of you to come here and live with us. Mama, I wish I could see you and kiss you and put my baby girl in your arms. I know that you are forbidden to write to me, but I will not put my name on the envelope and I will find someone who can send this letter to you from Helsinki. Maybe then you can see the pictures of us that I have included. You see me there with my cello playing for my little girl. She loves music.

Mama, please find some way to send me just a few words. Tell me you are well and that you receive my letters. Mama, please do not forget me. I never forget you, Leo, Nadja, Alex. I love you all. Tell Papa I never forget him. I wish he could hear me play.

Love, Grisha

Chapter Thirty-five

Germans take Sudetenland
Arrests of Communists and Jews Begins.
Jewish shops looted and burned in Berlin
German youths roam Berlin streets shouting obscenities.
British Prime Minister calls for peace.

Paris, France
October 1938

Gregor inched forward in line. For over an hour he had alternately stared down at the bald spot on the head of the man in front of him, or read the grim newspaper reports from Prague. Neither activity made the wait easier. He closed his eyes and leaned against the wall. The newspaper held not a glimmer of hope. Five years since the Nazis took Berlin. Five years he had hoped the Fascists would grow weary and return to Bavaria. For a time it seemed Hitler was satisfied with speeches and parades. Then came arrests, prisons, labor camps for unionists and students, even artists and musicians. How much more did the madman want?

"Move!" someone shouted. "You're holding up the line."

His head snapped up and he saw that the gap had widened between himself and the bald man. He hurried forward. The queue turned the corner into a narrow hall, almost to their destination. The black door with the words, *Permis de séjour* in official-looking gold letters graced the portal. But there was nothing golden about this place.

"Pardon me." He felt a tug on his jacket. "Could you tell me what is the time?"

He turned, expecting to see the nervous Austrian who had stood behind him for the past hour. Instead, an elderly woman and a little girl clutching her hand had taken the man's place.

Glancing down at his wristwatch. "It is half past three."

The old woman's face sagged. "That is why so many have left. In thirty minutes they will tell us all to go home." She shook her head and shuffled toward the exit.

"Wait," Gregor called out. "Surely they will not turn you and the child away."

She didn't respond, but he saw her shoulders sag.

"Let her go," said the little man with a Slovakian accent. "If more leave, we may yet make it inside."

"What does it matter?" Gregor sighed and looked at his watch again. "They can't complete our applications today."

"But they must." A worried frown creased the little man's forehead. "I've been trying for a week to get my residency permit renewed." He ran a hand over his few wisps of remaining hair. "Every time I present myself, the inspector says I must obtain yet another document, one that I don't have."

Gregor felt a wave of nausea. Each time he applied for a permit, the interrogation grew longer. Was he any different than this man? "What will become of you if you don't get your permit today?"

"My papers expired last week." The man's voice dropped. "If it's not renewed, I will be sent back to Sudetenland."

"But Czechoslovakia is under attack." Gregor handed him the folded newspaper. "The German army has already crossed the border. Here, show them this."

"It matters not to the French what the Germans do to Jews. Paris is protected by the Maginot Line." The man pressed his pudgy hands to his face and his shoulders shook. When he finally looked up, Gregor saw tears in his eyes.

"It's not as bad as it seems," Gregor offered. It was a lie and they both knew it. "I'm sure you will get your papers today."

The man seemed not to hear him. He slowly shook his head. "If they force us to return we'll be murdered. If we stay here without permission, my wife and daughter will be imprisoned and I will be sent to the front lines." He turned away so Gregor could not see him cry. "We are doomed."

* * *

The smell hit him first. He covered his nose with his hand. Someone was dead. No, many were dead. But in the darkness he could see nothing. He staggered forward, his eyes straining for a glimmer of light. Nothing. His foot hit something solid and he was thrown off balance. Arms flailing, he tried to catch himself. Instead he fell.

"Run Grisha!" Papa screamed. "Now!"

But he couldn't run. His legs and arms were trapped, tangled in heavy masses of soft flesh that dragged him down into the darkness of the cellar. No, not the cellar, it was a ditch, deep and slimy, filled with mud, a grave. The smell of rotting flesh overpowered him and he vomited.

The wrenching woke him. He rolled from the couch, newspapers falling from his lap to the library floor. His stomach heaved with spasms, but nothing came up. Exhausted, he sank face down on the carpet, inhaling bits of dust. Dust! It tickled his nose and he sneezed.

"*Nyet!*" he said. Pushing himself to his knees, he slumped against the wall, his breath coming in short gasps. Above him the hundreds of thick books loomed, somber and weighty. There was no place to hide, not even here in the Rothschild mansion. No place was safe enough now.

Across the room a small light glowed on the face of the radio. The news broadcaster's tone droned on, flat, as if he were reporting the price of potatoes.

"*Jewish refugees fleeing Berlin were turned back at the Polish border. Danzig has ordered the expulsion of both Polish and non-Polish Jews. Five hundred refugees were dispatched in buses and trucks to the German border. No visas were issued and all passports have reportedly been confiscated.*"

"Grisha?"

He looked up and saw Jacqueline standing in the bedroom doorway. The light behind her silhouetted her figure but left her face in shadow.

"The deportations have begun." Gregor pointed to the radio. "Danzig and Warsaw."

"You shouldn't listen to the radio." She moved across the room, her long silk robe swishing around her legs. She turned off the radio, then picked up the newspapers that had scattered across the floor.

He watched her gather them in a neat pile and place them on the table. As she started to turn away, he saw her pause. Something caught her eye. Her hand went to her mouth suppressing a little gasp.

Slowly, he pushed himself from the floor. Standing behind her, he wrapped his arms around her shoulders, as much for her warmth as to steady himself. The headline stretched across the front page. It demanded attention. *200,000 Gas Masks Ready for Parisians. Those failing to apply are subject to penalties.*

"This is nonsense." She turned the newspaper over. "Nothing is going to happen to us." She faced him, but he didn't let go of her. "Come to bed, Grisha. You need to sleep."

"How can I sleep?" He stepped back from her then walked to the window, hiding the fear that must be written on his face. "Tomorrow, maybe the day after tomorrow, they'll revoke my residency permit."

"But this evening you said everything was fine." She stood beside him, touching his arm. Her fingers felt warm on his cold skin.

"Everything is not fine. It is . . ." For a moment the words eluded him. How could he possibly convey the disaster that was bearing down on them? She had never seen war, never lived through starvation and never met a Nazi. He pulled her close, pressing his cheek into her soft hair.

"Today I saw the army take a man away." He held her at arm's length. The window allowed enough light for him to see the worried frown on her face. "He was in front of me in line. His permit had expired. The soldiers were everywhere, watching, all the time, just watching." He took a deep breath and squeezed his eyes shut.

"But you're not a French citizen. How can they—?"

"The police can do whatever they want." He looked out the window. Through the trees, he saw the glow of streetlights. Everything had changed, yet the streetlights remained unaffected.

"All men over eighteen must register for military service, but aliens, those of us without papers, are taken first." He turned back. Did she understand what was coming? Did she really know? In the pale light she stood as still as a statue.

"The man was from Prague." He reached out and touched her cheek, feeling the soft warmth beneath his fingers. "He cried and begged them to let him stay, but it made no difference. He is a dead man." He covered his face with his hands. "So am I."

"Your permit hasn't expired. I'll call Father in the morning. He can talk to the Minister of Immigration and . . ."

"No." Gregor shook his head and began pacing. "No. I'm not a coward who hides behind an old man."

"But we're leaving for America in a few weeks," she pleaded. "Surely they won't do anything that soon."

"If we leave tomorrow morning, we can be in New York in five days," he said. "When I get there I'll go to the French Consulate and apply for my American residency permit. Maybe they will be more understanding."

Jacqueline frowned and shook her head. "Jephta is still at Meautry with Mother. They won't be home until Thursday." She crossed her arms and hugged herself as if she had grown cold. "You go to America. We can join you there in a few weeks. By then you'll have your papers in order." She stepped closer, rising onto her tiptoes and kissed him. "I want you to be safe."

He felt the warmth of her lips touch his cold skin, but he couldn't move.

"Go now," she whispered. "We'll join you in New York. Everything will be fine. I know it will."

* * *

On the upper deck Gregor propped his cello against a stanchion then leaned on the railing. He smoked one cigarette, then another while watching a hazy sun inch its way above the horizon. To the west, dark clouds piled up over the Atlantic. This would not be a smooth voyage.

Sounds drifted up from the dock. The port city of Le Havre was waking. Below, a line of taxis disgorged passengers and luggage. Everyone seemed in a hurry. Even the crew rushed back and forth making the ship ready for departure.

At the far end of the pier he saw a police car round the corner. For a moment he held his breath. Had they discovered he was leaving? No. The dock master had not asked for his papers. The police couldn't possibly know he was on board. Still, the sound of footsteps approaching from behind made him cringe. A well-dressed, middle-aged man stopped at the railing and nodded in Gregor's direction.

"Bonjour," he said in American-accented French.

"Bonjour." Gregor replied and was glad for the company. "Are you traveling alone?"

"I am," the man replied with a smile, the first smile Gregor had seen all morning. "I can't wait to get back to the States."

"You are an American?" Gregor asked, feeling the sudden urge to talk to someone not French.

"Yes. Born in New York, but my father's French." He extended his hand and Gregor shook it. "Philip Le Clerq. I write for the New York Times."

"You are a newspaper man? Can you tell me what is happening?" He extended his cigarette case and Le Clerq accepted the offer. "Everyone seems to have gone mad."

"I only know what I report, but do I understand it? No. No one understands anything anymore."

"I think perhaps no one ever will," Gregor said. He took another drag on the cigarette and felt the relief that always came when he smoked.

"You may be right," said Le Clerq as he exhaled a plume of smoke. "But I'm certainly glad to be on board. This is probably the last ship they will allow to leave."

"What do you mean?" Gregor pushed back from the rail, his hands suddenly cold.

"I mean the war could start tomorrow or the next day." Despite his words, Le Clerq's tone was casual. "Once Germany, England or France decides to attack there won't be any more ships going to America. The French government will take them for troop transports. You're wise to be on board."

Gregor's hand froze in midair, the cigarette burning toward his fingertips. No more ships? Jacqueline and Jephta would be trapped. He would be on one side of the ocean and they would be on the other. The war would begin. The Germans would attack.

His wife and child would be rounded up with the other Jews, arrested, loaded into trucks, deported, sent to labor camps, imprisoned, starved, beaten and killed while he waited for them in New York, helpless. He closed his eyes and in that instant saw Aunt Rosie lying in the road, her belly slit, her unborn child spilling into the dust.

"Monsieur?" Le Clerq's voice came from far away. Gregor didn't answer. The glowing embers of the cigarette touched his fingers. The pain was excruciating.

"Are you all right, monsieur?"

Gregor dropped the cigarette, picked up his cello then turned and hurried toward the stairs.

"Monsieur," he heard Le Clerq call. "Where are you going?"

Jacqueline was aware of the cold long before she woke. She rolled onto her side and reached across the sheets for Grisha's warmth. It wasn't there. Still groggy, she slid her hand along the pillow, searching. Nothing but cold, crisp linen. His side of the bed was empty. She remembered the fear in his eyes. Not just fear. Terror. Where was he now? Did he feel safe? Could he sleep?

Outside the bedroom window she heard the hiss of rain on the glass. Was it raining on him too? In her mind she saw him talking, laughing, playing cards with his friends. He loved being with people. They were attracted to him and he loved their attention. Once on board the ship, he would become his usual, confident self.

What had made him so fearful? He never spoke of Russia and rarely of Poland or Berlin. Of course he had left Germany. Hitler had made it impossible to stay. But in Paris he was safe. The German craziness couldn't reach him. But no amount of reassurance made any difference.

Lying in the dark, she tried to find him, searching with her mind, imagining him on board. His ship would have left port last night or early this morning. He would stand on the deck, watch the waves and smoke a cigarette. Was he looking forward toward America or backward to France? He would look forward, she decided. Grisha never looked back.

He was happiest when he was in America. That huge country invigorated him. If it weren't for her he would have already made America his home. Instead, the pull of Paris and grandparents, of all things familiar kept her in Paris.

Rolling off the bed, she turned on the reading lamp and looked at the clock. Six o'clock. She slipped out of her nightgown, took a hot bath, but still couldn't relax. The rain made it feel like night. Wrapping herself in a Chinese silk robe, she propped up several pillows and sat in bed with a list of tasks resting on her knee.

In little more than a week she, Jephta and Kate would leave for America. Thank God Kate was there to help take care of Jephta.

Jacqueline looked down at her list. The telegram had already gone out to the Hotel Pierre in New York City, informing them of their arrival, but she had forgotten to ask for a pram for Jephta. She and Kate would need boots and heavy coats. New York in March was a cold, wet place.

From somewhere downstairs she heard a door slam shut. At this hour? Before she could call out, footsteps pounded on the stairs then stopped outside her door. She slid off the bed, but before she could reach the door, it flew open. He stood there, dripping wet, hair matted to his forehead, a disheveled mess.

"Grisha!"

The cello case slid off his shoulder and dropped to the floor, as if he were too tired to hold onto it any longer.

"I couldn't leave——." The words tumbled from his lips. "I didn't know what might happen. Tomorrow, maybe the next day, all ships could be stopped. I couldn't leave. Please forgive me. I am such a coward." He pressed his face into the side of her cheek.

"You're soaking wet." She tried to soothe him the way one comforts a child, stroking his damp hair. It felt icy on her fingers. "You must get out of these wet clothes or you'll be sick."

He allowed her to lead him to the bed. Let her unbutton his coat, his shirt and loosen his tie. He was soaked to the skin. Naked, he crawled under the blankets and she lay beside him, pulling the blankets up over him. He clung to her, silent, his head resting on her shoulder.

"I couldn't leave," he whispered. "If I had—if I had, we would have been lost."

"Didn't you believe I would come?"

"It is not that easy." He rolled onto his back. She curled her leg over his thighs and stretched her arm across his bare chest trying to warm him. In profile she saw his face, handsome and anguished.

"Why?" she asked.

"When the war begins." He hesitated then searched for Jacqueline's hand under the blankets. "When the war begins, ships will no longer sail for America. I could not return to France and you would not be allowed to leave."

"Do you really think that's going to happen?"

"I think already it is happening." He rolled back toward her and laid his cheek against her chest. "They may come to arrest me tomorrow or the next day. I couldn't bear to wait in America knowing that you and Jephta—."

"What could possibly happen to us?" His fear seemed out of proportion to the news she had heard that morning. "The Germans are not barbarians. You've lived in Berlin. The people there mean us no harm." She lifted his hands to her lips and kissed his fingers. They were like ice.

His hand slid from hers and he covered his eyes, as if blocking something unbearable.

"What are you afraid of? Tell me."

For a moment he lay very still with his hand over his face. When he finally spoke, his voice sounded distant, as if he were seeing something she could not see.

"They caught Rosie outside our gate. She was carrying a child." His hands remained over his eyes. "They cut her open. The baby's head was severed. I thought purple snakes were crawling from her belly."

He lowered his hands and Jacqueline saw his eyes, but they were looking at something far away.

"I was six years old," he said, his voice barely a whisper.

Chapter Thirty-six

German Jews forbidden to own property or hold government jobs
Gold and silver forcibly collected from Jews by Nazis
German schools closed to Jewish children
Hitler signs pact with Mussolini
Fascists control Madrid
US orders Jewish refugee ship returned to Europe

Elizabethtown, New York
May 1939

"You're going to love this place." Ed Campe negotiated the big Chevrolet through a sharp turn then sped downhill toward the single-lane bridge. The hood of the vehicle dipped and Gregor grabbed the door handle. Below him the river dropped away as foamy white water cascaded over boulders the size of cars.

"This is very . ." The automobile hit a rut in the rough concrete and Gregor felt himself momentarily leave his seat. "A very exciting place."

"I've been coming up here every year since 1924." Campe downshifted and the engine whined. "We bought Ledgewood for next to nothing. It was in rough shape, but I've had a lot of work done."

The road straightened and Gregor gradually released his grip on the door handle. Ahead, both sides of the road were lined with towering pines, creating dark green shadows though it was still early afternoon. "I love mountains," he said as he looked up at the peaks hugging both sides of the road. "I go many summers to Switzerland with Horowitz and Milstein." His eyes were drawn to a pond with a mirror-like surface that reflected the mountains behind it. "We take holiday at Lake d'Annecy."

"You should have brought Jacqueline along. My wife would love to meet her."

"Yes, but our daughter is a little bit sick. Jacqueline says she must rest before we return to Paris."

"You're going back? I would have thought you'd rather stay here." The big engine purred as Campe maneuvered the car through a series of tight turns.

"I must return. I have only one month left on my French work permit." The car picked up speed as it rolled down a steep incline. "But the newspapers report there is no more fighting in Spain."

"I hope so. My wife and I would love to see Madrid again."

Gregor kept his eyes focused on the landscape. He had not seen the likes of such a clear blue sky since last summer's trip to the Alps. He allowed himself to relax. The grueling schedule of five concerts a week had taken its toll on all of them. Jephta was coughing and Kate wasn't feeling well either.

"Go," Jacqueline had insisted when Mr. Campe invited them to his mountain lodge for a few days' rest. "I just want to sleep in the same room for the next three nights without packing and unpacking my suitcase." She kissed him then handed him his hat and coat. "Jephta is still sick and Kate will keep me company. Have a wonderful time and tell us all about it on Monday."

Now, two hundred miles north of New York City, in the midst of the Adirondack wilderness, Gregor felt the tension melting away. "Look," he cried, pointing to the trees that stood like bright sentinels against the dark green of the forest. "We have these trees in Russia. What do you call them?"

"You mean the white ones? Those are birch trees."

"I remember such trees in Sokolniki forest. My brother and I skied there when the snow was deep."

"The snow gets plenty deep up here too. See, there's still some there in the woods. Some folks ski at Otis Mountain. There's even a rope tow to pull you up the hill."

Campe slowed the car as a cluster of houses came into view. "We're almost there. This is our post office and general store all rolled into one."

The American flag fluttered on a slender pole over a small white building. Above the porch, in neat lettering, a sign read DENTON'S GROCERY, New Russia, New York.

"Stop!"

Campe hit the brakes, but before the car came to a complete halt Gregor opened the door and jumped out. "What are you doing?"

"You see this?" Gregor stared at the sign. "The name of this place? New Russia? How can this be? Are there Russians here?"

"None that I know of," Campe said, and laughed. "This village has been called New Russia for over a hundred years, and you, my friend, are probably the first Russian to ever set foot in it."

* * *

Gregor followed Campe up the wide steps of the porch and into Ledgewood Lodge. It towered above him, a huge, rustic building perched on the side of a mountain in the midst of an evergreen forest. Inside, the dark wood paneling reminded him of the hunting lodges he had visited in Switzerland. Standing by the massive stone fireplace was a small man with a quick smile.

"Mr. Levitt," said Campe. "This is Gregor Piatigorsky, the cellist I told you about."

"I'd like to hear you play," said Levitt as he extended his hand.

Gregor shook the man's hand. "I would be happy to play, but I left my cello at the hotel." He held out his empty hands. "Mr. Campe is very persuasive. Another time, if I return."

"I hope you do come back," Campe said. "We'd like to add some culture to our little hamlet. Levitt here knows a lot about land and property in this area."

"Ahhh," Gregor said, grinning at the not so subtle ploy. "You have invited me to dinner for a purpose."

"Let's have a drink." Campe opened the liquor cabinet. "Sit outside. Enjoy the sunset until dinner is served."

They retreated to the porch, armed with a tall glass of Scotch for Gregor and bourbon for the Americans.

"You have a beautiful home in a wonderful place." Gregor stood at the log railing, his eyes following the undulating line of mountaintops across the valley. Below the green peaks, a delicate white spire of a church stood in a nest of tiny houses. He wished Jacqueline had come. "It is Switzerland, only softer."

"It certainly is a retreat from the city," said Campe sinking into a wooden chair.

Gregor followed and found the wide arms of the chair a perfect place for holding his glass. "You are fortunate to have such a home and no fear of losing it."

"Not much chance of that up here," Campe lit a cigarette and offered the gold case to Gregor. "I hate to talk politics, but how are things in France?"

"Not good," Gregor paused, wondering how he could possibly explain the insanity that had taken over Berlin and now infected Paris.

"Is Hitler as bad as the newspapers say?" asked Levitt. "The Germans seem to think he's going to get rid of the Communists. Doesn't sound like a half bad idea to me."

"Communists and Nazis are not so different." Gregor swallowed the whiskey. "Either group makes trouble for people without citizenship."

"Aren't you a Russian citizen?" said Levitt.

"I am a citizen of the world."

"But your wife is French?"

"It makes no difference. Every three months, like all other stateless persons, I must go to the Paris police and beg to stay with my family."

"Have you considered applying for U.S. citizenship?"

"I have. Two years ago I signed papers at immigration office in New York City. But I must wait three years more to become citizen. Many people are leaving Europe. I think American government is not so anxious to give citizenship to strangers."

"It wouldn't hurt if you showed Uncle Sam you owned property and paid taxes." Levitt puffed on a slim cigar. "That would show your good intention."

"Uncle Sam? Who is this?"

"He means the government of the United States," said Campe. "But he's right. Property owners and taxpayers get treated with a lot more respect than your ordinary immigrant."

"But I spend most of my time on tour and I have a home in Paris."

"What you need is a summer place." Campe motioned to the peaks. "You could stay here between tours instead of traveling back and forth across the Atlantic every few months."

Gregor reached for the liquor bottle, but Campe beat him to it and poured three fingers of Scotch. He settled back in his chair with his drink and stared at the pink and orange clouds just touching the mountaintops to the east. A home in the Adirondacks, Jacqueline would love it. She and Jephta could stay here instead of following him from hotel to hotel. He could travel to concerts, even take the train to New York City and still come home in less than a day.

In three years, just three short years, he could apply for citizenship. He tried to imagine what it would feel like to walk through customs and present his American passport to the officers.

"*Yes, Mr. Piatigorsky, your papers are all in order,*" the officer would say. "*Welcome home.*"

With an American passport no one, not the police, not the army, not even immigration officers could stop him. *Welcome home.* Those words would be the sweetest music he would ever hear.

* * *

"The driveway's steep." said Levitt as he pulled the Ford onto the shoulder of the road. "We'll park here and walk up."

"We only need a small house, a cottage. Nothing more." Gregor wondered what this man was leading him into. "Must we climb the hillside like goats?"

"In the summer you can drive up," said Levitt. "But right now there're still icy patches on the driveway, but the caretaker did give me the house keys."

Gregor followed Levitt along the edge of the narrow macadam road. Ahead of them the morning sun illuminated massive stone walls that surrounded two large barns. A metal gate sagged on its hinges, secured by a rusty chain. Levitt pulled the gate back, allowing just enough space for the two of them to squeeze through.

"This place was built over fifty years ago." Levitt took the lead, moving with ease. "Back in the old days, carriages and wagons were kept down here in these barns. Then the owners used a little horse cart to carry people up to the top."

"Where is the cart now?" Gregor found his breath coming hard.

"Long gone." Levitt paused to point through the trees at a small gray-green house. "Will Cauley looks after the place, at least he did until the owner died. That was a couple of years ago. No one's paid him or the property taxes since. Last month I put the whole place up for sale. It's the only way the town can collect the back taxes."

"Does anyone work here now?"

"Cauley still keeps the keys, but he doesn't do any work."

Ahead, faint tire tracks disappeared under a thick mat of dead leaves and patches of wet snow. Above, pines and hemlocks blocked the sun, creating a cave-like sensation. Slender white birches, their leaves just starting to bud, arced like dancers over the road in front of them. As the road grew steeper, their climb slowed. Gregor paused more often to catch his breath. Never before had he been in such a secluded place.

"Is this house small?" Gregor removed his hat and loosened his shirt collar. Despite the cool mountain air, he was perspiring. "I will only spend five thousand dollars, no more."

"Its just the kind of place for a man like you. Your fans and the newspapers won't bother you."

That and the police, Gregor thought, but didn't say it. Instead, he smiled and tried to slow his breathing. "I am not a movie star like Rudolph Valentino or Errol Flynn. Admirers of my music need only buy recordings to be satisfied."

They continued climbing. As their ascent slowed, Gregor found himself looking down at the ground. Along the edge of the road, a stone wall held back huge moss-covered rocks, which towered above them.

"What do you think?" Levitt stopped and lit a cigar. "Pretty impressive, huh?"

Gregor looked up. Above him a massive fortress, like that of an English castle, rose from the mountainside. Stone buttresses supported a half-timbered balcony that wrapped around the structure. Heavy arches led to a tunnel beneath the parapet wall and a riot of new ferns and evergreens surrounded the base.

"It is—." Gregor stared up at the structure. " It is very big."

"I have the keys," Levitt said. "Let's take a look inside."

Up they went, climbing a narrow stone staircase that led to a landing just below the balcony. There was a flash of movement as a small brown creature darted between two large Grecian urns, which stood like sentinels at the top of the stairs.

"I have never seen such creatures." Gregor stepped under a covered walkway. To his right, another short flight of stairs led to the balcony and the larger portion of the house. On the left, another building stretched into the forest.

"This is the dining room and kitchen," Levitt said as he tried several keys, before finally unlocking the big wooden door. "Behind this room are the servants quarters and laundry. The next building is the guesthouse. Up above us, on that rock, is a screened in summerhouse that overlooks the rest of the place."

It took a moment for Gregor's eyes to adjust to the low light as he stepped inside. The first thing he noticed was a massive stone fireplace that filled the back wall of the room. Across from it, tall diamond-paned windows looked over the valley below. A long table and rustic chairs took up most of the middle of the floor. Every surface in the place was covered with a fine layer of dust and a few lethargic flies buzzed against the windows, hoping to escape.

"Certainly could use a good cleaning." Levitt said as he moved through the dining room into the kitchen. Gregor followed.

A large, black iron stove squatted in the center of the room, behind it, stacks of firewood. Along the wall stretched a white enamel sink and a fat spider spun a web over the hanging lamp.

"It is like a castle in the Alps." Gregor said, remembering his vacations in Switzerland.

"Let me show you the rest of it," Levitt moved quickly out of the dusty kitchen.

Outside, Gregor followed his guide up the short flight of stairs to the larger part of the building. A great hall opened onto the balcony and overlooked the river below. The view was incredible. As far as he could see, there were forests and fields dotted with the occasional tiny house or barn. The silver thread of a river curved and twisted along the valley floor. Close beside it, a narrow ribbon of pavement turned with every bend of the river.

"Is it true?" Gregor stretched his arm up and touched the thick beam supporting the roof of the balcony. "There are no Russians in New Russia?"

"I've never heard of any." Levitt flicked his cigar butt over the wooden railing. "If you made this your castle, then you would be the Tsar of New Russia." He chuckled. "And your wife would be the Tsarina."

"My wife already has a castle in France." Gregor was growing weary of the man's cheerfulness.

"Let me show you the rest of the place. You're going to love it." Levitt used the same key to unlock the door of the great hall. Inside, the first thing Gregor noticed was a musty animal odor that filled the air. The room had no ceiling, but was open to the peak of the roof.

Gregor leaned back and stared up at rafters. They were made from whole tree trunks. Like the dining room, this part of the house had also been built around a massive stone fireplace. But the thing that caught his eye was the face of the ugliest animal he had ever seen.

"What is this beast?" He stared up at the creature whose enormous head hung over the fireplace.

"A moose," Levitt said and chuckled. "Haven't you ever seen one before?"

"I have seen reindeer and elk, even a buffalo when I visited Denver, but never such a hideous creature as this."

"He comes with the place, but you could take him down if you wanted to."

"No one should remove him." Gregor tugged at the long whiskers hanging from the animal's chin. "This is his home."

"So what do you think?"

"I think this is not a small cottage and it will cost more than five thousand dollars."

"I believe the owners are flexible."

"Or perhaps desperate?" Gregor tried to imagine what Jacqueline would say if she were here. "I would like to find a smaller house with not so many steps."

"I think this place is perfect for you, but I can keep on looking when you go back to France. I'll need you to leave me a cash deposit."

"I will give you five thousand dollars," Gregor said, feeling reluctant but not brave enough to say no. "But I cannot leave more than that."

"That will be fine. I will deposit it in escrow at the bank in Albany." Levitt locked the front door and they headed back down the stone staircase. "But Mr. Piatigorsky, I really think this is the place for you."

Chapter Thirty-seven

WESTERN UNION: To G. PIATIGORSKY-PARIS, FRANCE
YOUR ESCROW DEPOSIT OF $5,OOO IS ACCEPTED BY ESSEX
COUNTY CLERK! WINDY CLIFF PROPERTY WILL CONVEY
IMMEDIATELY! MONEY ON DEPOSIT WILL COVER ALL FEES. J.
LEVITT

Lake d'Annecy, Switzerland
August 31, 1939

"*Chancellor Hitler is willing to negotiate, but France must acquiesce to his demand for control of Danzig. Berlin says the door is still open to a peaceful solution. In Paris the president waits for a British . . .*" The broadcast broke up in a rattle of static.

Gregor stubbed out his cigarette. He leaned over the kitchen table and adjusted the tuner a fraction, hoping to pick up the rest of the news. It happened like this every day. In the early morning he could hear reports from Lyon and Marseilles, but by mid-day it became impossible.

"*...Chamberlain has ordered the mobilization of the British fleet and civilians are being evacuated . .* " Static swallowed up the rest. Once again he was cut off from the world.

He sank back in the big chair and ran his hands over his face. Sitting here trying to patch together the pieces of broadcasts was making him crazy. He needed to talk to someone, anyone who might know what was happening.

Frustrated, he went to the window and stared out at the peaceful valley below. How could the world be at the brink of war? No one here had the answer. Few people discussed world news in the village of d'Annecy. People came to the Alps to escape the city heat and political tensions.

Maybe Milstein would know. At least he might get better radio reception at his villa.

"I must call Marseilles," he told the operator when she finally came on the line.

"What is the exchange and number you wish to call?"

"Exchange Sabot. Number five, seven, zero, three." He paced but could only move two steps in each direction. The length of the telephone cord kept him in check.

"Pardon, monsieur," said the operator. "I cannot connect any calls into or out of France."

"What?" Gregor froze. "I called that number two days ago."

"The government has closed the border."

"That is not possible."

"I am sorry, monsieur, but this is what I am told. Perhaps it is only temporary." With a loud click the line went dead.

What had happened? Had war already begun? He picked up the newspaper then remembered it was already two days old. *HITLER BLUFFS—LONDON RELAXES,* read the headline. Could things have changed so much, so fast? Perhaps it was just a precaution. That was it. The French government was just being careful. Sooner or later the men in power would come to their senses and find some sort of compromise. They had to. Besides, the Maginot line was well fortified. No army could penetrate it.

He poured a half glass of Scotch and took a swallow. It was better if he tried not to think about the world and its problems. But the alcohol didn't help. Maybe fresh mountain air was the tonic he needed.

Stepping outside the chalet, he took a deep breath and closed his eyes. The warm air of late summer carried the smell of fresh cut hay. He remembered the same smell from the fields around Ekaterinoslav. Was Mama even now in the kitchen making supper? And Leo—?

"Grisha?"

Startled, he turned and saw Jacqueline standing in the doorway. She wore a light flowery dress that hung loose around her slim hips. He hugged her and let his hand slide down her breasts until he touched the slight roundness of her abdomen. It was the only thing about her that had changed.

"How do you feel, *Mumchik?*" He kissed her cheek and smelled the light scent of her perfume. How could anything be wrong in the world, he wondered?

"I'm a little tired." She laid her head on his shoulder. "Kate and Jephta are down at the lake picking flowers. I think I'll go upstairs and take a nap before lunch."

"I should practice," he said, but made no move to release her. "I have only two weeks left before tour."

"Everything will be fine." She squeezed his hand. "How goes the world?" she asked as she picked up the newspaper. "Is there any change?"

For a moment he hesitated. Should he tell her the border was closed and no phone calls could go in or out of France? "They're trying to negotiate an end to the difficulties. It will be over soon."

"I hope so. Father told me not to worry. He and Mother are going to London on Friday."

"You see, everything is good." He forced a smile. "When my tour ends, we'll take a vacation, maybe California." He kissed her cheek. "Go upstairs, rest. I can't practice if you're here distracting me." He turned her toward the stairs. "Take care of yourself and our baby."

He watched her slowly climb the stairs. When the bedroom door clicked shut, he sank down at the kitchen table and turned on the radio. The speaker crackled as he moved the dial to Geneva instead of Marseilles.

"*This morning—soldiers entered Warsaw —the capital—unable to report.*" The announcer's voice disappeared in a rattle of static. What had happened? What were they talking about? For a moment he closed his eyes, trying to block out the images with his hands. Soldiers in Warsaw? Were they Polish? French? Russian? Please don't let them be German. Anything but Germans.

He opened his eyes and turned the dial back to Marseilles. The voice was inaudible. Not knowing made him crazy. Giving up, he paced the length of the room then opened the kitchen door. The midday sun shone bright and the sky was milky blue. Two more weeks and they would leave for New York. Two more weeks and he could relax. Two more weeks and they would be safe.

* * *

Jacqueline leaned against the bedroom door to catch her breath. Thank God they had Kate to help with Jephta. She pushed open the bedroom window and the gauzy drapes billowed around her. Paris was unbearable, but here she could breathe. Across the meadow, she saw a spot of red near the woods. Jephta's sunbonnet bobbed up and down as the little girl ran along the edge of the flowerbeds. It was peaceful here and she wanted to savor every moment of it, stopping time for just a bit longer before the craziness of Grisha's tour began.

The big bed with the white coverlet looked so inviting. Stretching out, she sank into the softness. Eyes closed, she sighed and let every part of her body go limp. Downstairs the clock chimed eleven. It was much too early for a nap. Just half an hour, she promised herself. Then she would join Jephta and Kate by the lake for lunch.

Even with her eyes closed she could still see the smooth contours of the meadow stretching away from the chalet toward the blue expanse of Lake d'Annecy. The breeze from the open window washed over her like a caressing hand. Everything was going to be fine. Everything was going to be all right.

A waft of cool air moved across Jacqueline's legs. A summer thunderstorm? Maybe it would break the heat.

I must get up and close the windows or the rug will get wet, she thought. But the bed was so comfortable that she couldn't bring herself to move. Just one more minute.

On the horizon clouds grew dark. The summer breeze grew stronger and blew straight into her face. A faint odor, like burning wood, touched her nose.

Along the lake she saw a thin ribbon of yellow stretching as far as the eye could see. Fire! The black clouds were not harbingers of a storm, but billowing smoke. Tiny figures moved toward her, people running along the shore, escaping the approaching flames. The figures became a mob and stampeded toward her, panic etched on their faces.

"What is it?" she called out as a woman ran past her. "What's happening?" But the woman didn't answer. A man carried a little girl, her face buried in her father's shoulder. Blood trickled down the side of the man's face.

Jacqueline opened her mouth, but no sound escaped her lips. She tried to cover her eyes, but her arms and hands were frozen, no longer her own. People moved like zombies, some missing limbs, others eyes. Behind them great clouds of smoke spit red and yellow flames. Sparks ignited the grass. The air around her crackled. In another second the flames would engulf her. She would die and the child growing within her would never be born. With all her strength, she inhaled and screamed.

The sound of her own voice woke her and she sat up, her heart pounding. "Grisha, where are you?" She cried, sliding off the bed and stumbling to the top of the stairs. "We have to leave. Now!"

Chapter Thirty-eight

Nazis invade Poland
Chamberlain calls Parliament into emergency session
Poland mounts defense, calls on allies for help.
French President calls deputies to Paris
Reservists called to Maginot Line
U.S. Congress discusses neutrality

Northern France
September 2, 1939

Automobiles choked the narrow country road even at midnight. Everyone in France seemed to be on the move, but to where? No place was safe. Gregor glanced at Jacqueline and saw her rub her eyes. Fatigue etched lines on her face that were visible every time the headlights of an approaching car shone through the windshield. He should be the one at the wheel of the car, not her. At times like this he felt helpless and stupid.

Ahead, he saw a road sign, Le Havre 100 km. At this rate it would be dawn before they made it to the port. He tapped the last cigarette from the pack. Smoking didn't help, but there was nothing else to do with his hands.

"They'll send you to the front lines if we stay," Jacqueline said, taking her eyes off the road for a moment and meeting his gaze. "They have to reinforce the Maginot Line. It's the only defense."

He didn't reply. He had no answer.

They should never have left New York. At least in America they were safe. What would happen if they couldn't get onboard? For a moment he closed his eyes hoping for relief from the glare of headlights.

He saw her lying there, belly slit open, blood congealed in the dust. Only this time it wasn't Aunt Rosie. Shaking off the image, he opened his eyes and brought the cigarette to his lips. His hand shook so badly he could hardly hold it.

"Once we're onboard they won't put us off," Jacqueline said. "The ticket agent promised."

"I feel like a coward." He tossed the partially smoked cigarette out the window.

"Of course you're not. You have to leave. If you don't, they'll send you to the front lines. What good is a medal to us if you're dead?"

"If I were a citizen I would fight for France." He chewed his lip then rubbed his hands over his face. He glanced down at the newspaper on the seat. It was too dark to read, but the headline was there before his eyes. GERMANY ATTACKS POLAND!! BRITAIN DECLARES WAR!! FRANCE WILL FOLLOW!!

In the mirror he saw Kate's worried face. He turned, looking over the back seat and tried to give her a reassuring smile. "Do not be afraid. We will be there soon."

Her eyes and nervous stroking of Jephta's hair betrayed her fear. "I know," Kate said, her voice barely a whisper. "I know."

Talk was meaningless. Traveling with only one French passport among the four of them was risky. In normal times the Rothschild name on Jacqueline's documents counted for something. Not anymore.

Kate's labor card identified her as German, but the fact that she was Jewish made the situation more difficult. Gregor's Nansen passport was worthless.

At the Swiss border, the guard recorded his name, age and address, then told him to report to the Paris military command in Precinct Three. All male immigrants were needed to reinforce the front lines. If he failed to report as ordered, he would be sent to a labor camp. Instead of complying, Jacqueline bypassed Paris and drove straight for the coast.

"We should get something to eat," Jacqueline said.

"Don't stop," Kate cried, grabbing the seat back. "Please." She was almost sobbing. "You have no idea what they'll do. Please keep going."

"Jephta's sleeping," Gregor said. "We shouldn't stop." Food was the last thing he cared about.

"Can we make it?" Kate whispered. "Will they let us board the ship?"

"The agent said there was one inside cabin left." Jacqueline slowed the car as she approached a sagging farm truck loaded with passengers. "If we get there in time the cabin is ours."

"We can sleep on the deck if we must," said Kate. She rocked back and forth as if the motion of her body could make the car go faster. Jephta, blissfully unaware that the world had gone mad, wriggled on Kate's lap and sucked her thumb. "Don't let them put us off," Kate whispered. "Please, don't let them put us off."

* * *

The North Atlantic looked sour. Gray-green water reflected a hazy sun and the air smelled of diesel fuel. The stifling heat on land gave way to the damp clingy humidity of open sea. Even on deck Gregor felt a trickle of sweat run down the side of his neck.

As he stood at the bow of the ILE de FRANCE, a force like a giant hand rose beneath the hull and rolled the ship to port. Grabbing the rail he held on tight as he waited for the vessel to right itself. If he had eaten breakfast he might have lost it, but food no longer interested him.

Two sweltering days in port had passed while the authorities argued. Should the ship be allowed to leave with three thousand passengers, or would all able-bodied men be pressed into service? Male citizens had disembarked then been allowed to re-board.

Finally, on the third day, the overloaded vessel had slid out of Le Havre. Rumors were rampant. The ship would be turned back, they would all be taken prisoner, strafed by the Luftwaffe or sent to a watery grave by a German U-boat. No one rested and few could eat. Only Jephta was oblivious to the crisis. Her wobbly attempts at walking on the rolling deck kept some people amused.

With every pulse of the big engine, every turn of the screw, Gregor willed the ship forward. Now this ship was a giant bird on whose back his family would fly to safety. But the bird was as vulnerable as he was. Down there, beneath the dark waves, evil waited for him. Was it his turn to die?

He glanced at his watch. Two hours out of port, two hours closer to America, surely they wouldn't be turned back now. Five days to New York, no, four days and twenty-two hours. That was all they needed to reach safety.

When he closed his eyes, he felt cold. There, on the edge of memory, was the sound of heavy boots, the tickle of dust in his nose and the smell of burning flesh. That would not happen here. This time death came from beneath the greasy water. A muffled thud or maybe no sound at all. Would the ship suddenly pitch? Could he make it to a lifeboat? How fast would seawater pour though the hull? He would never survive, none of them would in the North Atlantic.

He felt motion at his elbow and opened his eyes, grateful for a reprieve. A small man with a dark moustache stood beside him. The man's right eye twitched and his fingers trembled as he tried and failed to put a match to his cigarette.

"Let me help you," Gregor offered, glad for something to do. He took a lighter from his pocket and held out the flame.

"*Merci, monsieur.*" The man took a long drag and held the smoke in his lungs. "*Merci.*"

"What more can we do but stand here and count the minutes?" Gregor lit his own cigarette.

The man nodded and he took another drag. "Did you hear? The German crew left us in Le Havre. Some say they sabotaged the vessel before they departed."

"Why would they do such a thing?" This was a possibility that hadn't occurred to him. Danger above and danger below. "Can a wine steward be a saboteur?"

"I don't know, but that's what I have been told. Did you know the Germans already torpedoed a passenger ship off the coast of Ireland?" The man rested his hand against the rail, but the trembling continued. "All passengers were lost."

"Surely our captain is taking every precaution," Gregor said.

"Ha! You see those men down there?" They both leaned forward and peered over the rail. Below them, tied to a cantilevered lifeboat, two crew members slapped black paint over the portholes. "That is so no light will shine in the darkness," said the man. "The Captain wants to make us invisible." He pointed up at the bridge. "You see, our ship flies no flag, so the Germans will not know we are a French vessel. Even the name has been painted over."

Hiding in plain sight? That was their only defense? Gregor wanted to run, to flee from this faceless, nameless enemy that would destroy everyone and everything. But he couldn't run. Here, in this wide-open place, he was trapped.

He looked at his watch again. Ten minutes had passed, ten minutes closer to America. "New York is only five days away," he said, trying to sound confident. "Once we are there, we will have nothing to fear."

"Nothing to fear unless you are traveling without papers." The man tapped his cigarette ash over the rail. "The Americans are not so welcoming as they once were. Do you have a passport and visa?"

"I have a contract to work for four months," Gregor said with a sinking heart. "Perhaps by April all trouble will be past."

"Do you really think Herr Hitler will be so easily appeased?" The man shook his head then tossed his cigarette into the waves. "I am traveling without documents. If the Americans try to send me back, I will jump into the sea."

Gregor stared. "You cannot mean that."

The man's deep-set eyes had a hollow, haunted look. "Sir, I am a Jew. Already many of my friends have gone to prison, turned in by my own government. France will not protect me." His eyes narrowed. "Nor will they protect you. Our only hope is America. If they betray us now, we will all be better off in a watery grave."

Chapter Thirty-nine

Germans attack Poland
German Jews forbidden to own radios
Nazis begin euthanasia of crippled and infirm
Britain, France, Australia and Canada declare war on Germany
Soviets honor commitment to Nazis and invade Poland
Nazi U-boats sink British and French ships
U.S. proclaims neutrality

Ellis Island, New York
September 7, 1939

"Passports," demanded the officer when it was finally their turn. Gregor saw the man's name printed in white letters on a black badge pinned to his jacket. REICHMAN.

"Your documents sir," the man repeated.

Gregor drew the stack of papers from his leather case and slid them across the counter. Jacqueline's French passport was on top along with Jephta's birth certificate. Beneath them lay the contract with Arthur Judson and his tattered Nansen passport. Kate had nothing. In a moment of panic she had thrown her German identity card into the sea.

Instead of examining them, the officer took the documents and passed them to another inspector. Neither of the men looked at Gregor, and Reichman kept his eyes glued on the thick rulebook before him. "The purpose of your visit?" It was a question, but his voice remained monotone.

"I will perform the Brahms Double Concerto with the Boston Symphony. I will also play with my good friends Nathan Milstein and —."

"Duration of your stay?" Reichman interrupted.

"What is duration?" Gregor tried to keep his own tone pleasant.

Behind him someone snickered and he was tempted to turn and chastise them for poor manners. Instead, he repeated, "I am sorry, my English is not good. What is duration?"

"How long will you stay in the United States?"

Gregor hesitated, momentarily lost for words. Should he tell the truth? Should he say they would stay in America for the rest of their lives, if possible, or at least until Hitler and his Nazis were no longer in power? But that might be the wrong thing to say.

"Until my contract is satisfied."

"How long will that be?"

"Four months."

"Then you will return home?"

"If it is possible to do so."

"Have you booked return passage for your party?"

"Return passage?" Hadn't this man heard what was happening in Europe? "Sir, do you expect us to—."

For the first time the man looked up and Gregor felt his stomach sink. America did not want even one boatload of refugees, much less an entire continent of them.

"If you have not purchased tickets, do you have adequate funds to buy such passages when your visa expires?"

"I have funds." Inside his coat pockets his hands were clenched. Still, he gave the man his best professional smile.

"How much money do you have?"

Gregor took a deep breath. "I have sufficient funds." He pulled his bankbook from his pocket and passed it to the inspector. The man studied the leather folder with the words CHASE MANHATTAN BANK embossed on the cover. Then he flipped it open and thumbed through the pages of deposits and withdrawals. "Is this your money?"

The insult was so egregious that Gregor opened his mouth to object. It would do no good. He bit his tongue and managed to say, "Yes." Anything more would have been an obscenity.

"Hmmmph," he grunted and handed the bankbook back.

"Do you have anyone who can vouch for you?"

Jacqueline stepped forward. "My father is Edouard de Rothschild."

"Is he an American citizen?"

"No. He is the president of the Banque de France."

"Then he can't vouch for you."

"He is currently in London with the Prime Minister. Shall I send a telegram and ask Mr. Chamberlain to vouch for us?"

The man paused and seemed to ponder Jacqueline's offer. Then he scribbled Nearest kin, Edouard Rothschild, on the document.

"How many people are traveling with you?"

"Three." Gregor motioned Kate and Jacqueline forward. "My wife and my daughter. She is not yet two years old. This is my daughter's nurse, Katherine Kuhlman. She must remain with us. My wife will soon be a new mother."

He put his arm around Jacqueline's shoulder as the officer looked up from his book. Jacqueline gave the man a weak smile and Gregor saw his eyes move down to her round belly, pause then return to his manifest list. He made four check marks, then scribbled something in the margin.

"Our record shows that there are no legible fingerprints on file."

"I have never needed such a thing before," Gregor snapped. Being pleasant wasn't helping. Now he was ready to argue. "I am not a criminal."

"All aliens must present a legible thumbprint on their visa. The law now requires it."

"How are we to obtain this fingerprint?"

"Officer Schmidt." The man motioned to his assistant. "See that they are all fingerprinted."

Gregor retrieved his cello and their single suitcase. Jacqueline carried his briefcase. Kate still held Jephta, who squirmed as she tried to look at everyone. In a narrow windowless room devoid of all furniture save a table, Schmidt produced an inkpad and started with Gregor. He rolled his thumb on the pad then pressed it in the little box on the visa.

"It is no different than Berlin," Gregor heard Kate mutter in German. His eyes moved up to Schmidt's face, but despite his name the man didn't seem to understand her remark.

"Do you have a chair?" Gregor asked. The man handed him a dirty ink stained rag to wipe his thumb. "My wife is very tired."

Schmidt glanced at Jacqueline then out the door toward the desk where his supervisor sat questioning the next group of passengers.

"I'm sorry, but there are no chairs except the one for my boss."

"I'm all right," Jacqueline said. She stretched out her right hand and Schmidt quickly rolled her finger in ink and pressed it on the form.

"You next." He motioned to Kate.

Gregor reached to take Jephta from her and saw Kate's face stiffen.

"Do it. *Schnell!*" He spoke to her in German. "He will not harm you."

She moved forward, her body wooden, her fingers trembling as the print was made.

"There now," Schmidt said. "You're all done."

They followed him back to Reichman's desk where again they waited until the officer finished with a Dutch couple whose knowledge of English was so bad that they were forced to repeat every answer several times.

Finally, when it was their turn, Reichman drew four blank forms from a thick folder and began laboriously filling them out.

Gregor felt Jacqueline lean against his arm. Exhaustion showed on her face and her skin looked gray. "Just a little longer, *Mumchik*," he whispered. "Soon we will be in our new home".

"I'm fine." She dropped her head against his shoulder. "Just tired."

"We will go to a hotel." He kept his voice low. "You can rest. Then we'll find a car. I know you will love Windy Cliff." He kissed her cheek. "We will be safe when we get there."

Chapter Forty

Germans attack Greece
Germans attack Yugoslavia
Germans attack Soviet Union
Germans deport Jews to Auschwitz
U.S. denies refuge to Jews

New Russia, New York
September 15, 1939

"You can't live at Windy Cliff," said William Cauley.

They all stood in a circle in front of the big dining room fireplace. Jacqueline knew it had been years since anyone kindled a fire. The carcass of a mummified duck lay on the hearth amid a pile of dusty kindling wood, curling brown leaves and sooty feathers. She shivered. Here, inside the stone and log kitchen, where the sun's rays didn't reach, it was chilly. The odor of old wood smoke and mildew hung in the stale air.

She watched Cauley try to roll another cigarette. There was a tremor in his fingers and crumbs of tobacco fluttered to the floor. It hardly mattered. The wooden boards, already caked with ground-in dirt, were mottled with mouse droppings. "Can't stay here much longer anyway. Pipes will freeze. In a month you won't have water either."

Jephta dropped to her knees and started crawling under the big table. "*Nein, nein,*" Kate scolded and scooped her up. "*Sehr* dirty, *sehr* dirty." She brushed the debris from Jephta's knees.

Jacqueline looked at Grisha and saw a worried frown crease his face. "It will be lovely," she said and squeezed his hand. "Once we get it cleaned. Mr. Cauley will you help us?"

"I'm a caretaker." He twisted the ends of the little paper and tucked the cigarette between his thin lips. "You've got over twenty rooms. You need a couple of cleaning ladies. Carpenters too. Roof in the big hall's been leaking since nineteen thirty-five. That's when Mrs. Norton died. Passed away right here in the kitchen."

"We will hire cleaners," Grisha said, a little too quickly. "And painters and carpenters. Whatever is needed, it will be done."

Jacqueline recognized the mask of confidence he used to hide fear. "This will be the finest home in the valley. All of our friends will come. No one will be turned away."

"Still," Cauley spoke around his cigarette. "Can't live here in winter."

"Where will we go?" Grisha asked. "We have no other home."

"Mary Partridge's house is empty. I caretake it too. Mary's gone to Florida. Probably she'll let you rent 'til May."

"The pipes will not freeze?" Grisha looked skeptical.

"No, sir. Place has a coal furnace and ten rooms. Right in town. 'Cross from the courthouse."

"Mary Partridge?" A smile lit up Grisha's face. "Yes. We will live in Mary Partridge's house. When it is spring we will return to Windy Cliff." He took Jacqueline's hand and gave it a gallant kiss. "Welcome to your new home."

* * *

Elizabethtown, New York
February 1940

It was a Moscow kind of cold, the kind that froze the inside of his nose with every breath. A sky, crystal blue. The kind of sky Muscovites saw only when the wind blew down hard from Siberia, pushing the smudge from wood fires and coal stoves south toward the river. The kind of day when new snow covered rubbish heaps and people could, for a day, believe the world was good. It was a beautiful Moscow kind of day, with none of the pain.

"I can't reach her feet." Jacqueline laughed at her own helplessness. "You put her skates on."

With arms outstretched, Gregor slid the last few feet across the ice, almost tumbling over the bench where Jephta sat.

Jephta leaned forward, trying to escape her mother's arms. "Papa. Let me." Off the bench she hopped, her little legs struggling to stand. She took only a few steps before her feet came out from under her and she plopped down on the ice.

"Come back." Jacqueline moved cautiously off the bench and reached for the little girl, but Jephta wouldn't wait. Rolling to her knees, Jephta pushed up, slipping and sliding her way back toward Gregor.

"Soon you will be skating like Sonja Henja." Gregor picked her up and sat her back on the bench. "But you will do better if you wear skates."

As Jacqueline unbuckled the skate straps, Gregor pushed his gloved hands under his arms and tried to keep his fingers warm. The sting of cold was there, not something he wanted to feel, this close to a performance. He caught Jacqueline's eye and saw the slight frown that told him she knew his hands were cold.

"I'll do it." She awkwardly lowered herself to the bench.

"No," he protested, pulling off his gloves. "My hands are warm." He knelt on the ice as Jephta stuck her legs straight out.

"Hurry, Papa." By the time he had the little metal skates clamped firmly to her shoes, his fingers were as numb as his knees. "There now, you can skate." He stood and pulled on his gloves. The wool lining was already cold, the leather stiff.

Jephta tried to stand, but her ankles bent, first one way then the other. Arms flailing, she grabbed at the bottom of his coat to stop her fall.

"I'll take one hand." Jacqueline pushed herself up from the bench. "You take the other."

With Jephta wobbling between them, they moved slowly across the ice. Across the rink, children bundled in thick wool hats and jackets, swooped and glided like a flock of birds. At the far end, a fire danced in a steel drum, warming the hands and bodies of the older children. The boys seemed less interested in skating than in showing off for the girls.

Gregor released Jephta's hand and turned in a complete circle, his arms outstretched. The smooth soles of his shoes let him spin as if he were on skates.

"Up there," Gregor said, pointing to the hillside just beyond the end of the rink. "It looks like Russia. I have not seen such beautiful snow since Leo and I skied in the Sokolniki Park." He inhaled the frigid air and it hurt his lungs. "We must find skis."

His eyes dropped to Jacqueline. The roundness of her belly made it impossible for her to button her overcoat. "Soon, very soon we will all go skiing together."

"I want to ski," Jephta cried, and let go of her mother's hand. She flung out her arms and tried to spin on her own. Instead, she fell forward and sprawled face down on the ice.

"I thought all Russians were born knowing how to skate," a voice called from across the ice. Gregor looked up as he returned Jephta to her feet. A small mustached man, wearing a fedora and earmuffs waved at them from the edge of the rink.

"Doctor Gerson," Jacqueline called at the sight of the man in a black coat and bowler hat. "Come join us."

"We had plenty of cold winters in the Baltic." He slid his way across the ice. "Riga was not such a good place to live, but it was a wonderful place to skate."

"We skated in Moscow," Gregor said. He took a few steps with his arms stretched out and slid toward Gerson. "I will do so again."

The doctor laughed. "Not much chance of finding skates big enough for your feet in this town."

"Then I will have some made for me when I go to New York City."

"Now Jacqueline," said the doctor pointing a gloved finger in her direction. "Don't get any ideas about skating in your condition."

"I feel fine." Jacqueline replied. "But I will wait to buy my skates." She glanced at Gregor. "And my skis."

"And Grisha, make sure she stays warm. It could go to twenty below tonight. My Chevrolet does not make housecalls at that temperature."

"Jacqueline will not trouble you." Gregor grinned. "And I will make certain there is coal in the furnace."

The doctor pulled out his pocket watch and tried to open it, but his gloved hands made it awkward. "I've had all the socializing I am allowed," he said when the cover finally popped open. "Frank Morris fell this morning while shoveling snow off his roof. His wife called me but said not to hurry. As long as he was in pain she was sure he wouldn't climb back onto the roof." With a wave Gerson slid back toward his car, where a plume of gray smoke floated skyward from the rear of the vehicle.

"Papa." Jephta tugged at his coat. "Skate some more."

Jacqueline let go of Jephta's mittened hand and Gregor noticed her fingers went instinctively to her belly.

"Papa, look at me." Jephta pressed forward on the ice, her legs splayed wide apart. Even as he caught her, he noticed a tiny wince play across Jacqueline's face. It was there, then gone. He steadied Jephta and glanced back at Jacqueline.

She smiled and waved them on. But she hadn't moved from her spot on the ice. He knew something was wrong.

"Jacqueline?" he called.

He saw her blink then close her eyes. Again her gloved hand pressed against her belly.

"What is it?" He turned Jephta to face her mother.

"Nothing." Jacqueline slid one foot forward, then the other, her movements too slow. "Let me see Jephta skate." Her smile was forced.

Jephta struggled to cross the ice, while Gregor kept a tight hold on her hand, a little too tight. "Let go, Papa." She tried to pull free of his grip. He released her hand when she was close enough to reach her mother.

"You are a wonderful skater." Jacqueline smiled.

Again, Gregor saw the wince cross her face. For the first time that day he felt a real chill. "You must sit down." He wrapped his arm around her shoulder. "Are you tired?"

"No. I am all right—." Before she could finish her eyes closed and she seemed to hold her breath.

"Jacqueline?" He leaned close to her. "I must call the doctor."

"He's busy right now. Just let me sit down."

Bending over, he picked Jephta up with one arm then slipped his other through Jacqueline's elbow. Should they try to walk the two blocks home then call the doctor? He looked around at the ice rink. Most of the skaters were congregated around the fire barrel, too far away to be of much help.

"We must go to the hospital," he said, keeping his voice calm or at least trying to sound that way. "We will walk across the street."

He felt her fingers dig into his arm and this time she nodded, as if speaking required too much of her strength.

The street was snow-covered, but packed hard by traffic. Gregor stopped at the corner as two smoke-belching trucks loaded with logs climbed the steep hill that led into town.

"I want down." Jephta kicked, digging the blades of her skates into his thigh.

"Stop it," he said. "You cannot walk in skates."

Jacqueline let go of his arm. "Take her home to Kate. I can go by myself."

"No. I will not let you go alone." The stench of diesel exhaust still hung heavy in the air as they crossed the street. "I'll call Kate from the hospital." He kept a firm grip on Jacqueline's arm, helping her over the rutted gray ice.

Gregor sat Jephta on the bench inside the front door of the Community House Hospital. Jacqueline lowered herself onto the bench. She was breathing heavily and her face had grown pale.

"I'll find the nurse." He headed down the hall, looking for someone, anyone that could help. The parlor, which served as a waiting room and the first-aid alcove, was empty.

"Please," he called out. "Is anyone here?" Footsteps sounded overhead and he looked up the staircase. A young nurse in a white uniform and cap peered over the railing. "My wife is not well," he said. "She needs help."

The nurse hurried down the stairs, her heels clicking against the polished wood. She knelt in front of Jacqueline and placed a hand on her abdomen. "Are you in labor?"

Jacqueline nodded then winced and squeezed her eyes shut.

"I'll take her upstairs to lie down," said the nurse. "You wait here."

Gregor lifted Jephta in one arm and took Jacqueline's hand. "Come, *Mumchik.*"

"I'll be fine," Jacqueline said, but took his hand as he helped her to her feet. "Take Jephta home."

"I'll get her settled and call Doctor Gerson. This is going to take some time."

Jephta twisted and turned in his arms. "I want down," she said. "I want to skate."

"Please, Grisha." Jacqueline paused midway up the stairs, her breathing hard. "Take her home."

"I will." He watched as she made her way to the second floor, still holding the nurse's arm. "I will come back," he said. "I won't leave you alone."

* * *

The young nurse kept shaking her head as she patted Jacqueline's hand. "Mrs. Piatigorsky, you have to wait for the doctor."

"I—I –can't."

"Try."

"Where's Doctor Gerson?" Jacqueline barely got the words out. "Call him."

"I did. He said you couldn't be too far along."

She grabbed the metal bed railing, the wave of pressure swelling inside. "I can't wait. Please!"

"Ethel?" the nurse called. "Ring up the doctor."

"How far apart are the contractions?" Ethel asked when she peered through the labor room door.

The young nurse looked at her watch, counting softly. The pressure came again and Jacqueline tried to breathe, but the pain was unbearable. She screamed.

"Less than a minute," the nurse said. "He'd better get here fast."

"You've been through this before, haven't you, honey?" Ethel stood looking down at Jacqueline.

"Once," was all she managed to say as the wave of pressure subsided. "It wasn't like this."

"You've probably forgotten." Ethel stroked her damp hair. "Just hold on. The doctor will give you something for the pain when he gets here."

Nothing about Jephta's birth had been like this. At home, in Paris, with plenty of medication, attended by two doctors and three nurses, giving birth had been hard enough. While she had held Renee's hand and cried, Grisha smoked cigars with her father in the salon.

Never before had she felt so alone. How was she going to manage in this foreign country with no family and no doctor? The wave of pressure began, welling up within her, threatening to rip her apart. "Please," she called out to the young nurse. "I can't bear it any longer."

* * *

Elizabethtown, New York
February 4, 1940

    Dearest Mama, Today you have a grandson and he is American, the first American in our family. I pray to God that being an American will keep him safe. No one here in this town cares if he is Jew or Christian, only that he is a little boy. You can see by the envelope that Elizabethtown is our new home. It looks so much like Russia I don't feel like I'm thousands of miles away. But I think of you Mama, and of Nadja and Leo and Alex. And I think of Papa too. Have you told him I am married and that he is a grandfather now? Tell him that I will teach his grandchildren about music and history and art, just as he taught me. Does he speak of me? Is he still angry with me?

    I will send you a package with violin strings and soap and photographs as soon as I can have them made. Please write to me. Please let me know you are alive and well. Please don't forget me.

    Love always, Your Grisha

Chapter Forty-one

Nazis rumored to have perfected poisonous gas
All German Jews must wear Yellow Stars
Nazi troops lay siege to Leningrad
30,000 Ukrainian Jews killed
Kiev falls to Germans
President Roosevelt reaffirms neutrality in European conflict

September 1941

"Morning, Mr. P." The feminine voice drifted out from behind the row of brass mailboxes that filled the corner of Denton's General Store. "Did Johnny bring you down? I didn't hear the car."

"Good morning, Mrs. Denton." Gregor dropped his head so he could look through the little window that opened into the mailroom. "It is a beautiful day, so I walk to your store."

"It is gorgeous, especially the sugar maples. It's like an artist painted the mountains orange and gold."

"A very good artist it would be. Tomorrow I will bring Jephta with me."

"Better make sure she wears red, both of you. Hunting season started today."

"Am I in danger?" He laughed at the idea. "Do I look like a bear?"

"Not a bear. This is deer season. My Albert is up at hunting camp already. These boys will take a shot at anything that moves."

"I will remember to be careful." He pulled two envelopes from his pocket and slid them across the scarred wooden counter. "I have letters to send. Also, Jacqueline would like apples if you have some."

"I've got two bushels out back. I'll fill you a sack." She peered around the corner, three envelopes in her hand. "You've got mail today too. Looks important."

"Thank you." He took the letters while she studied his outgoing mail.

"This one to New York City's no problem," she said shaking her head. "I don't know about London and Kiev. Things are pretty bad over there right now." "I know, but I cannot contact my friends by telephone or wire."

"I'll send them out, but it will cost you a dollar seventy-eight." She licked several stamps then postmarked each envelope. "I hope you're not wasting money. Do you still have family there?"

"My parents are in Russia." He paused before adding, "I am not certain of my sister and brothers. I write them many times, but I hear nothing."

"Terrible, terrible." She put the envelopes in the box labeled OUTGOING. "I'll get you those apples."

While he waited, he sat on the bench near the front door and studied his mail. The return address on the first letter said Arthur Judson, Concert Management. Hopefully good news. He slid his finger under the flap and pulled out a single sheet of paper.

Grisha, RCA will give you three days in the recording studio for the Saint-Saens and Brahms sonatas. Can you be here by Thursday October 4th? Steinway wants a photo shoot with you and Horowitz on the 9th. Please confirm. A. Judson.

The fourth? That was only a week away and Jephta's birthday was the fifth. The women in his family were not going to be happy with his absence. He slid that envelope into his jacket pocket. It was unlikely, but he'd try and convince Judson to postpone the session.

He recognized the shaky handwriting on the second letter. Lev. Once his student in Leipzig. A wonderful cellist.

The envelope was soiled and battered, like a piece of tired luggage, the stamps French. Someone had crossed out the original address, Carlyle Hotel, New York and rewritten General Delivery, New Russia, New York. He turned it over. *Station Sauve 12 France* was scrawled across the flap. He didn't want to open it, but he did.

Dearest Grisha, I pray this letter finds you and your family safely in America. Pray for us as well. Many of our friends have been arrested. All must now wear the yellow star. Alicia, Stephan and others fled to the countryside and hid in the forest, but the Germans hunted them down with dogs. I fear they were shot, or worse. Helene, Little Josef and I took the train from Gare de Lyon to Sauve before the Germans knew to look for us. We pray Petain will not betray us. Please, if you can find it in your heart to save the life of your student, wire the American Embassy in Lisbon assuring our support so we may come to America. Soon we will try to cross the mountains to Spain.

Ever your friend, Lev. 12 June 1941, Sauve, France.

He closed his eyes and sank back against the wall. Lev and Helene, the wedding at the small café near the Eiffel Tower. They were too young, but Lev loved Helene so much. And Little Josef, born after he and Jacqueline had fled Paris. We will be safe, Lev had written in his last letter. My father works for the Consulate Office. And Alica? No pianist he had ever met could play with her light touch. She and Stephan gone? Swallowed up by the monster.

In his mind he heard heavy boots, the breaking of glass, gunshots, maniacal laughter, the feel of dust in his nose. Only by forcing his eyes open, did he save himself.

He slid the letter back in the envelope. The sight of Lev's handwriting was too painful to bear. Three months had passed since he had written this letter. It may as well have been three years. In his heart he knew they had never made it over the mountains to Spain, never found their way to Lisbon, never made it to the American Embassy. If they had, he would have heard by now. A letter. A telegram. Something. But there had been nothing. They were gone, all of them.

The address on the last envelope was blurred. No. It was his eyes filling with tears. Impossible to read. He ran his hand over his face and took another deep breath. The letter bore the seal of the United States Government, Department of Immigration, Washington, D.C. He didn't want to open this one either.

The sound of voices outside was enough of a distraction to make him look up. A tall man pushed open the front door, a gust of cold autumn air following him inside. He was dressed for hunting in a red plaid shirt and black pants tucked into tall boots.

"Hey Marshall," the hunter called out. "Sharpen your knife. I got a big one."

The swinging door at the back of the store popped open and Marshall Blanchard emerged wiping his bloody hands on his soiled butcher's apron. He was dark haired man with thick arms, made strong by years of cutting meat.

"Didn't take you long," Marshall said then noticed Gregor and waved. "Hello, Mr. P."

"Good morning, Mr. Blanchard." Gregor hoped his face didn't betray his emotions.

"Took him down in under an hour," said red shirt. "This one must weigh almost two hundred pounds. You should get at least half that in good meat by the time you're done."

"You going to hang and drain him?" Blanchard asked. "Or you want me to do it?"

"If you'd string him up out back I'd appreciate it. My wife doesn't like staring at dead deer, but she sure loves those venison steaks."

"No problem." The wooden front door banged shut as the two men left.

Gregor looked down to the last envelope.

Gregor Piatigorsky
New Russia, New York

As a resident alien you are required to report to the Office of Immigration and Naturalization at 21 North Adams Street, Albany, New York, on November 5, 1941 at 1:00 pm pursuant to your application for citizenship. Please bring all previously filed documents, official passports, military identification cards, records of your most recent travel outside the United States, selective service classification card, social security card, birth certificate, marriage license if applicable, birth certificates for any and all dependents, contracts or verification of employment, two recent photographs and seven dollars U.S. currency. Failure to comply will result in revocation of your temporary visa or residency permit.
G.H. Verlach
Assistant Secretary, INS

The tone of the letter left him shaken. Before the war Americans had been friendly, always willing to help. But since the German invasion of Poland and the fall of France, things were different. Too many homeless refugees, too many hungry orphans, too many exiled Jews. Now the newspapers railed against immigrants. Congressmen made speeches warning of the danger of opening the floodgates to Europe's masses.

"Here you go, Mr. P." Mrs. Denton emerged with a bulging paper sack. "We've got more apples on the trees."

"Thank you." The reality of buying apples was a relief. "How much is the cost?"

"That's almost six pounds, but I'll charge you for five. Twenty-five cents."

"They look like good apples." He handed her the coins.

"Come back on Friday," she said. "Marshall will have fresh venison steaks by then."

"Thank you." He stepped onto the narrow porch and reached into the sack for an apple. As his hand touched the fruit, he stopped. Parked at the foot of the steps was a big Ford sedan. Draped across the hood, its head hanging over the left headlight was the deer, a black-rimmed hole drilled into the fur beside its ear. In death the animal's eyes remained open, staring at the sky. Blood ran from the animal's mouth, leaving a trail across the headlamp and forming a puddle on the ground beneath the bumper.

In that instant he remembered Aunt Rosie lying in the street, eyes wide open, staring at the sky, the thin line of blood leaving a trail in the dust. His legs went weak and he reached for the doorframe. A loud yelp shattered the air and he looked away from the image of death. A big yellow dog stuck his head out the car window, his tongue hanging out.

Gregor felt the bag of apples slide from his hand. Ripe fruit bounced down the wooden steps, some rolling under the parked car, one coming to rest in the little pool of blood.

"Mr. P.?" It was Mrs. Denton's voice but she sounded a long way off. "Are you all right?"

"I... don't..." He willed his legs not to collapse.

"Mr. P., you've dropped your apples. I hope they're not all bruised." Mrs. Denton moved past him and down the steps, picking up fruit as she went. Her body momentarily blocked his view of the slaughter.

"I am sorry." He stooped to retrieve the torn sack. Marshall Blanchard and the red-shirted hunter came around from the behind the car, their conversation interrupted.

"That sack must have had a hole in it." Marshall knelt to retrieve the blood stained apple. With the end of his apron he wiped the piece of fruit then handed it to Mrs. Denton who added it to the rest cupped in the fold of her apron.

"Must have." She held up the ripped bag. "I'll get you a new one." She disappeared into the store, leaving Gregor alone with the hunter and the butcher.

"What do you think, Mr. P.?" Marshall slapped the flank of the dead deer. "He's one big buck. Bet you've never seen the likes of this where you come from."

Gregor gave the men his best performance smile, the one he used when he was ready to collapse from exhaustion or fear, but didn't dare let it show. "You are right. I have never seen such a thing."

The sound of Mrs. Denton's footsteps allowed him to politely turn away from the men and their trophy. "But I am sure others have."

He took the sack of apples. "Thank you, Mrs. Denton." He kept the smile on his face for her benefit until he left the group behind.

The trail back to Windy Cliff followed the old road, a track long since abandoned for the newer, macadam highway that ran close to the river. Desperate to put distance between himself and visages of death, he walked fast. The crunch of dry leaves beneath his feet sounded enormously loud. A cloud passed in front of the sun and the warmth was suddenly gone. He shivered.

The crack of a gunshot shattered the chilly air, followed by another, then a third. The sound echoed off Otis Mountain on the other side of the river. He walked faster. Branches slapped his legs and face as they stretched across the trail. The thick mat of leaves grabbed at his feet. *Run, Grisha.* Papa's words rang in his ears.

No, he would not run. This was America. There was nothing to fear.

Nazi dogs, with sharp white teeth and drooling tongues, they could tear a human apart. The sack of apples dropped from his hand, the fruit rolling away in the red and brown leaves.

The old dirt road emerged from the woods intersecting with the new pavement. Ahead, he saw the barn roof that marked the entrance to Windy Cliff. Sagging, he leaned against the trunk of a maple. His breath, bottled up in his chest, felt like it would explode. Sweat coated his palms. He listened for the sound of the hunters, but the mountains were still, the dogs silent.

When the air finally felt cool against his damp skin and his breath slowed, he walked again. Near the stone pillars flanking the driveway, he saw something move.

"Papa," Jephta cried. "Papa." She waved her arms as she ran across the road to greet him.

At that moment, the deep-throated growl of a truck caught his ear. Reaching down, he scooped Jephta up and stepped back into the safety of the driveway.

"You see that truck?" He pointed to the big vehicle carrying whole tree trunks as it sped past, leaving a swirl of fine sawdust at their feet. "That truck will hurt you. Did *Mumchik* know you came down the hill alone?"

"She said I could wait for you at the barn."

He set her back down, then knelt and wrapped his arms around her. What difference did it make? He couldn't protect her from the world, not even here.

Chapter Forty-two

Germans take Rostov
Germans take Odessa
Germans take Kharkov
Germans reach Sebastopol
Germans advancing toward Moscow

Albany, New York
November 5, 1941

"Have a seat, Mr. Piatigorsky." The young man motioned to a chair then took one for himself.

Gregor sat and faced the immigration examiner across the narrow table. He had smoked eight cigarettes while waiting in the crowded lobby. Now his throat felt like sand.

"Lewis Johnson. U.S. Department of Immigration." The young man extended his hand. Gregor shook it. "I need to go over your Declaration of Intent."

"I have looked forward to this day for a long time," Gregor said.

The young man gave a noncommittal nod as he pulled a big envelope from the leather case. Gregor straightened up and tried to read the cover of the upside-down envelope. He wanted another cigarette, but there were no ashtrays.

Johnson unwound the string that kept the envelope closed, then pulled out a thick stack of papers. Gregor waited, his fingers gripping the top of his knees, grateful that the table hid his hands. The young man flipped through the first few sheets, sometimes nodding, sometimes shaking his head.

"Are you aware that the United States Government has imposed new regulations regarding aliens, immigration and naturalization?"

"I have heard such things. Please explain."

"With the war going on in Europe there are a lot of people trying to come to America. We have to be careful about who we let in."

"Please," Gregor asked. "Are my papers in order? May I see?"

"I'm sorry. These are official U.S. Government property." Johnson attached the top sheets with a clip and pulled several more forms from his bag. "Let's begin. These are standard questions."

"Everyone who becomes American citizen must answer this?"

"Well, not everyone," Johnson kept his eyes on the documents. "We take these on a case-by-case basis."

"What is case by case? What does this mean?"

"Why don't we get started?" Johnson removed a mechanical pencil from his jacket pocket. "Let me first warn you that all your answers must be truthful. Any attempt to give false information can and will result in the revocation of your visa. Do you understand?"

"I understand." Gregor studied the young man and was suddenly reminded of the two Bolshevik boys who interrogated him at the Bolshoi. Why do governments always use the young for these jobs?

"Let me review what we already have. You were born where?"

"Ekaterinoslav, near Kiev on the Dnieper River. April 20, 1903."

"That's the Soviet Union, isn't it?"

"Yes, then Russia was ruled by Romanovs. The Tsar and Tsarina."

"But now it's part of the Soviet Union."

"Yes." He watched Johnson write in big block letters, BORN IN USSR.

"So you're a Soviet citizen?"

"I have no citizenship." He slid his hand into his jacket pocket and felt the worn surface of his Nansen document.

"Do you have a passport?"

"I have Nansen identity papers issued in Paris by League of Nations."

"So it's a French passport? Are you a French citizen?"

"I have no citizenship. France will not allow me citizenship. First I must join French Foreign Legion and fight for France in Africa."

"And you're not willing to do that?" He saw Johnson scribble something, but the young man kept his arm at an angle so the words were hidden.

"It would be better that I become citizen before I am killed."

Johnson appeared to ignore information that didn't fit his question sheet. "Have you ever served in the armed forces of any nation?"

"When I was young, I serve in two Russian army regiments."

"In what capacity did you serve?"

"I was musician. I play for the soldiers in the barracks."

"But you were a soldier?" Johnson raised an eyebrow. "What was your rank?"

"I had the lowest rank."

"Did you receive an Honorable Discharge?"

"I escaped. I ran away." He leaned forward and tapped the table with his finger. "I think it was not honorable, but it was necessary."

"AWOL," the man mumbled as he wrote the letters on the form. Gregor had no idea what that meant but it didn't sound good.

"What's your present occupation?"

"I am cellist."

Johnson looked up, a quizzical frown on his face. "A what?"

"A cellist, I play cello."

"But what do you do to support your family?"

"I play music with the symphony orchestra. Have you heard of such a thing?"

"Of course." He sounded a bit offended. "I'm from Houston, Texas."

"I know Houston. A wonderful concert hall. I play with the Houston Symphony in 1934."

"I'm partial to cowboy music myself." Johnson looked hopeful. "Gene Autry is my favorite. I've got all his records."

"I do not know his music."

"If you're going to be an American, you'd better know who the great musicians are. He's one of the best."

"I will make sure to do so."

"How about your political affiliations?" Johnson turned to the next page in his stack of documents. "Have you now or have you ever belonged to any of the following organizations: The Workers Party, the Communist Party, the Socialist Party, the Nazi Party, a labor union or any anarchist organizations?"

Gregor felt his mouth go dry. If he told the truth he might be deported. If they caught him lying, the consequences would be worse.

Johnson's eyebrows went up and he leaned forward. "Do you want me to repeat those names?"

"It is not necessary." Gregor took a deep breath. "When I was young, I joined the Communist Party in Moscow. Everyone who wanted to eat belonged to the Party."

Johnson wrote, MEMBER OF COMMUNIST PARTY, in big letters clearly visible to Gregor from the other side of the table.

"Have you renounced your affiliation with that organization or are you still an active member?"

"I have not belonged to the Party since 1921."

Gregor expected more questions, but that seemed to satisfy him.

"Have you ever been arrested?"

Again he hesitated and Johnson's eyes met his. Perhaps the examiner already knew about his past and was testing his honesty. "Yes," he offered. "But the circumstances were difficult."

"All right. When, where and why?"

"The first time was the Cheka, the Bolshevik police. I think 1920. They said I was a deserter, but I talked to the Commissar and he set me free." He watched Johnson write,, *1920 CHARGED WITH DESERTION.*

"Go on."

"When I left Russia, I cross the Zbrunch River. Polish police put me in jail."

"What was the charge?"

"They say I am Russian spy."

"What happened next?"

"They send me back to Russia, but I escaped on railway and went to Warsaw."

Johnson wrote the words, *ACCUSED BY POLISH POLICE OF SPYING FOR RUSSIA.* "Are there any more?"

"The police in Berlin."

"What did they charge you with?"

"In Berlin it was only necessary to be a Jew. That was crime enough."

"Were you imprisoned?"

"For a short time. My landlady reported me because I did not pay rent."

Johnson wrote, *POLITICAL PRISONER, BERLIN.* "Is that all?"

"That is all," he said, deciding not to mention the incident in Japan when the police held him for twenty-four hours. A Nansen passport meant nothing there. Only the Emperor's intervention had saved him from deportation, but he dared not mention even meeting Hirohito.

"Do you have a well-founded fear of political, religious or ethnic persecution if you return to the country where you most recently resided?"

Gregor stared into the young man's face. "I will be killed if I return." He spoke slowly, pronouncing each word so there could be no misunderstanding. Johnson didn't blink.

"Have you ever advocated the overthrow of any established government or taken part in a revolution?"

"Are you asking me if I am Red or White?" This time he couldn't hide his anger.

Johnson pulled back. "I need to know if you're an anarchist or would actively advocate the overthrow of the United States Government." He spoke so fast his words ran together.

Gregor leaned forward, no longer trying to please. "The Tsar's soldiers tried to kill my family. The Bolsheviks tried to kill me."

He felt heat rising in his face. How could this young American possibly understand what it was like to live in constant fear? "Hitler wants me dead. I will do whatever is necessary to protect my family. Will the Government of the United States do the same?"

Johnson's eyes widened and a frown creased his smooth brow. He dropped his eyes and wrote something, paused, tapping the sharp point of his mechanical pencil on the tabletop. Finally, he flipped the pencil over and erased what he had written. Keeping his eyes on the form, he said, "When did you first enter the United States?"

"October 27, 1929. I remember the day. I lived in Berlin. My agent arranged for me to play with New York Philharmonic at Carnegie Hall. But first I traveled to Oberlin. That is Ohio." He paused hoping Johnson would say something, but the immigration officer kept scribbling on his note pad. "Then I play with Chicago Symphony and in Philadelphia."

"That was eleven years ago. Why didn't you petition for citizenship then?"

"I was principal soloist with the Berlin Philharmonic. Wilhelm Furtwangler allowed me to perform. I traveled to America for only three months." Gregor tried to remedy the disaster caused by his previous outburst by giving Johnson a hopeful smile. "But even then I like America very much."

"How do you spell that?"

"What?"

"Your employer's name?"

"Wilhelm Furtwangler?" Gregor wasn't sure if he understood. "*F-U-R-T-W-A-N-G-L-E-R.*"

"It sounds German."

Gregor stared at Johnson. Was he joking? No, the young man's face was serious. "Yes." He spoke slowly. "Maestro Wilhelm Furtwangler is German."

"*WORKED FOR GERMANS.*" Johnson filled in the next line. "Do you plan to make the United States your permanent home?"

"Yes. I own property in —." He paused then decided not to mention his New Russia address. "I own property near Elizabethtown, New York. I pay taxes to the government. I am never late in my payment."

"That's very wise." Johnson nodded. "Before moving here, what was your last legal residence?"

"I lived in Paris on Avenue Foch."

"And before that?"

"Berlin, and before that Leipzig."

Johnson paused for a moment, rubbing his hairless chin deep in thought. "You realize the application process for citizenship takes five years. When did you first file a residency application?"

"Four years ago, the fifth of February 1937, in New York City."

"Do you know that as a condition of your naturalization you must register for military service? Are you willing to serve this country if you become a citizen?"

Gregor swallowed hard and took a deep breath. "I have already signed papers with the military officials in Elizabethtown. If I receive citizenship, I will serve my new country any way I can."

Johnson appeared satisfied. "In order for this application to be valid, you must make the United States your permanent residence. I advise you not to leave the country."

"But I am a musician. I must travel in order to perform. I have engagements scheduled in Tokyo, Singapore and Hong Kong." Again he felt like he was speaking to a child. "I have been invited to play with the Montreal Symphony in support of the Canadians fighting in Europe."

"You'd better not go. The United States is still neutral in this war. You must have a legal passport or citizenship papers to cross the border. If you leave, you might not be allowed back in."

"But my home is in Elizabethtown. My wife and children live there. My son Joram was born in Elizabethtown Community Hospital."

"Lucky for him," Johnson said. He closed the folder and slid it back into the big envelope. "At least he's an American citizen. As for your wife and daughter, I'd advise them not to leave the country either."

* * *

Dearest Lev:

I pray this letter finds you, though I know not where. I have wired the American consulate in Lisbon pledging my support for you to come here. Use my name any way you must. We have room for all your family here. Horowitz and Milstein are safe. Pavlovsky and his new wife are here also. They took a house in our village. I will bring all of you to Windy Cliff if I can.

Lev, what has happened to the world? On radio we hear Japanese attack at Pearl Harbor and every day my despair grows deeper. On all sides now, West and East, we are besieged. The world is not big enough. There are no hiding places left. Those of us who fled are classified and titled by the papers we carry in our pockets. Even here I am an alien and suspect. I have filed papers for American citizenship. I want so much to belong to this country, but I fear the Nazis will take the Atlantic. Then we will all be hunted down like rats.

I am required to register for the army. I do so with heavy heart. If I am called I will fight for America and protect my family. Death no longer frightens me. But if I go to war I fear I will face my friends, Bernard or Herman or any of the boys I taught in Leipzig. Or even you, Lev. How can I be a good soldier and kill my friends? I would drop my gun and rush forward to embrace you all. I would make a very poor soldier. Still, it is the price I must pay for the sanctuary America offers.

When I look at my hands I see blood. German blood, Russian blood, French blood. All the same blood. I know that bloody hands can never hold the bow or touch the strings. Music and the cello are my only weapons. If I am forced to kill, I will never be able to touch the instrument again. Life without music is too painful. My heart would stop and breath would go out of me. Lev, for my family

or my friends I would gladly give up my life and my music, if only to bring you to safety. Tell me what you need and I will send it to you.
    Grisha

Gregor slid the envelope into his pocket then opened the passenger side door and stepped out of the Ford.

"I will not be long," he said.

"I'll keep the engine running," Johnny called after him as he opened the wooden screen door to Denton's store.

"Mr. P., I'm so glad you stopped by." Mrs. Denton climbed down from the stepladder and wiped her hands on her blue apron.

"I must go to Vermont," Gregor said, forcing a polite smile. "I will take the train to Boston."

"Are you performing again? Seems like you hardly get home before you have to leave. I don't know how your wife stands it, you being gone so much."

"Jacqueline is the most patient woman in the world."

"She must be. I guess she's used to all your traveling. I'd go crazy if Albert left that much."

"Please, Mrs. Denton, Johnny Hooper waits with the car." He slid the four envelopes across the counter. "Please send this letter?"

"Certainly."

"Thank you." Gregor watched her pull open the stamp drawer. "How much must I pay?"

"That will be three cents each." She paused. "Mr. P,. this letter is addressed to France. You can't send a letter to France. Surely you know that."

"Please, Mrs. Denton." He handed her a one-dollar bill. "Please send it. I have to try."

"But you're wasting your money. It can't possibly go through."

"There must be a way."

Mrs. Denton's pressed her thin lips together in a frown. "I really hate to take your money. It's not like it will do any good."

"I am willing to pay." He couldn't smile anmore. "Please." He was willing to beg. "Perhaps through some other nation." He slid a second dollar across the counter.

"Craziness, craziness," she muttered. Still, she took a black pen and made a notation next to the address, *c/o U.S. Embassy, Geneva ,Switzerland.* "It's the best I can do. I'm sorry, Mr. P."

"Thank you, Mrs. Denton." He turned toward the door. "That is all any of us can do."

Chapter Forty-three

Japanese attack Americans at Bataan
Japanese take central Burma
Japanese occupy Mandalay
Japanese take Corregidor
Japanese take Tulagi
Japanese reach India
U.S. troops surrender to Japanese in Philippines

New Russia, New York
June 1942

"Papa! Papa!" Jephta cried. "Johnny's here. He brought the car." Gregor heard her pounding feet as she ran through the great hall then burst into the bedroom. "Mama, can I go with Papa and Johnny?" She climbed onto the bed where Jacqueline was trying to pull socks onto Joram's wriggling feet.

"Already? He's here so soon?" Gregor picked up his wristwatch from the bedside table. "But it is only eight thirty."

"He called last night," Jacqueline said. "He wanted to start early." She sat Joram on the floor, where he immediately rolled to his knees and grabbed Gregor's leg, pulling himself to standing.

"I want to drive with you." Jephta bounced up and down on the bed. "Papa's going driving. Papa's going driving."

"How can I drive with you singing in the car?" He scooped her off the bed. "You play with your friends, Sis and Tom. I will learn to drive."

"You won't take the car down the hill, will you?" A frown creased Jacqueline's face.

"Johnny will instruct me." Gregor finished buttoning his shirt and slipped on his jacket. "But I will let him drive down the mountain."

* * *

"Okay, Mr. P." Johnny stepped from the driver's seat of the 1935 Ford sedan. "Your turn."

Gregor exited the passenger side and moved around the front of the car. "You are very brave, Johnny Hooper." He slid behind the wheel. "Can a man as old as I learn to drive?"

"Sure." Johnny slid into the passenger seat. "But forget last summer's lesson. Let's start from scratch."

"From scratch?"

"From the beginning. Pretend this is your first time."

Gregor put both hands on the steering wheel and looked ahead through the dusty windshield. At the end of the lane he saw Jephta and her friends running around the barn. Leaning out the window, he waved.

"Keep your hands inside the car." Johnny pointed to the floor. "Push the clutch with your left foot."

Gregor looked at the floorboard and saw his two big feet and three pedals. Why did they make cars this way? He did as instructed.

"Now, your right foot, push the accelerator. Give it some gas and hit the starter button."

Gregor looked over at the steering column and saw the tiny button on the dashboard, above the knob labeled "lights." But he didn't release his grip on the steering wheel.

"Keep one hand on the wheel while you start the car."

Gregor inhaled and released his right hand. "It does not feel safe."

"Don't worry." Johnny grinned. "We're not moving yet."

"I will do it quickly." He pushed the button. The engine growled, then sputtered.

"Give it some gas."

He pushed again then pressed the gas pedal to the floor. The engine died.

"Give it some gas while you press the button."

He tried again. It started and the roar of the engine filled the car.

"Back off," Johnny shouted. "Give it just enough to keep it going."

The roar dropped and they were able to speak normally again.

"Okay," Johnny said. "One hand on the gear shift, the other on the wheel."

Gregor wrapped his right hand around the cold metal stick that protruded from the floor like a spindly tree.

Johnny put his hand on top of Gregor's. "I'm going to help you until you get the feel." Johnny wiggled the metal stick back and forth. "This is neutral. Do you remember?"

"*Da.*" It felt like a loose music stand.

"Okay, let's find first." Johnny pushed the stick left. "This is first. It feels different."

"Much better," Gregor said. The stem hardly moved at all. "I like it."

"They're all good. Now, let out the clutch. Slowly."

He hated this part. The last dozen times he had tried to drive, let out the clutch were words he dreaded. Fear made him look at his feet.

"Look up," Johnny said. "Keep your eyes on the road."

Johnny's words caught him by surprise. He obeyed and the clutch popped up too fast. The car lurched forward.

"Give it some gas," Johnny cried.

He pushed it too hard. The engine roared. The car dipped. His head snapped back as the vehicle swerved off the road and into the pasture. Johnny reached over, switched off the ignition and sighed.

"I'm sorry." Gregor felt foolish.

"Let's try again."

They repeated the ritual, each step causing Gregor's knuckles to whiten as he gripped the wheel. But he smiled. He couldn't let Johnny see what a poor excuse for a man he was.

"Now you've got it." The car crept toward the bridge.

In fits and starts, Gregor pressed the accelerator, giving enough gas to keep the engine from stalling. Ahead, the wooden bridge loomed like the executioner's dock. Would they plunge into the river and drown?

The nose of the car pointed up. *CLUNK.* The front tires dropped over the lip of the first plank. Gregor stared ahead, his eyes locked on an apple tree on the opposite bank. As long as he kept his eyes fixed on that tree, he couldn't see the dark water through the spaces between the planks.

"Watch it," Johnny screamed, and grabbed the wheel. Gregor glanced left and saw the fender just miss the guardrail. The front of the car dropped and they were over the bridge.

"I did it."

"Jesus! Keep your hands on the wheel."

Gregor gripped the wheel and stared straight ahead. Several cows interrupted their grazing to stare. He pushed the gas pedal harder and the car picked up speed. "How fast?"

"Fifteen miles an hour. Push in the clutch. Go to second."

Gregor obeyed. The car went faster. Twenty. "I'm driving," he cried.

"Sure you are. Now slow down and turn here. Nice and easy."

Gregor felt the car move smoothly over the packed earth.

"Now remember," Johnny said. "When you turn, you have to signal. Put your hand out the window and point up."

He released his grip on the steering wheel and stretched his arm out the window.

"Very good." Johnny motioned right. "Now bring it around."

"This is wonderful." Now Gregor faced the bridge without fear. "Johnny, I can drive." This time he didn't even look at the water. Soon he would be able to travel anywhere he wanted.

They passed the Otis farmhouse and he looked for Jephta. She and two other children stood on the porch waving. Before he could wave back, Johnny leaned forward, blocking his view.

"Get ready to slow down. Now, Mr. P. Now!"

The car came to a violent stop. The engine died. Gregor looked at Johnny and saw the young man's wide-eyed expression. "What is wrong?"

"You almost ran onto Route 9." Johnny's white-knuckled hand gripped the emergency brake. Gregor turned and stared out the windshield. Sure enough the nose of the car was sticking onto the main road.

"Don't get distracted." Johnny released the brake. "Keep your eyes straight ahead. Understand?"

"I'm sorry." He looked down at his own hands, feeling helpless.

"All right. Now start the engine. Turn left and head down toward your place."

Step by step they went through the sequence again.

"Okay, signal left. Not that way, that means right. Just keep your arm straight out."

"I forget," Gregor said. He felt sweat dampening his shirt.

"Now, see if anyone is coming." For the first time, Johnny sounded tense.

Gregor looked down the road toward the brown barns that marked the end of the Windy Cliff driveway. Route 9 was empty. It wasn't that far to the barns. He had walked this distance many times. Now the ribbon of black macadam stretched like all eternity.

"Papa. Papa." Jephta was suddenly right beside him. "Can we ride with you?"

"Get back on the porch," Johnny said before Gregor could reply.

The children retreated and Gregor faced the road. Having an audience now was not a good thing.

When he pressed the gas pedal the car lurched forward, hitting the edge of the black top. He turned the wheel left. Something moved at the edge of his vision. Johnny gasped. There was a shrill scream of a horn. The car lunged right as Johnny jerked the wheel. Bright chrome and a flash of red passed by them on the left.

"Swine!" Gregor screamed at the rear of a pickup truck speeding away.

"Mother of God!" Johnny sank back in the seat. "You almost got us killed." Beads of sweat dotted the young man's smooth face.

"I did not—I never—." Gregor's heart pounded so hard he couldn't speak. The children stood on the porch, Jephta's eyes were wide, her mouth open.

Mrs. Otis stepped onto the porch, a broom in her hand. "Are you all right?" she called. "Can you get the car back on the road?"

"It's okay." Johnny exited the vehicle. "I'll take care of it."

"Come inside, children," Mrs. Otis said. "He doesn't need you watching him."

"Johnny." Gregor pushed open the door but was too shaken to stand. "I will never learn to drive. I cannot put your life at risk any longer."

"That was too damned close." Johnny settled behind the wheel. "I need a drink."

"You drive, Johnny. I will drink enough for both of us."

* * *

The resident deer glared down from above the bar of the Deer's Head Inn, his black eyes malevolent. Other than the deer, the place was empty.

"I think we're too early." Johnny peered around the end of the ornate bar. "Ben hasn't even opened."

"Mr. Stetson." Gregor slapped his hand on the bar. "Mr. Stetson, we are your first customers in need of a drink."

There was a scuffling in the back room and Ben Stetson emerged, his shirttail hanging out of his pants, his hair uncombed. "Mr. Piatigorsky, I knew that was you." He frowned, his meaty forehead wrinkling above bushy brows. "My bartender doesn't come in until noon."

"Mr. Stetson, I would have waited until then to buy a drink, but a truck almost killed us." Gregor leaned forward and pointed to the bottle of Scotch. "Please, we must have something for our nerves."

Stetson looked at Johnny over the top of his glasses. "Trying to teach him to drive again?" Ben placed two glasses on the bar. "Didn't you try last summer?" He placed the Scotch bottle beside the glasses. "And the summer before that?"

Johnny shrugged. "I really thought he could do it this time."

"Be careful, Mr. Piatigorsky. Johnny once worked for Marvin's funeral home. Things have been a little slow lately."

Gregor took the bottle and handed the glasses to Johnny. "We will not disturb you, Mr. Stetson." They took a table near the window and sank into a couple of Windsor chairs.

Johnny waited patiently as he always did. Only the pallor of his skin betrayed his feeling. Gregor poured half a glass of the amber liquid for Johnny, stopping only when the young man held up his hand.

"You're a brave man, Johnny Hooper," he said. He poured twice as much Scotch into his own glass, leaned back and closed his eyes. "Driving is dangerous. It is best left to experts like yourself." He took a sip and held the liquor in his mouth and let it roll around his tongue.

"I don't get it. You play the cello. That seems a whole lot harder than shifting gears."

"When I play, I feel the music. Can I drive a car by feeling only? No. Two feet and two hands and two eyes are not enough to drive a car. A man must have three feet, three hands and three eyes."

"Does it bother you that your wife can drive?"

"Jacqueline can do many things that I cannot. Last week she told me she wants to fly an airplane."

"Fly? You must be kidding?"

"No, Johnny. She already has a teacher in Westport. On Saturday her lessons begin."

"Aren't you afraid she'll kill herself?"

"I am terrified." He leaned forward. "But I would be more terrified if I told her no. Jacqueline is strong woman and she is very smart. She wins chess every time we play."

"My father wouldn't like that." Johnny sipped his Scotch. "He said there are some things a woman shouldn't do."

"Is this the American way? Are there rules about such things?"

"No, it's just custom." Johnny took another sip, then pulled out a pack of Lucky Strikes. "You wouldn't let her become a soldier?"

"I think she would make a far better soldier than me. Her father taught her to ride and shoot when she was young." He accepted the cigarette Johnny offered.

"Do you think you'll get called up?" Johnny lit his own cigarette.

"I gave my name for military service." Gregor held a match to his own cigarette. "That is the price of freedom."

"My brother got called up. Mom's scared. She said I should go first because I'm older."

"Will you go Johnny? Will you fight?"

Johnny swirled the liquor in his glass. "I'd rather fight Japs than Germans, wouldn't you?"

Gregor studied the innocent face. Did it matter what nationality made the speeches, held the guns or controlled the mobs? "Johnny, I will tell you this." He leaned forward and moved the Scotch bottle so it sat in the center of the table. "I have played my cello in Tokyo and Berlin. The Germans always tell me if my performance is bad or good. When they enjoy a concert they applaud loudly and give me all manner of gifts." He tapped a finger on the table. "But if they feel the performance is poor, they do not withhold criticism. With Germans I always know how they feel." He moved his empty glass to the right of the bottle.

"The Japanese are very polite people. I played a most excellent program for the Emperor and his court and they applauded my performance. They bow and say 'Very nice. Thank you very much.' Always it is the same, every year." He took a drag on his cigarette then ground the remains in the ashtray. "One day I play the piece badly and they applaud just the same."

He moved Johnny's glass to the left of the whiskey bottle. "So you see, Johnny, here are the Japanese." He lifted the empty glass in his right hand. "And here are the Germans." He lifted the other glass in his left, then placed them both on the table, a little too hard. Johnny flinched.

"We are in the middle." He lifted the whiskey bottle and held it between them. "Tell me, Johnny, who would you rather fight? The enemy you understand or the enemy you do not?"

Chapter Forty-four

New York Times
August 29, 1942

The Nazis have ordered all foreign Jews in France sent to labor camps in Germany. The deportation of 25,000 Jews held in southern France has begun. All Jews living in occupied zones are required to wear the yellow star. Jews are forbidden to appear in public places such as restaurants or theaters. London estimates over one million Jews have already been put to death. Jewish uprisings in Warsaw have been crushed by the Nazis. Jewish leaders appealed to the United States for help. Allied leaders open discussions on whether to accept 1,500 Jewish refugees into the US next year.

The US Congress has passed a bill changing the military draft age. Effective immediately, all men 18 to 50 are eligible for induction. A Federal court in Chicago sentenced a draft evader to a two-year prison term at hard labor.

German Luftwaffe bombs London, estimated one thousand causalities. British RAF retaliates by bombing Cologne. Germans shoot down six heavy bombers.

Gregor pushed the pile of newspapers aside. The more he read, the worse it got. Closing his eyes, he pressed his hands to his face. The dining room walls were closing in on him. Even here at Windy Cliff he could not escape the Nazis. They stared at him from newspapers, their names and deeds crackled across the airwaves on the radio. They invaded his sleep. Letters, not just correspondence but desperate pleas, arrived almost daily. There was nothing he could do.

How could he concentrate, how could he think? He couldn't read. Music was impossible, not composing or playing. For the first time in his life the cello offered no solace.

Practicing was out of the question. He hadn't tried in weeks. How could he think of music? Once he had tried, sitting alone in the great hall, his cello between his knees. But his hands trembled so badly that he couldn't hold the bow, much less draw a single note. Before him, even with his eyes open, all he could see was blood, flames and death.

With each newspaper and every evening broadcast the world grew smaller. Reports from Russia were the worst. The Nazis were advancing on Kiev. Mama. Papa. Leo. Nadja. Alex. This time the cellar would not save them. How much longer before they came for him? Even here in America. There was no safe place, no refuge, no sanctuary far enough away.

Every friend who managed to flee Europe, every student who escaped the Nazis, each new arrival to Elizabethtown, he pumped for information. Who was alive? Who was dead? How long could this go on?

"*Nyet*," he cried, and pushed back from the table. Jacqueline was right, there was nothing he could do about the world. Especially not today.

He carried the newspapers to the fireplace and dumped them on the hearth. Heat still rose from the coals. Pushing the papers in with his foot, he waited for the flames to catch. A thin feather of smoke drifted up the chimney, nothing more. Impatient, he reached for a match, struck it on the rough stone then dropped it onto the pile of paper. It flared for a moment then flickered out. Kneeling, he struck a second match then crumbled a sheet and set the flame against it. This time the paper caught. With satisfaction, he watched Hitler's face turn brown, curl then disappear as the fire consumed him. If only it were that easy.

Behind him the kitchen door opened. "Grisha, are you ready?"

He stood and saw Jacqueline in the doorway, Joram squirming in her arms. Jephta slid past her mother's leg and ran to him.

"Papa, Johnny's here with the car. Can I ride up front with you?"

"*Da*, yes. You ride with me." He retrieved his suit jacket from the back of the chair. "Do I look . . . acceptable?" He slipped into his coat, then straightened his tie.

"You look wonderful," Jacqueline said as she sat Joram in the playpen. "Are you happy today?" She adjusted the white handkerchief in his suit pocket.

"Is it a concert, Papa?" Jephta looked up at him. "Are you going to play cello?"

"No concert." He ran his hand over her dark curls. "Today I become citizen. Today I will be American."

"Can I be American too? And Mama and Joram?"

"Joram is American." Gregor lifted Jephta into his arms. "He was born here."

"That's not fair." Her lip turned down. "I'm bigger than he is. I want to be American."

"You will." He took her hand. "Right now Johnny will take us to the courthouse. Watch carefully. You will learn how to become American."

* * *

"All rise," the bailiff called. Everyone in the crowded courtroom stood.

Gregor looked down at the children sitting between him and Jacqueline on the narrow, slatted benches. Jephta turned and stood on the seat, peering at the row of spectators behind her.

"Come down," Jacqueline whispered and turned her around.

Anxious to see what was happening, Jephta stood on tiptoes, holding onto Gregor's arm as she tried to see over the heads of the people in front of her.

Lost in a sea of knees, Joram clung to his father's leg. Jacqueline knelt and pried his fingers loose. He started to whimper so she picked him up and patted his back. Teary eyed, the child scanned the sea of strangers around him.

"New York Superior Court is now in session," announced the bailiff, as the judge entered the courtroom. "The Honorable Judge Byron Brewster presiding." The middle-aged man in a black robe took his seat and the bailiff motioned the crowd to sit.

"The following petitioners step forward," the bailiff read from a sheet of paper. "Fannie Smyth Treg-gett." He paused, waiting until a small woman emerged from the back row. "Sophia Mark-i-vica." The bailiff struggled with that one. "Andrea Plis-kof-sky." This time he paused even longer. Gregor felt his fists tighten. Why hadn't the man called his name?

The bailiff leaned to Judge Brewster and whispered in his ear. The judge took the sheet of paper, looked at it and whispered something back.

Gregor wiped the dampness from his palms on his thighs.

The bailiff straightened up. "Kath-ar-zyna Wo-jew-odzic." Again he paused as Katharzyna excused her way past a crowd of spectators. "Gregor Pi-at-ti-gor-sky. Come forward to the bench." He handed the list to the judge.

The relief at hearing his name weakened his knees and he gripped the back of the bench in front of him. As the other four petitioners moved forward to the railing, he waited. Glancing at Jacqueline, he wondered if she could see his fear. She smiled, her face radiant, her confidence in him absolute. Taking a deep breath, he followed the others to the front of the courtroom.

Judge Brewster's face was expressionless. For a moment Gregor watched as the judge's eyes surveyed the group standing before him, then with a slight nod he looked down at the list of names. He set it aside.

"Those of you who have come before me today have completed a long and difficult journey." His voice sounded serious and very official. "That journey ends here in this courtroom. You have left your homes and loved ones far behind, faced wars and deprivation, experienced persecution and prejudice." He paused, adjusted his glasses then continued.

"From this day forward you will no longer have to run, no longer have to hide, no longer have to live in fear. In taking this oath of allegiance, I ask you to leave all that behind and look to the future. America gives you that opportunity and in return asks you to give this nation the very best that you have."

For a moment Gregor felt lightheaded, dizzy. His eyes moved to the right of the room and settled on the American flag. Focusing on it anchored him. He took a deep breath.

"You will now receive a copy of the oath of allegiance." The bailiff handed each petitioner a printed card. "Raise your right hand and read along with me."

Gregor raised his hand and looked down at the card. For a moment his hand shook and the words blurred. But as he read out loud and repeated each phrase, his voice grew steady.

"I hereby declare, on oath, that I absolutely and entirely renounce and abjure all allegiance and fidelity to any foreign prince, potentate, state, or sovereignty, which I have heretofore been a subject or citizen.

That I will support and defend the Constitution and laws of the United States of America against all enemies, foreign and domestic.

That I will bear true faith and allegiance to the same.

That I will bear arms on behalf of the United States when required by law.

That I will perform noncombatant service in the Armed Forces of the United States when required by the law.

That I will perform work of national importance under civilian direction when required by law.

I take this obligation freely, without any reservation or purpose of evasion.

"So help me God."

"So help me God," Gregor repeated.

"You are now citizens of the United States." Judge Brewster's somber faced softened and a slight smile turned the corners of his lips. "And as such you are afforded all the privileges and protections of American citizenship as outlined in the United States Constitution. This privilege cannot be altered, revoked or denied."

"I am American," Gregor whispered.

The judge rose and stepped from behind his bench. Pronouncing each new American's name correctly, he worked his way down the line shaking hands. As he reached for Gregor, the Judge smiled. "Better face the cameras Mr. Piatigorsky."

Gregor turned and the flashbulbs went off, momentarily blinding him.

"Mr. Piatigorsky," shouted a reporter. "How does it feel to be an American?"

"How long have you been in this country?" cried another.

"Will you ever go home to France again?" said a third.

"America is a wonderful country." He smiled into the camera. "It is now my home."

New Russia, New York
August 29, 1942

Dearest Papa,
    Today I have become an American. I write to you now so you will know that
this is a wonderful day and to tell you that all you ever believed about America
is not true. America is a great country and I know that if you could find it in your
heart to forgive your foolish son, to forgive me for my pride and my arrogance,
then you can also find it in your heart to forgive America for being less than you
wanted. There are musicians and concert halls here. I know many people and
can make the opportunity for you to play with a fine orchestra. Please write to
me and tell me that you are healthy, and that Mama is well and Nadja is happy,
and Leo too. Papa, so much time has passed. Tell me what I can do for you now.
Do you need anything? I know that life for you is difficult, but someday the war
will be finished. Then Papa, you and Mama will come here to my home and live
with us. Please ,Papa, write to me.
    Your son always, Grisha.

Artist Wayman Adams paints Gregor Piatigorsky at the Old Mill Art School, Elizabethtown, NY 1942. The painting now hangs at Shepherd School of Music, Rice University

Gregor Piatigorsky and Ivan Galamian, founders of the Meadowmount School of Music. Piatigorsky was the school's first cello teacher

GRISHA

EPILOGUE

In the late 1940s, Gregor Piatigorsky was exhausted after more than two decades of nearly year round performing, recording and teaching. He decided to pull back and take a year off. Resigning from his position at the Curtis Institute of Music in Philadelphia, he turned down most performance requests and moved his family to Los Angeles. There he spent time writing his memoirs, which were eventually published in 1965 and titled simply Cellist.

In 1949 he joined pianist Artur Rubinstein and violinist Jascha Heifetz in a series of summer concerts. The three made several notable recordings, which since 1950 have never been out of circulation. In the 1960s Gregor joined Heifetz in creating the Heifetz-Piatigorsky Concert Series where the two virtuosos performed with many of the world's greatest musical artists.

In 1962, with a thaw in the cold war, Gregor was invited by the Soviet government to represent the United States as a judge in the Tchaikovsky International Music Competition in Moscow. Along with his wife Jacqueline and son Joram, he returned to the country of his birth. For the first time since the age of twelve, he met his father and brother Alexander. He also met Anatole, a brother who had been born after Gregor had left home. Sadly, his mother and other family members had passed away.

In 1968, Gregor was named professor emeritus at the University of Southern California where he taught for the remainder of his life. He gave a master class in Switzerland and played several concerts in his final months, though seriously ill with cancer. On August 6, 1976, he died at age 73 of lung cancer at his home in California.

Gregor Piatigorsky left a rich musical legacy through his teaching and recordings. He is best remembered as the artist who popularized the cello, excelling as a soloist and bringing this rich instrument to people who had never heard it before.

RECOMMENDED RECORDINGS

The following CDs feature some of Gregor Piatigorsky's best known cello performances, as well as four of his cello compositions. They are available at www.musicandarts.com, www.amazon.com, www.towerrecords.com

Dvorak Concerto, Gregor Piatigorsky with the Boston Symphony (BMG 09026-61498-2).

Dvorak Concerto, Gregor Piatigorsky with the Chicago Symphony (Sony MHK 62876).

Schumann: Cello Concerto, Gregor Piatigorsky with the London Philharmonic (Music & Arts 4674).

Brahms Sonata No. 1, Shostakovitch Sonata, short pieces by Gregor Piatigorsky with piano (Music & Arts 644).

Brahms Double Concerto, Gregor Piatigorsky with the RCA Victor Symphony Orchestra, conductor Alfred Wallenstein (BMG/ RCA 6778 or 63531).

Shostakovitch Sonata, Haydn Divertimento, Schumann Fantasiestucke, short pieces by Gregor Piatigorsky with piano (Biddulph LAB 117). Piatigorsky Legacy Volume 1, Tchaikovsky Rococo Variations, Shostakovitch Sonata, short pieces performed by Gregor Piatigorsky (Arlecchino ARLA74).

Cello America, Volume III, includes four solo cello pieces composed by Gregor Piatigorsky and performed by his assistant, Terry King, released February 2001 (Music & Arts 1076).

Historic Piatigorsky concert recorded at the courthouse in Elizabethtown, New York August 2002 on the 60th anniversary of the concert Piatigorsky gave in 1942. A performance by Piatigorsky students Terry King and Doris Stevenson. (Available from Otis Mountain Press) Contact mail@Otismountainpress.com or call 301-467-0261.

SELECTED BIBLIOGRAPHY AND SOURCES

Cellist by Gregor Piatigorsky Doubleday 1965

Jump in the Waves by Jacqueline Piatigorsky St. Martin's Press 1985

"Sanctuary Among the Birches" Adirondack Life magazine   June 2001

Before the Revolution : a view of Russia under the last Tsar
by FitzLyon, Kyril & Browning, Tatiana. 1978

A Century of Ambivalence: The Jews of Russia and the Soviet Union;   by
Zvi Gitelman, YIVO Institute 1988

Before the Deluge: A Portrait of Berlin in the 1920s by Otto Friedrich 1972

Koussevitzky Collection-Piatigorsky Correspondence: Music Division and
Manuscript Division Library of Congress, Washington D.C.

Records from the Glinka Museum of Culture: Moscow, Russia

Records from the Moscow Music Conservatory: Moscow, Russia

Ships manifests: National Archives: Washington, D.C.

Elizabethtown Post: Adirondack History Museum, Elizabethtown, N.Y.

Interviews and correspondence with: Jacqueline Piatigorsky, Jephta
Piatigorsky Drachman, Joram Piatigorsky, Lona Piatigorsky Gregory Piatigorsky,
Terry King, Doris Stevenson, Adele Seigal, Jacob Lateiner, John Barnett,
Ralph Berkowitz, Judith Galamian, Elsa Hilger, Jeffrey Solow, Stephen Kates,
Ethel Johnson, Nathaniel Rosen, Grant Beglarian, Faylene Hooper,Dennis Brott,
Erling Bengtsson, John Fonda Fournier, Gary Graffman, Marion Davies,
Laslo Varga, Dr. Sergi Zhuk, Dorothy Singer and many others.

Gregor Piatigorsky

Otis Mountain Press
Otis Lane
New Russia, New York 12964

**Additional copies of this book
may be purchased from Otis Mountain Press**

$19.95 + $5.00 Priority Mail
($2.50 shipping for each additional copy shipped to the same address)

8% sales tax for New York State Residents

**Check or Money Order
Credit cards accepted through Pay Pal on webpage**

Name_____

Address_____

_____

**Website: www.otismountainpress.com
E-mail: mail@otismountainpress.com
Phone: 301-467-0261**

Discounts for Schools, Churches and Synagogues